FOURTH EDITION

SOCIAL WELFARE

A Response to Human Need

Louise C. Johnson
Professor Emeritus
University of South Dakota

Charles L. Schwartz
University of South Dakota

Donald S. Tate
University of South Dakota

Allyn and Bacon
Boston • London • Toronto • Sydney • Tokyo • Singapore

Editor-in-Chief, Social Sciences: Karen Hanson
Series Editor: Judy Fifer
Editorial Assistant: Mary Visco
Marketing Manager: Quinn Perkson
Editorial-Production Service: Chestnut Hill Enterprises, Inc.
Manufacturing Buyer: Megan Cochran
Cover Administrator: Suzanne Harbison

Copyright © 1997, 1994, 1991, 1988 by Allyn & Bacon
A Viacom Company
Needham Heights, Massachusetts 02194

Library of Congress Cataloging-in-Publication Data

Johnson, Louise C.
     Social welfare : a response to human need / Louise C. Johnson,
Charles L. Schwartz, Donald S. Tate. — 4th ed.
        p.   cm.
     Includes bibliographical references and index.
     ISBN 0-205-19729-9 (hardcover)
     1. Social service—United States.   2. Public welfare—United
States.   3. Social workers—United States.   I. Schwartz, Charles
L.   II. Tate, Donald S.   III. Title.
HV91.J625   1997
361.973—dc20   96–12679
                                                                                    CIP

Printed in the United States of America

10   9   8   7   6   5   4   3   2   1   01   00   99   98   97   96

Photo Credits: Page 64, © AP/Wide World Photos; Page 120, From the Archives of the National League
of Nursing; Page 151, Miro Vintoniv/Stock, Boston.

CONTENTS

    Groups, Communities, and Families   275
    Group Services   276
    Social Work and the Group Services Field   277
    Community Practice as a Field of Practice   280
    Social Workers and Community Practice   283
    Services to Families   284
    Social Work and the Family: A Historical Perspective   285
    Family Social Policy   286
    Family-Centered Problems   288
    Social Work Practice and the Family   291
    Summary   293
    Key Terms   293
    References   294
    Suggested Readings   295

14 Old–New Fields of Practice: Industrial and Rural   297
    Industrial Social Work: A Historical Perspective   298
    Practice in the Industrial Setting   301
    Issues in Industrial Social Work   303
    Rural Social Work: A Historical Perspective   304
    Practice in Rural Settings   308
    Issues in Rural Social Work   310
    Summary   311
    Key Terms   311
    References   311
    Suggested Readings   312

15 The Contemporary Social Welfare System   315
    A Framework for Analysis   316
    Contemporary Social Problems   320
    Structure of the System   322
    The Future of Social Work   324
    A Student's Next Step   326
    Summary   327
    Key Terms   327
    References   327
    Suggested Readings   328

    Name Index   329

    Subject Index   333

PREFACE

We have written this book for students in introductory social work courses and social service courses that focus on understanding the nature of the social welfare system in the United States. As a background for these courses and the book, an introductory course in sociology or social problems and some understanding of U.S. history are helpful but not necessary. In developing the materials for inclusion in the book, we have been cognizant of the requirements of the new Curriculum Policy Statement of the Council on Social Work Education. Of particular significance are those that relate to content regarding minorities, women, and social work values. We have also attempted to include material from significant research studies relative to the social welfare system.

We view the social welfare system as one way we, as a people, attempt to respond to human needs within our society. Although these needs are individual in nature, they also have a universal quality. The social welfare system, then, is defined as a system of arrangements, programs, and mechanisms—formal or informal, governmental or nongovernmental—that try to meet the needs of individuals and families who cannot fulfill such needs through their own resources. The theme carried throughout our book is society's response to human needs. We examine the social welfare system from a historical as well as a contemporary perspective. History is presented in a way that emphasizes its relevance to the current functioning of the system.

We have divided the book into two major parts. In Part One, we consider how societal values and philosophies, as well as the needs of the times, have influenced the development of the social welfare system. We deal with the conditions that make it difficult for individuals and families to meet their needs and thus force them to rely on the social welfare system. We discuss the availability of resources to meet these needs, and we conclude with a discussion of specific types of prejudice and discrimination.

In Part Two, we first consider two attributes of the social welfare system: the profession of social work and the organization of that system into fields of practice. Chapter 6 on the social work profession provides both a history of the development of the profession within the social welfare system and a discussion of contemporary social work practice. A thorough view of the fields of practice or service areas that constitute the social welfare system follows. First to be discussed, in Chapters 7 through 12, are the traditional fields of income maintenance, child welfare, health care, mental health, criminal justice, and gerontology. Next, Chapter 13 considers the organization of social work practice and, in turn, the social welfare system into fields that focus on specific social systems: the group, the community, and the family. Last among the fields of practice are two that relate to a specific context, industrial and rural, discussed in Chapter 14. Chapter 15 provides a summary that develops an organizing framework for considering social welfare programs and services. It also considers contemporary problems that have been noted throughout the book, with emphasis on the capacity of the U.S. social welfare system, as it is now organized, to respond to those problems.

Retained in the fourth edition of *Social Welfare: A Response to Human Need* are Learning Expectations. These begin each chapter and outline the chapter objectives. At the end of each chapter is a list of Key Terms that are developed for the first time within that chapter, as well as a list of Suggested Readings for those who want to further develop their understanding of the material presented.

New to the fourth edition of the text is a presentation of paradigms that explain social change and their effects on individuals, groups, and communities in Chapter 2. We forward the notion that much social change has occurred as a result of paradigmatic shifts (changes in ideologies and ways of thinking about people's relationship with the environment and each other), which in turn influence the social welfare response to human need. Also introduced in this chapter, is the theme that social change, as contributed to by paradigmatic shifts, has resulted in problems in the distribution of rights and resources for certain societal groups, leading to the oppression of these groups. The concept of empowerment of people, as a way to deal with oppression and to ensure social justice, is also introduced in this chapter, and is discussed in detail in Chapter 5, and in the fields of practice chapters, as the concept relates to social policy and social work practice in that field. We believe that these additions fulfill the intent of the new CSWE Curriculum Policy Statement.

Updates are provided on relevant statistics presented throughout the text, as well as new case examples for several of the fields of practice chapters.

For those familiar with previous editions of this text, you will note that the reference citation style for the fourth edition has changed from the Chicago style to the style of the American Psychological Association.

Our hope is that, through the use of this book, students of social work will develop sufficient knowledge, values, and skills needed for analyzing policy issues, understanding the various roles and functions of professional social workers, and working within the structure of the contemporary social welfare system. The book is dedicated to all students who are beginning your journey toward becoming effective social work practitioners. We hope that you become excited about joining a host of social workers who labor to meet human need and to help those who, for whatever reason, cannot help themselves.

SOCIAL WELFARE AS A RESPONSE TO SOCIETAL CONCERN

Part One introduces the basic concepts and gives a framework for understanding the social welfare system in the United States. In Chapter 1, six different arrangements that our society uses to provide for the needs of its members are defined and discussed. These arrangements are one facet of the framework of the book. A second facet is the history of the development of the U.S. social welfare system. This history will be expanded in later sections of the book, but important milestones are introduced in Chapter 1. A third facet is a discussion of the motivations that influence decisions that affect our social welfare programs and policies.

Subsequent chapters discuss human needs and the reasons that individuals, families, and personal networks cannot always meet their needs. Social change and an increasingly complex society are shown to be basic reasons that there must be societal provision of social welfare programs and services. It will help the student understand why some people are unable to provide for all of their own needs and those of their family.

Chapter 2 considers changes that have taken place in society in the United States and how those changes have affected people who live in that society. Chapter 3 examines poverty as one of the major contributors to people's inability to meet their own or their family's needs. Chapter 4 considers the resources people need to function in contemporary society. Chapter 5 looks at racism and discrimination as they affect individuals and interfere with meeting human needs.

1

AN INTRODUCTION TO THE SOCIAL WELFARE SYSTEM IN THE UNITED STATES

Learning Expectations

- Ability to define human needs
- Knowledge about areas of human need and of the factors that influence specification of need
- Identification and understanding of six societal arrangements used in meeting human needs
- Capacity to give examples of each arrangement for meeting human needs used in the U.S. social welfare system
- Identification of the major milestones in the development of the U.S. social welfare system
- Capacity to explain the event and circumstances that led to the change reflected by each of the milestones
- Identification of five motivators that have influenced the development of the U.S. social welfare system
- Understanding of how each motivator influences the contemporary U.S. social welfare system

This chapter introduces the theme of this book—the social welfare system as a response to human needs. It starts by considering human needs as a part of the human condition and moves through how people meet their needs. Throughout history, people in their collectives or through their social structures have created mechanisms or systems of organizing their responses to human needs. In a complex technological society, not all human needs can be met through personal effort or reliance upon one's family or associates. This chapter gives an overview of these mechanisms as they affect the system in the United States from three perspectives: first, approaches used in providing for human needs; second, historical milestones that changed the structure and philosophy underlying the contemporary U.S. social welfare system; and, finally, the motivations that influence decisions about how human needs should be met. Later chapters will develop these themes in more depth.

Human Needs

Human needs are those resources people need to survive as individuals and to function appropriately in their society. No definitive list of needs can be given. Needs vary depending on the specific individual and the specific situations. The same person will have different needs at different stages of development. For example, a child with an enzyme deficiency has different nutritional needs than does a child of a similar age with no such problem. The needs of young children for protection and care are very different from those of young adults. For individuals to develop self-esteem (a sense of self-worth that allows people to function comfortably in their environment), one culture may require considerable freedom of choice; another culture may require considerable conformity to societal expectations about roles and behaviors. Families with an unemployed breadwinner in densely populated cities do not have the means to raise a portion of their food, while a rural family living in poverty may be able to. Every individual and family has needs that, if provided for, would enable the family and its members to function more adequately. But these needs differ depending on the individual and the situation.

Human needs usually include the following:

1. Sufficient food, clothing, and shelter for physical survival
2. A safe environment and adequate health care for protection from and treatment for illness and accidents
3. Relationships with other people that provide a sense of being cared for, of being loved, and of belonging
4. Opportunities for emotional, intellectual, and spiritual growth and development, including the opportunity for individuals to make use of their innate talents and interests
5. Opportunities for participation in making decisions about the common life of one's own society, including the ability to make appropriate contributions to the maintenance of life together

Any specification of some need of any particular group of people must consider its life-style, culture, and value system. It must also consider the physical, emotional, cognitive, social, and spiritual attributes of the individual being helped. Need must also be considered in the light of issues of responsibility for self, others, and the general social condition.

In the United States, a theme of *rugged individualism* has influenced our thinking about social welfare—the belief that each person should be responsible for meeting his or her own needs. This situation is neither possible in contemporary society nor desirable in terms of optimal human growth and development. Human beings have always depended on others to provide for their needs. These others may have been family, clan, tribe, neighbors, co-workers, or a part of some organized structure such as church, city-state, or governmental unit.

Human beings have always had some means for meeting human needs. The means for meeting human needs that serve the common good are known collectively as *social welfare*. The network of services resulting from custom and public policy forms what is known as the social welfare system. This system is particularly concerned with individuals and families who cannot meet their needs with their own resources. Children, older people, and the handicapped are of particular concern. The system includes government programs, private nonprofit organizations, and informal helping endeavors. This is a broader definition than the one often used, which includes only formal or organizational components of the system. Another very narrow definition might include only the governmental segments. This broad definition reflects a belief that human needs have never been met exclusively by an individual's own effort or solely through the efforts of a family unit. There have always been mechanisms in the larger social unit that enable individuals and families to meet basic needs. Thus it seems important when examining how a society (for example, the United States) meets individual and family needs that cannot be or are not being met within the resources of the family unit to also examine all efforts, not just governmental mechanisms.

Important questions dealt with by this social welfare system are: Which needs should be met by individuals and families in caring for themselves and each other (personal system)? Which needs should be met through relationships among people outside formal structures (the informal system)? And which needs are the responsibility of the formal social welfare systems (government and other formal organizations)? The search for this balance in meeting human needs is ever-present in the development and functioning of the contemporary social welfare system in the United States.

Societal Responses

Society has developed six different kinds of societal arrangements for meeting human needs: mutual aid, charity-philanthropy, public welfare, social insurance, social services, and universal provisions (Handel, 1982). Each arrangement has developed from people's responses to societal structures and from beliefs about human needs, the reasons people are unable to meet their needs, and what society's responsibility is in meeting these unmet needs. Each arrangement has particular qualities that make it especially appropriate for meeting particular kinds of needs under differing circumstances. Each has advantages and disadvantages. Today's social welfare system makes use of all six arrangements (see Table 1-1 for definitions of these arrangements). Thus, in evaluating the U.S. social welfare system, it is important to understand the uses of each and to consider which arrangement is most appropriate to meet the specific needs of a particular circumstance.

Mutual Aid

Mutual aid is the oldest form of social welfare. It probably has been used ever since humans banded together in extended families or loose social groups. It is, however, the least recognized and documented in social welfare literature. Mutual aid is the expression of people's need to take responsibility for each other's well-being. Friends and neighbors have provided for children when family capacity for care has broken down. Social groups have cared for their own aged, weak, and deviant members. Studies show that mutual aid mechanisms are present in primitive

TABLE 1-1   **Arrangements for Delivery of Social Welfare Service**

Mutual aid	The expression of mutual responsibility for one another that occurs outside formal community structures. Helper and recipient of help are peers who may change roles, depending on the situation.
Charity-philanthropy	Redistribution of wealth by some mechanism outside the government through voluntary giving. Usually givers have higher status than receivers. Benefits may be tangible or intangible.
Public welfare	Provision of tangible support (food, clothing, shelter, health care) for those unable to make such provision for themselves that uses the mechanisms of government (taxation, etc.).
Social insurance	Required contribution to funds used for money payments to individuals contributing to the program (or their beneficiaries) who meet the criteria for which the program is intended (over age sixty-five, disabled, widowed). The program is administered by the government.
Social services	Intangible benefits provided by agencies and institutions (governmental and nongovernmental) that ameliorate dysfunctioning and prevent problems in social functioning.
Universal provision	Fiscal support or services by governmental units, available to everyone within particular categories, with no special contribution or other limitations.

Source: Based in part on work by Gerald Handel, *Social Welfare in Western Society* (New York: Random House, 1982). Definitions differ somewhat from Handel's.

societies. Imperatives for mutual aid are a strong part of the traditions of Judaism and Christianity. Mutual aid was present in the craft guilds of the Middle Ages when they provided funds for the burial of members and the support of their widows and children. It was present in various immigrant groups as they settled in ethnic enclaves in the United States and together provided for their own needs.

Ferdinand Tonnies (1855–1936), an early German sociologist, explored the relationships among people in the industrialization of society and used the term *Gemeinschaft* (a society using mutual aid to meet human needs) and the contrasting term *Gesellschaft* (individuals related through structures in the community) (Loomis, 1940). In U.S. society, mutual aid is still very apparent in rural communities. Farmers help each other during harvests. Neighbors in small towns often come to depend on each other during a crisis such as a death or illness in a family.

Another good example of mutual aid is the self-help groups that have been particularly useful in meeting the needs of individuals in transition (such as Widow to Widow), those who are isolated and lonely (Parents Without Partners), and those who share similar problems (Alcoholics Anonymous) (Pancoast, Parker, and Froland, 1983). The recognition of natural helpers as a resource is another manifestation of mutual aid. In many communities (particularly in rural communities and in some urban neighborhoods) there are individuals who have won the trust and respect of the community and to whom people go for advice or for help in solving problems. Another example of mutual aid is giving a fund-raising benefit for someone who has been injured or who has lost property through a disaster.

Mutual aid seems to work most effectively when the people helping and those being helped hold similar values, come from a similar culture, or have a similar lifestyle. Such people have an egalitarian and reciprocal relationship in which a person is sometimes the helper, sometimes the one being helped. Mutual aid has the advantages of being relatively nonintrusive, culturally relevant, fiscally inexpensive, nonstigmatizing, and relatively autonomous. It seems to be less effective among people of different cultures, lifestyles, or ethnic groups. It is usually short term and of limited financial commitment—for example, providing food for a family in times of illness or other distress, or providing shelter after a fire. It requires a situation in which the helper has sufficient motivation, energy, and resources to provide the needed help. It also requires that the helpee respond in a way that provides satisfaction to the helper. Mutual aid is not appropriate for meeting all human needs, but it is a very important arrangement that has always been a part of human society and one that deserves more understanding, attention, and appropriate use within the current U.S. social welfare system.

Mutual aid is usually found within a single class or group. When stratification causes one group to acquire greater wealth and power, the mutual aid ethic is often transformed into the belief that the richer should help the poorer—or *charity-philanthropy*.

Charity-Philanthropy

When societies began to stratify and develop a class structure, new means of helping became necessary. With stratification came a differential distribution of power and resources, but the mutual aid ethic of responsibility for others persisted. Two early European examples of this kind of social welfare are the feudal system and the Roman Catholic church. Within the feudal system the lord of the manor was responsible for the well-being of those who lived on the manor: his underlings and serfs. With the breakup of this economic system came a breakdown in the meeting of human needs that caused much unrest in the countryside. During feudal times, the church also developed ways of meeting needs: hospitals, almshouses, and schools. Gifts to the church were seen as gifts to the poor. The tithe (giving one-tenth of one's income to the church) became expected of all. Although this means of redistributing wealth was a way of carrying out society's social welfare function, it was also a means of social control. To receive help meant, at least in part, adhering to accepted norms and behaviors. For example, in response to help from the church, individuals were expected to live by the teachings of the church and provide for their own needs as much as possible. They were not to waste resources by indulging in pleasure. It is important to note that the church's charity was not governmentally administered or controlled. It was a means for providing help based on the relationship of one social class to another. Thus the helper assumed a position of power over the recipient of help.

In the nineteenth century, the U.S. social welfare system developed institutions and organizations that laid the foundations for the use of charity-philanthropy. Individuals with wealth established and endowed schools and colleges, libraries, hospitals, orphanages, and homes for the aged. Some people believed that those who were privileged with wealth should share with the less fortunate, particularly through the establishment and maintenance of institutions for the "uplift of the masses" or for those who needed care through no fault of their own. On the other hand, society made sure that no help was given that would in any way deter the able-bodied from working to provide for themselves and their families (Bremner, 1960).

Two organizations are particularly important in describing the charity-philanthropy arrangement in the United States: the Charity Organization Societies and the settlement houses. Although different in underlying philosophy, both originated in Great Britain in the latter part of the nineteenth century and were quickly copied in the United States.

The *Charity Organization Societies* (COS), forerunner of the present-day Family Service America, originally functioned with "friendly visitors," usually women of the upper class who carried out their charitable responsibility by visiting poor women in an attempt to motivate them toward better ways of living. The friendly visitor gave advice about such things as child-rearing and housekeeping and warned against the evils of drink and idleness. The system was based on the belief that poverty came from wrong living, misuse of money, excessive drinking, and immorality. Money or other concrete aid was supplied only in exceptional situations and for very short periods of time. An extensive system of coordination and supervision developed. The individual or "case" was the focus of attention, with emphasis on finding out why the person was having difficulty. But the friendly visitor believed that the source of the difficulty rested within the individual's ways of functioning, that the poor had the means to overcome their problems, and that the friendly visitor could help the needy find their own means for overcoming difficulty. This method of giving help became known as *scientific charity*. It provided the beginnings of social work as a profession—the friendly visitor evolved into the caseworker.

On the other hand, the *settlement house* was a place in the neighborhoods of low-income families, usually immigrants, where wealthy and privileged people could live among the poor. Socially conscious clergy and university women were also apt to be found living in settlement houses. They believed that by becoming neighbors, they could bring about needed changes and thus meet human needs. Another method was to invite neighbors into the settlement house for clubs and classes (group activities) that helped immigrants adapt to the new country and its way of life. It was hoped that this would also demonstrate a caring attitude. The settlement house workers believed that through club activities people could find enrichment and education that would lead them to a higher quality of life. Rather than seeing the cause of problems as originating in individuals and their lifestyles, the cause was seen as resting in the environment and stemming from a lack of understanding about how to cope in new surroundings. The settlement workers were also heavily involved in research to identify the factors causing need and in activities intended to eliminate the factors that caused the need (Bremner, 1964).

The COS and the settlement houses engendered numerous *private agencies*. This term emphasizes that the support and governance of such agencies come from private citizens, not government sources. Included in this group of agencies are those supported by religious groups. Today many of these agencies do receive support from governmental funds through grants and purchase-of-service contracts. Some examples of private agencies include those concerned with the welfare of children (e.g., Children's Aid Societies), family counseling agencies (e.g., Family Services), child guidance clinics and other mental health services, and community center and group service agencies (e.g., YWCAs). The advantages of private agencies are that they voluntarily redistribute resources and let people carry out their responsibilities for others in ways that are more personal than are government-controlled mechanisms. The private approach has more flexibility, focuses on particular cases, and provides relative autonomy for the helper. Because of the flexibility and autonomy, there is a capacity for experimentation and development of pilot programs not always possible in the government sector. The private agencies have enjoyed an absence of government control, but as government has made its presence felt in many parts of our society, so it also has developed regulations for these agencies.

There are, however, disadvantages to the charity-philanthropy arrangement. It does seem to reinforce class structure and thus can stigmatize the people receiving help. With limited funds and other resources, it cannot meet all existing needs. Because of its independent functioning, coordination of services has been difficult to achieve. In addition, private agencies often seem to have difficulty responding to different cultural groups. Finally, this arrangement can lead to an overemphasis on professionalism and an elitism that can be dysfunctional.

Despite its limitations, the charity-philanthropy arrangement remains an important component of our social welfare system. Like mutual aid, it cannot provide for all human needs, but it can best provide for some needs, such as counseling people with problems in interpersonal functioning and developing new services, that mutual aid and government-controlled systems have difficulty providing. It has been a means for identifying unmet needs and exploring or demonstrating through new programs and strategies means that might be useful in meeting the need. However charity-philanthropy cannot be expected to universally meet the need.

Public Welfare

The third arrangement used in meeting human need is *public welfare*. The essence of this component is government-regulated provision for and control of the needy by tax-supported financial aid and institutional care. The arrangement uses local, state, or federal tax monies to provide minimal support for people unable to provide for themselves.

The U.S. public welfare system generally traces its roots to the *English Poor Law* of 1601. This law, discussed in greater detail later in this chapter, was a codification of laws that the British Parliament had passed during the previous century to regulate begging and to establish government involvement in provision for the needy. It reinforced the notion that the local community was responsible for the care of its poor. The thrust of the English Poor Law was carried over to the American colonies and their provision for their own poor.

What became known as *indoor relief*, or the care of certain persons in congregate-care institutions, became popular in the seventeenth and eighteenth centuries. Poorhouses, hospitals, and orphanages were established. Although many of these were privately supported and thus fall within the charity-philanthropy arrangement, many were also partially government supported. State governments, in particular, became responsible for the care of some groups of people. States established separate institutions for the retarded, the blind, the deaf, and the mentally ill. In 1845, President Franklin Pierce vetoed a bill that would have provided support for the care of "indigent insane persons" by the federal government, saying the federal Constitution did not provide power for this activity. Thus the principle of local and state responsibility for care of the poor remained operational until the 1930s.

The present U.S. public welfare arrangement began with the federal government's response to the Great Depression of the 1930s. President Franklin Delano Roosevelt's New Deal policy, which provided work relief, reversed the thinking of the Pierce veto and established the involvement of the federal government in providing public welfare. The *Social Security Act* of 1935 with its numerous amendments is the basis for the U.S. public welfare system. This act was an important part of the New Deal. Certain categories of poor became the joint responsibility of state and federal government. These include mothers (families in some cases) with dependent children (ADC, Aid to Dependent Children, and AFDC, Aid to Families with Dependent Children), the aged (OAA, Old Age Assistance), the blind (AB, Aid to the Blind), and the disabled (AD, Aid to the Disabled). This approach has come to be known as *categorical assistance*. More recently (1972) all but ADC and AFDC have become the responsibility of the federal government. General assistance, help given to those who do not fall into one of these categories, falls to state and local governments. General assistance can be both money or in-kind provision. Institutional care has been deemphasized and for the most part remains the responsibility of state and often of local governments. In 1965, the Medicaid program (Title XIX) was added to the Social Security Act. This amendment pays for medical care for the poor. Fiscal responsibility for the program is shared by the federal government and the states (Day, 1989).

The public welfare system has two major strengths. The first is its universal quality: Anyone who meets stated criteria is covered. Mutual aid and charity-philanthropy do not have this quality. Thus, the public welfare approach provides a specified level of help to all who have an established degree of need. This scope can be possible only with a relatively large and relatively stable fiscal base. Thus the second major advantage of this arrangement is its dependence on a tax base, providing a large and stable source of funds.

Because the federal government operates with a system of bureaucracies, such impersonal service delivery is not capable of responding flexibly to individuals in need. Bureaucracies often create a proliferation of rules, regulations, red tape, and paperwork. All this reduces the government's capacity to respond to human need and increases the costs of supplying needed assistance.

It has been argued that a limiting feature of public welfare has been the principle of less eligibility—that is, the idea that individuals should not be provided for at a level equal to or higher than the level an individual working for a living can attain. This policy developed mostly from the belief that citizens do not want to pay taxes to maintain others in a equal or better lifestyle than they maintain for themselves. The principle of less eligibility served as a "unwritten policy" for many years, keeping public assistance benefits generally at low levels. Recently it has been argued that the combined benefits of welfare assistance, food stamps, and Medicaid, discussed in detail in subsequent chapters, have, in some instances, made public welfare recipients "better off" than some people who work at low-paying jobs with no fringe benefits. This issue has added to the controversy surrounding this arrangement for meeting human needs.

Another disadvantage of public welfare is the stigma that the dominant culture attaches to receiving public assistance of any kind. This stigmatization is a major cause of the prejudice and discrimination that people who receive public assistance often experience. This prejudice in turn affects their feelings of self-worth and thus further increases their need for support. Inflexibility in the government's response to diverse populations and diverse needs is another important limitation. Thus, despite its mandate, public welfare does not serve all segments of U.S. society equally. For example, under some circumstances it is not responsive to middle-aged adults who are unable to work because of mental or physical handicaps.

Currently, much discussion and debate has centered on public welfare, most particularly "welfare reform." A political vow made by the Clinton Administration shortly after the 1992 national election was to "end welfare as we know it." More recently, in the aftermath of the 1994 congressional elections, both houses of Congress have gone on record, promising to pass welfare reform legislation. The current debate largely focuses on the concern that some poor people should be able to help themselves or may not be victims of circumstances beyond their control. Behind this concern is an assumption that assistance for these "undeserving" poor should at best be minimal. Some of the questions involved include: Should such assistance be given only to those in certain particularly vulnerable categories—the aged, widows, children, or handicapped persons? Does public welfare discourage the able-bodied from working? What should be the response to extensive unemployment caused by disruptions in the economic system? Should help be in the form of institutional care, or should public welfare provide subsistence within the community? If the latter, should subsistence be in the form of cash payments to the poor or needy, provision of commodities like surplus food, or payment of selected caregivers? What level of care should be provided? What are the responsibilities of relatives and the local communities for the care of their own? Which level of government should be responsible for providing financial resources to support the disadvantaged? Should welfare recipients be required to work as one condition of receiving aid? Despite many questions and limitations, public welfare is the core of the current U.S. social welfare system, for it provides the *income maintenance* segment of the system. Income maintenance provides financial assistance in the form of cash or a voucher given by government agencies to individuals and families when their incomes fall below a predetermined level (Wyers, 1987). Examples of income maintenance services are Aid to Dependent Children, food stamps, and Supplementary Security Income for the aged. Without income maintenance, human needs cannot be met in contemporary U.S. society.

Social Insurance

The fourth arrangement used in the social welfare system is social insurance. *Social insurance* is a mechanism whereby citizens (or employers and employees) are required to contribute to government-administered funds. These funds then pay out benefits when the insured condition or status is reached by any contributor. In the United States a group of insurance programs, including old-age and survivors insurance, disability insurance, and Medicare (medical insurance for those over sixty-five years of age) are provided under the Social Security Act and its amendments (the same act that provides for social welfare benefits). Workers have a certain percentage of their paychecks deducted, and employers are required to contribute; this money is paid into a fund that in turn pays benefits to qualified aged and disabled people.

This arrangement had its beginnings in Europe during the latter part of the nineteenth century, when first Germany and then Great Britain introduced health, old age, and accident insurance. In the United States the first social insurance was Workers' Compensation. This developed in response to the rise of industrial accidents that disabled breadwinners and thus plunged families into poverty. Between 1910 and 1920 many states passed laws providing insurance and protection against the risk of income loss due to industrial accidents, and for the medical care needed as a result of such accidents.

Other types of social insurance are also a part of the contemporary U.S. social welfare system. These are Old Age and Survivors Insurance, Unemployment Insurance, and Medicare. Old Age and Survivors Insurance, now referred to as Old Age, Survivors, Disability, and Health Insurance (OASDHI), provides three types of benefits: retirement income, income to families of deceased workers, and income to workers who are permanently and totally disabled. The benefits received depend in part on the worker's contributions to the fund: Those who have worked little receive little. Since its inception in 1935, the program has gradually expanded to include more and more of the work force, but it is still not universal. Unemployment Insurance operates from funds collected by a payroll tax, with each state setting up its own program. Medicare, which came into being as a result of the 1965 amendments to the Social Security Act, provides health insurance for people over sixty-five. It is co-insurance; that is, the recipient pays a part of the cost of health care. The Medicare program is federally administered (Day, 1989).

Social insurance has several advantages. Because individuals contribute to the funds they draw on when they meet the requirements for obtaining benefits, social insurance does not carry the stigma that other arrangements do. This arrangement also has a universal quality, although it is somewhat limited in that some people do not contribute and thus are not eligible for benefits. However, the extent of the coverage is now so broad that social insurance can be considered almost universal. It is also nonintrusive. There is no investigation to establish need and there are relatively simple eligibility requirements.

There are, however, some disadvantages to social insurance. Of current concern is the shifting population pattern, with many more older people receiving Social Security and fewer younger people contributing to the plan. Whether the OASDHI fund can continue to provide the present benefits without increasing the level of contributions, raising the eligibility age, or finding new sources of funds is a real concern. Also, as noted before, the rules and regulations of bureaucracy are often unresponsive to human needs in their individual and diverse forms. The system has difficulty adjusting to these inequalities and to changing social patterns. The exclusion of housewives from primary benefits is an example. Another limitation is that not everyone is part of the system. Certain individuals "fall between the cracks." Housewives, some seasonal workers, some state and local government employees, and some agricultural workers do not have Social Security coverage. The program is not as universal as many would desire. But social insurance, despite its limitations, has become a very important part of the social welfare system by providing income at times when people might otherwise have to depend on public welfare income maintenance programs.

Social Services

Not all the social welfare needs that people have can be fulfilled merely by providing money. Traditionally, nonmonetary types of help have come from mutual aid and charity-philanthropy. Although mutual aid and private agencies have done a fine job, they have not been able to provide for all the needs or to provide universal coverage for even some of the needs.

The heart of social services comprises a wide variety of counseling services known as casework. However, it also includes other kinds of services, such as information and referral, socialization and other group services, and supportive services. In addition, services that increase the capacity of communities to meet human needs are included in this arrangement. *Social services* can then be defined as supplying nonmonetary help that directly or indirectly increases people's abilities to function in society (Kahn, 1979).

The roots of contemporary social services lie in the work of the COS and the settlement houses. From these origins many agencies, services, and other provisions have grown to meet a wide variety of needs. From the COS came the concept of helping people through a one-to-one relationship. This led to an emphasis on casework as the vehicle for the delivery of social services. The COS also pioneered much of the community organization approach, with its emphasis on coordinating services. The settlement house movement initiated services to groups and to communities, to help people change their environment. The many and varying uses of the social service model will become apparent in Part Two of this book, where the various fields of service are examined.

Until recently, social services tended to remain primarily within the charity-philanthropy arrangement. Then some services, especially in the areas of child welfare and mental health, began to be provided by government agencies. There was a gradual recognition that income maintenance programs alone could not fulfill everyone's needs. The 1967 Social Security amendments allowed state governments to provide services to ADC recipients. Thus the Social

Security Act was broadened to recognize social services as a distinct arrangement. When Title XX of the Social Security Act was passed by Congress, this amendment broadened the kinds of services offered and the criteria for who could receive such services. Services like family planning and information and referral could be provided to everyone regardless of income. With the rise of public social service and the use of public funds for grants and contracts for services, the social service arrangement seems a more accurate designation for many services provided by agencies formerly supported by the charity-philanthropy arrangement.

One of the advantages of social services is their individualized attention to the need and their specific response to the person in the situation. Response to diversity is much more possible than with other arrangements. This arrangement also recognizes that needs exist that are not caused simply by inadequate income. Social services also place an emphasis on the need for voluntary acceptance of services.

There are, however, disadvantages to social service. In many instances, it is a very intrusive kind of help, calling for delving into very personal aspects of people's lives. Professionalism has produced other negative spin-offs. One of them is that some social services tend to discourage the use of mutual aid or the informal helping system; professionalism has given helping an elitist flavor. It has made certain kinds of help very expensive. Sometimes it places a stigma on those who turn to it for help. Also, help has not been available to all who need and could use it. It should be recognized, on the other hand, that the professionalism of the social services has brought about a higher level of care and a greater capacity to help in circumstances that are beyond the capacity of the informal system.

Universal Provision

Universal provision is fiscal support or services given by governments to enhance the social functioning of all the people within a society. Universal provision requires no means test; people do not have to show that they or their family fall below a predetermined income level to receive benefits. No eligibility requirements are necessary other than that recipients belong to a particular category of people (those over sixty-five, children, etc.). This arrangement has not been used in the United States to the extent it has in many other countries. It must, however, be recognized as an option when discussing how the U.S. social welfare system can be more responsive to human needs.

Primary examples of universal provision in the United States are such public health services as the Poison Control Centers or the Centers for Disease Control in Atlanta, particularly as they safeguard everyone's health. The Older Americans Act of 1965 provides planning, social, and nutritional services for anyone over sixty years old, regardless of income. This program, however, has never been adequately funded and currently targets only those with income or social need.

Canada has three major universal provisions: Family Allowances, Old Age Security, and Medicare. Family Allowances pays a set sum for every dependent child in a family. Old Age Security pays a basic allowance to every person over sixty-five years of age. Medicare covers medical and hospital costs for everyone. These programs are supported from the federal and provincial general tax funds.

One advantage of universal provision is that administrative costs are cut because everyone is covered, so eligibility processing is minimal. Some of the cost is reclaimed since this income

TABLE 1-2   **Summary of Social Welfare Arrangements**

Arrangement	Government Involvement	Relationship	Stigma	Strength	Limitation
Mutual aid	No	Reciprocal	No	Quickly available if given within cultural context	Limited to persons who are culturally similar
Charity-philanthropy	No	Superordinate or subordinate	Yes	Individualization Development of new approaches	Limited by scope of resources available Tends to be controlled by dominant groups' expectations
Public welfare	Yes	Superordinate, subordinate, or impersonal	Yes	Breadth of coverage	Controlled by dominant groups' expectations Bureaucratization
Social insurance	Yes	Impersonal	No	Breadth of coverage Lack of stigma	Bureaucratization Some individuals left out
Social services	Yes	Depends on situation	Probably in some cases	Breadth of coverage	Limited funding Bureaucratization
Universal provision	Yes	Limited	No	Breadth of coverage	Cost

is taxable. No stigma is placed on those receiving universal benefits; in fact, society recognizes that people through no fault of their own need subsidies. In many countries, these provisions have become rights.

The major disadvantage is, of course, cost. At issue is the question: Is it better to pay taxes and be protected, or is it better to provide for need on an individual basis (through each individual's personal effort and also through government programs)?

Each of the six arrangements with its strengths and limitations has developed within the U.S. social welfare system to deliver a particular set of benefits and services that meets certain needs in our society. Understanding each arrangement is necessary for understanding the total social welfare system (see Table 1-2).

Development of the U.S. Social Welfare System

The milestones set within the history of the social welfare system show how it has developed. The following material examines the major historical points at which the system changed in some significant way (Trattner, 1989). In Part Two, the development of fields of practice will be considered. Fields of practice are services to specific groups, such as children or families or the aged, and services within specific settings such as health care or corrections facilities. Although the study of fields of practice shows how the identification of a group (class) of people in need and the provision of resources and services to that group has been an important influence on the evolution of the overall social welfare system, a look at the general historical background of the system provides a necessary framework for understanding the development of the fields of practice.

Two historical milestones are the passage of specific social welfare legislation and the development of the institutions, agencies, and programs within the system. The former can be tied to specific dates; the latter cannot. Both, however, grew over time. With institution/ agency development, it is difficult to specify a precise date when a new service or philosophy was generally accepted throughout the system. Specific legislation of the type being discussed usually was preceded by other legislation or by legislation at another level of government. The passage of this legislation was the climax of a process or movement toward a new way of providing for need.

In understanding how the system grew and changed, it is important to note not only the milestones but also the influences involved in the changes. There are two types of influences: situational and philosophical. Situational influences include the historic context: the economic, social, and political events in the country at the time. Philosophical influences are the values, beliefs, and prevailing philosophic constructs that influenced the process of change resulting in a milestone.

English Poor Law of 1601

The English Poor Law of 1601 is generally considered the first milestone because it was the basis of the social welfare system in both colonial and post-Revolutionary America. The sense of this law formed the foundation of the system until the passage of the Social Security Act in 1935, and its philosophy influences attitudes toward social welfare even today. This law became necessary as England changed from an agricultural society to an industrial one. It regulated the poor and dealt with the many wandering beggars. The introduction of sheep raising and the enclosure of property had pushed people off the land and into a new way of life in the cities. Vagrancy became intolerable. The old system whereby the landholder was responsible for those who lived on his land was breaking down. Further, England had embraced Protestantism, and the monasteries and other Roman Catholic institutions that had met the needs of the poor were abolished by the Crown. It was a time of unrest and uncertainty about responsibility for those in need.

The response was restrictive. Social control was the intent of the poor law. The poor were not allowed freedom to move around the country at will. Begging was controlled, and people in need were returned to or required to remain in the locality where they held residency. Residency was established by birth or by living and working in a locale for a period of time before becoming indigent.

Another provision of this law was *local control*. The poor and dependent were the responsibility of the local government unit, which was responsible for all who held residency or settlement in that area. The law also required that people be responsible for the care of their relatives in need; this is the principle of *relative responsibility*. Differentiation was made between the able-bodied poor, those able to work, and the other poor. The able-bodied could be required to work. Categorical assistance, or the practice of providing assistance to various categories of people such as children, the aged, or disabled adults, has its roots in this differentiation.

This law continued the churches' involvement in caring for the poor. The churches were made responsible for administering the welfare system. Funding came largely through required tithes to the church. What was new was that the government now regulated the system. This change came about not from concern for poor people but from political expediency: the growing numbers of poor people and the desire to control the unrest this had created.

In the New World, this system of social control and local control was culturally appealing. Puritan-Calvinism, with its well-known work ethic, found the approach congruent with its beliefs. In the new environment everyone had to work. There was scarcity and a belief in equality. With little social stratification, there was no concern about a class structure. The smallness and isolation of settlements made local control appropriate. Differentiating the able-bodied from the sick, the disabled, and widows with children also fit the values and beliefs of the people. The major unsolved problem was that of outsiders who might require assistance, and they were now dealt with through residency laws. Needy strangers were sent back to their place of legal residence. The social welfare system of the Old World fit the needs of the new situation; thus it was adopted and still influences the contemporary system.

Institutional Care, 1820 to 1850

As the nation of the United States grew out of the colonial period politically, it also grew geographically and economically. Its population increased dramatically, from 3,929,000 in 1790 to 23,261,000 in 1850. During this period, immigration from Ireland and Germany were responsible for a substantial amount of the population growth. Vast amounts of new territory were opened for settlement. Roads, canals, and railroads opened the West. Cities expanded rapidly, and the factory system became an important economic factor. No longer could subsistence economy and local care provide adequately for all human needs. People worried that the able-bodied poor were not being reformed (i.e., were not forced to be self-supporting) under the prevailing system. Also, it was increasingly difficult for local communities to provide care for their special classes of dependent people (the mentally ill, children, etc.). A belief was growing that these dependent people needed a special environment that would encourage them to grow or change. This in turn stemmed from a belief that people were perfectible. Few recognized that changes in society could be responsible for people's inability to provide for their needs. Instead, the causes of need were seen as lying within individuals and their own responses to changing conditions. The answer was institutions that would care for and train dependent persons so they could become self-supporting. Gradually, *institutional care* became an accepted means for helping needy people.

Originally all dependent people were placed in institutions, the local *almshouse* or poorhouse. This practice became known as *indoor relief,* care in an institution, as opposed to *outside relief,* care within a community. It later became evident that some of the needy required more specialized care or, in the case of children, separate care from other dependent people.

In the beginning, great emphasis was placed on the institution as a place of refuge or asylum that would substitute for the family in providing needed socialization and protection for vulnerable individuals. This was why the institution was seen as a progressive development for the social welfare system. By the mid-1800s, however, most institutions had lost this emphasis on protection and socialization and had developed a custodial approach, concerned with protecting society by removing troublesome individuals (Rothman, 1971).

Local communities often were unable to provide specialized institutions. Thus, from the 1820s on, states began to establish institutions to care for children, the mentally ill, the blind, the deaf, and the retarded. Correctional institutions were established to deal with criminals. Some of these institutions, particularly hospitals and those caring for children, were established by wealthy individuals as their charity work, thus falling under the charity-philanthropy category. Others, financed by the state tax base, fell under the public welfare arrangement.

In the development of the institutional care we see three additions to the social welfare system (still dominated by the principles of the English Poor Law):

1. The widespread use of the charity-philanthropy arrangement
2. The acceptance by state governments of the responsibility of caring for certain categories of needy people
3. The beginning of the recognition that a social welfare system developed for a subsistence economy could not meet human needs in an industrial society

The goals of social welfare in this era were expressed as helping people develop self-respect and dignity through self-support and by protecting vulnerable people from temptation. These goals were translated into the social control goals of "making people behave themselves and keep working."

The system in the United States was developing and taking on a unique character, responding not only to individual needs but also to its citizens' beliefs about dependency. People were beginning to realize that the needs of some members of the society were not being met and that this was due not to these people's lack of moral character but to circumstances beyond their control. This was a response to the nation's unique social, political, and economic reality.

The Charity Organization Societies and Settlement Houses, 1885 to 1900

After the Civil War the movement toward industrialization and urbanization continued. Also, immigration continued to bring more and more people into the United States. Many were from rural backgrounds and had difficulty adjusting not only to a new country but to a new, urban way of life as well. Some new immigrants were from southern and eastern Europe, and their lifestyles differed from those of the northern and western Europeans who had up to this time made up the majority of immigrants to the United States. In addition, a stratified class society had developed, with some people having considerable wealth and power and others having very little of either. The large city slums that housed the families of poorly paid workers, many of whom were immigrants, became the concern of the wealthy, who saw it as their Christian duty to help meet the needs of the poverty-stricken. Two very different types of agencies, both imported from Great Britain, were founded to work with the residents from the slums. These were the Charity Organization Societies and settlement houses discussed earlier in this chapter.

Although the two systems were based on very different beliefs about the cause of unmet needs and responded in very different ways, both were reacting to the same situation: the increasing number of poor and immigrant people struggling to adapt to life in large cities, suffering from a frightening range of problems. Both agencies also came into being because of the newly stratified social class structure. They were expressions of concern by the wealthy for the well-being of their fellow men and women. Generally, both agencies were an expression of a religious conviction that those who had should share with those who did not. They were new systems of helping, within the charity-philanthropy category, that formed a basis for an important segment of our social welfare system. They both furthered the dual system whereby private charity complemented public provision. Most important, they emphasized that need was more than financial need.

During the era when the COS and settlement houses were prime systems for delivering social welfare services, organizations that addressed the needs of particular minority groups began to emerge. Included in this group of organizations were the National Association for the Advancement of Colored People (NAACP) and the Urban League. The Woman's Suffrage movement was successful in obtaining the vote for women. Settlement House workers such as Jane Addams and Lillian Wald were active both in helping minority groups to organize and in the suffrage movement (Cox, Erlich, Rothman, and Tropman, 1987).

Both the COS and the settlement houses accomplished a great deal. From those working in these agencies came a concern about human needs that, along with the progressive reform movement of the early twentieth century, gave rise to laws addressing such problems as child labor, mothers' aid, widows' pensions, and juveniles. Settlement house workers, concerned about the plight of labor, were involved in the formation of unions and in advocating labor legislation. From the settlement houses came the innovation of working with groups. Most important, the settlement houses and the COS produced leadership for developing the profession of social work and for devising new approaches to meeting human need. From these agencies the private sector of the social welfare system came into being.

The Social Security Act of 1935

This act and its subsequent amendments are the major source of U.S. public social welfare policy today. The passage of the act in 1935 marked the beginning of a major shift in the social welfare system. The act relates primarily to three of the mechanisms discussed in the last section: public welfare, social insurance, and social services. (For a summary of its provisions and amendments, see Table 1-3.) After a time of relative prosperity following World War I, a severe economic depression heralded by the 1929 stock market crash plunged the nation into economic disruption. There had been other such periods, but none so extensive as what has come to be known as the Great Depression. It affected all classes of society—the rich, whose investments were now worthless; the growing middle class, whose jobs disappeared and whose savings were lost when banks closed; and of course those with chronically low incomes, who suffered greatly. The usual sources of income and other help for the poor, traditionally provided by the charity-philanthropy arrangement, dried up as these sources were financially overwhelmed by the extent of need. Everyone knew people who were considered moral and upstanding but who were suddenly out of work, had no resources to fall back on, and were now among the needy. Thus, it quickly became apparent that individuals could be unable to meet basic needs for themselves and their families through no fault of their own.

The short-term response to this situation was a package of federal programs known as the New Deal. This overall program contained legislation to improve the economy and provide jobs for the unemployed. But the measure that permanently and basically changed the social welfare system was the Social Security Act of 1935.

TABLE 1-3   Provisions of the Social Security Act and Its Amendments

Year	Legislation	Category
1935	Social Security Act passed.	
	Title I: Grants to states for Old Age Assistance (OAA)	Public welfare
	Title II: Federal old-age benefits	Social insurance
	Title III: Grants to states for Unemployment Compensation	Social insurance
	Title IV: Grants to states for Aid to Dependent Children (ADC)	Public welfare
	Title V: Grants to states for maternal and child welfare	Health and some social services
	Title X: Grants to states for Aid to the Blind (AB)	Public welfare
1939	Old-age insurance expanded to include survivors and eligible family members.	Social insurance
1950	ADC broadened to include relative with whom child is living; becomes Aid to Families with Dependent Children (AFDC).	Public welfare
1956	Disability insurance added to the insurance package.	Social insurance
1962	Provision of social services to AFDC families added.	Social services
1965	Title XVIII: Medicare providing federal health insurance for aged and disabled	Social insurance
	Title XIX: Medicaid providing grants to states to use with matching funds for health care for public welfare recipients and the medically indigent	Public welfare
1972	Title VI: Supplemental Security Income (SSI), federally administered means-tested income maintenance program that supplants OAA, AB, and AD	Public welfare
1975	Title XX: Social services amendments, comprehensive social services program	Social services
1981	Social service block grant, amended Title XX, consolidates social service programs and gives greater state discretion.	Social services
1988	Family Support Act	Public welfare

This act with its subsequent amendments provides the basic income maintenance structure still in use today. It provides two types of benefits: social insurance for people who are a part of the labor force and public welfare for people outside the labor force. These provisions were introduced earlier in this chapter and will be discussed more fully in Chapter 7. The act represents unprecedented public involvement in the social welfare system and significant movement away from local control of and responsibility for those in need.

In 1935, workers were covered for old-age benefits; in 1939, survivors' benefits were added. In addition, grants were made to the states for the partial funding of unemployment insurance programs.

Under the public welfare arrangement, grants were made to states to provide an income maintenance program for mothers of dependent children without fathers' support (ADC), for the blind (AB), and old-age assistance for those over sixty-five with insufficient income from other sources (OAA). In 1956 a program for the totally and permanently disabled was added (AD). In 1961 further aid became available for needy dependent children whose father was in the home (AFDC). All of these programs were state administered.

In addition, certain services were provided in the areas of child welfare and maternal and child health through grants to state-administered programs. Thus, the social service category really originated as a part of the provisions of the Social Security Act.

In 1965, amendments to the Social Security Act added Medicare and Medicaid. Provision for additional social services was made in 1962 and 1974. In 1974, Old Age Assistance, Aid to the Blind, and Aid to the Disabled were converted into a single federal program called Supplementary Security Income (SSI). This is a federally funded and administered program that provides income to those with insufficient resources.

The federal government—through social insurance programs that are federally administered, through public welfare programs that are both federally and state administered, and through social service programs that are largely state administered—provides a basic system for social welfare in the United States. State governments are required to administer programs within specified guidelines and to provide matching funds for most state-administered programs. This system is supplemented and complemented by mutual aid and charity-philanthropy arrangements.

Although since 1960 many new and important programs, such as low-income housing, food stamps, and so on, have supplemented the social security programs, none, except the limited program under the Older Americans Act that introduced universal provision, has changed the basic system.

The social welfare system, then, is a combination of six arrangements. Questions about the system, therefore, should not address which arrangement should be used to provide for all needs or which level of government should be responsible for meeting needs. Rather, the question should be: Which arrangement and which level of government is appropriate for meeting specific needs?

Motivators of Social Welfare Decisions

To understand how decisions about which type of program and which level of government should be responsible for meeting some particular need, one must first know what factors have influenced those decisions. To do this, one more analytical framework is useful. This framework was developed by David Macarov (1978) of the Hebrew University of Jerusalem. He identifies the motivators for social welfare programs as mutual aid, religion, politics, economics, and ideology. It should be apparent by now that each of the arrangements and each of the milestones in the social welfare system came about in response to changes, not only changes in need but changes in our society's beliefs about the nature of need. For example, mutual aid is not only a way to meet human needs; it is also a natural caring response that motivates the development of other services and programs. The formal social welfare system evolved because it became apparent that in a complex industrial or postindustrial society the collective needs of citizens are dependent on meeting at least minimal needs for everyone within society.

Mutual aid is an important motivator permeating our social welfare system. As discussed earlier in this chapter, the impetus to help other people, particularly those most like ourselves, is an innate part of human functioning. It underlies family care and concern, neighborliness, volunteerism, and other self-help activities. It is an expression of the social nature of the human condition and a motivator for the development of mechanisms for helping others (the social welfare system and its component parts) when the mutual aid mechanism cannot meet the existing needs.

Both the mutual aid and charity-philanthropy arrangements had a strong religious motivation. Most of the people involved in developing charitable and philanthropic institutions and agencies were in part satisfying their religious beliefs as they dedicated time and money to developing those responses to human need. The work of Charles Loring Brace, who founded the Children's Aid Society, is an example of social welfare work influenced by religious motivation. Brace first became aware of the plight of poor children in New York City when, as a student at Union Theological Seminary, he visited the Five Points area and conducted religious meetings and classes for street children. When he formed the Children's Aid Society, he was supported in his work by various Protestant denominations (Lieby, 1978, p. 83).

The two major religions that most influenced our system, Judaism and Christianity, place considerable emphasis on mutual aid. Judaic scripture, particularly the Old Testament books of Leviticus and Deuteronomy, provides commandments calling for charity to the poor, the sick, the aged, and strangers. Later, a more formalized system of relief was created in the Talmud, a collection of Jewish laws and traditions. The Talmud set forth directives on how resources should be gathered and distributed, and how much should be given. Thus, Jewish tradition was one root of the beginning institutionalization of social welfare.

These traditions continued with the development of Christianity. Christian teachings also emphasized charity and service to others. The parable of the Good Samaritan (Luke 10:25–37) is an example of this teaching. At first, Christian responses were in the form of mutual aid, but by the second century Christian charity had become more formally organized, and granting relief had become a function of churches or church-related groups. The clergy, particularly with the development of the monastery system in Europe, were charged with this responsibility. The clergy were seen as leaders in carrying out the social welfare function of the churches. In a sense they became the first helping professionals. Their work was inspired by altruism, a sense of calling and commitment to serve the interests of people. This altruism and commitment are still considered characteristics of a modern professional helping person. Within the Roman Catholic church, Saint Vincent de Paul organized groups of volunteers to serve the needy; these groups came to be known as the Ladies of Charity (1617), and eventually became the Society of Saint Vincent de Paul (1833). Protestants also made extensive use of their laity in carrying out charitable work (Trattner, 1989).

In contemporary U.S. society, the influence of religion and spirituality on the social welfare system has lessened considerably, perhaps due to concern about the separation of church and state, in that government is the largest provider of social welfare services. However, religious and spiritual influence on this system is still present in several important ways.

On a more narrow and direct level, some religious groups are involved in the social welfare response because they see it as integral to living out their faith and spiritual beliefs, a sense of purpose and commitment that calls them to promote the development of the human potential (Canda and Chambers, 1994). Similarly, there still exist private agencies supported in whole or in part by organized religious groups (e.g., Catholic, Lutheran, and Jewish social services and some neighborhood and community centers). Other groups participate in various community efforts to relieve needs not met by government sources. These efforts include food pantries, shelters for the homeless, and home delivery of meals for the elderly. Canda and

Chambers (1994) forward that "All human endeavors are driven by just such concepts and become manifestations of the spirituality of individuals and collectives" (p. 54).

On a broader, social policy level, decisions must be made about how to allocate economic and social resources that are scarce, because the need for them usually exceeds their supply. Policy makers who must make these important decisions are influenced by their own spiritual values, that is, their perceptions about life's meaning and purpose, what is "just and right," and their moral views as to what is in the best interests of the public. Questions such as, Should unmarried women under the age of eighteen be denied AFDC benefits? Should government fund the cost of abortions? Is certain parental behavior (e.g., homosexuality) not in the best interests of children? all have been raised recently in regard to social policy decisions, and have brought into play the influence of the spiritual beliefs of those who make social policy. More often than not, the beliefs of the individual policy makers are in conflict with each other. Consequently, it is clear that social welfare policy, and the social programs that are created from them, reflect the expression of rival religious and spiritual beliefs, and continue to be important motivators of social welfare (Canda and Chambers, 1994).

The prevailing political climate has a considerable influence on the social welfare system. For example, the political events in Europe that brought about the Protestant Reformation disrupted the Roman Catholic church's role in caring for the needy. Likewise, the creation of the social security system was politically expedient in the 1930s. Because of the immensity of the economic problems and the number of people affected, the political system had to devise some means for dealing with the effects of the Great Depression if a political party expected to remain in power.

Political motivators originate in the body politic (voters and elected and appointed officials), and the body politic reflects concern about human needs and the unrest related to unmet needs. The concern is particularly related to the ability of a given political party to be elected and reelected, to the government's capacity to exercise its various powers, and, more generally, to the stability of the political system.

The influence of the political system is often apparent in political party platform items relative to social welfare issues, in voting patterns of the electorate, and in statements by political figures about human need and its resolution. Political motivation strongly influences the manner in which a government structures its social welfare system. In the United States, the mixture of state and national administration of social welfare is directly related to political concerns about the balance between state and federal governmental powers.

Government involvement in the development and administration of social welfare mechanisms (policies, programs, services) has always been closely tied to the current political philosophy about the responsibilities of government.

There are two prevailing political views regarding the role of government in the social welfare arena, the conservative and liberal. Also included here is an alternative perspective, the radical, a minority view albeit, but with tacit implications for understanding the nature of social welfare. It is imperative to note here that neither the conservative nor liberal view represents an absolute constellation of beliefs, but rather tendencies to think and act in accordance with the general belief system forwarded by each view. The perspectives held by people about social welfare are dualistic, meaning that they generally fall into one or the other of the above camps, rather than on a continuum from conservative to liberal (Kerlinger, 1984). For example, those who identify and affiliate with the Republican party tend to have more conservative views regarding social welfare. Conversely, Democrats generally tend to hold more liberal views about social welfare (Popple and Leighninger, 1990).

Conservatives believe that the role of government in social welfare should be limited to providing a basic "safety net" for those who cannot on their own, or through natural channels such as the family and economic marketplace, meet their needs and become dependent on society. Liberals, on the other hand, believe that the capitalistic market place cannot provide equally for the needs of all, causing some people's needs to go unmet. Therefore, according to this view, government should have the responsibility to intervene via social welfare to provide for unmet need (Popple and Leighninger, 1990). Radicals, in deference to the above views and in line with the perspectives of Karl Marx and other "conflict theorists," believe that the role of government in social welfare has been to use it's power to control and oppress certain societal groups by providing just enough assistance to sustain them, but keep them poor, and thereby advantaging the power elite (Karger and Stoesz, 1994). Radicals hold that the remedy to this is a complete restructuring of the economic, political, and social systems with redistribution of power and control. There is disagreement, however, as to what role government would serve in social welfare after the reform (Popple and Leighninger, 1990).

Historically, the conservative and liberal views on social welfare have held prominence at given points in time. The conservative view can be said to have been dominant prior to the 1930s, where the social welfare response consisted mainly of the charity-philanthropy arrangement, with some minor involvement of state government, based primarily on the old world poor law perspective as noted earlier. The liberal view became the prevailing perspective after 1935, with the passage and implementation of the Social Security Act, and has been touted by some to be the beginning of the "modern welfare state." During this time (1935 to present), the role of the federal and state governments in social welfare has gradually expanded and replaced earlier arrangements as the major societal mechanism for meeting the human needs of those unable to do so on their own.

Currently, there is evidence that points to the erosion of the liberal view of government's role in social welfare and a swing in the political pendulum more to the conservative view. This will be discussed in more detail in Chapters 3 and 7.

Although the radical view has never prevailed as a dominant perspective, it has served to further the understanding of the modern social welfare system. Its greatest contribution has been to keep at the forefront the notion that the social welfare response has become an enforcer of societal social control, by only providing benefits to the poor at a minimum level of subsistence, thereby reducing its intended effect as an income redistribution mechanism.

Economic motivators of social welfare are difficult to separate from political motivators because each have direct bearing and impact on each other. The political scene is responsive to economic factors, and economic policy is, in turn, responsive to political influence. For example, in the early 1930s, the serious economic condition of the country caused by the Great Depression had considerable influence in motivating political leaders to create economic and social policy that would be responsive to the mass human need of the times (e.g., the New Deal Programs and eventually the Social Security Act of 1935). Perhaps the best example of the reciprocal relationship between the economic and political motivators of social welfare is the current scene. Lingering concerns about government spending, the federal budget deficit, taxation, and the perceived intrusive role of government in the lives of people have festered to the point of motivating the Clinton Administration, and Congress, to create a course of economic policy that will reduce the size and roles of government. One role of government that is particularly germane here is responsibility for social welfare, in which reductions in government funding are imminent.

At the heart of the matter regarding economic motivators for social welfare is cost. Social problems, such as poverty, mental illness, health care, and crime and juvenile delinquency, are expensive to society, both in fiscal and human costs. One of the compelling arguments posed for government spending in social welfare is to reduce the long-term expenses to society by alleviation or elimination of social problems. In this vain, government spending in social welfare is seen to provide stability, which offsets the effects of an economic system that contributes to social problems, and is an investment in human capital that will eventually increase the nation's well-being (Karger and Stoesz, 1994).

The economic costs of social welfare have been of long-standing concern, and a source of debate among those who make public social welfare policy. Although agreeing in principle that some government response to human need and social problems is needed, the ongoing economic motivation and effort have been more to reduce the costs of social welfare. Historically, social welfare programs that have promised to eventually reduce the costs associated with a particular social problem have had greater acceptance. For instance, work-related programs (e.g., WIN, Workfare, and JOBS), discussed in detail in later chapters, that have had as a goal to reduce the number of people on welfare, strongly reflect this intent. The prevailing philosophy behind this economic motivation is that when people do not or cannot work, they become a drag on the economy. Therefore, the purpose of work-related public assistance programs has been to prepare or return people to work (Macarov, 1978). As P. Nelson Reid (1992) puts it, "The welfare state, particularly as it exists in the United States, is concerned not so much with reducing dissatisfaction or making people happy, as with rendering them useful. The continuing pressures to put welfare mothers to work . . . attests to the strength of this passion" (p. 45).

Ideology, or the prevailing belief system of a society, also affects the social welfare system. From time to time, the ideologies of altruism and humanitarianism have been strong motivators for the development of new programs and services. The 1960s was such a time. During this period, for example, many people protested actively against laws and practices that discriminated against people of a minority race, color, or religion. The civil rights movement grew out of this concern and resulted in new legislation prohibiting discrimination in the workplace and in any public facility.

U.S. society has also been built on a strong emphasis on individualism and free enterprise. Both of these ideologies have argued against the creation of universal provision arrangements. This ideology, combined with the economic situation beginning in the late 1970s (reflected in a growing national debt and in concern about taxes), motivated a political stance that called for major cutbacks in social welfare spending. An ideology that reflected a concern for national power and thus for a strong military defense also drained support from the social welfare system since the 1980s.

To this point, the discussion has reflected a view that the U.S. social welfare system responds to needs in similar ways throughout the entire United States. While it is true that federal legislation either is the source of or highly regulates the contemporary social welfare system, significant differences exist from region to region, partly because many programs are implemented at the state level. Another, often overlooked, factor is the ideological differences toward "welfare" that exist in different areas of the United States

The historian David H. Fischer (1989) has identified four British folkways that were transplanted to the New World: those of the Puritans of East England who settled in New England, the Cavaliers and their indentured servants from the English West Country who settled in Virginia, the Friends (Quakers) of the North Midlands who settled in the Delaware River Valley, and the border country folk (England, Scotland, and, to some degree, Scotch-Irish) who settled in the back country (Tennessee, Kentucky, and western Virginia). Fischer develops the thesis that each of the four cultures are very much alive today in the various regions of the United States and are of major importance in the cultural and political functioning of each region. Although he does not specifically apply this material to the social welfare system, his work suggests the possibility of developing greater understanding about a number of regional differences within the U.S. social welfare system: for instance, the very low social welfare grants in the Old South, the heavy reliance on private social agencies in the Northeast, and the strong development of public social welfare in the upper Midwest.

Of course these four original English cultures cannot be credited or blamed for all differential attitudes toward social welfare. The United States has been populated by peoples from many parts of the world. Non-English Europeans have brought important customs and ideals about the care of those who cannot provide for their own basic needs. Of particular importance in parts of the upper Midwest are socialistic trends that were appearing in the homelands of the late nineteenth century Scandinavian and German immigrants.

The presence of various minority groups (particularly people of color) in a region has led to other ideological influences. Minority groups have culturally specific patterns for providing for the needs of individuals and families. The attitudes of majority people toward the needs of minority people has greatly influenced local implementation of governmental social welfare programs. Often this influence has had a negative effect as it openly or subtly helps to shape the local or regional systems.

One of the best documented regional differences has been in the rural social work movement. Not only do we find the specificity of differences based on the nature of the rural environment, but literature, also, can be used to identify differences due to regional factors and to the economic base of the area (Jirovec, 1984).

In summary, we have identified some motivational influences of a locality's specific social welfare system. The U.S. system as a whole is made up of many of these systems that have differing impacts on the delivery of benefits and services. This diversity is an area of study that deserves considerable development in the future.

Since the 1980s, ideological, economic, and political motivators have combined to support a policy of promoting economic growth. Important parts of this approach have included a tax cut, particularly for the highest income group; a large defense buildup; an anti-inflationary monetary policy; privatization of many endeavors that had become the responsibility of government; a lessening of government regulations; and the goal of a balanced budget through substantial cuts in domestic spending (Jirovec, 1984). This has resulted in the shifting of some programs from the federal level to state and local governments and the private sector. Since the early 1990s there has been a rise in the number of individuals and families who can no longer provide for their own basic needs. Many families can no longer find affordable housing.

TABLE 1-4   **Motivators for the Social Welfare System**

Motivator	Source	Characteristics	Expressions
Mutual aid	Innate part of human functioning	Collective need is often met by meeting individual need Care, concern for needs of others	Family care, concern, Volunteerism, Neighborliness, Self-help groups
Religion	Imperatives to help others embedded in religious faiths	A deep belief in a higher power that places expectations about care of the less fortunate on the believer	Charitable and religious institutions of concern and care Outreach and social action programs of religious groups Personal expression of many who work in the social welfare system
Body politic	The body politic's concern about unmet need and unrest resulting from unmet need Beliefs of the body politic about the source of unmet need	Statements by political figures about the nature of need and its resolution Influences on voting patterns Political party platform statements Political structures that define human need; its sources and means of mitigation	Governmental policies that influence, shape and define social welfare programs
Economy	Monetary capacity to meet basic needs Definition of accepted level of basic need Beliefs about social class, employment structures	Relative to economic conditions Relative to beliefs about basic need Relative to inherent rights and responsibilities about wealth	Income replacement programs (SSI, AFDC) Government insurance programs (Social Security) Regulations re health care costs
Ideology	Beliefs about others and relationships among people Expected cultural patterns of behavior	Strongly held cultural and regional differences Attitudes toward minorities	Humanitarianism Individualism Conservatism Liberalism Civil rights movement Women's movement Attitudes toward abortion, rights for homosexuals

Cuts in federal subsidies for housing have resulted in grave limitations in the availability of low-cost housing and a staggering growth of homelessness. The result for the social welfare system has been a greatly limited capacity to meet these growing needs for housing. Further discussion of the impact of changes in federal policy on the social welfare system will be discussed in subsequent chapters. The focus here is an understanding of how changing ideology has changed the capacity of the social welfare system to meet needs while not yet changing its basic structure.

Depending on the strength of particular motivators, the social welfare system may be strengthened or weakened in its capacity to meet needs; its structure and functioning may be modified. Thus, understanding the influence of the various modifiers is important for under-standing the social welfare system in its current form, as well as in its historical context. Each of the five motivators—mutual aid, religion, the body politic, the economy, and ideological factors—has influenced the development of the contemporary social welfare system. At any point, one or more of these motivators may predominate. Usually several, if not all, are re-sponsible for any change in our social welfare system.

While the discussion of motivators has classified them as separate entities, it should now be very apparent that this is an arbitrary division. Each classification influences and is influ-enced by every other classification; they are interdependent. Table 1-4 provides an overview of the five motivators discussed.

Summary

The contemporary social welfare system has developed as our society's response to its unique forms of human need. To understand that system, it is important to first understand the mech-anisms created to deliver resources and services to the people who need them. Six mechanisms have been identified: mutual aid, charity-philanthropy, public welfare, social insurance, social service, and universal provision.

How and why did these mechanisms develop? Certain milestones stand out as keys to un-derstanding this evolution. These include the English Poor Law of 1601, the roots of institu-tional care, the Community Organization Societies and settlement houses, and the Social Security Act of 1935.

A third way of analyzing the system is to identify the factors in a society that motivate a particular kind of response to an identified need. Mutual aid, religious, political, economic, and ideological motivators seem to be the most influential.

Key Terms

almshouse
categorical assistance
Charity Organization Societies (COS)
charity-philanthropy
conservative
English Poor Law
fields of practice
human needs
ideology
income maintenance
indoor relief
institutional care
less eligibility
liberal
local control

mutual aid
outside relief
private agencies
public welfare
radical
rugged individualism
scientific charity
settlement house
social insurance
Social Security Act
social services
social welfare
spirituality
universal provision

References

Bremner, R.H. (1960). *American Philanthropy*. Chicago: University of Chicago Press.

Bremner, R.H. (1964). *From the Depths: The Discovery of Poverty in the United States*. New York: New York University Press, 60–66.

Canda, E.R., and Chambers, D. (1994). Should Spiritual Principles Guide Social Policy? in *Controversial Issues in Social Policy*. Needham Heights, MA: Allyn and Bacon, 63–78.

Cox, F.M., Erlich, J. L., Rothman, J., and Tropman, J.E. (1987). *Strategies of Community Organization*. Itaska, IL: F.E. Peacock.

Day, P.J. (1989). *A New History of Social Welfare*. Englewood Cliffs: Prentice Hall.

Fischer, D.H. (1989). *Albions's Seed*. New York: Oxford University Press.

Handel, G. (1982). *Social Welfare in Western Society*. New York: Random House.

Jirovec, R.L. (1984). Reaganomics and Social Welfare: An Annotated Bibliography. *Public Welfare 42*: 23–27.

Kahn, A.J. (1979). *Social Policy and Social Services*. New York: Random House.

Karger, H.J., and Stoesz, D. (1994). *American Social Welfare Policy: A Pluralist Approach*. New York: Longman.

Kerlinger, F.N. (1984). *Liberalism and Conservatism: The Nature and Structure of Social Attitudes*. Hillsdale, NJ: Lawrence E. Erlbaum.

Lieby, J. (1978). *A History of Social Welfare in the United States*. New York: Columbia University Press, 83.

Loomis, C.P. (1940). *Ferdinand Tonnies, Fundamental Concepts of Sociology (Gemeinschaft and Gesellschaft)*. New York: American Books.

Macarov, D. (1978). *The Design of Social Welfare*. New York: Holt, Rinehart, and Winston.

Pancoast, D.L., Parker, P., and Froland, C. (1983). *Rediscovering Self-Help: It's Role in Social Care*. Beverly Hills: Sage Publications.

Popple, P.R., and Leighninger, L.H. (1990). *Social Work, Social Welfare, and American Society*. Boston: Allyn and Bacon.

Reid, P.N. (1992). The Social Function and Social Morality of Social Work: A Utilitarian Perspective, in *The Moral Purposes of Social Work: The Character and Intentions of a Profession*. Chicago: Nelson-Hall Inc.

Rothman, D.J. (1971). *The Discovery of the Asylum*. Boston: Little Brown.

Trattner, W.I. (1989). *From Poor Law To Welfare State: A History of Social Welfare in America*. New York: Free Press.

Wyers, N.L. (1987). Income Maintenance Systems. *Encyclopedia of Social Work*. Silver Springs, MD: National Association of Social Workers, 888–898.

Suggested Readings

American Public Welfare Association. (1992). The New Paternalism. *Public Welfare 50 (2)*: 4–5.

Amidei, N. (1991). Tax Policy and the Public Welfare: Becoming Tax Literate Is More Than Reading Lips. *Public Welfare 49*: 13–19.

Atherton, C. (1990). Liberalism's Decline and the Threat to the Welfare State. *Social Work 35*: 163–67.

Atherton, C. (1990). A Pragmatic Defense of the Welfare State Against the Ideological Challenge From the Right. *Social Work 35*: 41–45.

Blau, J. (1992). A Paralysis of Social Policy? *Social Work 37 (6)*: 558–562.

Bremner, R. (1960). *American Philanthropy*. Chicago: University of Chicago Press.

Day, P.J. (1989). *A New History of Social Welfare*. Englewood Cliffs: Prentice Hall.

Greenstein, R. (1992). Cutting Benefits vs. Changing Behavior. *Public Welfare 50 (2)*: 22–23.

Groskind, F. (1994). Ideological Influences on Public Support for Assistance to Poor Families. *Social Work 39 (1)*: 81–89.

Guest, G. (1989). The Boarding of the Dependent Poor in Colonial America. *Social Service Review 63*: 92–112.

Handel, G. (1982). *Social Welfare in Western Society*. New York: Random House.

Hartman, A. (1993). Writing A New Story About America. *Social Work 38 (2)*: 125–126.

Husock, H. (1993). Bringing Back The Settlement House: Settlements See Poor People As Citizens, Not Clients. *Public Welfare 51* (*4*): 16–25.

Jirovec, R.L. (1984). Reaganomics and Social Welfare: An Annotated Bibliography. *Public Welfare 42*: 23–27.

Karger, H.J., and Stoesz, D. (1994). *American Social Welfare Policy: A Pluralist Approach*. New York: Longman.

Karger, H.J., and Stoesz, D. (1993). Retreat and Retrenchment: Progressiveness and the Welfare State. *Social Work 38* (*2*): 212–20.

Lieby, J. (1985). Moral Foundations of Social Welfare and Social Work: A Historical View. *Social Work 30*: 323–330.

Macarov, D. (1978). *The Design of Social Welfare*. New York: Holt, Rinehart, and Winston.

Michielse, J.C.M. (1990). Policing the Poor: J.L. Vives and the Sixteenth Century Origins of Modern Social Administration. *Social Service Review 64*: 1–21.

Midgley, J. (1992). Society, Social Policy and the Ideology of Reaganism. *Journal of Sociology and Social Welfare 19* (*1*): 13–28.

National Association of Social Workers. (1987). History of Social Welfare. *Encyclopedia of Social Work*. Silver Spring, MD: National Association of Social Workers.

Newdom, F. (1994). Beyond Hard Times. *Journal of Progressive Human Services 4* (*2*): 65–77.

Rose, N.E. (1989). Work Relief in the 1930's and the Origins of the Social Security Act. *Social Service Review 63*: 63–91.

Schorr, A.L. (1988). Other Times, Other Strategies. *Social Work 33*: 249–250.

Stoesz, D., and Karger, H.J. (1992). Deconstructing Welfare: The Reagan Legacy and the Welfare State. *Social Work 38* (*5*): 619–28.

Trattner, W.I. (1989). *From Poor Law To Welfare State: A History of Social Welfare in America*. New York: Free Press.

2

SOCIAL CHANGE

Learning Expectations

- Understanding of the societal paradigms and ideologies that have guided societal social change and provisions for meeting human need

- Beginning of understanding of a social systems approach as one means for explaining social problems and how society responds to change

- Understanding of how population changes have influenced the development of the U.S. social welfare system

- Understanding of how the change from a subsistence economy to a monetary economy has affected individual and family capacity to meet basic needs

- Capacity to identify the changes that have taken place in family structure and how these changes impact the family's capacity to meet the basic needs of its members

- Understanding that some people become victims of social change; ability to identify examples in contemporary U.S. society; and discussion of the impact of such examples on individual and family functioning

- Understanding of empowerment and how it can be used by social workers to assist those who struggle with social change, or are members of a devalued group, to increase personal or collective self-efficacy

The contemporary social welfare system is in part a response to social changes surrounding the development of modern society in the United States. This society has been heavily influenced by the Industrial Revolution and scientific technology. This chapter explores some important areas of change and how those changes have affected our society and the individuals in it. It develops the theme that both problems in meeting human needs and societal responses to human needs increase during times of accelerated social change. The chapter presents the viewpoint that our social welfare system's development is related not only to the provision for human needs but also to social control and that in fact the two are inextricably related. *Social control* is the use of legal means to control the lives of people who are devalued by the larger society.

While there is no general consensus on a definition of social change, one is provided here to guide thinking about the context in which the material in this chapter is presented. *Social change* is alteration, modification, or substitution in the institutions, structures, patterns of organization, and exchanges and relationships between people in a given society. When one considers the above definition in light of U.S society, it is clear that change in institutions, structures, patterns of organization, and in exchanges and relationships between various groups of people, can and does become quite complex and can involve almost anything. What causes social change? Social change is often precipitated by economic, political, technological, ideological, and environmental changes, events, and developments. Changes or new developments in any of the above may in turn call for change in the ways human needs are met. Often there is a lag in time between the change event or development, and society's response to it. This may place further stress on those who find it difficult to meet their needs because they have been caught in the "winds of social change." A very strong component of any social change that takes place is development of new ideologies, or change in current societal ideology, preferred philosophy, or ways of thinking about or responding to something. As can be seen in what follows, social control has been one ideology that has influenced responses to human need caused by social change.

Chapter 1 pointed out that the English Poor Laws were, in part, a result of the movement away from an agricultural society to a society based on factory production—technological advancement. Ideologically, it also noted that poor laws developed out of the need for social control, for control of vagrancy, and for a stable labor force in the new economic system.

Institutional care in the United States grew out of changes in population patterns and the change from a subsistence economy to a monetary economy. In a *subsistence economy*, people meet their basic needs by hunting, fishing, or farming, or through other efforts directly tied to the natural resources that surround them. A *monetary economy*, on the other hand, uses currency in exchange for food, clothing, and shelter. Institutional care also involves concern not only for human needs but also for an element of social control, for segregating troublesome individuals from the general society. The Charity Organization Societies and settlement houses were responses to change brought about by massive immigration to the United States from Europe. Along with concern about the problems faced by these immigrants, there was also a social control component related to fear of cultural differences and a desire for the "Americanization" of the immigrants.

Social change and resulting political and economic conditions also influenced the development of the Social Security Act. The conversion from a subsistence economy to a monetary economy made it necessary to provide monetary support for those unable to provide for themselves. The Depression with its massive unemployment made it difficult for many citizens to provide for the needs of their families. A government program that provided at least a minimal income became economically necessary and politically expedient (Trattner, 1983).

In this chapter *social change* will be considered from five perspectives.

1. Societal paradigms and ideologies that have influenced responses to social change and provisions for meeting human need
2. Society as a social system, the nature of change in systems, and the effect of such change on the functioning of the societal system

3. Change as it has affected the societal system in the United States, with emphasis on changes by economic, political, technological, and environmental advancements or events
4. Change as it has affected individuals and families in contemporary society
5. Empowerment of individuals, families, and other collectives of people whose lives are affected in negative ways by societal responses to social change and human need.

Paradigms, Ideology, and Social Change

Thomas Kuhn (1970) defines a paradigm as "the entire constellation of beliefs, values, techniques, and so on shared by the members of a given community" (p.175). Paradigms shape and are shaped by values, knowledge, and beliefs about the world in which we live; therefore they are world views (Schriver, 1995). U.S. society represents a given community within the above definition; therefore there are paradigms that have become accepted within our society. These societal paradigms have not emerged by osmosis. They have emerged as points along a historical continuum as U.S. society has attempted to both understand and manage control of the world in which we live. Paradigms form and reflect at the same time the institutions and processes that we all share in (Schriver, 1995).

Not all societal paradigms are accepted and shared by the various diverse cultural groups in U.S. society. However, some societal paradigms become dominant because they are accepted and supported by the majority, particularly those who are socially affluent and powerful. Diverse groups, such as ethnic minorities of color, women, gays and lesbians, the aged, the poor, and persons with physical and mental disabilities, who do not accept and adhere to dominant paradigms are those who become devalued by the majority society. Other paradigms that devalued persons share and adhere to are often suppressed (Logan, 1990). Dominant paradigms, or world views, have emerged about almost all aspects of life. For instance, there are the political paradigms of conservative and liberal; each at a particular point in history has had the most influence on the direction of political thought and action. There are the economic paradigms of capitalism and socialism and so on. There are dominant paradigms that influence the relationship between majority white society and minorities of color. The dominant paradigm of "whiteness," that will be discussed more thoroughly in Chapter 5, is an example of such a paradigm. The major point being made here is that when societal paradigms achieve dominance they become embedded in social structures that perform socialization, "the process of teaching new members the rules by which the larger group or society operates" (Schriver, 1995:14). Therefore, they shape thinking and action about the relationships between various societal groups, and societal responses to human need and social problems. Consequently, the actions and responses that are shaped by societal dominant paradigms have the potential to oppress some groups of people.

Paradigms are not set in stone. Because they are socially constructed by people, they can and in fact have been changed or restructured (Capra, 1983). These changes are referred to as "paradigm shifts." According to Kuhn (1970), paradigm shifts "come about when a segment of a community, often a small segment, has a growing sense that existing institutions are unable to adequately address or solve problems in the environment" (p.92). The actions taken in this regard can result in replacement of all or parts of the existing paradigm. This constitutes social change. An example or two of paradigm shifts to illustrate this point are in order. An example of a paradigm shift that has recently altered the nature of sexual relationships between men and women is a change in both attitudes and behaviors regarding sex. Due to the presence of HIV and AIDS, the more liberal and permissive attitudes and behaviors about sexual relations of ten years ago are now being replaced by more conservative attitudes and safer sex practices. An older example of a paradigm shift involves government responsibility for social welfare. This occurred during the depression years of the 1930s. Prior to 1935, assisting the poor was believed to be the responsibility of private charity, with assistance being provided by the churches and other private voluntary organizations. Because these systems were unable to adequately respond to the massive amount of poverty that existed during these years, the federal government began to assume responsibility for social welfare, as authorized by the Social Security Act of 1935. This represented a paradigm shift, a change in ideology about societal responsibility for meeting human need.

As paradigm shifts occur, not all people are given a voice in the changes that result. This is because not all people are afforded equal power and control over what a new paradigm becomes, and whose beliefs and values give it substance. Paradigm shifts usually involve some amount of conflict and a struggle for power. When the dust finally settles, a new dominant societal paradigm takes form, supported by the majority, who then often use it as a measure of control to suppress alternative ideologies that are forwarded by other groups (Kuhn, 1970). This has largely been the case as it pertains to societal ideology about how responses to human need via the social welfare system should be made. Although society generally believes in the ideology of social provision, which emanates from a humanitarian paradigm, it also believes it has the right to control the means, the extent to which, and whose human needs will be met—a social control ideology.

It should now be clear that dominant societal paradigms have been shaped by social change, and in turn have shaped and influenced the ideologies out of which societal responses are made to human need and problems.

Society as a Social System

Considering society as a social system allows a view of social change that includes understanding how change in one part of a system calls for change in other parts of that system. A *social systems approach* gives a framework for discussing how social change affects both the society as a whole and individuals within that society. In other words, as change takes place in a part of society, some of the mechanisms developed to maintain that society must also change. Some individuals discover that their customary ways of functioning are no longer acceptable or no longer provide the resources they once did. Some members of the society may find that unless they change their customary ways of functioning, they may no longer be able to meet their human needs or fulfill their responsibilities for meeting the human needs of others. Some people may not have the resources or the motivation to make the necessary changes and thus require social welfare services. For example, a farm worker may realize he no longer has the skills needed for working in a highly mechanized agricultural system, or, even if he upgrades his skills, his services may no longer be needed in the new system. He then becomes unable to support himself and his family. His customary way of life is severely disrupted, and his capacity to function as a productive member of society is threatened. In addition, because his family members' needs are not being met, they too may be vulnerable to serious problems in social functioning. Change in one part of the system—the introduction of mechanized farming methods—brings about change in other parts of the system, resulting in many farm workers losing their jobs.

To take another example, as a result of changes in the economic system, such as inflation, the demand for a higher standard of living, and the lessening of economic contribution through home production, it has become necessary for many families to have two incomes in order to meet basic family needs. The employment of both parents outside the home then necessitates changes in the way child care is provided. Yet parts of the societal system continue to function on the basis of an ideology that the most appropriate care for children is provided in the home by a parent, usually the mother. This simplified explanation of a current conflict within the societal system illustrates another characteristic of times of accelerated social change: the lack of clear-cut patterns for social functioning. This in turn leads to lack of clarity about the proper focus of social welfare provision. Should the provision be one that supports families so mothers can stay home and care for young children (a stability response) or one that provides alternative care for children so mothers can work (a change response)? Of course, the solution also must consider other concurrent social changes, such as changes in the role and status of women in contemporary U.S. society.

Under some circumstances, change seems to be especially disruptive, placing various components of a society at considerable risk or even creating a crisis. The extent of the change—both the amount of change and the number of changes called for—is a primary consideration in assessing the risk posed by change. The rapidity of the change is another factor; the more rapid the change, the more disruptive it is apt to be. Change that results in feelings of bewilderment, uneasiness, and uncertainty about the future is apt to be disruptive to individual and family functioning. Also important are feelings of powerlessness or loss of control, which can lead to anger, to passive and dependent behavior, or to other destructive responses. A diversity of attitudes toward the change also can make resolution of the disruptions related to change more difficult. These circumstances in turn can lead to the development of social problems, difficulties that have the potential to affect the entire societal structure.

One means of explaining social problems is to use a cause–effect or linear framework for thinking about human functioning. As an example of this type of thinking, one might blame an unemployed father by saying that his lack of a job is attributable to sheer laziness, with no consideration of environmental factors that are at least in part responsible for his unemployment. (e.g., Perhaps no jobs are available because of a recession or plant closing, or perhaps he has obsolete skills and no opportunity for updating them, both factors that mitigate against relocation.) Linear thinking does not fully explain the functioning of society or the nature of social change, nor does it provide workable solutions for problems that develop in social functioning. In part because of this inadequacy, contemporary social work has adopted a social systems approach for understanding individuals, families, small groups, agencies and institutions, and communities in interaction with one another. This approach reveals not only the internal functioning of a system but also the interaction between the system and its environment in the broadest sense of the term. In the broadest dimension, society is seen as the environment; however, it too can be considered as a social system.

Defining the societal system can be problematic. Persell (1987, 47–48) defines society as a "group of people who share a heritage or history and ways of interacting," and culture as "that accumulation of customs, values, and artifacts shared by a people." This definition is too broad for the present discussion. The political entity of the United States is a more usable definition of the society's *boundary* when we refer to the society to which our social welfare system belongs. In fact, this entity as a system is almost too large and unwieldy, containing many subsystems of varying size and complexity. However, because of the important relationship between the federal political system and the social welfare system, we will find it useful for our discussion here. It provides a framework for thinking about strategies for alleviating social dysfunctioning.

A full discussion of social systems theory is beyond the scope of this book. We will present a cursory review of the major components of a social systems framework or way of considering a system's structure, functioning, and development. The first consideration is to identify the system of focus. Often, this system is identified in terms of its boundary. *Boundary* differentiates the system from its environment. The interactions within the boundary are more numerous and more intense than the interactions across the boundary lines. As stated earlier in this chapter, we are discussing the societal system of the United States. When considering a system of this size, however, it is also important to focus at times on other systems that are part of the societal system. It is important to identify the component parts of whatever system is the focus of attention. The identified societal system is made up of many overlapping and interlocking *subsystems:* states, communities, agencies, institutions, groups, families, and individuals. Also important are functional subsystems: economic, political, health, social welfare, and the like. In addition, various population groups, such as particular ethnic groups, disadvantaged groups, groups with a strong lobbying thrust, professional groups, and so on, may be important components of the system. When considering a system as complex as U.S. society, it is helpful to identify the subsystems that are important to the concern at hand. Once the appropriate systems have been identified, the next step is to identify the relationships between these systems and how these relationships affect the functioning of other subsystems. Another area for identification includes those systems in the environment of any one system that are important for its functioning. In the case of the U.S. societal system, for example, the systems of the world community are its environment. An economic consideration might be the availability of oil in the world market, which in turn could have an important impact on the ability of the U.S. societal system as it affects the cost of living index.

The concept of *steady state* is important because it deals with the way various parts of a system relate to each other. Steady state is concerned with the balance between parts, or an equilibrium in which various parts work together to complement, counteract, enhance, and support one another. The system is not static but, rather, is in constant movement. What is important is the degree of movement or change that a system can tolerate without disintegrating. One result of massive social change is that the societal system's steady state is placed at risk. The various subsystems must then seek a new pattern of relationships in order to maintain the steady state. These subsystems also must accommodate the change by changing their ways of functioning. The various changes in the social welfare system that were discussed in Chapter 1 came about as accommodations to changing social conditions.

Another area for consideration is the way a system operates to carry out its assigned functions. Each subsystem has its own means of decision-making, which in one way or another is validated by the larger system. Communication among subsystems is another important function. Each system also must create some means of allocating resources and energy to its various subsystems for carrying out assigned tasks. Understanding the way any system carries out its assigned functions and the way in which the various subsystems relate to one another is crucial for understanding that system.

As large systems develop, they tend to move toward a higher degree of organization and specialization in carrying out necessary tasks. The development of governmental bureaucracy is a good example. Bureaucratization can lead to a situation where preserving the stability of the organization (subsystem) takes precedence over carrying out its assigned function in meeting the needs of the total system or of other subsystems. In the social welfare system this has contributed to a social control stance rather than a focus on meeting human needs.

The so-called cultural lag that often exists in times of change can be explained by knowing that some parts of the system are operating under old rules while other parts have made the adaptation needed to accommodate the change. This lag allows confusion about how people are expected to function. The confusion that exists today about women's roles is an example. Societal change (economic and other) has made it necessary for many women to join the labor force. Yet women are also expected to continue to fill traditional roles in the home. The result is confusion about women's role in contemporary society. This confusion also can reduce people's capacity for social functioning as energy that could be available for such functioning is siphoned off for use in trying to meet conflicting demands (Chess and Norlin, 1991).

This brief description of a social system, with specific application to the U.S. societal system, is a cursory one at best. It does, however, provide a sense of how social change or change in any of the functional subsystems (political, economic, etc.) demands change in other parts of the system. Understanding how the societal system functions from a social systems point of view is one way of understanding the relationship between provision for human needs and provision for social control as they operate in the social welfare system. It also provides a framework for thinking about strategies for alleviating social dysfunctioning. It helps us appreciate the complexity and the interrelationships of the mechanisms that have been developed to provide for the well-being of individuals and their society.

Change as It Affects the Societal System

Two major changes that have greatly affected the U.S. societal system are changes in population characteristics and changes in the economic system. To develop further understanding of how each major change has affected the nature of the social welfare system, they will be considered from three perspectives: the nature of the change, how the change has affected social functioning within the societal system, and how the social welfare system has changed in response to these changes.

Population Change

Changes in the population can best be seen by examining census data. Since 1800 the profile of the U.S. population has changed in many ways, including geographic distribution, immigration and migration patterns, and employment patterns. Three major changes of particular interest when considering human service delivery issues are size of population, rural–urban residence patterns, and age distribution patterns.

The sheer growth in population has been complemented by a growth in the geographic area of the United States. Despite the geographic expansion, population density, or the number of people per square mile, increased as well. Table 2-1 depicts this growth from 1800 to 1990.

This population change has given rise to many accommodations within the societal system. Of particular interest is the change in the social welfare system (see Chapter 1 for an outline of the major changes). As the population grew, the number of individuals and families who could not provide for all their human needs also grew. As people came to live in closer proximity to others, their needs became more apparent and opportunities to meet these needs by using land for subsistence farming, or simply moving west, became unavailable. In addition, population growth was due in part to immigration. Immigrants brought with them special needs, which called for new responses. As the societal system and its component parts became aware of this rise in numbers of people with unmet needs, efforts developed to resolve the threat to steady state posed by this change. Some responses that developed included the following:

1. The establishment of institutions in which to care for those in need, but also as a means of isolating and controlling those who were troublesome to the general population
2. Attempts to categorize those in need as to whether they were worthy or unworthy of help, and to develop differential responses to the needs of these two categories of needy persons
3. The development of formal organizations to meet human needs (the COS and settlement houses) and increased acceptance of state and local government responsibility for social welfare functions

Table 2-2 shows the shift of the U.S. population from a rural to an urban society. In 1800 only 6 percent of the U.S. population lived in urban areas. In 1992, 79.7 percent of the U.S. population lived in metropolitan areas (U.S. Bureau of the Census, 1995). This growth has been steady, slowing only during the 1930–1940 Depression years. While census data after 1970 have not been tabulated to show the trends shown in Table 2-1, the trends from rural to urban living have continued. The growth in population and the shift from a rural, agricultural society to an urban, industrial society brought many people into new and unfamiliar environments. Many immigrants came from rural areas. Often both immigrants and migrants from rural areas in the United States were driven to the new urban life by harsh economic and political conditions. They came to the new situation under stress and were not prepared for the further stresses caused by many people (often strangers) living closely together. They had little knowledge of the sanitary measures necessitated by overcrowding. Factory jobs demanded long hours doing monotonous tasks under close supervision, very different from life in an agricultural setting. Factory workers suffered not only from poverty and hazardous health conditions, but also from disruption of family life and from a lack of understanding of what they needed to do to survive in their new surroundings. The immigrants often could not speak English and thus had additional trouble understanding how to use those resources and opportunities available to them. Once social change had disrupted their usual pattern of functioning, the newly urban poor had difficulty meeting their needs, and their social behavior often did not adhere to the norms of the established society in

TABLE 2-1   Population and Area of the United States, 1800–1990

Census Date	Number	Number per Square Mile of Land Area	Increase over Preceding Census	
			Number	Percentage
1800	5,929,483	6.1	1,379,269	35.1
1810	7,239,881	4.3	1,931,398	36.4
1820	9,638,453	5.5	2,398,572	33.1
1830	12,866,020	7.4	3,227,567	33.5
1840	17,069,453	9.8	4,203,433	32.7
1850	23,191,876	7.9	6,122,423	35.9
1860	31,443,321	10.6	8,251,445	35.6
1870	39,818,449	13.5	8,375,128	26.6
1880	50,155,783	16.9	10,337,334	26.0
1890	62,947,714	21.2	12,791,931	25.5
1900	75,994,575	25.6	13,046,861	20.7
1910	91,972,266	31.0	15,977,691	21.0
1920	105,710,620	35.6	13,738,354	14.9
1930	122,775,046	41.2	17,064,426	16.1
1940	131,669,275	44.2	8,894,229	7.2
1950[a]	151,325,798	42.6	19,161,229	14.5
1960	179,323,175	50.6	27,997,377	18.5
1970	203,302,031	57.6	23,978,856	13.4
1980	226,504,825	64.0	23,202,794	11.4
1990	248,709,873	70.3	22,164,068	9.8

Source: U.S. Department of Commerce, Bureau of Census, *Statistical Abstract of the United States, 1981* (Washington, D.C.: U.S. Government Printing Office, 1991), p. 7.

[a]Reflects inclusion of Alaska and Hawaii.

which they found themselves. The dominant classes of society were pressed to find ways to meet migrants' and immigrants' needs and to control their misunderstood behavior (Nichols and Reimers, 1979).

It was on this group of unadapted, newly urbanized people caught up in the turmoil of a changing societal system that the Charity Organization Societies and the settlement houses focused their concern. Both had a goal of helping these people establish a lifestyle congruent with the needs and demands of living in an urban U.S. societal system. Their goal spoke not only to the concern for the individual and the family but to the larger needs of society as well. They responded to the needs of a societal system in a state of change as it assimilated new subsystems. They spoke to the need for a system to stabilize its steady state.

Table 2-3 shows the shift in age distribution between 1900 and 1989. Of particular note is the dramatic rise in the number of elderly. The 65-and-over group was three times greater in 1989 than in 1900. In 1994, the population of persons age 65 and older stood at 33.1 million (U.S. Bureau of the Census, 1995). The percentage of people under 14 years old has continued to drop, except for the baby boom years of the 1950s and 1960s. The expected life span has also increased. In 1900 a person could expect to live 48.2 years. By 1959 this had risen to 69.9 years, and by 1976 to 72.8 years (U.S. Bureau of the Census, 1991). By 1993 life expectancy had risen to 75.5 years with a prediction that by 2010 it would be 77.9 years (U.S. Bureau of

TABLE 2-2   Urban–Rural Population in the United States, 1800–1970

Census Date	Urban		Rural	
	Number	Percentage	Number	Percentage
1800	322,000	6.0	4,986,000	93.9
1810	525,000	7.2	6,714,000	92.7
1820	693,000	7.2	8,945,000	92.8
1830	1,127,000	8.7	11,739,000	91.2
1840	1,845,000	10.8	15,224,000	89.2
1850	3,544,000	15.3	19,648,000	84.7
1860	6,217,000	19.9	25,656,000	80.2
1870	9,902,000	25.7	28,656,000	74.3
1880	14,130,000	28.2	36,026,000	71.8
1890	22,106,000	35.1	40,841,000	64.9
1900	30,160,000	39.6	45,835,000	60.3
1910	41,999,000	45.6	49,973,000	54.3
1920	54,158,000	51.2	51,522,000	48.7
1930	68,955,000	56.2	53,821,000	43.8
1940	74,424,000	56.5	57,245,000	43.5
1950[a]	96,468,000	64.0	54,479,000	36.0
1960	125,269,000	69.9	54,054,000	30.1
1970[b]	149,325,000	73.5	53,887,000	26.5

Source: 1800–1940: U.S. Department of Commerce, Bureau of Census, *A Statistical Abstract Supplement, Historical Statistics of the United States, Colonial Times to 1957* (Washington, D.C.:U.S. Government Printing Office), p. 8. 1950–1970: U.S. Department of Commerce, Bureau of Census, *Statistical Abstract of the United States, 1981* (Washington, D.C.: U.S. Government Printing Office, 1981), p. 14.

[a]From 1950 a slightly different definition has been used.

[b]Census records after 1970 do not reflect this population shift.

the Census, 1995). These facts indicate an enormous change in the characteristics of the population of the United States. Now it is important to identify how those changes have affected human needs.

With the aging of the population have come pressures to develop new support systems for the elderly. If elders remain in the work force, they fill jobs needed by younger workers. If they are removed from the work force, they can no longer support themselves, and some societal provision must be made for their support. The Social Security Act provides the major mechanisms used since 1935 to support those over 65 years of age. It provides monetary and health care support for meeting individual needs while providing for societal needs by allowing older workers to leave the work force.

In recent years, as medical advances have further lengthened the life span, we now have a new group of elderly, those over 75 years of age known as the *frail elderly*. This population stood at 14.5 million persons in 1994 (U.S. Bureau of the Census, 1995). This group often needs more than income support. The frail elderly may need other services either in the home or in institutions: help with many tasks of daily living such as self-care and care of the home, considerable health care, and often opportunities for social contact with others. One of the challenges of the 1990s is the development of mechanisms that respond to the needs of this

TABLE 2-3 Age Distribution of Population of the United States, 1900–1989

Population by Age

Census Year	Total Population	14 and under	Percentage	15–24	Percentage	25–34	Percentage
1900	76,094,000	24,581,000	32.3	16,514,000	21.7	12,162,000	16.0
1910	92,407,000	27,806,000	30.0	20,024,000	21.7	15,276,000	16.5
1920	106,466,000	31,756,000	29.8	28,858,000	19.6	17,417,000	16.4
1930	123,077,000	33,638,000	27.3	24,852,000	20.1	19,039,000	15.5
1940	132,122,000	30,521,000	23.1	26,454,000	20.0	21,446,000	16.2
1950	151,683,000	38,605,000	25.5	24,458,000	16.1	23,926,000	15.8
1960	179,323,000	55,786,000	31.1	24,020,000	13.3	22,818,000	12.7
1970	203,235,000	57,936,000	28.5	35,467,000	17.5	24,923,000	12.3
1980	226,505,000	51,282,000	22.6	42,475,000	18.5	37,076,000	16.4
1989	248,239,000	53,941,000	21.7	36,514,000	14.7	43,834,000	16.8

Population by Age

35–44	Percentage	45–54	Percentage	55–64	Percentage	65 and over	Percentage
9,271,000	12.2	6,439,000	8.5	4,027,000	5.3	3,100,000	4.0
11,761,000	12.7	8,454,000	9.1	5,101,000	5.5	3,985,000	4.3
14,383,000	13.5	10,503,000	9.9	6,620,000	6.2	4,929,000	4.6
17,270,000	14.0	13,096,000	10.6	8,477,000	6.9	6,706,000	5.4
18,422,000	13.9	15,555,000	11.8	10,694,000	8.1	9,031,000	6.8
21,569,000	14.2	17,413,000	11.5	13,424,000	8.8	12,287,000	8.1
24,081,000	13.4	20,485,000	11.4	15,572,000	8.7	16,560,000	9.2
23,101,000	11.4	23,235,000	11.4	18,602,000	9.2	19,972,000	9.8
25,336,000	11.2	22,797,000	10.1	21,700,000	9.6	25,544,000	11.3
36,283,000	14.7	24,896,000	10.0	21,593,000	8.7	30,964,000	12.5

Source: 1900–1950: U.S. Department of Commerce, *Historical Statistics of the United States, Colonial Times to 1957* (Washington, D.C.: U.S. Government Printing Office), p. 6. 1960–1980: U.S. Department of Commerce, *Statistical Abstract of the United States, 1991* (Washington, D.C.: U.S. Government Printing Office, 1991), p. 18.

growing group of frail elderly. Again, a change in one aspect of society, the population, calls for change in its social welfare system.

Growth of a Monetary Economy

With the movement from rural to urban living came the movement from a subsistence economy to a monetary economy. Most people no longer had land available to use to provide a major portion of their food supply. A family could not take in individuals in unfortunate circumstances as live-in servants or apprentices. Often families could not even provide for a relative who had no means of support. Costs of essentials, such as food, shelter, clothing, and medical care, rose dramatically. The availability of money became essential for survival in our contemporary, money-based society. Since older traditional means of taking care of oneself and others are no longer possible in today's societal system, social welfare mechanisms must provide monetary means for needy people. Thus the social welfare system has had to change because of social and economic changes. Economic changes affect not only how people provide for their own basic needs, but also how society provides for the needs of those who cannot provide for themselves.

The growth of a government social welfare system is related to the growth of the necessity to make monetary provision for human needs. That means the system must be set up not only to provide for human needs but also to control costs and to control decisions about whose needs and which needs are provided for.

One important contemporary issue is how much income and how many services can be provided through monetary mechanisms by the various supporting political entities. This can be translated: How much tax money is available for providing for the welfare of individuals in U.S. society? A related question is: How much of a contribution through taxes and other means are citizens willing to make to help meet the needs of others? A third question is: Who are to be helped—those who are unable to meet their basic needs (the poor) or those who create concerns about social control (all citizens)? In other words, how much welfare must be provided to prevent riots, uprisings, and other civil strife? Economic change has disrupted an earlier steady state. Society is using the social welfare system to bring about a new balance by providing for new areas of human needs, some of which are a result of the economic change. At the same time, society is using that system as a form of social control, control that is needed if a steady state is to be maintained.

It is thus apparent that changes in the economic system have brought about changes in how people meet their needs, both individually and collectively.

In the 1990s there is a movement toward what had been developing since the 1960s and 1970s, called a *service society*. This movement is characterized by the growth of many low-paying jobs of a service nature. These jobs are often found in the food industry, and they tend to be part-time with no fringe benefits. In addition, there has been a loss of blue-collar factory jobs and a widening gap in the economic structure between what has been characterized as the "haves" and the "have-nots." The result has been a rise in the "employed poor," that is, employed people unable to meet their basic needs through their employment. During the process of change, old means for meeting needs become either unusable or ineffective. Until new means are developed, some people, through no fault of their own, are unable to meet their own or their family's needs.

Social Change as It Affects Individuals and Families

Social change not only has an impact on the larger societal subsystems (e.g., the economic and social welfare systems), but it also affects smaller subsystems. Of particular importance to the discussion are families and individuals who seek to meet their needs and who carry out their functions in the changing societal system.

Changes in Family Structure and Functioning

Although the family is the primary social unit within our society, it takes on many forms. In light of this, Hartman and Laird (1987: 576) offer a broad definition of the *family* as it exists in the United States today:

> *. . . when two or more people construct an intimate environment that they define as a family, an environment in which they generally will share a living space, commitment, and a variety of the roles and functions usually considered part of family.*

Within the family, individuals are socialized, protected, and nurtured so they can develop the skills necessary for their well-being and survival. To meet the needs of individuals, the family unit in whatever form must first have its needs met. Prior to the turn of the present century, the family was the primary social and economic unit within society. The basic family structure was the *extended family* system. Families were large, with several generations that included brothers and sisters, cousins, great aunts and uncles all working closely together, all living in close proximity to one another. People were raised, lived, and died close to their birthplace. Most needs were met within the family system. Families needed to be large: the larger the family, the more producers available, and the better off the family became. When family problems occurred, the response was mutual aid within the extended family structure. But the Industrial Revolution brought about vast changes. The change from an agricultural economy to a monetary industrial economy meant that families did not produce all their necessities (food, clothing, shelter) on the family farm or in the local community. Large families were no longer an asset. Extended families broke up as the younger generations relocated to the large industrial cities in search of new opportunities and higher wages. This resulted in the eventual change from the extended family to a new form of family structure, the *nuclear family*, usually consisting of only the two parents and one or more children.

The nuclear family remains the ideal family type today. However, in contemporary U.S. society, particularly since the beginning of the 1970s, several alternative family forms have emerged.

A common variant family form is the *single-parent family*, where only one parent is present in the home. A number of circumstances have brought about its appearance: out-of-wedlock births, desertion, separation, divorce, death, or incarceration. Single-parent families have also resulted from adoptions of children by unmarried individuals. These families are growing in number. In 1994, there were approximately 15.3 million single-parent families, compared with 10.4 million in 1980. By 1994 the number of families with single mothers was approaching 12.4 million. In 1994, 9% of children under 18 lived in mother-only households.

The *step-family*, or what has recently been termed the *blended* or *reconstituted family*, is another variant. A step-family is created when one or both partners in a marriage bring with them children from a former relationship. There are approximately 10 million of these families in the United States, and they too are growing in number. For some of these families, the process of blending together as a single, cohesive family unit has been difficult, giving rise to relationship problems among family members. In recent years, professional helpers have begun reaching out to reconstituted families who are experiencing difficulties, to help them with the problems that prevent them from achieving harmonious relationships and family cohesiveness.

The childless family is another family form, which many couples in recent years have chosen as a lifestyle. Cohabitation without marriage, with children present, is another form, as is the homosexual family arrangement.

The family is supposed to provide its individual members with opportunities for growth and development, and to teach them the physical, social, intellectual, and emotional skills necessary to prepare them for membership in the larger society. That process of growth and development for individual family members depends on the growth and development of the family itself. Just as individuals grow and develop through predictable phases in their life cycle, so does the family (e.g., marriage, birth of children, children reaching adolescence, and eventual separation of children from the family unit). Each phase of family development brings new tasks, different societal demands and expectations. The family's ability to perform its roles and functions depends on its successful transition through the developmental life cycle.

Effectiveness in performing roles and functions is also measured by the extent to which the family is able to meet its needs as a unit and the needs of its individual members (Goldenberg and Goldenberg, 1996). The social and technological advances of the twentieth century have affected the family's ability to do this. The family's roles and functions have changed, as have the ways in which they perform them.

In the past, the family—whether immediate or extended—was responsible for meeting all the needs of its members. These needs included needs for protection and safety; physical needs (food, clothing, shelter); emotional needs; and needs relating to health, education, religion, and leisure and recreation. Today it is no longer necessary for families to assume total responsibility for meeting these needs. Societal structures have assumed many of these responsibilities, of which education and health care are just two examples.

Despite changes, the family has retained some of its traditional roles and functions. These include reproduction, meeting the basic physical and emotional needs of family members, and early socialization of children (Longres, 1995). However, even some of these family roles are now being challenged. Changes in family values, technological advances, and economic pressures have brought this about. For example, parenting roles have changed. Traditionally, women had major responsibility for the care and socialization of preschool children. But today many women, out of either economic necessity or the desire to pursue a career, are employed. This has resulted in role sharing, not only in providing for the family's economic needs, but in childrearing responsibilities as well. Responsibility for child care has shifted to individual child care providers or other community arrangements such as day-care centers and preschools. Even the role of reproduction is now being challenged by such developments as surrogate parenting. Advances in medical technology have made it possible for reproduction to occur in laboratory test tubes. These new phenomena have the potential to further alter the family's responsibilities.

The family's structure and functioning have changed in response to societal change. Whether these changes will bring about further deterioration of the family's influence on the individual remains to be seen. If the family, despite the continuing erosion of its roles, can continue to meet the emotional needs of its members effectively, it has a reasonable chance of remaining the primary social unit in society.

The industrial, money-based economy operating in contemporary society has sometimes caused economic stress on families. Economic security for families has always been tied to the functioning of the marketplace. Since 1900, the U.S. economy has fluctuated with cycles of depression, recession, inflation, and relative prosperity. With each fluctuation, families have had to find ways to protect their own economic stability. Not all have been successful. Poverty complicates the problems experienced by these families in coping with economic fluctuations. Adequate income and economic supports are essential to successful family functioning. In families where there is not enough money, much family energy is spent in securing the resources necessary to sustain life. What can result is *role overload*, where more energy is spent in just making ends meet than in providing emotional support to family members. Families headed by single parents are particularly vulnerable to this problem, because the single parent is required to fulfill all expected family roles with limited energy and time. Inadequate economic support and the role overload associated with it often lead to tension and conflict within the family and to possible family dysfunction.

For many families, economic reality demands that both parents work. In some families, this has led to a weakening of family cohesiveness. If both parents spend most of their energy and time in obtaining financial support, the emotional and socializing roles may suffer. In many dual-career families, this is not a problem because parents make a conscious effort, through role division and role sharing, to ensure that the needs of family members are met. But when this does not occur, family stress and conflict may result in weakened family relationships and eventual problems in family functioning. Stressed families are those who most often come to the attention of the social welfare system, and they are in need of supportive help.

One question that should be raised about social change is whether a particular change is desirable or whether change should be resisted in an effort to achieve a steady state. The conservative political stance is usually to minimize change. The more liberal or progressive stance is to work for change. When political power rests with those who are comfortable with the current situation, the pull is for minimal change. When a significant group in the country is being adversely affected by social and economic conditions, the push is for change. Societal change has affected not only the population distribution and the economy of our society, but also the ways families function. Large families are no longer as desirable as when the economic base was the family farm or small family business. Then, many children were an asset, providing extra hands to carry out the work to be done. Today, with an economic base that requires many women to work outside the home, children are often an economic liability. Advances in maternal and child health have resulted in more children surviving their early years and fewer women dying in childbirth. Thus we find many families choosing to limit the number of children they produce. For women, this has led to a shorter period of child care and a greater opportunity to enter the labor force outside the home.

Women enter the labor force for more than just economic reasons. Today, women have more opportunity for education and thus more of the skills needed in the labor market. Labor-saving devices have freed women of much of the drudgery of caring for the home and have given them time for other activities. These women also contribute to family change as they develop new mothering patterns and new patterns of sharing household tasks.

The changed economic system also has a need for a mobile work force. As a result, family members often find themselves relocated at some distance from their extended family. These families must often seek new means for the sort of help once given by extended families, such as a grandmother's care of a sick child when the mother is employed outside the home, or the support of a caring network in times of stress. For the dual career family, additional stress may result when relocation is advantageous to one partner but calls for the other partner to give up a job for the move.

It is not the purpose of this discussion to note all the changes that have occurred in family life. Rather, the point is that social change has brought about change in the functioning of families and thus altered their capacity to meet some of the needs of family members through mutual aid. It has led to more dependence by families on the functioning of the economic marketplace to meet most of their needs. For some families, changes have forced an increased reliance on social welfare services to meet the needs of their members.

Some families are more vulnerable than others to problems in meeting their members' needs: those with the least capacity and opportunity to function in the job market, those with single parents, minority group families, those composed of aging people (sixty-five years of age or older), and those containing individuals with special medical and other needs. These families often cannot earn enough money to meet their basic needs. They are also the families who have been affected the most by social change—the ones whom social welfare must assist.

Some people see the solution to these problems as a return to an idealized family of some earlier day. They should remember that such an idealized family never existed for more than a few people, even in earlier times. The history of social welfare provides examples of many situations in which the family by itself was insufficient to meet human needs. The families of the poor, the widowed and orphaned, the sick, the aged, the immigrant often could not provide for all their members' needs. So the social welfare system developed mechanisms to meet at least some of these needs, first through institutions, then through settlement houses and the COS, and finally through some provisions of the Social Security Act. The solution for today's family in stress does not lie in a return to an outdated, idealized family structure, but in seeking new ways to balance the role of the family and the role of the social welfare system.

The mechanisms for meeting family needs have changed as society has changed. In the past, most family needs were taken care of by the immediate or extended family network. But as social change has altered traditional family structures, responsibility for families who cannot function on their own has shifted to the U.S. social welfare system and the public and private social service agencies that are part of it.

Changes in the structure of the family have affected the ways families seek and receive help with needs and problems. The shift from the extended family system to the nuclear family and other family forms has reduced the availability of family mutual aid as a resource. Families with problems cannot usually call on their extended family to provide immediate help because of the geographical distances that separate so many families from their relatives. In contemporary society, families needing help often must turn to public and private social welfare agencies.

Rapid social, economic, and technological change—particularly in the latter half of this century—has challenged the contemporary family. Some authorities argue that the family as the primary social unit is rapidly disintegrating, and some evidence does suggest that this is true. For example, it is estimated that one in two marriages ends in divorce. A slightly more positive viewpoint is that the family's ability to adjust and cope with social expectations and demands has simply not kept pace with the social changes that have occurred; this has placed stresses on families and has threatened the stability of some (Sedgwick, 1981). Family stability and cohesiveness depend in part on the degree to which individuals in a family feel connected to each other. Social change and technological advancement have given individuals more opportunities and choices about family lifestyle, including types of career, marriage partners, and whether or not to have children. Values about the importance of the family to the individual have also changed as a result of this. Society currently places a high value on individual growth and self-actualization, on the self-oriented individual as opposed to the group-oriented individual with a sense of connectedness to the family. The focus of socialization within the family has been on preparing family members for participation in a society that emphasizes the individual more than the family unit. In some families, this has led to a feeling of detachment and weak emotional bonding, undermining their solidarity. The problems individual family members experience as a consequence of this change have not gone unnoticed. The social welfare system has responded to family situations where children need protection from abuse or neglect, and has provided assistance to aged family members. However, these efforts have often been designed to assist individuals, rather than to strengthen the family as a social unit. A system of response directed at maintaining the family unit has not been developed. This is due largely to the absence of a national family social policy that clearly demonstrates society's responsibility to support families by providing resources and services aimed at ameliorating the social conditions and problems that jeopardize their well-being.

The Individual and Social Change

As a society changes, individuals in that society must also make changes. These changes involve the way a person provides for personal needs, such as earning a living; the kind of formal education a person obtains; and the roles and norms for functioning in the family and other social systems. In other words, a change in lifestyle may be necessary. Often the social change is gradual enough to allow a series of small personal changes that are within the coping capacity of an individual, with minimal disruption to how that individual functions. At other times the required change is sudden or outside the capacity of the individual. Automation of an industry may cause people to lose essential employment. In a day of intensive job specialization, skill obsolescence can come swiftly and unexpectedly. In the early 1980s, auto industry workers were placed in this kind of situation. Hard-working, productive people found themselves no longer needed by their society. People with outdated skills and knowledge may have little opportunity for learning new ones. Change may require moving to a new, strange environment. Cultural patterns of behavior, developed in a different time and place, may hinder a person's ability to adapt easily to change. People may feel tension between the need to adhere to the patterns of their cultural group and the need to develop new and different ways of functioning in relation to other societal institutions. Some people will be caught by change and find themselves unable to meet their needs or their family's.

     For example, some family farmers are finding they can no longer provide for their family's needs from a farm income. Like other displaced workers, including both "blue collar" and "white collar professionals," who may have been laid off due to factory shutdowns, down-sizing in business because of a slowdown in the economy, or technological advancement that no longer requires human skill, family farmers may find themselves dependent on social welfare arrangements, at least for a temporary period of time.

In the 1990s, young people who are finishing their educations and are ready to enter the labor force may find that the demand for jobs far exceeds the number of jobs available. The adaptations that these young people will need to make remains unclear. What is known is that society will expect them to find some means for meeting their basic needs.

It is important to consider what happens to victims of progress, people left behind by change. These people often feel alienated from others. They feel powerless to deal with the impact of negative circumstances and see no way to meet their needs. They are often resentful. Perhaps they believe they have lost that which is most meaningful to them. With no job or with little opportunity to participate in a meaningful human enterprise, they may seem to "drop out" or to isolate themselves from people and activities that would give them a sense of self-worth. Their new social milieu provides them with few indicators of expected behaviors. They have a sense of normlessness. With their low self-esteem and hopelessness comes a lessened ability to adapt. Thus, they feel caught in a vicious cycle. In extreme cases this can lead to substance abuse, violence, or other criminal behaviors, or to homelessness. It can also contribute to mental illness and other dysfunctional behaviors. The societal response to these dysfunctional behaviors often is to try to control the behaviors, rather than to provide services that might prevent or alleviate the dysfunctional behaviors.

People may need more than income maintenance services from the social welfare system. They need social and educational services to help them reenter the mainstream of society. With this kind of assistance, these people may be able to break out of their dysfunctional cycle and thus to better themselves and society.

In the contemporary social welfare system, people may not receive the services they need; they may "fall between the cracks" between programs because of programmatic eligibility requirements. This is due in part to the fact that the social welfare system finds it difficult to respond to needs for new services and programs brought on by social change. The social welfare system's structure and way of functioning developed to meet past social problems. Change and adaptation must continue if the needs that exist in the contemporary societal system—the needs of individuals and families who are negatively affected by the change process—are to be met.

Empowerment, Social Work, and Social Change

Although it is essential for social workers to care about how social change affects people in negative ways, it is not enough to just care. Nor is it sufficient to merely observe and describe social conditions and problems that are caused by social change. Social workers need to adopt a critical perspective about social change, that is, to critically analyze it, and identify problems and offer solutions (Longres, 1995). According to Anderson and Gibson (1978: 17) the *critical perspective* is "the dual task of developing a critique of all forms of social oppression [and] . . . assist[ing] in the development of alternative social forms that uphold human dignity and provide the conditions for the positive cultivation of human mental and physical ability." The question then is, how do social workers assist individuals, families, and other groups, particularly devalued groups, who are victims of societal progress and change? The answer is by adopting an empowerment orientation in practice with these groups. Through empowerment, individuals, families, communities, and organizations can gain control and have voice in decision making about their well-being. Specifically, empowerment is a process through which people become strong enough to participate within, share control of, and influence events and institutions that affect their lives (Torre, 1985).

On an individual person or family level, an empowerment orientation allows the social worker to view the helping process as a partnership, in which both worker and the individual or family are involved in mutual assessment of problems in functioning, need definition, and problem solving. The focus of the helping process is on peoples' strengths, adaptive capacities, and potentialities (Saleebey, 1992). By doing this, social workers are respecting peoples' strengths and attempts to cope, and the helping process becomes one that supports and reinforces the notion that people are capable of assuming control over their lives and can adapt and cope with the negative affects of social change. In essence, it gives people the personal power and self efficacy to rid themselves of the victim status (DuBois and Miley, 1992). However, in order for the above to occur, societal social structures and institutions must also change as per earlier material discussed on social systems theory that posits that change in one part of a social system will neccessitate changes in other parts of the system. Therefore, ways must be developed to change the way that social structures and institutions respond to social change. As noted earlier, U.S. society's traditional way of responding to social change that causes human need is through mechanisms of social control, often restricting or denying the resources needed by the affected groups. Empowerment can also be used by social workers to assist social institutions and social structures to respond more humanely to the needs of people. Empowerment, in this sense, implies or refers to the reallocation of power to citizens, particularly devalued societal groups, through modification of existing social structures that will provide increased opportunities for their participation in decisions affecting their welfare. This calls for change or alteration in dominant societal paradigms and the ideologies that flow from them, such as social control and others that will be discussed throughout the remainder of the text. Social workers need to be concerned with the empowerment of devalued groups who are not proportionally represented in dominant societal paradigms. As Schriver (1995) states

> *. . . when some of us are denied opportunities to influence decision-making processes that affect our lives, we all are hurt. We all lose when the voices and visions of some of us are excluded. . . . By listening to the voices and seeing the world through the eyes of those who differ . . . in gender, color, sexual orientation, age, ablement, culture, income, and class we can learn much about new paradigms or world views that can enrich all our lives (15–16).*

Summary

Social change is one of the reasons we need a social welfare system. Social change is a necessary ingredient of any society's growth and development. Change does, however, disrupt the functioning of a society's subsystems, its institutions, families, and individuals. When change occurs, customary methods of meeting human needs become inadequate and new mechanisms by which these needs can be met must be created. The disruption of the lives of individuals and families leads to losses in social functioning, that ultimately have a social cost to society. The social welfare system has developed mechanisms for responding to disrupted lives and unmet need that also contain provisions for social control. Although some amount of social control is desirable and perhaps necessary when responding to unmet need caused by social change, it becomes dysfunctional and oppressive when it serves to exclude and disadvantage certain societal groups.

One way to understand the contemporary social welfare system in the United States is to study the effects of social change on its development. In this chapter, dominant societal paradigms and ideologies that have influenced society's responses to social change and human need were examined. In addition, a social systems perspective has been used to discuss how social change has affected both the societal system and its functioning and the individual who is a part of that system. This chapter has also focused on population profile change and economic change. The impact of change on the contemporary family system and on individuals has also been considered. Lastly, the profession of social work's involvement through empowerment of individuals, families, devalued societal groups, and other collectives of people whose lives have been most affected by social change was discussed.

Key Terms

boundary
critical perspective
dominant paradigm
empowerment
extended family
family
frail elderly
ideology
monetary economy
nuclear family
paradigm
reconstituted family

role overload
service society
single-parent family
social change
social control
social systems approach
societal system
steady state
step-family
subsistence economy
subsystems

References

Anderson, C.H., and Gibson, J.R. (1978). *Toward a New Sociology.* Homewood, IL: Dorsey Press, p. 17.

Capra, F. (1983). *The Turning Point: Science, Society, and the Rising Culture.* Toronto: Bantam Books.

Chess, W.A., and Norlin, J.M. (1991). *Human Behavior and the Social Environment: A Social Systems Model.* Boston: Allyn and Bacon.

DuBois, B., and Miley, K.K. (1992). *Social Work: An Empowering Profession.* Boston: Allyn and Bacon.

Goldenberg, I., and Goldenberg, H. (1996). *Family Therapy: An Overview.* Monterey, CA: Brooks/Cole.

Hartman, A., and Laird, J. (1987). Family Practice, in *Encyclopedia of Social Work, 18th ed., Vol. 1.* Silver Spring, MD: National Association of Social Workers.

Kuhn, T.S. ([1962]1970). *The Structure of Scientific Revolutions.* Chicago: University of Chicago Press.

Logan, S. (1990). Black Families: Race, Ethnicity, Culture, Social Class, and Gender Issues, in Sadye Logan, Edith Freemen, and Ruth McCoy. *Social Work Practice with Black Families.* New York: Longman.

Longres, J.F. (1995). *Human Behavior in the Social Environment.* Itaska, IL: F.E. Peacock.

Nichols, R.L., and Reimers, D.M. (1979). *Natives and Strangers*. New York: Oxford University Press.

Persell, C.H. (1987). *Understanding Society: An Introduction to Sociology*. New York: Harper and Row.

Saleebey, D. (1992). *The Strengths Perspective in Social Work Practice*. New York: Longman.

Schriver, J.M. (1995). *Human Behavior and the Social Environment: Shifting Paradigms in Essential Knowledge for Social Work Practice*. Boston: Allyn and Bacon.

Sedgwick, R. (1981). *Family Mental Health: Theory and Practice*. St. Louis, MO: C.V. Mosby.

Torre, D. (1985). *Empowerment: Structured Conceptualization and Instrument Development*. Unpublished Doctoral Dissertation, Cornell University. Ithaca, New York.

Trattner, W.I. (1983). *Social Welfare or Social Control? Some Historical Reflection on "Regulating the Poor"*. Knoxville, TN.: University of Tennessee Press.

U.S. Bureau of the Census, *Statistical Abstacts of the U.S. 1991*. Washington, D.C.: U.S. Government Printing Office.

U.S. Bureau of the Census, *Statistical Abstacts of the U.S. 1995*. Washington, D.C.: U.S. Government Printing Office.

Suggested Readings

Chess, W.A., and Norlin, J.M. (1991). *Human Behavior and the Social Environment: A Social Systems Model*. Boston: Allyn and Bacon.

Day, P.J. (1981). Social Welfare: Context for Social Control. *Journal of Sociology and Social Welfare, 8*, 29–44.

DuBois, B., and Miley, K.K. (1996). *Social Work: An Empowering Profession*. Boston: Allyn and Bacon.

Longres, J.F. (1995). *Human Behavior in the Social Environment*. Itaska, IL: F.E. Peacock.

Saleebey, D. (1992). *The Strengths Perspective in Social Work Practice*. New York: Longman.

Schriver, J.M. (1995). *Human Behavior and the Social Environment: Shifting Paradigms in Essential Knowledge for Social Work Practice*. Boston: Allyn and Bacon.

3

POVERTY, HUMAN NEEDS,
AND SOCIAL WELFARE

Learning Expectations

- Ability to define poverty from several points of view
- Understanding of the way the federal poverty line is determined
- Ability to define three sociological theories of poverty and to discuss the implications of using each
- Understanding of how the viewpoints, culture of poverty, and racial inferiority influence societal views of poverty
- Ability to identify specific oppressed groups within the U.S. society that are particularly in danger of being in a poverty situation
- Understanding of why the groups identified in the expectation above are particularly prone to poverty
- Understanding of the causes of homelessness and of its various forms
- Capacity to discuss the economic causes of poverty
- Understanding as to how political views affect the concern for poverty as a social problem
- Ability to identify social and situational factors that affect the societal view of poverty
- Ability to trace the history of concern for poverty in the United States, including the societal responses to the situation
- Ability to identify some of the professional responses to the presence of poverty in U.S. society

Poverty is a serious social problem that contributes to the inability of individuals to meet their basic needs. According to the U.S. Census Bureau (U.S. Bureau of the Census, 1995), in 1993, 15 percent of the U.S. population had incomes below the poverty line. No single social problem has been more troublesome in its effects on the social system.

Throughout this country's history, numerous attempts have been made to reduce or eliminate poverty in the United States. The social welfare system has been the primary mechanism for doing this because it is designed to assist those members of society whose needs exceed their means to satisfy them. Yet poverty persists, despite public welfare and other antipoverty programs and services. Poverty is a complex and destructive social problem, deeply rooted in the total social structure of our society, a problem that distorts our nation's image as the land of plenty and promise.

This chapter is devoted to an extensive discussion of the phenomenon of poverty, with the aim of helping the reader understand the relationship between poverty and human needs and the societal responses made through the social welfare system to deal with the effects of that relationship. It examines the definitions of poverty, how poverty is measured, who the poor are, the causes of poverty, the discovery and rediscovery of poverty, and societal and professional responses to poverty. The problem of homelessness, a related social problem that has a cause and effect relationship with poverty, also will be discussed.

What Is Poverty?

Defining poverty is difficult. It can be defined loosely from commonly accepted perceptions, or it can be defined more strictly in terms of governmental laws and regulations. Poverty can also be defined by the individuals or groups who experience it. Furthermore, poverty can be described by the use of selected economic, political, and cultural theories. Some of these definitions are discussed next.

Individual Perspective

Some individuals consider themselves poor, even though they may not fit the established economic measures of poverty. These individuals base their perceptions of being poor on comparison of themselves to others. Conversely, other individuals considered poor by standard measures do not consider themselves poor. This suggests that poverty and deprivation are relative, depending on individual perceptions. But this self-definition of poverty is not very useful. If this were accepted as the sole definition of poverty, almost all people might consider themselves poor, which would add nothing to our understanding. Therefore, relative definitions are not very useful for describing poverty.

Societal Perspective

Some people's view of the poor is based on stereotypical perceptions or value judgments. They categorize the poor as people from the "wrong side" of town, or as recipients of public assistance, or even solely as members of certain racial or ethnic groups. Sometimes the poor are lumped together by society into one large homogeneous group, without considering the diversity that exists among them. All that is seen is the lifestyle of poverty, without considering the true causes of the conditions under which poor people live. To define poverty on the basis of stereotypes, without considering its causes, distorts our understanding of poverty.

Institutional Perspective

U.S. society has provided official definitions of poverty. The federal government was charged with this responsibility and first offered a definition of poverty in 1964, when the president's Council of Economic Advisors in its annual report stated, "By the poor we mean those who are now not maintaining a decent standard of living; those whose basic needs exceed their means to satisfy them." An alternative definition, also offered by the Council of Economic Advisors, was, "Poverty is the inability to satisfy minimum needs" (Haxlitt, 1973). These two definitions are sufficiently vague to have provoked a great deal of debate about what constitutes a decent standard of living, or what should be considered a person's minimum needs. Nevertheless, these definitions provided the impetus for establishing an official poverty line used to distinguish the poor from the nonpoor. The *poverty line* acts as the official measure of poverty in considering the incomes of individuals or families. Since 1965, the responsibility for establishing the official poverty line has rested with the Social Security Administration. The original 1964 poverty line was set at an annual income of $3,000 for a family of four, and $1,500 per year for an individual (Wisconsin State Journal, 1992). The poverty line has risen steadily since 1964. In 1993 it stood at $14,763 for a family of four (U.S. Bureau of the Census, 1995).

Economic Perspective

Poverty has been most often defined in economic terms, with personal or family income as a determinant. It is often classified as a problem of low income. It is best understood as a lack of the necessary income for people to meet their needs for food, clothing, shelter, energy, transportation, and medical care. In a monetary society like ours, a family's ability to meet these needs depends on the structure and functioning of the economic marketplace and not on the family's own ability to produce food and goods. But as the monetary society attempts to achieve a balance between meeting human needs and providing for social control, as discussed in the previous chapter, it has become difficult for some families to meet their daily needs for survival.

Sociological Perspective

Poverty can also be viewed from a sociological perspective. A number of sociological theories have offered explanations for its existence. One theory views poverty as a more or less permanent fixture of the social structure. The structuralist view places importance on the needs of society rather than on those of the individual, and the orderly functioning of society depends upon the performance of tasks deemed necessary to the overall welfare of the society. In this view only certain individuals, intelligent and talented, are capable of performing these tasks, for which they receive greater levels of social rewards. Those who perform tasks of lesser importance and deemed lower value, receive fewer social rewards. Through this structure order, control and stability are supposedly achieved, preventing disruption in the functioning of society by keeping in check conflict and competition for resources. Theorists admit that this kind of societal structure by design creates social inequality, but they believe that inequality is necessary to maintain the welfare and existence of society. This fatalistic and pessimistic view is not particularly useful in explaining poverty. Although it somewhat explains inequality, structural theorists do not agree on how much inequality is necessary, and they are unable to determine what useful function in society poverty serves (Perry and Perry, 1988).

A related theory, the *social stratification* theory (Coser, 1965), holds that the poor are assigned special status by society through a system of stratification. This theory assumes that social benefits, such as wealth, power, and status cannot be equally distributed throughout the social strata, thus creating a clear distinction between the "haves and have nots." Although providing a description of poverty, stratification theory fails to adequately explain poverty but, instead, merely explains the tendency for human societies to organize in a hierarchical fashion according to certain human traits in order to distribute its resources (Perry and Perry, 1988).

Another theory, the *labeling* theory (Longres, 1990), asserts that the poor occupy their position in society either as a result of achieved labeling, earned through negative interaction with others, or through ascribed labeling, born into or occupying a social position on the basis of some trait they possess, e.g., race or gender. Labeling theory, although useful in explaining the difficulty of the poor to escape poverty, attributes the process of labeling to human nature, adding little to the understanding about the complexities involved in explaining poverty.

Another sociological theory explaining poverty comes from a "radical position." *Marxian* theory (Longres, 1990), for instance, puts forth the notion that poverty exists as a result of the goals of capitalism to engage in alienation and exploitation of certain groups in an effort to maintain social control and order in the society. Marxian theory, perhaps due to its radical nature and its tie to Communism, has not found favor as an explanation for poverty.

Two other points of view that help to define poverty on a more practical level are the concepts of absolute and relative deprivation (Plotnik and Skidmore, 1975). Absolute measures of deprivation are based on established, fixed standards of living. Those individuals or families whose resources fail to meet these minimum standards are considered deprived. One problem with absolute measures of deprivation is that the standards being fixed make no adjustments to account for increases in the cost of living or for special circumstances such as fixed incomes for the aged, or physical, mental, or health-related disabilities that can potentially reduce an individual's or a family's income. Absolute measures of deprivation also fail to account for adequacy in the distribution of income and resources.

Relative measures of deprivation view poverty as a problem of unequal distribution of income in the population. With this measure, the poor are those whose income falls below a level established by comparing all incomes and the selection of a cut-off point in a range of incomes. Relative measures are flexible; adjustments are made in the cut-off point as incomes change. These two measures of deprivation are involved in the establishment of the official poverty line, which is discussed later in this chapter.

Political

Poverty can be studied as a political problem. The poor in the United States have not been sufficiently mobilized to exert their political influence and their power to make known and bring about changes in the economic system that would provide the income resources they need. The poor are placed in a difficult situation. With economic affluence comes social status, and with social status comes the power to use society's resources for one's own goals. Today's poor have the potential to become a powerful political constituency if they could be collectively organized. This was demonstrated in the 1960s, when the poor became a powerful force for change. The involvement of poor African Americans was a turning point in the civil rights movement, adding both numbers and a *raison d'être*. The voter registration activity associated with Jesse Jackson's 1984 and 1988 bids for the Democratic presidential nomination was an attempt to organize the poor, other disenfranchised groups, and people of all colors into a collective political voice (the Rainbow Coalition) with respect to issues of poverty and social justice.

Attempts to break the control of the politically affluent over policies concerning poverty and social justice are not new. Even when concern for these issues was politically popular (e.g., the New Deal era of the 1930s and the Great Society of the 1960s), the political support needed to muster an effective national social policy to eradicate poverty was insufficient. There appears to be a love/hate perception about public social welfare support for the poor. Paradoxically, most Americans favor public or government assistance for the poor, but at the same time they dislike social welfare programs that exclusively help the poor (Heclo, 1986).

The politics of poverty may well change in light of the civil disturbance that occurred in Los Angeles, California, following the acquittal of several police officers accused in the brutal beating of African American motorist Rodney King. This event was more than a protest against the business-as-usual position in race relations but rather decisively indicates the vehement dissatisfaction that disenfranchised groups have with the lack of change in their quality of life over the last twenty-five years, and the potential for additional civil unrest. Consequently, poverty and other quality of life issues will more than likely be put on the national political agenda as dissatisfaction grows in the inner city.

Cultural and Racial

Poverty has sometimes been defined as a cultural or a racial problem. Two theories behind such explanations are expressed as the *culture of poverty* and the theory of *racial inferiority*.

The anthropologist Oscar Lewis (1966) was a proponent of the culture of poverty viewpoint. According to this view, poverty forms the basis for a separate, distinct culture. Lewis contended that in the groups he studied, Mexican Americans and Puerto Ricans, poverty served as a foundation for their culture. The poor, according to this theory, have developed norms, values, attitudes, and lifestyles different from those of the rest of the society. As a result, "the poor are impoverished because their 'culture' prevents them from taking advantage of opportunities to escape poverty" (Schiller, 1989). Schiller contends that if this is the case, the effort to eliminate poverty will be more difficult and time consuming.

The racial inferiority theory of poverty is based on the notion that members of certain racial groups have low levels of motivation and suffer from genetic deficiencies that constrain them from achieving economic success. Although these cultural and racial theories of poverty are not as well accepted today as they once were, they have recently reemerged as explanations of poverty (Herrnstein and Murray, 1994). Although these theories do not represent our own view about poverty, we mention them here to stimulate thought and debate. In our view, defining poverty in cultural or racial terms is narrow and inappropriately pessimistic. Instead, poverty should be defined in a comprehensive manner, which includes the influence of economic, social, and political factors.

How Poverty Is Measured

Since 1964, the responsibility for establishing the official poverty line in the United States has rested with the Social Security Administration (SSA). Mollie Orshansky of the SSA first developed the formula by which the official poverty line is calculated (Orshansky, 1993). It was determined that the amount of income needed to be above the poverty threshold was equal to three times the cost of the economy food plan, which was based on a 1955 survey conducted by the U.S. Department of Agriculture (USDA) that indicated that families of three or more spent one-third of their income after taxes on food (Congressional Budget Office, 1989). The poverty line has been adjusted each year since 1964 to reflect inflation in food prices and the overall cost of living. For example, in 1964 a family of four needed at least $3,000 to be above the poverty threshold. Allowing for inflation, in 1993 that same family would have needed an income of $14,763.

The poverty line is treated as an absolute measure of poverty and is frequently used to determine an individual's or family's eligibility for public social welfare programs and services (U.S. Department of Commerce, 1983).

Several criticisms have been made of the way the poverty line is calculated. One criticism is that absolute measures of poverty, such as the current poverty index, fail to account for the disparity in the distribution of income and resources. Although the overall standard of living has increased, the line does not reflect the differences of income throughout the population, which are as great as or greater than ever (Ellwood, 1988). Another criticism is that the poverty line is adjusted only for changes in prices, and leaves the standard of living of the poor unchanged (Schiller, 1989). This is true because the poor use the majority of their income for purchasing the necessities of life, and thus they realize no real gains in income. A related factor is that the poverty line does not account for regional cost-of-living differences. Officially classified poor families who live in areas with a low cost of living may be better off than similar families with incomes above the poverty threshold living in areas where the cost of living is high (Congressional Budget Office, 1989). Similarly, poverty rates as determined by the current poverty line do not provide accurate indicators of the condition of low-income families. The question is: How much better off are families with incomes just above the poverty line than families just below the line, or than families with no earned income? Poverty rates, as determined by official measures, cannot answer these questions (Congressional Budget Office, 1989).

The process used to arrive at poverty rates has also been attacked on the grounds that it does not account for "in-kind or noncash income (e.g., food stamps, subsidized public housing, and health insurance)" (Heisler, 1991). It is thought that if these items were considered, a more accurate and realistic measure of the incidence of poverty would be obtained.

Who Are the Poor?

To understand poverty fully in terms of its relationship to human needs, it is necessary to understand who the poor are. Societal ignorance, oppression, and insensitivity have created stereotypical perceptions of the poor. Often they are thought of as a homogeneous group, perhaps varying with geographic location. Poverty is often seen to be confined to specific oppressed ethnic groups: African Americans, Native Americans, and Hispanics, or as mainly an urban problem. If it is perceived as a rural problem at all, it is thought to be restricted to the Native American reservations of the west, Appalachia, the rural south, or to migrant farm workers. Most Americans do not understand that the poor are a diverse group made up of a wide spectrum of the population. Although racial and ethnic minorities make up a significant proportion of the poor, there are over twenty-six million poor whites in the United States (U.S. Bureau of the Census, 1995).

For some people, poverty is situational, caused by environmental or situational events such as temporary unemployment or underemployment, a catastrophic event, or as a consequence of one's position in the life cycle. Some groups of people—the aged, women, children, and the working poor—are particularly vulnerable to becoming impoverished, due to their status in society.

For another, smaller group of people, poverty is a persistent, permanent reality of life. This group is referred to as the *underclass* (Heisler, 1991). They are oppressed people who have not been able, due to barriers and obstacles in society, to escape poverty. Recent studies have concluded that a segment of the population (the underclass) have been socially and politically disenfranchised from receiving the benefits of societal, economic, and political institutions. The causes of this phenomenon are debatable. Some attribute it to cultural characteristics of persons who comprise this group, while others argue that the causes are inherent in the social structures of society. For whatever reasons, the underclass appears to be growing in numbers and moving in the direction of becoming a permanent underclass (Heisler, 1991).

To understand who the poor are, one must examine the effects of poverty on all of the aforementioned groups.

Racial Minorities

African Americans

All racial minorities are overrepresented in the ranks of the poor, a result of long-standing racial discrimination and oppression in our society toward these groups. Among them, African Americans represent the largest group classified as living in poverty. In 1993 almost 11 million African Americans or 33 percent had incomes below the poverty line (U.S. Bureau of the Census, 1995).

In the last twenty years, some African Americans have gained greater economic affluence, primarily as a result of civil rights legislation that opened doors to schools and jobs. However, societal discrimination and oppression continues to handicap the efforts to achieve economic equality.

Native Americans

In 1990, 31.2 percent of all Native Americans had incomes below the poverty line (U.S. Bureau of the Census, 1995). Three factors are important in discussing the causes of their poverty. The first is unemployment. Unemployment rates on Native American reservations are high because most reservations were placed in geographically undesirable, economically depressed areas, with little or no industry to provide employment. Therefore, Native American people are heavily dependent on assistance from the U.S. Bureau of Indian Affairs and other local and state welfare agencies. Their dependency is a result of more than one hundred years of paternalistic practices by the federal government, sanctioned by laws passed in the 1800s that forced, and continue to force, dependence today. Native Americans are also handicapped by their lack of educational opportunities and job-related skills, both on and off the reservations. Finally, discrimination against Native Americans contributes to the perception of their poverty. Despite this gloomy scenario, the current economic situation for many Native Americans is changing. A recent change in federal legislation and policy in the U.S. Department of the Interior, allows for the development of a tribal gaming (gambling) industry. Native Americans throughout the United States have opened gambling casinos, which are seen as an economic boon, creating employment for tribal members, with the profits used for the development of tribal services that benefit members. This situation is too new for any speculation or evaluation of its merits, or lack thereof.

Hispanic Americans

Spanish-speaking people, or Hispanic Americans, include Mexican Americans, Puerto Ricans, Cubans, Filipinos, and others. Hispanic Americans are significantly represented among the American poor. In 1993 over 8 million Hispanics, representing 30.6 percent of this population, are living in poverty (U.S. Bureau of the Census, 1995). They face much of the same type of discrimination in the employment market as do other minorities. One group, the migrant farm workers of the southwestern and western United States, is particularly at risk of living in poverty. Because their employment is seasonal and requires a transient lifestyle, their lives are apt to become disorganized and chaotic. They are often exploited by unscrupulous growers. Adaptation to the migrant way of life creates a subculture with special problems of access to the social and health services that would interrupt the poverty cycle.

The Aged

According to 1993 U.S. census data, 12 percent of all people aged sixty-five or older live below the poverty line (U.S. Bureau of the Census, 1995). Several factors are associated with poverty and the aged. Generally, the elderly have limited or fixed sources of income, which may consist of Social Security benefits, Supplemental Security Income, veterans' benefits, some form of pension or retirement benefits, or income from a combination of those sources. In many instances the income is near or below the poverty line, a line that is set too low for the elderly.

Some researchers believe the poverty line for the elderly is set artificially low. According to Rogers, Brown, and Cook (1994), the poverty line for the elderly was originally based on the cost of an adequate diet. The lower standard for the elderly was based on the erroneous "fact" that the elderly consume less calories than younger adults. Rogers et al. go on to state the overall nutrient requirements for the elderly are not lower, and the elderly spend a higher proportion of their budgets on food than nonelderly. Consequently, many more elderly are below the poverty line than is reported in government statistics.

To make matters more bleak, programs to help the elderly have imposed limits on additional earned income as eligibility standards for participation. Thus the elderly cannot legally bolster their income in any way if they depend on those programs. Limited income curtails their purchasing power, forcing many elderly people into a life of poverty. Other problems the aged face as a result of inadequate income are poor housing, lack of medical care, poor nutrition, and lack of transportation.

Women

Women are another diverse group who experience the detrimental effects of poverty. In families in which a woman is the head of the household, there is a particularly great risk of living in poverty. This phenomenon is often referred to as the "feminization of poverty." In families headed by a woman in 1993, 38.7 percent were below the poverty line (U.S. Bureau of the Census, 1995).

It is speculated that a major cause of this situation is the increased breakup of two-parent families as a result of divorce (Mauldin, 1991). A study by Mauldin has identified a number of factors that shed light on women's inability to move out of poverty, particularly in the year following a divorce. These factors include a lack of adequate employment, job training, and education skills, and the presence of pre-school-age children: factors that make it difficult for single mothers to seek employment outside the home (Mauldin, 1991).

Even if they were able to work, women would earn less than their male counterparts, and this contributes to their difficulty in rising above a poverty level income (Levitan, 1990). This fact was also confirmed in studies by Woody (1991), and Kerlin (1993), who reported that even though most of the recent growth in the U.S. economy was in the service sector (an area of employment dominated by females) these jobs provide low compensation, are usually part-time with no or reduced fringe benefits, and provide little job security. Discrimination against women is another factor with which they must contend. This is a particular problem for single-mother families. It has been reported that factors that place these families at risk for poverty cannot be identified and be dealt with without understanding the inequalities with respect to race, gender, and social status, faced by female head-of-household families (Scanlan, Watson, McLanahan, and Sorenson, 1991).

Given these factors, many of these families are recipients of economic assistance programs, but these have not improved their quality of life because they do not provide other essential support services, such as health care, child care assistance and housing services needed by these families.

On the positive side, Segal (1991) found a number of states have started programs in the form of "family development projects" designed to assist female-headed welfare families to achieve economic independence. These projects take a total family-centered approach in service delivery and provide many of the above mentioned support services that are lacking in traditional welfare programs (Segal, 1991).

Children

One of the largest and most diverse groups among the poor are children. It is estimated that 22 percent of all children are considered poor (U.S. Bureau of the Census, 1995). According to Knitzer and Abner (1995), this is the highest rate of poverty among children in 25 years. What is tragic about this is that the children do not have a choice in the matter. They are trapped in poverty as a result of their status as children and are unable to break away from its destructive effects. Poverty affects children in physical, social, psychological, and emotional ways. It predisposes children to the risks of mental illness, juvenile delinquency, alcoholism and drug abuse, child abuse, and family violence, in addition to nutritional and health problems associated with deprivation. These effects cause poor children to function inadequately in the educational system. In this way, a cycle of generational poverty often develops in families in which the cycle of poverty is not interrupted, and the deprivation is carried into adulthood. Has the picture become brighter for children in recent years? Census data reveal that the poverty rate among children has steadily increased since 1970. See Table 3-1 (U.S. Bureau of the Census, 1995).

The Family Support Act of 1988, P.L. 100-485, which has as a goal to break the cycle of dependence of families on public assistance, may have an impact in the future, but early results are not encouraging. In a recent study, Martha Ozawa (1991) reports that the Family Support Act has not produced improvement in the economic well-being of children in welfare-assisted families.

The Working Poor

The working poor also feel the grip of poverty. The *working poor* are those individuals and families who are employed but who earn insufficient wages to meet their basic needs. In 1993, 3.9 million people whose income was below the poverty line worked at least part-time, and 1.2 million worked full time (U.S. Bureau of the Census, 1995). A distressing factor unique to this group is that although they work hard and earn an income, however insufficient, they usually are not eligible for any sort of public assistance because eligibility standards for most assistance programs are based on income. Sadly, this perpetuates the lifestyle of poverty for the working poor. Also, some of the working poor do not apply for programs that are available to them, such as food stamps, in order to avoid the stigma associated with receiving financial aid.

Some farmers make up another group of people who might be considered working poor. The continuing farm crisis affects the ability of some farming families to meet even their most basic human needs as they struggle to maintain their farms, some of which have supported their families for several generations. Because these people own land, they are considered to have resources; however, if they dispose of the resources, then they no longer can farm and are thrown into the ranks of the unemployed, often with no other marketable skills.

The Geography of Poverty: Urban? Rural?

In identifying the poor, it is useful to become aware of the geography of poverty. Is poverty mainly an urban phenomenon, or is it prevalent in rural areas as well? Poverty is commonly

TABLE 3-1   Percent of Children below the Poverty Level

Year	Percent
1970	14.9
1975	16.8
1980	16.0
1985	20.1
1989	19.0
1993	22.0

Source: U.S. Bureau of the Census, *Statistical Abstracts of the United States, 1995.*

thought to be more prevalent in urban than rural areas because it is more readily seen in metropolitan areas, as a result of high concentrations of population. In rural areas, where people live at considerable distances from one another, poverty is more difficult to observe. But contrary to popular belief, poverty is proportionately more common in rural areas than in urban centers. In nonmetropolitan areas, 16.3 percent of the population live below the poverty level, whereas in metropolitan areas, 12.7 percent are below the poverty level (U.S. Bureau of the Census, 1990). There are also differences in the causes of poverty in urban versus rural areas, as well as in the people who make up the populations of poor in each of these areas.

Leif Jensen (1989) has identified causes of rural poverty to be low wages, rising unemployment, an economic recession in the agribusiness economy, and exclusionary welfare eligibility requirements that render ineligible a large proportion of poor persons and families. The poor in rural areas are more often employed, a member of a married-couple family, an elderly person or couple, and disabled. They are less likely to be a child, or a minority. One of the most significant differences is that the poor in urban areas are more likely to be recipients of some form of public assistance than are persons in rural areas. There are two factors operating here. One is simply a matter of numbers—differences in the density of population between urban and rural areas. A recent study shows a correlation between population density and participation in welfare programs. Areas with lower population density (rural areas) have fewer public assistance recipients. The second factor has to do with the above-mentioned eligibility requirements in rural areas. Some programs are local, nonfederal programs that do not have legally mandated eligibility requirements, leaving decisions on rendering assistance to local authorities who often base their decisions on local norms or other locally relevant cultural determinants (Jensen, 1989).

The Homeless

Causally related to poverty, the social problem of homelessness continues to be of major concern. When the homeless began to capture the attention of policymakers and social welfare professionals in the early 1980s, it was first believed that their growth in numbers was related to deinstitutionalization policies (to be discussed in Chapter 10). These policies affected primarily the mentally ill and the developmentally disabled. Substance abusers were also thought to make up a large percentage of the homeless. Soon, however, studies began to show that the homeless were a heterogeneous group of individuals, with a growing number of family groups involved (Hagen, 1987).

More recently, studies have pointed to high poverty, economic recession, and the unavailability of low-income housing as major factors associated with high levels of homelessness. It was also thought that this problem was more common in urban centers. However, Fitchen (1991) reported that "rural homelessness" was found to be due to the unavailability of low-cost housing, lack of employment, and an increase in single-parent households in rural up-state New York where the field research was conducted.

Regardless of what causes homelessness, or where it exists, what is of more practical concern is what is being done to ameliorate this problem. Responses to this problem in the form of services appear to be connected to the living patterns of homeless people. A study by First, Roth, and Arewa (1988) identified three living patterns: on the street, in a shelter, and using resources. The latter includes individuals and families who use a variety of short-term resources,

Shelters for the homeless provide the only place many poverty-stricken people can find protection from the cold, rain, or snow.

including family and friends, for shelter. Resources to address the needs of those who live on the street or in shelter situations include a variety of temporary services, such as soup kitchens, store-front missions, and homeless shelters under the auspices of private, charitable, and religious organizations. Some federal funding for services to the homeless has also been made available to municipalities and other public-governmental agencies.

Recently, concern has turned to the high cost of housing for poor people. A 1989 report states that 45 percent of poor renters and one-third of poor homeowners are paying more than 70 percent of their incomes for housing. It is usually accepted that housing costs should not exceed 30 percent of income (U.S. Bureau of the Census and U.S. Department of Housing, 1989). Frederic G. Reamer (1989) has stated that homelessness is merely a symptom of a far broader crisis of affordable housing. He locates some of the causes of this crisis in current federal housing policy. He notes that there is an inadequate housing supply, particularly for the low-income segment of the population. At the same time, there is growing demand for housing, due in part to the growth in the number of households as compared with the population. Several demographic factors, including the presence of more single people and the growth of the aging population, contribute to this situation. Economic growth has led to increased competition for the housing that does exist, while federal housing policy has removed incentives for investing in low-income housing. It now seems clear that a major response to the housing crisis should be a revision of federal housing policy.

Causes of Poverty

The definitions of poverty are complex and its causes even more so. To try to understand this complexity, three broad areas of causation will be discussed: economic, political, and social situational.

Economic Causes

The economic causes of poverty, as agreed on by most authorities, are income distribution, inadequate income supports, and unemployment and underemployment. Too often, poverty is thought of merely as a result of low or inadequate income, but to identify this as the only economic cause of poverty is too simplistic. It is more meaningful to examine why large proportions of the U.S. population have low or inadequate incomes, and thus are considered poor.

Income Distribution

The chief factor is income distribution, according to Tussing (1975). The *gross national product* (GNP), roughly defined as the total income of the country and the indicator of a nation's wealth, is divided among a number of economic units. (One economic unit is the personal household, either an individual or a family household.) The *distribution of income*, the way that income is distributed, is what causes poverty. Although a minority of U.S. households are poor, those that are "are poor not because of inadequate total output or gross national product, but because of inequalities in the distribution of income and wealth" (Tussing, 1975).

Table 3-2 displays the share of total income received by each quintile of families in the United States in 1993, ranging from the wealthiest to the poorest families. As shown, 46.2 percent of total income was held by the top 20 percent of families; 4.2 percent of total income was held by the lowest 20 percent of families (U.S. Bureau of the Census, 1995).

This, most assuredly, illustrates the current inequality in the distribution of wealth, which has not changed substantially over the years. To illustrate, Table 3-3 shows the percent distribution of households for various income levels for the years 1970 through 1993. As can be seen,

TABLE 3-2   Percent Distribution of Wealth in each Quintile of Families in the U.S. in 1993

Lowest Quintile	Second Quintile	Third Quintile	Fourth Quintile	Highest Quintile
4.2%	10.1%	15.9%	23.6%	46.2%

Source: U.S. Bureau of the Census, *Statistical Abstracts of the United States, 1995.*

TABLE 3-3   **Percent Distribution of Households by Income Level for the Years 1970, 1980, 1990, and 1993**

	Under $10,000	$10,000– $14,999	$15,000– $24,999	$25,000– $34,999	$35,000– $49,999	$50,000– $74,999	$75,000 and over
1970	8.2%	7.3%	16.6%	19.6%	23.6%	17.3%	7.5%
1980	8.0%	7.1%	16.1%	15.6%	22.2%	20.0%	10.9%
1990	8.3%	6.5%	14.8%	14.6%	19.8%	20.0%	15.9%
1993	9.6%	7.2%	15.5%	14.8%	17.9%	19.4%	15.5%

Source: U.S. Bureau of the Census, *Statistical Abstracts of the United States, 1995.*

little shift or change in the distribution of income has occurred within the population, except in the highest income strata.

How is this inequality in the distribution of wealth explained, and how does it contribute to the perpetuation of poverty? Explanations can be found in some of the philosophical values that underlie a capitalistic economy. Capitalism does not place a high value on sharing wealth or on an equal distribution of income; competition and self sufficiency are believed to be more valuable. From this conservative viewpoint, inequality is acceptable. This is in tune with the structuralist view of poverty presented earlier. Conservatives such as Gilder (1981) and others argue that the wealthy serve an important function in economic spheres because they are willing to risk investment of capital with the hope and goal of earning greater wealth, creating employment and economic growth that will ultimately benefit everyone, including the poor. Empirical evidence supporting this notion is nonexistent; in fact, economic trends have been the opposite of this so-called *trickle-down* paradigm. Wealth and income have increased among the affluent and decreased among other groups in society (Popple and Leighninger, 1990). There is no tested evidence to suggest that persons or families in income strata below the most wealthy, particularly the poor, have benefited from the entrepreneurial enterprises of the wealthy.

Another economic measure for redistributing wealth to the poor involves income transfers through public income maintenance programs and other social programs. The source of the income transfer payments is revenue from personal and corporate income taxes collected by the federal government. But this measure has not provided sufficient redistribution of wealth to move large numbers of people out of poverty. Contributing to this failure is the fact that the philosophies that have influenced income transfers have not changed. Those who hold the wealth are affluent, not only in wealth, but also in social and political influence. The affluent exercise their influence in the marketplace and in political spheres, thus dominating decision-making on national social policy and social programs for the poor. The United States is a prosperous nation, yet poverty abounds.

Inadequate Income Supports

Inadequate income supports as a cause of poverty are a side effect of our economic system. Within this system the ability to obtain goods and services is called *purchasing power* (Schiller, 1989). The poor have very low incomes; thus their purchasing power is negligible or nonexistent. Most of their income, in whatever form it is received, is spent on necessities.

Income supports for some of the poor are provided through income maintenance assistance and other in-kind, noncash assistance, as described earlier. In theory, these programs should increase purchasing power, as they provide recipients with additional cash. However, because of the low levels of income assistance they provide, these programs fail to significantly increase the purchasing power of the poor, thus contributing to the perpetuation of a life of poverty for many poor people (Macarov, 1978).

Unemployment and Underemployment

Temporary or seasonal unemployment, although it may cause short-term poverty, is only a small part of the problem. Chronic or permanent unemployment and underemployment are the biggest contributors to poverty. *Underemployment*, working at a job that provides insufficient income, is another cause of poverty. Underemployment occurs when a low-income head of household, during times when jobs are scarce, accepts employment that does not fully utilize his or her time or employment skills.

Underemployment is occurring with increased frequency in recent years due to the changing nature of employment in the United States. As the American economy becomes more a service economy and less an industrial economy, jobs will require less technical skill and training. Many will be part-time, and they usually pay low wages. This has particularly affected female heads of household, as discussed earlier. Unemployment has always been a side effect of the U.S. economy. There are several views as to why this is so. A conservative view is that unemployment occurs because some people do not want to be employed despite available employment opportunities. Gilder (1981) has suggested that in order for the poor to escape poverty they must work and work harder than the classes above them, which he contends is not happening. Also related to this is the concept of the "flawed character," which assumes that individuals are in control of their own destinies and choose poverty as their lifestyle.

Another somewhat radical-conservative view is based on the argument that government, through offering unemployment benefits and welfare services, subverts the poor's incentive to work (Schiller, 1989). This is the "big brother" argument that promotes the perspective that government should do less, therefore increasing self-initiative and self-reliance in the unemployed and eventually leading to the elimination of poverty.

A more liberal view of unemployment argues that unemployment is caused by factors outside the control of the individual. In this view it is not the notion that the poor do not want to work, it is, rather, that they are provided limited and restricted employment opportunities. Supportive of this view is Shiller's restrictive opportunity argument in which he claims that "the poor are poor because they do not have access to good schools, jobs, and income; because they are discriminated against on the basis of color, sex, or income and because they are not furnished with a fair share of government protection, subsidy or services."

These views have been presented as different ways in which the unemployment-poverty relationship has been explained and do not, necessarily, represent the views of the authors regarding this matter. The conservative view is, in our estimation, the least valid, as there is no empirical data to support the claim that the poor choose not to work and to live in poverty. This view is also based on value judgments made about the poor that we find pessimistic and degrading. The radical-conservative view is also based on negative value judgments made about the current social welfare system, which lack empirical evidence to support such claims. The restrictive opportunity argument, we believe, best describes the realities of the unemployment-poverty connection.

Political Causes

The poor are politically disadvantaged, a result of years of unjust and inadequate social policies that were in fact designed to be mechanisms of social control. The poor are disenfranchised from the political institutions that determine social welfare policy. Therefore, they are not represented and have little or no voice in the determination of social welfare policy at the local, state, and national levels. This has contributed to the maintenance of the status quo. Changes in social policy or the creation of new policies more favorably affecting the poor have not occurred as often as they might if the poor themselves were more involved in the decision-making process.

Politicians are influenced by many interest groups. It has been suggested that "political leaders must obviously strive to accommodate groups that will provide them the votes to win elections" (Cloward and Piven, 1969). Therefore, knowing that the poor often do not vote and cannot contribute very much to campaign funds, some political leaders feel no particular obligation to represent their interests. According to Elinor Graham (1965), the rise of interest in issues of poverty during the 1960s occurred not because of a public outcry but because poverty became a popular political issue. Even though the poor gained some political influence as a result of the antipoverty movement in the 1960s, it was not sufficient to bring forth any lasting improvements in social policies that affect the poor. In the 1970s and 80s, concern emerged about the nation's general economic well-being. With the swing of the political pendulum toward the conservative side, politicians were unwilling to vote for expensive social welfare programs. The efficiency and efficacy of the social welfare system was seriously questioned by politicians, as well as who the poor are, whether they are truly needy, and what the response of government should be to their needs.

In the 1990s, poverty has become more of a political issue than it was in the previous two decades. Following earlier trends, conservative politicians advocated for and managed to pass restrictive social welfare legislation in particular regions of the country (discussed in more detail in Chapter 7).

On the national scene, the Family Support Act of 1988, on the one hand heralded as a positive movement that would break the status quo in welfare reform, has not produced significant results in the elimination of poverty. Although, in general, social welfare programs have benefited some of the nation's poor over the past two decades, the number of people remaining in poverty has actually increased.

Poverty is a prominent national political issue in the 1990s. This renewed interest in poverty was fueled by conservative elected officials heeding what they perceived as a public cry for "less government" and less taxes. Dismantling of the welfare system is number one on the political agenda nationally.

Social Situational

Poverty can also be described as a social and situational phenomenon. Various social and situational factors can be identified as causes of poverty. Among social factors, negative societal attitudes toward the poor stand out as important contributors to the incidence of poverty. The high value placed on self-sufficiency and society's infatuation with the Protestant work ethic have played a part in this. This virtue of self-reliance in U.S. society has as its core the philosophy that "society does not owe anyone a living; people make their own living" (Tussing, 1975). Success and making one's own way are measured in terms of hard work. Many wrongly believe that poor people have low incomes not because of membership in an economic class or from other circumstances beyond their control, but because they are not useful to society, are less hard-working, frugal, and responsible. Poverty then is seen as a failure to adhere to the values of hard work and self-sufficiency, and the result is to blame the victim of poverty for his or her condition. These attitudes and values operate in social interaction and form the basis of prejudice and discrimination toward the poor. We refer here to discrimination on a more structural or institutional level tied specifically to the status of being poor. The poor are discriminated against throughout the whole structure of society, which restricts and even denies them opportunities for living a satisfying life. Although it is true that certain racial groups are overrepresented in the ranks of the poor, no one can deny that societal discrimination has had a devastating effect on all poor people. Discrimination perpetuates the vicious cycle of poverty that the poor struggle daily to escape.

In addition to societal values and attitudes, individual situational factors cause and sustain poverty (Little, 1971). Seldom discussed is the fact that poverty can be caused by physical or mental handicaps, poor health, status, or age. Little has described two types of poverty related to individual situational factors. One is *crisis poverty*, caused by a catastrophic traumatic event, such as injury, illness, or divorce, that renders the person unable to work for a living, thus causing poverty. He also describes *life-cycle poverty*, which results from changes associated with stages of life—for example, the case of a person who is too old to work and may lack adequate retirement resources. Although these factors might be considered only temporary causes of poverty, they nonetheless contribute significantly to its incidence, according to Little.

Along with individual factors, environmental situational factors are also among the causes of poverty. Environmentally caused poverty can best be described by discussing the effects of poverty on families. One's immediate social environment influences and shapes one's future. In U.S. society the family serves as the primary system of socialization. It is where children are taught attitudes, values, and skills that they later use to survive as adults. Poor families often lack appropriate values, attitudes, and skills, and transmit instead attitudes that are self-defeating and tend to perpetuate the cycle of poverty. Little (1971) also has described this as *inherited poverty*, not in the sense of genetic inheritance, but inheritance of the lifestyle of poverty through family socialization.

Poverty is a complex social phenomenon with many social situational causes. These causes are as important as economic causes when developing an understanding of the roots of poverty.

Discovery and Rediscovery of Poverty: Societal Responses

In the late 1800s and early 1900s poverty was discovered as a significant social problem. Several factors influenced that discovery. The United States was a country in transition, experiencing rapid social change. The Industrial Revolution was having an impact, driving a surge of population growth in the large industrial cities that brought with it a host of social ills—overcrowding, disease, unemployment, crime, and poverty. In addition, the nation was experiencing an influx of immigrants, many of whom were poor, and all of whom were involved in a lifestyle change. Society became stratified, with a more definite class structure than had previously existed in the United States. Poverty became a threat to society's equilibrium, an unavoidable social problem that had to be dealt with. Societal responses to poverty up to this time had consisted largely of mutual aid, some forms of local assistance, and various institutions. For a time, as the nation grew during the early 1900s, these responses proved to be sufficient to deal with the needs of the poor. However, all this came to a halt in the early 1930s.

First Rediscovery

In 1929, the stock market crashed, and in the next few years many banks failed and industries and businesses shut down. Millions of Americans lost their source of livelihood, including farmers who lost their farms and land. The country was thrown into the depths of an unprecedented economic depression. Poverty then became not a problem for a few, but one for millions. What the Great Depression clearly demonstrated is that poverty is not solely a problem of the individual, as had been thought earlier. It is instead a social and economic problem with the potential to affect large numbers of people.

Responses to the poverty caused by the Depression were slow to come. Sentiment in support of federal intervention and assistance grew. But Hoover administration officials, believers in *laissez-faire economics*, were reluctant to intervene, convinced that the economy by itself would reactivate, stabilize, and return the United States to prosperity. Americans were reluctant to wait for this to occur, and in the 1932 presidential election, the Democrat, Franklin D. Roosevelt, was elected. During the early years of Roosevelt's presidency, federal intervention in the economy was accomplished through legislation designed to ease the burdens of the Depression. First came the *New Deal* programs, which provided unemployment relief and public works employment, in hopes that the economy would quickly recover. By 1935, it had become evident that, despite federal intervention, a more long-term solution to poverty was needed, and that year Congress passed the Social Security Act. It provided both social insurance and public welfare programs designed to be permanent responses to poverty. Despite these programs, comprehensive solutions to the poverty of the Great Depression remained elusive. By 1939, the United States was on the verge of entering World War II. The demand for war goods by our European allies stimulated some economic recovery, which was fully realized in 1941 when the country entered the war. Spurred by the war effort, the economy improved vastly, and prosperity returned for most Americans.

From the time the United States entered the war in 1941 until the end of the decade of the 1950s, poverty slipped away into obscurity. It was not that poverty didn't exist, but with the general economic well-being of the nation, poverty was thought to be limited. This view was widely supported in the literature of the day, an example of which is John Kenneth Galbraith's *Affluent Society*, published in 1958. Galbraith contended that the United States had become an affluent nation. In his view, poverty was again deemed a matter of individual circumstances, and not the general mass problem it had been during the Depression. Although conceding that some poverty existed, people assumed it was geographically isolated. By the end of the decade, the poor had for all practical purposes become invisible. This view, however, would soon change, and change rapidly. The beginning of the new decade of the 1960s brought with it a sense of restlessness among the American people, particularly among youths and African Americans. What was to follow was a second rediscovery of poverty.

Second Rediscovery

In 1960, John F. Kennedy was elected president. He brought to the job an awareness of the unrest among the people and of the impending change it was about to bring. He had become popular with youths and African Americans during his candidacy because of his humanitarian concerns. Continuing in this spirit, in his inaugural address Kennedy urged the United States to rise up and fight the common enemies of humankind—tyranny and poverty. This sparked renewed interest in poverty as a significant social problem and political issue. Literature emerged that called attention to the seriousness of the problem of poverty. Michael Harrington's book *The Other America* (1962) was especially important and caught the interest of the Kennedy administration, which was seeking new ways to approach the problem of poverty. Unfortunately, Kennedy's aspirations to find solutions were not realized during his lifetime, but the Johnson administration was able to carry out the spirit of these aspirations.

Other events also began to shape renewed interest in poverty. The civil rights movement called attention to racism and poverty, as did Martin Luther King's Poor People's March on Washington. Before his reelection to the presidency in 1964, Lyndon B. Johnson, in a message to Congress on March 3, 1964, unveiled a plan to declare a national *War on Poverty*. In this message, Johnson asked Congress to consider a piece of legislation entitled the *Economic Opportunity Act* of 1964, which, he stated, "strikes at the causes, not just the consequences of poverty" (Johnson, 1966).

The Economic Opportunity Act called for the creation of new programs to combat poverty, under the direction of a new separate federal agency, the *Office of Economic Opportunity* (OEO). This agency would in turn be under the direct administration of the president. The Economic Opportunity Act became law on August 20, 1964. Several new programs were created under this act: the Job Corps, a work training and work study program for youth; the *Community Action Program*, an opportunity given to local communities to design *antipoverty programs* suited to their needs, with primary funding from the OEO; and VISTA, or Volunteers in Service to America, a volunteer group that works in areas of the country where poverty is prevalent. As these programs developed, particularly the community action programs, many local antipoverty programs came into existence. The underlying premise on which the whole War on Poverty and its programs were based was maximum feasible participation. This meant that it was not government's role to do for the poor, but the role of the poor, with government assistance, to do for themselves. The poor, then, were to be involved in the planning, administration, and delivery of the antipoverty programs. With the funding provided by the Office of Economic Opportunity, and the planning and development of programs by state and local community action organizations, the War on Poverty machinery was set in place in both urban and rural areas across the country.

The success or failure of the antipoverty programs of the 1960s is a subject of debate. Several factors detracted from their success, most importantly inadequate funding. The United States by this time was heavily involved in the Vietnam War, and during these years the Johnson administration and Congress faced dilemmas over priorities in spending.

The philosophy of "guns versus butter"—that is, the nation's ability to engage in a war and still provide for its citizens—was the source of this dilemma. The result was that the War on Poverty took a back seat to the war in Vietnam in priorities in funding. Sundquist, in evaluating the antipoverty efforts, states, "Hardly had its central theme, the War on Poverty, been accepted by Congress and enacted into law than funds, attention, and leadership were diverted to the morass of Vietnam" (Sundquist, 1969: 235).

Another problem with the administration's War on Poverty programs was that eventually the program became administratively top-heavy. More dollars were spent administering the programs than in actually serving the impoverished. There was also no uniformity in administrative models, particularly among the local community action programs. Some were controlled by the local political power structure. Others were dominated by professionals, with no semblance of the philosophy of maximum feasible participation by the poor. The programs were prone to political infighting that produced chaos in their administration. It has been pointed out by Sundquist (1969) that "No single appraisal of community action is possible, because the one thousand CAAs [community action agencies] include all kinds—the militant and the tame, the rigorously managed and the sloppily managed, and professionally dominated and the poor dominated, the centralized, the decentralized, the respected, and the disdained, and all shadings in between all these poles."

In addition, it would seem that the antipoverty programs did not emerge from public support with a demand for launching a concerted attack on poverty even from certain political interest groups. Rather, it appears that the antipoverty programs adopted the Democratic party (Heclo, 1968). Lampman (1974), in an overall evaluation of the War on Poverty, found there was one point on which most agree: "the expectations engendered by the promises were far beyond anything the program had the capacity to deliver."

With the change in presidential administration in 1968, Richard Nixon declared an end to the War on Poverty. The end was not abrupt, but a gradual, piece-by-piece dismantling of the programs. Some parts of the Office of Economic Opportunity and its programs (e.g., Head Start, Job Corps) had proved their viability and have been transferred into other structures of the federal government.

The War on Poverty did leave some positive contributions that have become permanent features of the societal response to poverty through the social welfare system. One of these is the right of the community and of the service consumer to have input into decisions about community service delivery. Consumers' awareness of their rights and of access to information about services has also grown. Educational, job training, and legal services, now readily available to the poor, all resulted from the antipoverty programs. The questions now are: How far have we come in providing adequate responses to poverty? Have we done enough? Indications are that we have not.

Since the beginning of the 1970s, interest in alleviating poverty has declined and has not been a part of the national policy agenda. Poverty persists, however, alive and well as always. As Michael Harrington (1984) stated in *The New American Poverty*, "Two decades after the President of the United States declared an 'unconditional war on poverty,' poverty does not simply continue to exist; worse, we must deal with structures of misery, with a new poverty much more tenacious than the old" (p. 1).

Professional Responses to Poverty

Historically, formal responses to poverty in the 1800s brought forth the development of social work as a profession. Until the 1920s, social workers remained committed to the poor. But as knowledge of psychological and social functioning expanded, the profession slowly began to move away from exclusive work with the poor. During the 1930s the demands of the Depression involved some social workers with the poor. Again in the 1960s, the War on Poverty had the same effect.

Professional organizations such as the American Public Welfare Association and the National Association of Social Workers (NASW) all have made the issue of poverty a priority. A large proportion of the membership of these organizations, particularly NASW, are professional social workers. Yet today, the argument continues concerning what social work as a profession is and is not doing about issues of poverty. Some accuse social work of abandoning the poor.

Walz and Groze (1991) have suggested that factors such as expansion in private agencies and a dominant middle class in which there are many problems have changed the clientele served by social workers, capturing more of social work's attention and resources. The result is a weakening in the advocacy and political missions in social work practice. Further evidence of this, as suggested by Abramovitz (1991), is the "harmful language" used by some social workers when referring to the poor and other oppressed groups. This, she believes, is reflective of today's conservative climate and the presence of stereotypical attitudes that shape the consciousness and actions of some social workers. In a more positive tone, others speak of empowerment of the poor, combining the clinical and activist components of practice that some believe will fulfill the original ideals and aspirations of the professions founders. Leadership in the development of social policy and programming to deal with poverty must come from dedicated professionals. Professionals again need to assume leadership roles in the development of a sound national policy for dealing with poverty.

Summary

This chapter has focused on developing an understanding of poverty and its effects on and consequences for U.S. society. Poverty remains a complex and destructive social problem. We have not been able to show progress toward solving the problems of poverty, because the solutions remain elusive and complicated. Other interests have captured the attention of policymakers and of the general citizenry. Shortly after his election, former President George Bush called for the United States to become a "kinder and gentler" society. But this vision has not become reality. What is needed is a rearrangement of national priorities, with a concerted effort on the part of the general citizenry, the government, and the helping professions to take whatever steps are necessary to remove the barriers preventing those who live in poverty from obtaining sufficient income to meet their needs and live a personally satisfying life.

Key Terms

absolute deprivation	Economic Opportunity Act
antipoverty programs	feminization of poverty
Community Action Program	gross national product
crisis poverty	homelessness
culture of poverty	inherited poverty
distribution of income	laissez-faire economics

life-cycle poverty
New Deal
Office of Economic Opportunity
poverty
poverty line
purchasing power

relative deprivation
underclass
underemployment
unemployment
War on Poverty
working poor

References

Abramovitz, M. (1991). Putting an end to doublespeak about race, gender, and poverty: an annotated glossary for social workers. *Social Work, 36*(5), 380–384.

Cloward, R., & Piven, F. F. (1969). Politics in the welfare system and poverty. In L. A. Ferman et al. (Eds.), *Poverty in America.* Ann Arbor: University of Michigan Press, p. 223.

Congressional Budget Office (1989). Measuring poverty. In I. Colby (Ed.), *Social welfare policy: perspectives, patterns, insights.* Chicago: Dorsey Press, p. 205.

Coser, L. (1965). The sociology of poverty. *Social Problems, 13*(Fall), 140–148.

Ellwood, D.T. (1988). *Poor support: poverty in the American family.* New York: Basic Books.

First, R. J., Roth, D., & Arewa, B. D. (1988). Homelessness: understanding the dimensions of the problem of minorities. *Social Work, 33*(2), 120–122.

Fitchen, J. M. (1991). Homelessness in rural places: perspectives from upstate New York. *Urban Anthropology, 20*(2), 177–210.

Galbraith, J. K. (1958). *The affluent society.* Boston: Houghton Mifflin.

Gilder, G. (1981). *Wealth and poverty.* New York: Basic Books Inc. Publishers.

Graham, E. (1965). The politics of poverty. In B. B. Seligman (Ed.), *Poverty: a public issue.* New York: Free Press.

Hagen, J. L. (1987). The heterogeneity of homelessness. *Social Casework, 68*(October), 451–457.

Harrington, M. (1984). *The new American poverty.* New York: Holt, Rinehart and Winston.

Haxlitt, H. (1973). *The conquest of poverty.* New Rochelle, NY: Arlington House.

Heclo, H. (1986). The political foundations of antipoverty policy. In D. H. Weinberg (Ed.), *Fighting poverty.* Cambridge, MA: Harvard University Press, p. 330.

Heisler, B. (1991). A comparative perspective on the underclass: questions of urban poverty, race and citizenship. *Theory and Society, 20*(4), 455–483.

Herrnstein, R. J., & Murray, C. (1994). *The bell curve: the reshaping of American life by differences in intelligence.* New York: Free Press.

Jensen, L. (1989). Rural-urban differences in the utilization and ameliorative effects of welfare programs. In H. Rodgers & G. Weiher (Eds.), *Rural poverty: special causes and policy reforms.* New York: Greenwood Press, pp. 25–39.

Johnson, L. B. (1966). Message to Congress. In H. H. Meissner (Ed.), *Poverty: the affluent society.* New York: Harper & Row, p. 204.

Kerlin, A.E. (1993). From welfare to work: does it make sense? *Journal of Sociology & Social Welfare, 20*(1), 71–85.

Knitzer, J., & Abner, J.L. (1995). Young children in poverty: facing the facts. *American Journal of Orthopsychiatry, 65*(2), 174–76.

Lampman, R. J. (1974). What does it do for the poor? A new test for national policy. *The Public Interest, 34*(Winter), 66–82.

Levitan, S. A. (1990). *Programs in aid of the poor.* Baltimore, MD: The Johns Hopkins University Press.

Lewis, O. (1966). *La vida.* New York: Random House.

Little, A. (1971). Poverty types. *Encyclopedia of Social Work,* Washington, DC: National Association of Social Workers.

Longres, J.F. (1990). *Human behavior in the social environment* (1st ed.). Itasca, IL: F.E. Peacock Publishers, Inc.

Macarov, D. (1978). *The design of social welfare.* New York: Holt, Rinehart and Winston.

Mauldin, T.A. (1991). Economic consequences of divorce or separation among women in poverty. *Journal of Divorce and Remarriage, 14*(3–4), 163–177.

Orshansky, M. (1993). Measuring poverty. *Public Welfare, 51*(1), 27–28.

Ozawa, M. N. (1991). Basis of income support for children: a time for change. *Children and Youth Services Review, 13*(1), 7–27.

Perry, J.A., & Perry, E.R. (1988). *Contemporary society: an introduction to social science.* New York: Harper and Row Publishers.

Plotnik, R., & Skidmore, F. (1975). *Progress against poverty: a review of the 1964–1974 decade.* New York: Academic Press.

Popple, P. R., & Leighninger, L. (1990). *Social work, social welfare, and American society.* Boston, MA: Allyn and Bacon.

Reamer, F. G. (1989). The affordable housing crisis and social work. *Social Work, 34*(1), 5–9.

Rogers, B.L., Brown, J.L., & Cook, J. (1994). Unifying the poverty line: a critique of maintaining lower poverty standards for the elderly. *Journal of Aging & Social Policy, 6*(1/2), 143–66.

Scanlan, J., Watson, D., McLanahan, S. S., & Sorensen, A. (1991). Comment on McLanahan, Sorensen and Watson's sex differences in poverty. *Signs, 16*(2), 409–413.

Schiller, B. (1989). *The economics of poverty and discrimination.* Englewood Cliffs, NJ: Prentice-Hall.

Segal, E.A. (1991). A progressive service approach for women on welfare. *Affilia, 6*(3), 85–89.

Sundquist, J. L. (Ed.). (1969). *On fighting poverty.* New York: Basic Books.

Tussing, D. A. (1975). *Poverty in a dual economy.* New York: St. Martin's Press.

U.S. Bureau of the Census (1990). *Poverty in the United States: 1990.* Washington, DC: U.S. Government Printing Office.

U.S. Bureau of the Census (1995). *Statistical Abstract of the United States: 1995* (115th ed.). Washington, DC: U.S. Government Printing Office.

U. S. Bureau of the Census and U. S. Department of Housing (1989, June). A place to call home: the crisis on housing for the poor. *NASW News,* p. 9.

U. S. Department of Commerce, Bureau of the Census (1983). *Money, income and poverty status of families and persons in the United States.* Washington, DC: U.S. Government Printing Office. Series P-60, No. 145.

Walz, T., & Groze, V. (1991). The mission of social work revisited: an agenda for the 1990's. *Social Work, 36*(6), 500–504.

Wisconsin State Journal, (1992, August 16), p. 1G.

Woody, B. (1991). Recent employment experience of black women workers in the services economy: implications for policy and practice. *Sociological Practice and Review, 2*(3), 188–199.

Suggested Readings

Andersen, Sandra C.; Boe, Tome; and Smith, Sharon. "Homeless Women." *Affilia,* 3 (Summer 1988), 62–70.

Danzinger, Sheldon, and Weinberg, Daniel H. *Fighting Poverty: What Works and What Doesn't* (Cambridge, MA: Harvard University Press, 1986).

Ellwood, David T. *Poor Support: Poverty in the American Family* (New York: Basic Books, 1988).

Harrington, Michael. *The New American Poverty* (New York: Holt, Rinehart and Winston, 1984).

Human Services in the Rural Environment, 10–11 (Spring–Summer 1987). Special Double Issue on Rural Poverty.

Levitan, Sar A. *Programs in Aid of the Poor* (Baltimore MD: The Johns Hopkins University Press, 1990).

Patterson, James T. *America's Struggle against Poverty, 1900–1985* (Cambridge, Mass: Harvard University Press, 1986).

Reamer, Frederic G. "The Affordable Housing Crisis and Social Work." *Social Work,* 34 (January 1989), 5–9.

Rodgers, Harrell R. and Gregory Weiher, eds. *Rural Poverty: Special Causes and Policy Reforms* (New York: Greenwood Press, 1989).

Schiller, Bradley. *The Economics of Poverty and Discrimination* (Englewood Cliffs, NJ: Prentice-Hall, 1989).

4

SOCIAL WELFARE RESOURCES

Learning Expectations

- Identify and describe five mechanisms for meeting human need in U.S. society.
- Define resources.
- Define services.
- Describe the range of resources that the social welfare system provides in the United States.
- Describe how needs differ at each of the various stages of the life cycle.
- Define social support network. Discuss its importance for individual functioning.
- Discuss how social support networks influence individual functioning.
- Define prevention. Identify three types of prevention.
- Discuss barriers to developing a preventive stance in the delivery of social welfare services.

Human beings have a variety of needs that must be filled if they are to live functional, satisfying lives. These needs include food, shelter, health care, safety, opportunity for emotional and intellectual growth, relationships with others, and spiritual fulfillment. Usually, many of these needs are met through an individual's personal resources, or within family and friendship networks. But when an individual's resources are inadequate, these needs must be met through societal mechanisms. The social welfare system contains mechanisms to meet these needs. The lack of financial resources to provide for basic needs is known as poverty and was examined in the previous chapter. This chapter looks at the resources and services not directly related to financial provision that individuals and families need in order to be functioning members of society. It considers two related concepts, *social support* and *prevention*. This chapter explores different ways of classifying these resources by function and through life-span frameworks. It will address conditions and attitudes that influence availability and that may block the use of resources and services for those who need them. Issues of accessibility and acceptability and resource usability by groups with diverse characteristics will also be discussed.

Need for Resources

Within contemporary U.S. society, the mechanisms used for meeting human needs can be categorized as:

Personal: Self, family, friends, work colleagues

Informal: Natural helpers in the community, self-help groups, community grass-roots groups, clubs and other groups that function informally

Institutional: Schools, churches, and other formal organizations

Societal: Services, agencies, and institutions set up to meet specific human needs (DuBois and Miley, 1992; Federico, 1990).

Usually, people first attempt to meet their needs within the personal system and, if that is not possible, move to the informal, to the institutional, and finally to the societal system. For example, if parents are seeking information about how to deal with their child's discipline problem, they will probably first discuss the problem with a family member or a friend. If no solution to the problem is found, they may seek an informal source such as a group of like-minded parents. If that is impossible or does not yield a solution, they may then discuss the problem with a teacher or a school counselor. Finally, after all else has failed, they may seek out a social agency that offers counseling services to parents.

As social change evolved, as discussed in Chapter 2, change in how people satisfy their needs for socialization, for intellectual and emotional growth, and for satisfying relationships also took place, from depending on self and family (mutual aid) to depending on a broader social network and on societal provision.

With these changes grew the need for resources or services to help people facing problems of social functioning. *Resources* are what individuals and families need so they can carry out the roles and tasks assigned to them by society and can lead reasonably satisfying lives. *Social services* are those resources requiring the activity of a person employed within the social welfare system. According to DuBois and Miley (1992), the needs of most people are met through day to day interaction with their immediate environment. However, needs are met only to the extent to which there is a congruence between the needs of the person and societal resources. One factor that has increased the need for social services is the mobility of the population and the breakdown of personal resource networks. For example, a family with two young children moves two thousand miles to a large city, where the only people they know are work colleagues of the husband and the wife, none of whom have young children. One of the children becomes seriously ill and requires hospitalization. The family is faced not only with the problems of the sick child but also with the need for additional child care for their other child. The family may not yet have developed a personal friendship network through neighbors, clubs, or churches on whom they can depend for support. Both parents are already emotionally stressed in adjusting to new jobs and living arrangements. This family may need some help from a social agency in coping with this situation, because they have an inadequate personal network and few if any contacts with informal or other resources.

When adequate resources and services are not available to such families, there is danger that impaired social functioning will result. It may take the form of inadequate parenting, marital dysfunction, or inability to function in the workplace, to name a few. This impaired functioning can then lead to a need for expensive resources, such as income maintenance, psychological counseling, or other long-term services. Such problems in turn can result in further deterioration of both individual and family social functioning.

Range of Resources

A vast range of services and resources is needed by a person or a family to maintain an optimal level of social functioning within U.S. society. The specific needs change from time to time and from community to community, depending on a wide range of circumstances. Far too many services and resources exist to be specified in this discussion. What will be presented is a formulation that provides a means for determining the range of needed resources (Johnson, 1995). Areas of need include the following:

1. *Economic:* This area includes job training, career counseling and employment searches, counseling on work-related problems, training in money management and retirement planning, and information about where and how to receive financial assistance. In other words, this area covers those services and resources that either enable individuals to become economically self-sufficient or enable them to find and use alternative means of providing for their economic needs.
2. *Parenting:* This area includes parent–child counseling; supportive services for parents of children with special needs or for parents who are not able to carry out the parenting role independently; educational services focused on the parenting role; and substitute child care (day care or foster care) for children needing part-time or full-time care outside the family setting. In other words, this area includes all those services that help parents fulfill their parenting responsibilities or that provide alternative child care.
3. *Marital relationship:* This area includes premarital counseling, marital counseling, and services for divorcing couples. Services in this area include all those aimed at strengthening the marital relationship or at helping people recover from the negative consequences of a breakdown in a marital relationship.
4. *Interpersonal and community relationships:* This area includes resources that enable people to participate meaningfully in group activities; services to help newcomers become acquainted with the community; activities that provide opportunities for participation in religious, cultural, political, and educational events; and social activities for children and youth. It includes those services that provide education for and experience in working with others, in activities that are personally satisfying and also enhance the functioning of the environment.
5. *Physically and mentally disabled persons:* This area includes support services, training, transportation, special housing, and specialized care and health services. It includes services that enable individuals with disabling conditions to lead a satisfying life and to participate as much as they can in mainstream activities.

6. *Schools, hospitals, and institutions:* Social services in these institutions enable individuals to make maximum use of the institutions, their facilities, and their personnel. These services include counseling services in the schools and social work in medical settings. They are ancillary to the primary service of the institution in which they are housed.

7. *Community organization:* These are indirect services to agencies, such as unified funding, coordinating existing services, modifying services not effectively responding to the needs for which they are responsible, and developing new services when necessary.

8. *Other services:* These include information and referral services that link persons to a wide variety of resources, supportive services, problem-solving services for coping with personal and environmental problems, crisis services, and counseling and therapy for people experiencing severe social functioning problems. These services are aimed at preventing the need for more expensive services, such as income maintenance, institutionalization, or long-term therapeutic intervention.

Although this classification and the examples given do not include all the resources a complex society provides for its members, they do illustrate the variety of resources that can be provided. More specific discussion of resources needed will be presented in Part Two of this book. Many people can purchase these services, if they have sufficient income, but people living near or below the poverty line do not have the money to obtain this kind of help. A social welfare system that provides these resources often prevents the development of deep and pervasive social dysfunctioning.

A single mother with two elementary school-aged children takes a job in an accounting firm in a city some distance from the place she has always lived and from her family and friends. She is immediately faced with finding substitute child care after school and during school vacations. She also needs to find social outlets for herself. She may have difficulty dealing with the loss of the familiar and supportive environment she has left behind. She may need problem-solving or counseling services. Without these needed services, she may not function adequately either as a parent or at work. She may even lose her job, the sole economic resource for her family. Even more important, she may lose the capacity to function as a self-sufficient person and a role model for her children. Not every single parent moving to a new community will have trouble finding needed resources or will risk more serious problems. However, some individuals may, and an information and referral service and other services for single parents can help meet their special needs before problems develop.

Life Span Needs

Another way of categorizing resources is to identify the resources that are often needed at various stages in a person's life span. These stages are early childhood (birth to age 5), late childhood (ages 6 to 12), adolescence (ages 13 to 19), young adulthood (ages 20 to 35), middle adulthood (ages 36 to 60), and older adulthood (ages 61 and up). This classification is not rigid, and some people may need the services listed at particular stages in their life, either when younger or older.

1. *Early childhood:* Services for young children may include services to their parents that develop and enhance parenting skills; services for children with disabilities that help over-

come or compensate for the disability and encourage maximum social functioning; and alternative child care services for families who cannot or will not give full-time care, including day care, foster care, and adoption services.

2. *Late childhood:* Services for elementary school-age children include the services listed above plus services that help children maximize their use of important educational opportunities, services that develop socialization skills and constructive use of leisure time, after-school and vacation day care when needed by families with working parents, and therapeutic counseling and other psychological services needed by children displaying behavior problems. Foster care, adoption, or residential treatment may be needed for a few children.

3. *Adolescence:* Services needed by adolescents may include remedial teaching and counseling to help youth remain in school, location of appropriate educational or vocational programs, services that prevent and treat problems of delinquency and of alcohol and drug abuse, programs that help adolescents deal with and make needed decisions about sexuality, and career planning. Some adolescents need help with out-of-wedlock pregnancy and single parenting. Some adolescents cannot live with their own families and need alternative living opportunities such as foster homes, group homes, or institutional care. Adolescents with disabilities need special services to help them cope with their changing bodies and social lives.

4. *Young adulthood:* Services in this category are those that help individuals take on adult roles and tasks in a competent and satisfying manner, such as finding a mate, developing a satisfying marriage and a healthy parenting style, pursuing a work role or career that meets the needs of self and family, and participating in their community and in its decision-making process. People with disabilities need special resources and services to participate as fully as possible in all aspects of their lives; these include specialized transportation and barrier-free housing and workplaces.

5. *Middle adulthood:* Services needed by individuals in this category include those that enable them to deal with midlife changes of a physical, cognitive, and emotional nature while continuing to carry out their roles as spouse, parent, and worker. These include such concerns as living with adolescent children, children leaving home, midlife physical and emotional changes, career changes, loss of employment, and severe or disabling illness or disability. People in this category also often have to care for aging parents—a responsibility that requires some support. Also, services are needed that enable preretirement planning.

6. *Older adulthood:* Services for older adults help them adjust to the changes that come with old age, such as physical change and disability and retirement from the work force; services that provide satisfying use of leisure time and continued participation in community life; supportive and protective services that allow older people to remain in the community; transportation services and housing adapted to elderly needs; and services that maximize use of the available health services, including home health and institutional services.

Obviously, living in contemporary U.S. society often requires resources from outside a personal network, a community's mutual aid network, or the available institutional resources. However, these services are neither universally available nor always adequate. Not all of these services can or should be the responsibility of the government. Some can and should continue to be provided by personal networks, community mutual aid, or community institutions (Karger and Stoesz, 1994). But so far, no one can agree on the resources and the individuals for which the social welfare system should be responsible. In order to prevent serious dysfunctioning and overdependence, it is important that the social welfare system provide resources and services. It also makes sense for the social welfare system to support personal, natural, and community systems or networks of resources and services.

Social Support

Still another way of understanding the need for resource provision is to consider the *social support network* that well-functioning individuals seem to develop. Whittaker and Garbarino (1983) define a social support network as "a range of interpersonal exchanges that provide an individual with information, emotional reassurance, physical or material assistance, and a sense of self as an object of concern" (p. 4). In many ways this social support network resembles or is a manifestation of the mutual aid arrangement discussed in Chapter 1. Discussion of social support networks in this chapter focuses on identifying those resources usually provided to individuals and families in a personal social support network, the absence of which can lead to social dysfunction. It also assumes that social problems and dysfunctional behavior can likewise undermine a weakened, maladaptive, or otherwise disrupted social support system. It is when the resources usually provided by a personal social support system are absent or have a negative influence, or when the need is beyond the capacity of the support system to provide, that resources from the social welfare system become important (Vosler, 1990).

Recently there has been concern about and research into the nature and purpose of social supports and the social support network (Maguire, 1983). Furthermore, recent studies have shown the role that these supports play in the maintenance and promotion of health (Auslander, 1988). Collins and Pancoast (1974) have described several systems that seem to provide considerable social support for those who participate in them. These include tavern culture, single-room occupancy buildings, the Mexican American community, the relationship of boarding home residents and providers in the field of mental health, and the relationship of child-care providers and parents. The study of the role and function of natural helpers and considerations for linking these informal helpers with more formal social welfare providers has also yielded an understanding of the role and function of social support systems in providing help to individuals and families (Hoch and Hemmens, 1987).

The social support network provides both tangible and intangible help. Tangible supports include such activities as child care, help with housekeeping, meals, escort services, and social activities. Intangible supports include information and advice, informal teaching, emotional support and the opportunity to release feelings, mutual problem-solving activities, and the like. The particular support provided depends, of course, on life stage and life situation. Older people need different kinds of help than do young parents. People from different cultural and socioeconomic groups require help that addresses their specific situation. One of the advantages of social support is that the help is usually given by like-minded people who often have faced the same concerns and problems. This enhances the likelihood that the help provided will be useful.

In contemporary U.S. society, some individuals and families find their social support networks disrupted. Social change, mobility, an increased life span, and economic insufficiency, to name but a few, are all factors that contribute to the disruption of individual social support systems. When this disruption occurs, individuals and families are placed at risk of not having their needs fulfilled. They become vulnerable to problems that disrupt their capacity to care for themselves and their families. Resources provided by the social welfare system then become an important means of helping people cope with the demands of daily living.

Sometimes, because of the changes and stresses of the contemporary world (such as poverty), social support systems or elements of those systems become stressed or unable to provide supports they formerly provided. At this point the appropriate provision may be one that restores the support system's ability to carry out its traditional function. For instance, children of elderly parents may be provided with information about the needs of their parents, with problem-solving help to determine how best to meet these needs, or perhaps with respite care for the parent to lessen the stress on their adult children.

Making sure that the resources usually provided by social support systems are available to all people is one way to prevent problems that can cause even greater disruption in the lives of individuals and families. As greater understanding is developed about social support networks and how they function, there will be increased understanding of the resources needed in a contemporary society if individual and family needs are to be met, and of how to provide those resources in the best and least disruptive manner possible.

Prevention

The discussion of support systems leads to the notion that preserving and strengthening support systems, as well as providing resources, is a means for preventing both the breakdown of social functioning and further dysfunctioning when some breakdown has already occurred. Not only do resources provided by the social welfare system help meet human needs, they also are preventive in nature. In order to clarify this more fully, a discussion of prevention is in order.

Prevention includes activities aimed at stopping a noxious circumstance from happening while also protecting strengths and competencies and promoting desirable goals or ends. Knowledge from the field of public health provides further understanding of the nature of prevention. There are three types of prevention: primary, secondary, and tertiary. *Primary prevention* stops a condition or circumstance from happening at all. *Secondary prevention* includes early detection and intervention aimed at stopping more serious damage from occurring. *Tertiary prevention* provides rehabilitative assistance (Bloom, 1987). For example, suppose a husband and wife are having serious marital difficulties. The husband threatens not only to leave the family but also to move to another part of the country. Two school-age children are involved. Primary prevention would be the provision of services (resources) that would allow the married couple to find ways of overcoming their problems and resolving issues surrounding the possible move. Secondary prevention would focus on allowing the wife to begin to function as a single parent. It might include provision of adequate financial resources or job counseling, provision of counseling resources to mother and children to help them deal with feelings about their new situation and status, provision of substitute care for the children while the mother is working, and provision of a resource that can compensate in part for the missing father. Tertiary prevention would take place if family or individual dysfunctioning occurred and might take the form of counseling.

Another public health concept is that prevention is carried out through a process of identifying the source of problems, minimizing hazards, and developing an awareness of the *at-risk population* and targeting them for concern (Schlesinger, 1985). For example, in the area of child abuse, attention would be paid to discovering why children are abused (stress intergenerational relationship patterns, etc.); identifying ways in which stress can be minimized and intergenerational relationship patterns changed (substitute child care, adequate income, education about children's needs and discipline strategies, etc.); and identifying situations in which parents and child-care providers are stressed or have questionable patterns of child care or parenting.

Still another public health concept is that three elements are involved in the condition to be prevented:

1. *The host:* The element (individual or group of individuals) that is at risk for or experiencing dysfunctioning
2. *The agent:* The element or elements that can trigger or contribute to the dysfunctioning
3. *The environment:* The situation in which the dysfunctioning can be supported (Schlesinger, 1985).

Prevention, particularly primary prevention, seeks to reduce stress, promote growth, support environments that minimize opportunities for negative agents, teach people how to avoid undesirable behavior and situations, and modify environments to provide more healthful situations.

It seems, then, that the provision of resources is an important aspect of prevention on all three levels. When considering the primary and secondary levels, the site of resource delivery becomes important. Resources need to be provided in a place where early entry is possible, one that is nonstigmatizing and culturally acceptable. The service should include outreach. It should enhance and strengthen the functioning of individuals and families and should preserve and strengthen their social support systems. One idea might be to place resources or services at places where people are apt to be present who are dealing with transitions from one life situation to another, such places as maternity wards, kindergartens (for parents), middle schools or junior high schools (for parents of early adolescents), and hospitals, as well as grocery stores, shopping centers, and so on (DuBois and Miley, 1992).

Although lip service is paid to the development and enhancement of a preventive stance toward the delivery of services in the U.S. social welfare system, little real progress has been made in this area. During the Reagan and Bush administrations in the 1980s, there was discussion of prevention as a way to reduce social services. However, it became apparent that preventive social policy, thus social programs, would call for the development of new resources and services and add to fiscal expenditures in social welfare, the idea of which was politically unacceptable at the time. Currently, there is interest in reducing the number of births out of wedlock among teenagers through preventive health and education programs. It is this group at which current social welfare reform proposals are largely directed. This comes at a time when the current political climate, as discussed in Chapter 1 and elsewhere in this text, is not supportive of increasing spending on social welfare programs, but more inclined to cut or substantially reduce expenditures. It must be noted here that preventive programs, particularly primary prevention programs, cost more than maintenance or rehabilitation programs. True, in the long run, a preventive stance has the potential to reduce the need for more expensive rehabilitation services, but the results are not immediately seen. To get to that point, an investment in the form of additional spending must be made. Currently there seems to be considerably more interest in achieving instantaneous results through cuts in social welfare spending rather than long-term investment.

There are two other barriers to the development of a preventive stance. The first is the problem of accountability. Primary prevention, in particular, is very difficult to prove. That is, in many situations it is difficult to identify just what it was that prevented something from happening. For example, a community center might say that it is preventing delinquency and enabling youths to be better prepared for a satisfying life. But is it the activity of the community center, the educational system, the youths' families, the general atmosphere of the community, or some other factor that is the prevention agent? In a society in which accountability is of prime concern, it is difficult to sell programs that cannot prove their worth.

Another barrier has been the lack of professional interest in preventive activities. Although a few professionals have seen the values of prevention and have been willing to engage in such activities, many have not. Part of the reason probably lies in the lack of funding available for such activities. In addition, many professionals seem to have a need to engage in the more dramatic activity of rehabilitation.

Gilbert (1982) suggested that there are three basic policy issues that need to be addressed in relation to primary prevention. First is the issue of identifying appropriate clients. Does identification as "at risk" stigmatize a client or even become a self-fulfilling prophecy? Is primary prevention too intrusive in a free society? Second is the issue of unanticipated consequences. This is best explained by an example given by Gilbert. In the attempt to prevent adolescent pregnancy, does provision of easy access to free family planning services lead to more sexual activity among teens and hence to more pregnancies? Last is the issue of implementation. Gilbert questions whether the technology of prevention has been sufficiently developed and calls for careful consideration of this concern.

It would seem that the provision of resources—not only resources for those who have needs they cannot meet themselves but also resources aimed at prevention of social dysfunctioning—would be an appropriate activity for the U.S. social welfare system. However, this development will not be easy from either a political or a professional viewpoint. Many important policy issues must be considered if prevention is to become a reality within the U.S. system.

Availability of Resources

If a wide variety of resources, including service, are needed to support people with their social functioning, then these resources must be available for use. *Availability* means that the resources are present in sufficient quantity for all who need them. However, quantity is not the only factor in defining availability. Distribution, accessibility, usability, and coordination must also be considered.

Distribution of the resources within the social welfare system remains a difficult problem. Resources are usually more readily available in large metropolitan areas than in rural or sparsely populated areas. They are more readily available in affluent cities and states than in areas with lower tax bases or poorer populations. They are more likely to be present where citizens have a high level of social consciousness than where citizens believe strongly in "rugged individual-ism." People who need resources and services usually are too poor to travel long distances to receive services. They may find it difficult to take time off from work or from child care responsibilities. They may be physically unable to travel. All of these circumstances contribute to the problems of distribution of resources within the U.S. social welfare system.

A second and related factor in resource availability is *accessibility*. Resources may be located geographically near to the people needing them and still not be accessible. If needy people do not know about them, they are not accessible. If they cannot be reached by public transportation, then they are not accessible to people without cars. If there is a fee for the use of the resources, then they are not accessible to people on limited incomes. If the hours when the resource or service is available are those when some people needing the service must be at work, at school, or taking care of children, then the service may not be accessible to them.

Another factor in availability is *usability*. Resources are not usable if the people needing the resource and the people responsible for its distribution do not speak the same language. DuBois and Miley (1992) have pointed out the need for differential resources and service delivery strategies for minority people. They note that cultural lifestyles and values must be considered, along with experiences of prejudice and discrimination. For example, Spanish-speaking clients may not be able to find services available in Spanish. They may not find a professional helper who not only understands the language but also understands the Hispanic family structure or the traditional use of folk medicine and healing by some Hispanics. If family structure or the traditional healing methods are not considered when developing a service plan, that plan may be incongruent with the client's lifestyle and therefore unusable.

Resources need to be congruent with the culture of the people needing them. For example, in Native American culture, it is important that family members share what they have; thus nutrition programs for older people are often unusable. Traditional Native Americans would rather go without than break their cultural mores of sharing.

Racist attitudes or practices of workers and agencies regarding people from different cultures can be another barrier to usability. These attitudes can arise from subtle unrecognized feelings, from lack of knowledge about a client's culture, or from discriminatory or unrealistic expectations on the part of the agency or worker.

Resources and services delivered from outside the user's frame of reference are often not easily used by people of other economic groups. For example, blue-collar families may avoid using resources in white-collar, downtown settings because they feel uncomfortable outside their own neighborhood or environment. Our current social welfare system is biased toward the culture and value systems of middle-class people. It makes assumptions about individuals' and families' needs that are based on middle-class perceptions. The resources and services are structured to conform to middle-class preferences. But contemporary U.S. society contains diverse cultures and lifestyles (Schriver, 1995). If the waiting room of an agency reflects a standard different from standards familiar to clients, they may become uncomfortable and avoid future contact with the agency. For resources and services to be available, they must be in a form usable by the people who need them.

A final element of availability has to do with *coordination* of resources. People often need several different resources that may not all be available in one place or agency. Conflicting information or conflicting demands may confuse people who need resources. This can add an additional burden to already burdened people, for it may call for them to sort out and find ways to deal with the conflicting information or demands, which places additional responsibility on the resource user (Schriver, 1995). If services are not coordinated, people may find the resulting confusion overwhelming and either withdraw from the helping situation altogether or use only part of the needed services.

For resources to be available, they must be appropriately distributed, accessible to, and usable by those who need them. And someone must coordinate them. Attention must be paid to issues of availability within the social welfare system.

Summary

This chapter discussed the wide range of resources and services that individuals and families may need. These services and resources can be categorized by functions or tasks, or they can be categorized by life span stages. The concepts of social support and prevention were also considered. Factors affecting availability of resources were also discussed: These include distribution, accessibility, usability, and coordination. Discontinuity between the culture and lifestyle of ethnic minorities and the way resources and services are delivered is another problem of availability.

Key Terms

accessibility

at-risk population

availability

coordination

distribution

prevention

primary prevention

resources

secondary prevention

services

social support

social support network

tertiary prevention

usability

References

Auslander, G.K. (1988). Social Networks and Health Status of the Unemployed. *Health and Social Work. 13* 191–200.

Bloom, M. (1987). Prevention. *Encyclopedia of Social Work, Vol. 2.* Silver Springs, MD: National Association of Social Workers, p. 303.

DuBois, B., and Miley, K.K. (1992). *Social Work: An Empowering Profession.* Boston: Allyn and Bacon.

Federico, R.C. (1990). *Social Welfare in Today's World.* New York: McGraw-Hill.

Gilbert, N. (1982). Policy Issues in Primary Prevention. *Social Work 27,* 293–297.

Hoch, C., and Hemmens, G.C. (1987). Linking Informal and Formal Help: Conflict Along the Continuum of Care. *Social Service Review 61,* 432–446.

Johnson, H.W. (1995). *The Social Services: An Introduction.* Itaska IL: F.E. Peacock.

Karger, H.J., and Stoesz, D. (1994). *American Social Welfare: A Pluralist Approach.* New York: Longman.

Maguire, L. (1983). *Understanding Social Networks.* Beverly Hills, CA: Sage Publications.

Schlesinger, E.G. (1985). *Health Care Social Work Practice.* St. Louis: Mosby, p.131.

Schriver, J.M. (1995). *Human Behavior and the Social Environment: Shifting Paradigms in Essential Knowledge for Social Work Practice.* Boston: Allyn and Bacon.

Vosler, N.R. (1990). Assessing Family Access to Basic Resources: An Essential Component of Social Work Practice. *Social Work 35*, 434–441.

Whittaker, J.K., and Garbarino, J. (1983). *Social Support Networks: Informal Helping in the Human Services.* Chicago: Aldine.

Suggested Readings

Auslander, G.K., and Lirwin, H. (1988). Social Policy Networks and the Poor: Toward Effective Policy and Practice. *Social Work 33*, 21–34.

Bloom, M. (1987). Prevention. *Encyclopedia of Social Work, Vol. 2.* Silver Springs MD: National Association of Social Workers.

Maguire, L. (1983). *Understanding Social Networks.* Beverly Hills, CA: Sage Publications.

Martin, M.A. (1988). Creating Community: Groupwork to Develop Social Support Networks with Homeless Mentally Ill. *Social Work With Groups 11 (4)*, 79–93.

Richardson, M., West, M.A, Day, P., Stewart, S., and Cahn, K. (1989). Coordinating Services by Demand. *Public Welfare 47*, 31–36.

Rosenberg, D.E. (1991). Serving America's Newcomers. *Social Welfare 49*, 31–46.

Tracy, E.M. (1990). Identifying Social Support Resources of At-Risk Families. *Social Work 35,* 252–258.

Tracy, E., and Whittaker, J.K. (1990). The Social Support Network Map: Assessing Support in Clinical Practice. *Families in Society 71 (10)*, 461–470.

Vosler, N.R. Assessing Family Access to Basic Resources: An Essential Component of Social Work Practice. *Social Work 35*, 434–441.

Zippay, A. (1991). The Limits of Intimates: Social Networks and Economic Status Among Displaced Industrial Workers. *Journal of Applied Social Sciences 15*, 75–95.

5

DISCRIMINATION AND RACISM

Learning Expectations

- Understanding of the terms *prejudice*, *discrimination*, and *racism*, including the capacity to differentiate between them

- Capacity to differentiate between individual racism and institutional racism and give examples of each

- Knowledge of how racism affects individual social functioning

- Understanding of the history of racism in the United States

- Identification of four ideologies about the eradication of racism and knowledge of the usefulness of each

- Understanding of the historical relationship of each of the major racial groups in U.S. society (African American, Hispanic, Native American, and Asian) to the majority society

- Understanding of the nature of discrimination against other groups within U.S. society

- Identification of some responses to racism and discrimination that have been made by the U.S. social welfare system and the profession of social work

Chapter 2 dealt with social change, specifically how social change influenced the development of the U.S. social welfare system. It also noted how social change, at various points in U.S. history, brought about special social conditions and problems, which in turn called for a response from the social welfare system. This chapter considers social problems related to the social condition of racism and discrimination, problems that have had a powerful influence on the course of development of the social welfare system. Racism and discrimination have often caused denial of access to the resources including those of the social welfare system. Sometimes resources are delivered in a manner that makes them unavailable because they are unusable within a particular cultural framework. (See Chapter 4). This then must be an important factor when identifying and discussing need provision—psychological, social, and economic. This chapter focuses on developing an understanding of the relationship between racism and discrimination and the meeting of human need, an essential factor in understanding the nature of the U.S. social welfare system. After defining racism and discrimination and their causes, the chapter will specify some specific discriminatory actions taken against specific minority groups. Finally, the chapter will discuss responses of the social welfare system and the profession of social work to racism and discrimination in U.S. society. The human diversity perspective, a framework for considering the functioning of diverse groups in U. S. society, as well as empowerment as a strategy to combat racism and discrimination will be discussed.

Prejudice, Discrimination, and Racism: Definitions

Prejudice, discrimination, and *racism* are often used interchangeably to describe social conflict between majority (powerful) groups and minority groups, but little attention is paid to their individual meanings. For purposes of the present discussion, a definition of each is essential.

Prejudice refers to a set of negative beliefs that are held about someone or something. Prejudice is defined as "any set of ideas and beliefs that negatively prejudge groups or individuals on the basis of real or alleged group traits or characteristics" (Newman, 1973). Prejudice, then, consists of beliefs or cognitive thoughts about a particular group, not behaviors or actions. Prejudice often leads to discriminatory or racist behaviors but this is not necessarily the case. If one is honest, one must admit that all humans carry some prejudicial beliefs or attitudes. However, many humans seek to become aware of these beliefs and attitudes in themselves so as to explore them for validity to avoid acting on them in discriminatory ways. Prejudice is an attitude that resides within the individual.

Discrimination refers to action, usually based on prejudicial attitudes. *Discrimination* is the overt and deliberate *act* of affording differential treatment toward some group (Mack, 1968). Discrimination describes the actions of a group or an individual (usually dominant and powerful) toward another person or group, usually less powerful and of minority status. These actions often deny equal opportunity for members of the less powerful group. Discrimination reveals itself in the interaction between individuals and groups. Individuals can engage in discriminatory actions without being aware of prejudicial attitudes or even that their actions are discriminatory. For example, a white business owner who claims not to be prejudiced against minorities may try to discourage young blacks from entering his establishment for fear that his other customers may stay away. He sees this behavior as protective of his business interests, not as prejudicial. On the other hand one may be well aware of prejudice within a personal value system and not discriminate overtly. If one's business is dependent on funding from government sources, it may be essential to comply with equal opportunity employment policies that minorities be hired. This person will, of course, be susceptible to engaging in subtle discriminatory behaviors as a part of the ongoing interaction with the minority individual.

A major source of prejudice and discrimination is racism. *Racism* is the belief that a certain race or races are superior to all others (See and Wilson, 1987). In the United States, racism becomes the belief that northern European Caucasians are superior. Brieland, Costin, and Atherton state, "Color becomes the determinant for classifying people as insiders or outsiders"

(Brieland, Costin, and Atherton, 1980). Therefore, racism in the United States is a kind of white racism based on the concept of *ethnocentrism*, the belief that one's own group is superior to other groups. Two forms of racism exist in the United States, *individual racism* and *institutional racism*, as described by Carmichael and Hamilton: "Racism is both overt and covert. It takes two closely related forms: Individual whites acting against individual blacks, and acts by the total white community against the black community. We call these individual racism and institutional racism" (Carmichael and Hamilton, 1967). Although this discussion is in terms of the black experience, it has application to analyzing racism and its effect on all racial groups in U.S. society.

Another factor that must be considered is that of social economic class. While it is true that minorities of color tend to be greatly over represented in the lower social economic segment of society, there are people of color at all social economic levels (Longres, 1995). Often social economic class characteristics and ethnic characteristics are confused. Thus attitudes about a lower-class lifestyle are projected on all persons of color. These attitudes reinforce discriminatory behaviors; they intensify prejudicial attitudes and strengthen tendencies toward racism (individual and institutional).

Since the 1960s, individual racism has received considerable attention in the United States. Laws have been passed outlawing its many manifestations. More important, some people have become aware of their racist attitudes and have attempted to overcome them. Among some segments of the society, often depicted as liberals, racism is viewed as unacceptable. Various strategies have been developed in the educational system and among some religious groups to help individuals overcome racism. In the 1990s, certainly some gains have been made, but individual racism is still apparent in U.S. society. Recently it has raised its head on many college campuses. It also manifests itself as fear, fear of those who are different, and the equating of race with the violence so rampant in contemporary U.S. society. The April–May 1992 reaction to the acquittals of four Los Angeles policemen charged with the brutal beating of a black man provide another indication that racism, both individual and institutional, is alive and well in U.S. society. This reaction among blacks indicates the festering anger that is present as a result of racism in U.S. society.

The concept of institutional racism also needs further consideration. It reflects a strong power component. The majority society from a position of power imposes societal structures and ways of functioning that reflect the value and cultural concerns of the majority group. This can place a minority individual or group of individuals at a disadvantage when functioning within the societal institutions developed by the majority members of society. For example, many children of a minority background are placed at risk in an educational structure developed to serve the children of the majority culture. These minority students come to the educational system with different values and attitudes about education. They come with culturally different ways of learning. They may be more action oriented or more comfortable in an oral (story telling) mode than in an empirical, scientific mode. Thus they are not able to respond as expected, that is, to learn as readily as majority children.

Another example lies in the social welfare system. This system has developed on the premise that the nuclear family is of prime importance in the scheme of life. Thus, the primary concern in the provision of resources and services has been a focus on providing resources and services to individuals or nuclear families. In many minority cultures, the extended family, the tribe, the clan, or the community may be the primary structure. Delivery of resources and services to these minority groups often results either in resources and services that are unuseable or in the weakening or destruction of the natural resource structure, the means for mutual aid.

Institutional racism then is the use or imposition by a majority group, based on its inherent power, of its ways of functioning and its institutional structure on individuals and groups for whom a different way of functioning or different institutional structure is more culturally congruent. If racism and particularly institutional racism is to be eradicated from the scene in the United States, ways must be found to structure the social welfare system (as well as other societal systems) to respond to the diversity of cultural and other groups that now make up the population of the country. This will call for radical changes in the attitudes of those who hold the power, it will call for understanding the nature of the diversity of people who make up the population, it will call for tolerance of difference, and respect for those who are different. This has been a tall order given the recent contemporary political tenor, but it is a task that may be tackled in the Clinton administration. This is important if the United States is to have a social welfare system that supports our "national value" of liberty and justice for all.

Before proceeding with further discussion of these terms it is important to briefly point out some of the effects of racism on the individual being discriminated against. A major result is lowered self-concept. The lowered self-concept often results in difficulty in developing the interaction and technical skills so necessary for functioning in contemporary U.S. society (Zastrow and Kirst-Ashman, 1994). Another result is lessened opportunity. This is in part related to skill deficiency but is further exacerbated by limited or unuseable opportunities to participate in the mainstream U.S. society. Opportunities in the educational and economic (job) areas are particularly crucial. Discrimination and racism indeed impact the individual's ability to meet personal and family needs.

Causes of Discrimination and Racism

Racism has always existed in the United States. Our nation's image as the land of the free, its values of respect for human rights and dignity, have always been tarnished by the forces of racism. Some form of white supremacy, both ideological and institutional, has existed from the first day Europeans arrived in the Americas. Current concerns regarding the Columbus event brought to light the negative attitudes and racist behaviors that immediately succeeded his "discovery of America" (Schama, 1992). The English immigrants who came to North America also continued to see Native Americans as a lesser breed. Often these negative attitudes were connected to the religious beliefs of the Europeans. It should of course be noted that prejudice toward other races and ethnic groups began centuries before the discovery of the New World. Jewish scripture shows the presence of prejudice toward many other peoples. Jewish people themselves have suffered from much discriminatory behavior through the ages, the Holocaust in Germany in the 1930s and 1940s was only a continuation of this trend. The Romans discriminated against all whom they conquered, as noted in the reports of their campaigns. The right of the conqueror to the spoils of battle has been justified in many ways too numerous to discuss here. What is important is understanding the attitudinal factors present in contemporary U.S. society upon which collective societal thinking is based.

Individual Factors

Individual attitudes certainly contribute to racism; "Prejudice, like all culture, is learned, taught and transmitted through the process of socialization into one's group and society" (Newman, 1973: p. 197). Preference for one's own group, ethnocentrism, is learned through socialization, and it forms the basis for prejudice toward groups different from one's own. It must be made clear that socialization does not always cause prejudice: Prejudicial attitudes must be present in the social structures that perform the socialization function, such as the family, for prejudice to be transmitted. But unfortunately, when prejudice is present, it sustains and spreads prejudice from generation to generation.

The attitudes of prejudice and the tendency to engage in behaviors considered racially demeaning are also sustained and supported through an individual's reference groups and peers. This influence results from both socialization and social control mechanisms.

However, engaging in discrimination toward particular groups is a matter of individual choice, based on the perceived rewards or negative consequences of such action. Lipset and Schneider (1978) have suggested that whether or not an individual engages in discrimination depends on whether the person holds the value orientations of *egalitarianism* or those of *individualism*. The egalitarian value orientation embraces a democratic and humanitarian perspective, whereas the individualistic value orientation emphasizes self-reliance, hard work, and achievement. A person who has the value orientation of egalitarianism will be disposed to identify with the plight of minority groups and will tend not to discriminate against them. Those who adhere to the individualistic value orientation will tend either to be ambivalent toward minority groups or to engage in acts of discrimination based on *stereotyping* in their perceptions about the social problems experienced by members of minority groups—for example, unemployment, welfare dependency, crime, and drug addiction. Persons who value individualism will tend to see these problems as a threat to their values about self-reliance and individual achievement (pp. 38–40).

At least some of the resurgence of individual racism on the contemporary scene can be attributed to extreme attitudes of individualism present in the majority culture. When, as is true in the depressed economy of the early 1990s, self-reliance and individual achievement do not necessarily result in job security, the threat becomes great. Racist activity expands. Not only is prejudice based in irrational prejudgment, it is also based in experience. The 1990s have seen a rise in criminal behaviors particularly in large cities with large minority (particularly African American) populations. Often the crime is attributed to the minority population. Whether this is fact, it has led to unrest and fear in the general population. The feelings of fear support prejudicial beliefs. Manifestations of racism increase. Which comes first—the societal factors or individual factors—is difficult to discern. What can be stated is that both are present.

Societal Attitude Factors

Although individual factors contribute to racism, they are often the result of societal factors. Prejudice and discrimination occur on a collective level—that is, on a societal level. The influence of an individual's reference group is strong. This influence enables the translation of the individual prejudice to a societal prejudice and thus to racist behaviors. When individuals share with a reference group negative experiences they have had with a particular minority person or group, they are encouraging prejudicial attitudes of the entire group.

Although recent research has shown an apparent decrease in stereotypical racial attitudes among the general public, it is thought that this research overestimates the degree to which white America has reversed its disaffection for blacks and other minorities (Dividio and Gaertner, 1988). Specific groups continued to be targeted for prejudice and discrimination.

Which groups are the targets of these behaviors varies depending on location. In certain parts of the United States, African Americans are targeted; in other parts of the country, the targets are Native Americans or Hispanic Americans. Prejudice and discrimination are part of a learned response toward people, which in turn is a result of socialization that has occurred in a geographical and cultural context. Some whites in the southern United States have been taught prejudice toward blacks. People in the Dakotas are sometimes socialized to be prejudiced against Native Americans. The list of examples could go on and on. Although some might view racism as a problem isolated within specific geographic areas, this view is too simplistic. Racism is deeply embedded in the total U.S. social structure. It has become institutionalized. Racism is a collective response from many parts of society.

Societal institutions were created and designed to meet human needs through structured distribution of goods, resources, services, and other social benefits. As discussed in the chapter on poverty, the distribution is inequitable and unjust. Minority groups, like the poor, are discriminated against and denied equal opportunity to a share of the resources, and are often denied a voice in the policy decision-making affecting the control of the distribution of goods and services. However unintentional or unconscious it may be, society, through its institutional structure, rewards certain groups and penalizes others. Majority groups tend to be rewarded in society's political, economic, educational, legal, medical, and social welfare institutions. Minorities tend to be penalized by being denied fair and equitable treatment from these institutions.

The U.S. social welfare system as a societal institution is no more exempt from racism than any other institution. Social welfare programs and services, delivered in a white cultural mode and based on social policies developed from a middle-class bias, have maintained the status quo position of minority racial groups. Various ideologies inherent in the majority culture support the continuance of racism. Clinton administration appointments would indicate an official movement toward inclusiveness. This may lead the way toward the softening of societal discriminatory practices.

Ideologies that Support Racism

In order to further understand the existence of racism in U.S. society, it is important to examine some of those ideologies that have developed either in support of its continuation or as antidotes to its existence. *Ideology* is the system of beliefs and assumptions of a group or culture. Some believe that the culture of a predominantly white world is most desirable. Therefore, the dominant world view or paradigm is "whiteness." This view posits that all persons, white, but especially non-whites, are judged or evaluated in all life areas according to standards that reflect the values, attitudes, experiences, and historical perspectives of whites. Whiteness, then, becomes a powerful and pervasive force that perpetuates the illusion that "white is right" (Schriver, 1995: p. 24). Others believe that all racial groups must share equally in the overall framework of society. Although not completely contradictory, the operationalizing of the two has placed them in opposite political camps—the first being a more conservative stance and the latter a more liberal stance. Which one predominates depends on many economic and political factors, but when the liberal stance predominates, equality tends to have higher status; when conservatism predominates, the desirability of the "majority culture" tends to have higher status.

One prevalent ideology about the elimination of racism assumes that racism can be eradicated by the process of *assimilation*. This belief "holds that the existing culture or civilization, of the majority, is desirable, and other groups must change themselves to become like the existing, majority group" (Macarov, 1978). In this view, all minority groups are expected to assimilate into the majority culture. If this occurs, racism would cease to exist because the differences between cultures will fade away.

This view has proved to be invalid for several reasons. First, those minorities who have assimilated and have achieved educationally and economically, still find themselves discriminated against because of visible differences such as skin color. For example, a physician who served on the faculty of a medical school may be followed by police as he returns to his affluent residential community. An African-American boy returning to his middle income neighborhood from school is questioned by police about why he is in the area.

Another reason for the invalidity of assimilation lies in the fact that many people of minority status either do not want to or cannot give up strongly cherished values and ways of functioning. For example, Native Americans have strong traditions that support the extended family. Individual achievement in the majority culture "sense" simply is not congruent with communal functioning. Another example from Native American culture relates to beliefs about the relationship of humans and the land. Most Native Americans believe that humans and the land and other aspects of nature must be in harmony. The majority culture believes that humans are to have dominion over the land and thus its resources are for their benefit and to be consumed.

Assimilation has not led to the eradication of racism. In some cases it has failed because outward appearances provide an ongoing sign of difference. In other cases, the minority groups have not given up dearly cherished aspects of their culture and, in the view of the authors, should not be asked to give them up.

While the equal rights/equal treatment approach sounds like one that provides "liberty and justice" for all, it too has limitations in eradicating racism. The civil rights movement resulted in laws that legislate against discrimination in the workplace, in education, and in many other areas of society. However, laws do not change attitudes. For example, it may be the law that all children are to receive an equal education and that education is to be in a nonsegregated situation. But, if the teacher has preconceived ideas about the abilities of minority children, equality cannot be achieved. A blatant example of this is when an African-American high school student who has already had some of her work published is confronted by a teacher and asked who wrote her assigned paper because "blacks do not write well." Racism has its roots in prejudicial attitudes, thus the legal approach is incomplete. Also *equality*, "sameness in number, size, merit, etc.," may not be the appropriate criteria to use when considering "justice." Rather *equity*, fairness or impartiality, may be a more appropriate criteria. Equity would recognize that justice includes allowance for various racial and ethnic groups to receive societal resources and services from within a framework congruent with their experience and culture.

Another view, *mutual assimilation*, or the melting pot concept, holds that each group must give up part of its heritage, while another part is absorbed by and becomes integral to the remainder of society—in short, that from an amalgam of all groups a new entity arises (Macarov, 1978). Here, each group is expected to give up part of its heritage while sharing other parts of its culture with the total society. It has been argued that this view represents the situation in our country today. To some extent, the United States has become a melting pot for ethnic and cultural groups. For example, African Americans and Hispanic Americans have given us unique forms of music, and many Asian groups have introduced other Americans to a feast of new foods.

However, there are cracks in the melting pot. Minority racial groups face a skin color barrier when it comes to mutual assimilation. While certain cultural characteristics held by minority ethnic groups are sometimes more acceptable to society at large, white society has been slow to realize that all Americans, regardless of their complexions, accents, or behavior, are going to have a part in shaping our culture; they have not done their part in mutual assimilation. Blacks, Native Americans, Mexican Americans, and other groups continue to be victimized by the forces of racism and discrimination. Experience has shown that this is not a viable solution for either the majority culture or for minority groups. It just does not work.

A third view related to the belief that all groups should participate fully and equally in society is *cultural pluralism*. In this view, each group should retain desirable and essential parts of its cultural heritage while actively taking full part in the total society. In cultural pluralism, diversity and difference are accepted and rewarded, not punished. Society has made some movement toward acceptance of this perspective in recent years. Most minority groups see this as the most desirable solution to racism and continue to press for its adoption. This approach has much to recommend it but it does not speak to the modification of attitudes, an essential component of any strategy for the eradication of racism in U.S. society.

Attitudinal change will of necessity recognize the desirability of a multicultural or diverse society. Two techniques that hold promise for encouraging attitudinal change are, first, the development of an appreciation for and an understanding of the diverse cultures and their contributions (former and potential) in and to contemporary U.S. society. It follows then, that multicultural education is called for at all levels.

A second approach is the provision of positive opportunities for people of various backgrounds to get to know each other as human beings with needs, hopes, and dreams—as people who want the good life for themselves and their children within the framework of their beliefs about the nature of that "good life." Opportunities for this should be in a context in which cultural experiences can be shared and appreciated, in which contributions can be celebrated, and in which differences are not seen as negative.

No single ideology represents the total relationship between majority society and minority groups in the contemporary United States. The elimination of racism in the United States remains a pervasive and stubborn social problem. There are reasons for both optimism and concern about this problem for the future.

On the optimistic side, laws have been passed to prevent blatant discrimination against persons on the basis of race. Other laws have made it easier for persons of color to take advantage of educational and employment opportunities, thereby narrowing the gap in socioeconomic status between majority white society and minority groups on an individual level. In some respects racial prejudice has declined, and minority group members are seen in a more positive light than ever before. Increasing numbers of African Americans and members of other minority groups are being elected to public office, with some support from a white constituency (Dividio and Gaertner, 1986). Despite these phenomena, however, there are significant reasons to be concerned about progress toward the elimination of racism.

Although racial attitudes have improved, significant numbers of whites continue to hold racist and bigoted attitudes. In fact, it appears that there has been some backsliding in recent years in the progress toward eliminating negative racial attitudes. As the courts in the United States have become more conservative, there seems to be a trend toward reducing the power of Civil Rights legislation.

What may be happening is that although considerable progress has been made toward the elimination of discrimination from a legal point of view, the necessary changes in attitudes have been slower in coming. The present change can be seen as a backlash. There is no doubt that heightened racial tension exists. This may be due in part to the fact that racial minorities have developed an expectation of change that has not been forthcoming. They also may have developed increased sensitivity to discrimination and prejudice and a sense that, both legally and morally, certain discriminatory behaviors toward them are no longer tolerable. Another explanation for the backlash may be that in today's ultraindividualistic society, anyone or anything that gets in the way of individual achievement of goals must be pushed aside. For example, many white males believe they have been victims of what has come to be known as reverse discrimination. That is, they feel they have been passed over for promotion or other rewards in order that minority quotas might be met. There has been much debate recently concerning the efficacy of federal Affirmative Action/Equal Opportunity Employment law and policy. Some policymakers contend that this policy has become unwieldy and unfair and regulates beyond what were its original intents. Therefore, it would not be surprising to see major changes in or the elimination of this policy. One state, California, has just recently repealed state compliance with affirmative action policy.

The means for living together in a diverse society in which there is liberty and justice for all is a high ideal. Yet, an agenda that seeks this ideal deserves a major emphasis within the U.S. social welfare system if needs are to be truly met. Such an agenda is also important if the larger society is to accord liberty and justice to all groups and individuals who make up the society. The apparent openness of the Clinton administration to such an agenda holds hope that the United States will more nearly approach the high ideal of liberty and justice for all.

For a broader understanding of these problems, attention will now be given to the effects of discrimination on specific groups and the ways these groups have responded to it.

Discrimination toward African Americans

Discrimination, prejudice, inequality, and injustice are just a few terms that describe the historical relationship between majority white society and African Americans. Although the first African Americans were free persons, by the end of the 1700s, most were trapped in the chains of slavery.

The true impact of slavery upon U.S. society is only now beginning to be understood. Slavery developed as an economic strategy in the southern colonies. It was owners of large sugar and cotton plantations who needed cheap labor who supported it. It placed African Americans in a subservient position in a foreign culture. It has led to present day attitudes of prejudice, racism, and discrimination within the majority society and to feelings of lowered self-worth among African Americans. While politically the U.S. Civil War was fought to free the slaves, it should be noted that in reality it was a war between two economic systems. It left African Americans with a changed status; however, freedom still did not give them equality. They still experienced very significant discrimination and prejudice. Racism abounded (Day, 1989).

From the Civil War to World War II

The end of the U.S. Civil War was the beginning of African Americans' long journey to achieve integrity, dignity, and equality, a journey that today is still not fully realized. Although African Americans had been freed from slavery after the Civil War by the Thirteenth Amendment to the Constitution, they were ill prepared to deal with their newfound destiny as free citizens. During Reconstruction (1865–1877), the federal government for a short time attempted to prepare African Americans for their new status. But the freed slaves, lacking in education, land, and other resources, fell once again into second-class citizenship. In the aftermath of Reconstruction, despite guarantees of civil rights—such as equal protection under the law and the right to vote, as provided in the Fourteenth Amendment of the Constitution—the South returned to "home rule." State-passed laws, referred to as Jim Crow laws, called for the segregation of African Americans from whites in schools and public places. African Americans in all southern states were denied the right to vote under amendments to state constitutions. In the North during this time, they also were not accepted as equals, a further denial of their civil rights. From the turn of the century through the 1940s, African Americans were trapped in the forces of racial prejudice and discrimination in both the South and the North. In the South, the Jim Crow laws legitimized their inferior status. Any attempts to press for basic civil rights were dealt with harshly, even by lynching. White supremacy groups like the Ku Klux Klan effectively kept African Americans from collective action. In the North, they were subject to stereotyping and denied equal opportunities in education and employment. For a long time, African Americans had no alternative but to accept the inferior status society had so unjustly imposed.

During World War II, the status of African Americans did not improve significantly. There was widespread discrimination toward employing them in defense industries until, in response to pressures brought by their leaders, President Franklin Roosevelt signed into law Executive Order 8802, which forbade discrimination in the defense industries' employment policies on the basis of race, color, creed, or national origin. As with most laws, however, loopholes were found that weakened its effectiveness. This law did not significantly improve the situation, and employment opportunities for African Americans continued to be restricted.

Despite the prejudice and discrimination experienced particularly in educational opportunities, in political power structures, and in economic structures, a growing number of African Americans achieved what might be identified as a middle-class lifestyle (Day, 1989).

Growth of the Civil Rights Movement

Up to the end of World War II, the struggle for black civil rights had focused on constitutional change and court battles; during the 1950s this effort continued. One of the turning points in this struggle, which set the course for several events to follow, was the 1954 Supreme Court case *Brown* v. *Board of Education*. This case dealt with the issue of whether African American students should be admitted to predominantly white public schools. It arose out of similar situations in several states. The Supreme Court ruled that segregation in the public schools, permitted by state laws, was unconstitutional. Although states had been permitted to segregate the public schools—on the basis of the 1896 Supreme Court decision of *Plessy* v. *Ferguson*, which allowed separate but equal facilities for African American students—the *Brown* v. *Board of Education* case essentially voided this decision and is considered to have been an important step toward improving the quality of education for these students.

This victory added much fuel to the fire by fostering a growing awareness among African Americans that aggressive action toward achieving equality could be successful. Other major victories were won in the 1950s—in particular, the confrontation at Little Rock, Arkansas, where African American students were admitted to high school under a federal court order and with protection of federal troops. These events set the tone for the development of new pride among African Americans and for the emergence of new civil rights leaders.

At the beginning of the 1960s, the African American civil rights movement entered what has been termed its protest phase. African American protests consisted of both violent and nonviolent actions. Both kinds of protest had significant effects on the civil rights movement. The nonviolent movement led by Dr. Martin Luther King, Jr., of the Southern Christian Leadership Conference (SCLC) promoted the causes of the nonviolent protest groups such as the Congress of Racial Equality (CORE), the Student Nonviolent Coordinating Committee (SNCC), and the National Association for the Advancement of Colored People (NAACP). Many nonviolent protest demonstrations were held throughout the South and were frequently marked by violent actions by the white power structure. The most noted event was the 1963 Poor People's March on Washington, D.C. African Americans and whites alike participated in this march. Martin Luther King's famous and influential "I have a dream" speech was given there. His work captured the imagination of both African Americans and whites and inspired leadership and action in the nonviolent civil rights movement.

The protest phase also had a violent side. Some African-American leaders were not satisfied with the relatively slow gains of the nonviolent movement and believed that aggressive, violent action was necessary to achieve the aims of equality. Rioting in Detroit, Michigan, and in the Watts area of Los Angeles, California, were examples of this violent side. The African American power movement, characterized by radical, revolutionary militant groups like the Black Panthers, and cultural nationalist groups like the Black Muslims, was another component.

According to James Cone, noted liberation theologian, Malcolm X, leader of the Black Muslims, led northern urban blacks just as Martin Luther King, Jr., led southern blacks. Each worked within a specific context: the urban ghetto and the legally segregated south. Malcolm X sought to empower, to affirm the goodness of being black, to develop self-respect among a people who had political rights but still were forced to live in substandard housing, and were denied equal educational and job opportunities (Cone, 1992).

The widespread racial unrest encouraged by black power groups, as well as the nonviolent protest, prompted President John F. Kennedy in 1963 to introduce new civil rights legislation. In the aftermath of Kennedy's assassination, President Lyndon Johnson urged Congress to proceed with this legislation, and the Civil Rights Law of 1964 was passed. This law guarantees everyone equal protection under the law.

Another victory for desegregation occurred in 1965, when the Voting Rights Act was signed into law. This brought an end to the practice of so-called home rule engaged in by the southern states for many years. African Americans as a collective group now had the potential to become a political force.

The protest phase of the 1960s, if nothing else, brought to the forefront a public awareness of the social conflict bred by racism. In 1967 President Johnson authorized the President's Commission on Civil Disorders, the so-called Kerner commission, to study the issues and problems of civil unrest in the United States. Overwhelmingly, the commission stated as its number one finding the fact that white racism was at the heart of civil and racial unrest. Shortly after the assassination of Martin Luther King, Jr., the protest phase of the civil rights movement waned.

The period from the decade of the 1970s up to the present has been characterized by some positive gains for African Americans as discussed earlier. However, there appear to be false perceptions about the extent of their progress. Alphonso Pinkney, in his book *The Myth of Black Progress*, states, "at a time when there appeared to be some minor progress in improving the citizenship of black people in the United States, and some official commitment to racial equality, the national mood shifted rather abruptly to one of continued subjugation and racial oppression" (Pinkney, 1984). In contemporary U.S. society blacks continue to experience significant problems as a consequence of discrimination. They continue to be overrepresented in the ranks of the poor. It has been suggested that there is developing a permanent black underclass (Massey, 1994). Discrimination continues to impede progress in the areas of education, employment, housing, and health care. Institutional discrimination continues to exist.

The riots of April–May 1992 may indicate that the United States is entering a new phase of black/white relationships. A phase that will bring demands for justice. Equity rather than equality may be an ongoing concern. The focus may be on institutional racism rather than individual racism.

Discrimination toward Native Americans

Racism toward Native Americans has a long history, but it has its roots in different issues than discrimination against African Americans. The European quest in the New World for land and for control of its resources was the first act of discrimination. The values held by the white settlers were very different from those of the people they found in the new land. Just as there were differences of culture among the four English groups who came to North American shores before the American Revolution, so there were differences among the various Native American tribes or nations. While these differences led to different Native American/white relationships, a few generalities can be stated. White colonists did not appreciate Native Americans' love for their land or the high value that their society placed on sharing resources. The colonists believed that claiming new land and controlling its resources were their God-given rights. Some believed it was their duty to "convert the savages" to Christianity. Unfortunately, Native Americans also believed their use of the land was *their* God-given right. These two world views soon came into conflict.

As the colonist population grew and expanded its territory, whites and Native Americans could not live in harmony. Native Americans became pawns in the wars between France and Great Britain, and later between the American colonies and Great Britain. Following the American Revolution, the United States government continued its earlier practice of entering into treaties with various tribes. Although these treaties recognized Indian tribes as sovereign nations with land entitlements, they were systematically broken, provoking further conflict.

Pushed further and further west by the Europeans' greed for land and willingness to use force to get it, Native Americans stopped cooperating and began to strike back. From the mid-1800s to the turn of the century, whites and Native Americans fought over land rights.

During the 1830s, the federal government authorized the forced resettlement of Indian tribes to lands west of the Mississippi River. Thousands died of illness and exposure. In 1834 Congress created the United States Indian Service, which was placed in the U.S. War Department and eventually became the U.S. Bureau of Indian Affairs (BIA). White agents located on military outposts were charged with carrying out the programs and policies of the federal government. The real test of the government's control over the tribes came in 1862, when the Homestead Act was passed by Congress. This opened up the West to white settlement and broke the treaties made with the tribes that gave them all the land west of the Mississippi River. After another series of battles, the vanquished Native Americans were forcibly confined to reservations under the control of the BIA.

By the end of the nineteenth century, Native Americans had become a conquered people, far removed from their original homes. Many of their children were sent away to boarding school and forbidden to speak their native languages or engage in Indian cultural activities. This, in the name of Americanization. Also they were forced to accept a new form of tribal government that white society considered superior to older, traditional forms. With a great deal of their land gone and their cultural heritage threatened or destroyed, Native Americans were forced to accept and begin to live in the shadow of the dominant culture.

Native Americans have been driven into dependency on the government as their major source of means for survival. Uprooting entire cultures and relocating them far away from their usual sources of food, shelter, and trade forced the people to abandon their original cultures. To survive, they had little choice but to live more or less within the expectations of the dominant white culture. This is yet another vivid example of institutional racism.

Prior to the 1960s, the Native American struggle for equality and civil rights was a quiet one, largely jurisdictional and legal. But in the late 1960s, influenced by African-American protests, the struggle went through a protest phase marked by both nonviolent and violent efforts. Nonviolent protests included the 1972 takeover of the BIA building in Washington, D.C., and the occupation of Alcatraz Prison in San Francisco. Violence broke out in 1973 when militant American Indian Movement members occupied a building on the Pine Ridge Indian reservation at Wounded Knee, South Dakota, and a riot took place at the courthouse in Custer, South Dakota, over the alleged murder of a Native American by a white.

In recent years, renewed cultural pride and a sense of heritage have allowed some Native American people to return to traditional values and lifestyles, to the extent possible in a technologically advanced world. But the reservations, despite the many and varied human services programs offered, remain economically depressed areas, where poverty, disease, crime, alcoholism, and other social problems continue to exist. Open discrimination toward Native Americans exists outside the reservations. Native Americans who live in these areas are subjected to the same forces of prejudice as other minority groups.

Another growing source of tension is the development of various kinds of gambling on reservation land. This activity is providing significant income to impoverished tribes and jobs where there have been none. Yet there are concerns about crime and law enforcement issues related to gambling activities. Gains have been made by Native Americans in their struggle for equality in recent years. Landmark victories have been won in terms of ownership of land and mineral rights. Changes have also occurred in the relationship between Native American tribes and the BIA. The BIA has lessened its control over Indian affairs and is now moving toward a policy of Indian self-determination.

Discrimination toward Hispanic Americans

A third minority group experiencing significant societal discrimination and prejudice are Spanish-speaking Americans. Included in this group are the two largest subgroups, Mexican Americans and Puerto Ricans, plus Cuban Americans, as well as other smaller Spanish-speaking groups.

The most easily identified characteristic of the Hispanic-American population seems to be use of Spanish as their first language. Puerto Ricans and Cubans tend to be found along the East Coast; Mexicans in the West and Midwest. Another means for identifying Hispanic people is through identification of their heritage. A very small group of Hispanics can be considered as transplanted. That is, they are pure blood descendants from European Spanish people. Another small group are pure blood descendants from the indigenous people who populated Central and South America before the Spanish conquest. However the vast majority of Hispanics are what is known as mixed blood. Their heritage is part European Spanish, part indigenous native, and part black. The black heritage comes from Africans who came to the New World prior to 1492 or who were later brought as slaves by the Spanish. They are a people who were born out of the rape of African and indigenous mothers by the Spanish conquerors. They celebrate resistance and have a strong will to persist. They have lived with violence for five hundred years. Slowly new ethnic groups based on geography have emerged. We will consider only two of these groups but it must be remembered that Hispanic-American groups include Haitians, Cubans, and refugees from other Central and South American countries. Each group has its own subgroups based on original heritage and geographic location. Each has been exploited by absentee land owners, often supported by religious groups (Apolonaris, 1992).

Mexican Americans

The majority of Mexican Americans are concentrated in the southwestern United States. Some seventy-five thousand Mexicans were residents of the Southwest when this area became part of the United States in the aftermath of the Mexican-American War in 1848. While sharing and participating in the cultural history of this area, they were never afforded equal status and opportunity as U.S. citizens. Large-scale Mexican immigration to the United States began at the turn of the century, as a result of civil wars and economic chaos in Mexico, as well as attractive employment opportunities in the United States. Efforts to curtail immigration began in the 1930s and have continued since that time. However, each year large numbers of Mexicans continue to enter the United States as illegal aliens.

Life for Mexican Americans in the towns and cities of the southwestern United States was filled with the harsh realities of prejudice and discrimination. Excluded from the mainstream of community life, Mexican Americans were shunted into ghettos called *barrios*, which became pockets of poverty and a host of social problems. In many places in the Southwest during the 1940s and 1950s, Mexican Americans, like African Americans, were faced with public, institutionalized segregation. The lifestyle foisted upon them demonstrates that "the experience of discrimination is not an academic concept, rather it forms an integral part their life experiences" (Pachon and Moore, 1981).

The effects of prejudice and discrimination on Mexican Americans are clearly seen by examining their lack of equal opportunity within the social mainstream over the last two decades. They have suffered from unequal opportunities in employment and inadequate incomes. Many are employed in a "secondary labor market, characterized by relatively dead-end jobs paying low wages, offering little security, and providing limited choices of economic advancement" (Pachon and Moore, 1981). It is not surprising, then, that large numbers of Mexican American families have incomes below the poverty line. There is a large income gap between the median income for Mexican American families and for all families in the United States.

Through a form of institutionalized racism, Mexican Americans have been denied equal educational opportunities in part due to a need for bilingual education. They compare unfavorably to other groups in terms of numbers of years of school completed. It should be noted, however, that some improvement has been made among younger Mexican Americans. Language barriers have been at the heart of this struggle. Many Mexican American students still attend segregated schools, and schools are failing to provide youngsters with incentives to complete their education. Thus the vicious cycle continues; lack of education in turn results in fewer employment opportunities and reduced incomes.

Mexican Americans also have been denied their civil rights and equal protection under the law. They continue to be arrested more often, subjected to verbal and physical abuse, and denied due process of law. They also receive maximum penalties under the law more consistently than individuals from other groups (Mirande, 1987).

The civil rights movement for Mexican Americans has essentially been a nonviolent effort, characterized by political mobilization rather than protest. However, some nonviolent protest did occur. In the 1960s a migrant farm worker, Cesar Chavez, led a nonviolent movement to unionize migrant workers in the southwestern United States. The agribusiness system that employed thousands of Mexican Americans had victimized and taken advantage of them for years. Through the efforts of Chavez and his followers, plus successful boycotts across the country, the United Farm Workers, an affiliate of the AFL-CIO, became a reality. Today, the members of this union enjoy collective bargaining rights as a way of improving their quality of life.

In the political arena, Mexican Americans have become a highly mobilized entity and have made significant gains during the decade of the 1970s. This has come about through the efforts of local, state, and national coalitions and organizations. Such groups as the Mexican Political Organization, the Community Service Organization of Los Angeles, the Mexican American Legal Defense and Education Fund, and the National Council of La Raza have spearheaded this political movement. As a result, Mexican American individuals have been elected to local and state public offices, though not at the national level. The Mexican American vote is a powerful force that serious politicians must deal with. Although some gains have been made in the struggle for equality for Mexican Americans, particularly in politics, prejudice and discrimination against them continue today.

Puerto Ricans

Other Hispanic groups, such as Puerto Ricans and Cuban Americans, also suffer racism and discrimination from the dominant society. The case of Puerto Ricans is a special one. As citizens of the United States, they enjoy the freedom to move back and forth from the island to the mainland without immigration restrictions. However, "they come from an area that has its own strong cultural background and language. As a result the problems of cultural uprooting, intercultural misunderstanding, prejudice, and discrimination affect them as they have affected most newcomers before them" (Fitzpatrick and Parker, 1981). Poverty, unemployment, inequitable education, and unequal protection in the U.S. justice system are problems of life that are also faced by this group. A special characteristic of this group is a continuous movement from the island to the east coast cities and back to Puerto Rico.

Discrimination toward Asian Americans

Asian Americans are a group who have apparently assimilated themselves into the mainstream of society more than the groups previously discussed. However, Asian Americans were subjected to prejudice and discrimination in earlier days. To some extent this is still true today and should not be ignored. Large numbers of Asians, particularly the Chinese, began to enter the United States in the 1850s. The United States was a prospering nation that needed an inexpensive labor force to work in the construction of railroads and new industries.

Conflict between the Chinese immigrants and white society became a significant problem shortly thereafter. Acts of violence against Chinese people occurred in 1854 in the aftermath of a decision made by the California Supreme Court in *The People* v. *Hall*. The court ruled that Asians could not testify either for or against whites charged with a crime. The court's decision provided the impetus for abuse of the Chinese. Murder, lynching, destruction of property, and robbery were common acts of violence against the Asian community. In the 1880s, the efforts of Chinese Americans to improve their status through employment and property ownership was met with legislated exclusionary measures. In 1883, Congress passed the Chinese Exclusion Act, which brought an end to the immigration of Chinese into the United States and prevented the naturalization of Chinese already in residence.

Japanese immigrants, who began to enter the United States in the 1880s, found their situation no better. The Immigration Act of 1924 created a quota system that favored the immigration of white ethnic groups from Europe and excluded Asians.

In the aftermath of the Japanese attack on Pearl Harbor in 1941, Japanese American citizens and legal aliens on the West Coast were taken into custody by the federal government and confined in "relocation camps." Japanese Americans became targets of suspicion. This is another example of how discrimination based on race has dictated social responses to racial groups; the same practices were not employed in relation to German Americans during World War II, even though several German Americans were convicted of spying, whereas no Japanese Americans had ever been accused of disloyalty.

During the war years, two events eased the plight of Asian Americans. In 1943 all Asians residing in the United States were finally permitted to become naturalized citizens. This opened the door for further Asian immigration. And in 1944, the U.S. Supreme Court ruled that the policy of confining Japanese citizens should be revoked. Japanese citizens who had been forced to abandon their possessions and property during the period of confinement were faced with the task of rebuilding their lives. Recovery from this injustice was a slow and difficult process for Japanese citizens.

Since the end of World War II, efforts to improve the social status and quality of life for Asian Americans have met with varied results. Like other minorities in the United States, some Asian Americans have been able to achieve a satisfying quality of life, whereas others have continued to experience the disadvantages associated with prejudice, discrimination, and disenfranchisement from dominant society. Many Asian Americans continue to suffer from poverty, inadequate housing, inadequate education, poor health care, unemployment, and underemployment. Language and cultural barriers often prevent Asian Americans from taking advantage of human services that could help them. Second- and third-generation Asian Americans struggle with the dilemma of adhering to traditional cultural values while adopting the values of mainstream society.

In recent years, immigration of Asians to the United States has been on the increase, particularly for Vietnamese, Cambodians, Laotians, Thais, and Koreans. Often these new immigrants are destitute when they arrive in the U.S. Also, many have experienced the horrors of war or the experiences of living under a hostile government. Often they have had to leave a part of the important extended family behind. They are not understood by either the majority society or by other ethnic groups. The majority society tends to lump all Asians together. It also expects all Asians to understand one another, yet there are age-old animosities among the various groups. The social welfare system has responded to the needs of these people. The Refugee Act of 1980 allows eligible refugees to receive income maintenance assistance, including medical care, for a period of three years. Considerable debate ensued in 1982, when this legislation was reviewed with concerns about the refugees' possible dependence on this assistance.

Social service agencies and other organizations, particularly churches, have helped with aid in the resettlement of these refugees. Many of them are children, some of whom have special needs, which has stimulated the development of specialized adoption programs. The struggle for equality for Asian Americans, though not readily observed by most, continues as it has since the 1800's. This remains a problem, but concern about this in the past has been tempered by the awareness that resettlement requires more time than was originally anticipated (Kerpen, 1985). Currently, policymakers have become more concerned about this issue, particularly as it relates to the provision of welfare benefits to illegal aliens. The pending federal welfare reform legislation will permit individual states to deny public assistance benefits to foreign nationals who enter the U.S. illegally. This will affect all illegal immigrants, including those of Asian descent.

Prejudice and discrimination, as can be seen from the previous discussion of their effects on all minorities of color, have always been an integral part of the U.S. social and cultural structure. They have blighted and distorted our nation's image as the champion of human dignity and human rights. Leon Chestang (1974), an African-American social worker, says in response to this:

> *The realities are that the society stands for human dignity while at the same time it disrespects Blacks and other minorities; the society stands for human mutuality while it shuns integration for all its citizens. Few individuals reared in a society such as this can escape incorporating its practices; none can escape being touched by them. Each of us—all of us— shares or is affected by American racial attitudes (p. 393).*

Although minorities of color have made some gains toward equality, the consequences of prejudice continue to affect how well the society meets the human needs of those belonging to minority groups. Discussion in this chapter has focused largely on discrimination on the basis of race or ethnic heritage, but other forms of societal discrimination also exist and must be considered.

Discrimination toward Other Groups

Among the many "isms" that label the process of discrimination are "ageism" and "sexism." Discrimination based on age and sex are perhaps the most obvious and readily seen forms of discrimination other than racial discrimination. Of course, societal discrimination is not limited to these groups. Other groups, such as the mentally ill, the physically and mentally handicapped, homosexuals, and certain minority ethnic groups, often bear the burden of societal prejudice and discrimination. These groups are denied opportunity in some way within the U.S. social, economic, and political structure.

Ageism

Ageism is defined as the "process of systematic stereotyping and discrimination against people because they are old, just as racism and sexism accomplish this with skin color and gender" (Butler and Lewis, 1973). Discrimination against the elderly occurs in the marketplace, on the streets, in the institutional structures of society, in social policy and programs, and within the whole fabric of society. U.S. culture is characteristically youth-oriented and has left no meaningful function, role, status, or place for aged persons. Their wisdom is not valued as it is in many cultures. Society has developed stereotypes of the aged, such as the belief that the aged are less intelligent, senile, rigid and conservative in thought, unable to learn, or risky as employees. These false images justify the lack of societal responses to the needs of aged people. The consequences of these social attitudes about the aged are vividly seen when viewing their collective status. They are overrepresented among the poor, stripped of dignity and purpose through forced retirement, easy targets of crime, and generally not provided meaningful societal roles. It is only within the last few years that society has even begun to become concerned about the plight of the aged.

Sexism

Women have also been disadvantaged through social discrimination. Sexism, a term that describes discrimination based on gender (this could include both men and women) has been used most often to describe discrimination against women. What is involved is the following:

> *Sexism involves individual attitudes and institutional arrangements that discriminate against people, usually women and girls, because of sex role stereotyping and generalizations (Barker, 1991: p. 212).*

Sexism occurs throughout the structure of society, particularly in the marketplace, where women suffer unequal opportunities for employment, career advancement, and personal income. Discrimination also occurs in the educational system, where women have been socialized through the educational process to believe that they are incapable of pursuing certain careers, particularly those deemed socially acceptable for and dominated by men.

In large part, sexism is caused by societal attitudes, norms, and values that have fostered the illusion that women are inferior to men. These social attitudes are readily transmitted into messages that have become part of the socialization process whereby men are socialized to believe that they are dominant and superior to women in all respects. This socialization process is referred to as *sex-role stereotyping*. That is, sex roles, learned patterns of behavior, define how men and women should behave and interact with one another and in society (DuBois and Miley, 1996). Despite some changes in the traditional sex-role socialization process, sex-role stereotyping continues to perpetuate the forces of sexism operating in U.S. society.

There is, however, room for optimism when examining how the efforts of the women's movement and changes in societal structures, particularly the family, have changed the public perception of women's place in society. The public has become more aware of the destructiveness of sexism, and women have made some gains toward achieving equality.

Civil rights legislation that forbids discrimination on the basis of sex has been enacted. Although the Equal Rights Amendment (ERA) has not been ratified, efforts on its behalf have brought about a greater awareness of inequality between the sexes. Women are now pursuing careers and assuming roles different than they did just two decades ago, when traditional sex-role stereotypes imposed barriers to them. All this represents a positive step toward achieving change in the status of women in U.S. society. However, optimism should be guarded in light of recent Supreme Court decisions concerning affirmative action/equal opportunity laws.

Another area that is troublesome with respect to women's rights is the continuing debate on abortion. Many people feel very strongly that women's rights have been weakened by the 1989 Supreme Court decision that states have the right to decide who can legally obtain an abortion. Government regulations have made it all but impossible for poor women to obtain abortions or even to obtain information about reproductive choice. Many women are concerned that subsequent decisions may lead to the Court's setting aside the *Roe* v. *Wade* decision, which is the basis for the right to obtain a legal abortion. Others feel just as strongly that the unborn fetus has a right to life that supersedes the woman's right to obtain an abortion. This issue is a major one in the political arena of the 1990s. It is an issue that has polarized the public; there are two, strong, diametrically opposed views, with little room for constructive dialogue between those who hold opposing views on abortion. Very early in his administration, President Clinton issued executive orders to rescind former executive orders regarding the availability of abortion counseling, about the use of fetal tissue in research, and other reproductive issues. At least for a time this may heighten the debate and lead to continued strife.

It seems apparent, then, that issues concerning women's rights, many of which are directly related to issues of equality, equity, and discriminatory practices toward women, are in a state of flux. Although some progress has been made, serious threats to that progress may arise from recent and future court decisions.

Gays and Lesbians

Another group in the United States who face the effects of discrimination are *homosexuals*. In the last decade, considerable attention has been paid to issues of prejudice and discrimination against persons on the basis of their sexual orientation and lifestyle.

Although *gays* and *lesbians* constitute a minority of the total U.S. population (5 to 10 percent), and sexual expression is considered to be a private matter, these persons have come under a great deal of public scrutiny in recent years. This has come about as a result of *homophobia*, an irrational fear and hatred of homosexual persons. Homophobia has a long history but has been heightened by the connection between acquired immune deficiency syndrome (AIDS) and gay men. The extent of homophobia in U.S. society is evidenced by public opinion polls and studies, which have pointed out that the U.S. population has negative attitudes about homosexuality and feel that it is an unacceptable lifestyle (Green, Dixon, and Gold-Neil, 1993; Marsiglio, 1993). For gays and lesbians, the consequence of homophobic attitudes has been blatant discrimination against them. Not only have they become the targets of homophobic behaviors, including violent hate crimes referred to as gay bashing, but some, as a result of internalized homophobia, have developed a diminished self-image and a view that the problems they experience in living are unique to them and are a result of their sexual preference (Schoenberg and Goldberg, 1989). Gays and lesbians face the same kinds of problems in living as the rest of the population (e.g., alcoholism, mental health problems, and other health problems), but these problems are exacerbated by the discrimination and prejudice they encounter. Although some progress has been made in public enlightenment about homosexuality, in securing of legal rights for gays and lesbians, and in the removal of homosexuality as a mental illness or disorder by the American Psychiatric Association, discrimination continues to impose barriers to social justice for gay and lesbian persons. With regard to legal protection from discrimination, unlike other oppressed groups, gays and lesbians have no rights guarenteed them at the federal level. It is perfectly legal, in most instances, to discriminate against them. Where this diverse group has found some measures of protection has been at the state and local level, with some states and a number of cities having law or ordinance that forbids discrimination against persons on the basis of sexual orientation. Despite these, opponents of these laws continue to work towards their repeal. For instance, in 1993, the Colorado State Supreme Court upheld a lower court decision, that held that an amendment to the state's constitution that would have banned state and local laws prohibiting discrimination against homosexuals was unconstituional (Longres, 1995). Also recently, a constitutional amendment in the state of Maine that would have repealed that state's law which protects gays and lesbians from discrimination, was put to a vote, but was fortunately defeated. Notwithstanding, these attempts reflect the fervor that the opponents of the gay and lesbian rights movement have with respect to abolishing what little gains this group has made in rights to protection from discrimination. Homosexuality continues to spark controversy and debate, which is evidenced in political rhetoric forwarded by members of the conservative right who object to this sexual orientation on the basis of moral, religious, and family values. This has also become very evident in the recent debate over homosexuals in the military. The Clinton Administration early on seemed to be supportive of a policy that would protect the right of gays and lesbians to serve in the military without fear of being discharged if their sexual orientation became known, which was up to that point, the standard procedure of the military services. However, the Clinton Administration softened on their original position, which has resulted in the current policy of "don't ask, don't tell." It would seem the time has come for the United States to examine its value base and policy regarding homosexuality and recognize the inconsistencies in thinking that negate social justice for this diverse group of people.

Other Groups

Developmentally disabled people, those with either physical or mental handicaps, often suffer discrimination. The physically handicapped experience a subtle form of institutional discrimination, as evidenced by the fact that society does very little to accommodate their special needs in many parts of their daily lives. For example, the physically handicapped, especially those in wheelchairs, need special facilities in public buildings. This problem has in part been alleviated by the Americans with Disabilities Act of 1990 which guarantees access to employment, public services, public accommodations, and telecommunications to those with disabling conditions. This need often is ignored, despite laws and regulations mandating ramps, special parking places, and larger doorways for them. The mentally retarded are often ridiculed and taken advantage of. Mentally ill people face a painful stigma and harmful stereotyping that often prevents them from enjoying full opportunities for employment and education.

There are many other reasons that people experience discrimination. Some are discriminated against because they or their parents came from a different country, and thus, in some people's minds, their national allegiance is automatically thrown into doubt. Others may be discriminated against because of their religious beliefs (or lack of such beliefs).

Prejudice and discrimination against diverse groups affect the responses made by the social welfare system toward meeting human needs. They also have made it difficult for minorities and other groups outside the mainstream to take advantage of the resources of the social welfare system, since these tend to be structured by and for the majority culture and are not particularly responsive to the diversity that exists in contemporary U.S. society.

Social Welfare Responses to Racism and Discrimination

An early response by the social welfare system was that of the settlement houses in the late 1800s, which helped immigrants adjust to their new status as U.S. citizens. Settlement houses supported the Immigrant Protection League and other reform efforts. Jane Addams, for example, worked with reform groups that eventually developed into the National Association for the Advancement of Colored People (NAACP). This arose out of her long-standing relationship with Dr. W. E. B. DuBois, an African-American sociologist and the founder of this organization. Other social reform efforts by the settlement workers in areas of prejudice and discrimination included advocating education for the mentally retarded and physically handicapped and promoting laws to protect women and children in the labor market.

As the social work profession took shape within the social welfare system, it developed professional responses to prejudice and discrimination. Philosophically, social work as a profession has always been concerned with these issues; but in fact, concrete attempts to deal with the problem from the early 1900s through 1950 were largely indifferent, limited, and uncoordinated (Cox, Erlich, Rothman, and Tropman, 1984).

In the 1960s, during the social upheaval and civil unrest of that decade, the profession became increasingly aware of its need to change its practices and develop greater understanding of and sensitivity to the unique needs of minorities. The civil rights movement and the development of pride within minority groups pushed social work to develop a knowledge base and skills aimed at minority clients. Until then, the state of the art in social work knowledge, methodology, and skills had not dealt directly with the problems of discrimination or the special needs of minorities. It became evident during the 1960s and early 1970s that this would no longer be acceptable, and that new approaches to working with minorities must be developed. As a result, the profession committed itself to positive change in this area.

Providing the leadership in this effort were the National Association of Social Workers (NASW), and the Council on Social Work Education (CSWE). In 1960 the NASW adopted a formal code of ethics that expressed the commitment of the profession to work against the forces of discrimination. In 1967 the code was amended and included the following statement: "Social work is based on humanitarian and democratic ideals. Professional social workers are dedicated to the service of mankind, to the disciplined use of a recognized body of knowledge about human beings and their interactions, and to the marshalling of community resources to promote the well-being of all without discrimination" (NASW, 1967).

Even though the NASW took a stand on these issues, the association continued to be criticized for its reluctance to acknowledge that many of its own members continued to hold racist attitudes and continued to be a part of a human services system that perpetuated institutionalized racism and social control over minority groups. Much of the criticism came from within the profession itself, from minority practitioners, especially African Americans. The militancy that characterized the black civil rights movement found its way into the profession. Black practitioners were dissatisfied with what they perceived as the status quo position that the NASW was assuming on issues of racism. In 1966 this led to the formation of the National Association of Black Social Workers (NABSW). The NABSW, from its inception in 1966 until 1969, when it split away from the main body of the NASW, protested the lack of response to understanding the black experience. The NABSW continues today as a separate professional social work organization.

In the 1970s, the NASW intensified its efforts to develop new understanding and improvement of the quality of social work practice with minorities of color and other oppressed groups. One effort was to encourage the publication in its journals of articles dealing with how to work with oppressed clients. Before this time, little had been written on these issues. But since then, a wealth of literature dealing with social work practice and minorities of color has been published. NASW has, on a number of occasions, devoted entire issues of its journal, *Social Work*, to these topics. In addition, social work books written by minority practitioners have filled a void that existed in the knowledge base of the profession.

In 1979, the NASW revised the social work code of ethics. The new code is divided into several parts. One part of the code addresses the social worker's ethical responsibility to the client. It states: "The social worker should not practice, condone, facilitate or collaborate with any form of discrimination on the basis of race, color, sex, sexual orientation, age, religion, national origin, marital status, political belief, mental or physical handicap, or any other preference or personal characteristic, condition or status" (NASW, 1980). The expanded code of ethics reflected the profession's interest in working against discrimination.

Leadership in combating prejudice and discrimination and in developing a more viable response to them has also come from the Council of Social Work Education. The CSWE, since the 1970s, has improved social work education and training on these issues. Its efforts have focused on three issues: the recruitment of minority students, the recruitment of minority faculty, and curriculum development and curriculum content that prepare social workers to engage in practice with minorities of color and other oppressed groups. Accreditation standards for both graduate schools and undergraduate programs in social work have been developed that call for content in the curriculum on minorities of color, ethnic groups, women, gays and lesbians, and other oppressed groups. Schools have made a concerted effort to recruit minority students and faculty, and enrollment of minority students in these programs has increased steadily since 1970. Social work programs at both levels have supported minority students by offering financial aid and scholarships. There also has been a significant increase in the number of minority faculty teaching in these schools and programs. In addition, considerable effort has been expended to improve the ability of nonminority faculty to teach minority students and minority content. Curriculum development in both graduate and undergraduate schools in the area of ethnic and cultural diversity has improved significantly in the last several years. Specific courses in social work practice with diverse groups have been added to the curricula of the schools.

One of the more recent curricular developments has been the adoption by many schools of the *human diversity* perspective, a framework useful in organizing knowledge and skills needed to intervene with diverse groups. Human diversity refers to "the continuum of differences between people and groups resulting from biological, cultural, and social factors" (Skidmore and Thackeray, 1982). The human diversity perspective emphasizes viewing the range of human differences, which form the basis of diversity, as normal and acceptable, as opposed to making judgments about people's characteristics—race, ethnicity, or any other human characteristic or preference—as abnormal or unacceptable. The social worker is then freed from the trap of viewing human behavior and difference in a framework that narrowly defines normality. This framework also rejects the stereotyping of human characteristics that so often forms the basis for oppression, domination, control, and discrimination directed against diverse groups. In this view, the unique characteristics that people possess are considered strengths rather than weaknesses. Social workers are encouraged to use the strengths that people bring with them from their various racial, ethnic, cultural, and social backgrounds. These are the basic resources that should be used in intervention with anyone.

While the human diversity perspective tends to be more philosophical with regard to intent and purpose, there is another more pragmatic strategy that has emerged in recent years to combat racism, discrimination, and oppression. It is empowerment, as introduced in Chapter 2. Although "catching on" recently, empowerment, in the context of a strategy for work with minorities of color and oppressed groups, is not necessarily new. It has been discussed in the past as a process and a goal in work with minorities of color and oppressed groups of people. Solomon (1976) discussed empowerment as a process in which social workers engage in activities with people with the goal to reduce powerlessness that is caused by peoples' membership in devalued societal groups. More recently, Evans (1992), Freire (1990), Gutierrez (1990), and DuBois and Miley (1996) have discussed empowerment as a knowledge base and strategy for work with minority and oppressed groups. Empowerment is then a process whereby individuals from minority and oppressed groups, working with a social worker, can gain personal control and self-efficacy in their lives, and a process in which devalued groups collectively can gain social influence, political power, and legal rights. The later is based on the assumption that society is made up of various groups, each with differing degrees of power interests that compete and conflict with each other. Through empowerment, groups with less power than others become strong enough to effectively compete in the struggle to obtain resources that are compatible with their expectations and needs. In working with minority or oppressed groups, the empowerment activities of the social worker would be to identify the obstacles to power, and then to implement change strategy to eliminate or reduce their effects (Solomon, 1976).

Despite the fact that social workers in recent years have adopted the human diversity perspective and an empowerment orientation, the systems in which they work have not. The current system of social welfare and social services has ignored individual differences among the people whom it serves. Decisions about what social welfare benefits and which social service programs will be provided to meet human needs remain largely in the hands of majority groups, and others have little or no voice in these decisions. Social work in recent years has taken the lead and continues to push for change in the system through the efforts of the NASW, the CSWE, and other professional organizations concerned with social welfare and social service responses to human needs.

Summary

In this chapter, prejudice and discrimination against the many subgroups within U.S. society have been presented as destructive and complex social issues that have interfered with meeting human needs. An effort was made to bring about a clearer understanding of racism (both individual and institutional), prejudice, and discrimination, and to discuss phenomena such as ethnocentrism, societal attitudes, and ideologies that cause them to occur and perpetuate their existence. Discussion also focused on the effects of prejudice and discrimination on specific groups, and how these groups have attempted to achieve equality and a sense of social justice. The responses made by social work as a profession to prejudice and discrimination were also highlighted by showing how the profession has dealt with these social problems both within its own ranks and within the larger society. But unanswered questions remain. What will be the continued effects of these problems on meeting human needs in our society? It is hoped that the understandings developed in this chapter will stimulate thinking about what should be done in response to the issues raised.

Key Terms

ageism
assimilation
cultural pluralism
discrimination
egalitarianism
equity
ethnocentrism
gays
homophobia
homosexuals
human diversity

individualism
lesbians
minorities of color
mutual assimilation
oppression
prejudice
racism (individual and institutional)
sexism
sex-role stereotyping
stereotyping
whiteness

References

Apolonaris, Y. (1992). *Discrimination Against Refugees from Central and South America*. Madison WI: American Baptists of Puerto Rico.

Barker, R.L. (1991). *The Social Work Dictionary*. Silver Spring, MD: National Association of Social Workers.

Brieland, D., Costin, L.B., and Atherton, C. (1980). *Contemporary Social Work: An Introducton to Social Work and Social Welfare*. New York: McGraw-Hill, p.395.

Butler, R.N., and Lewis, M.I. (1973). *Aging and Mental Health: Positive Psychological Approaches*. St. Louis, MO: C.V. Mosby.

Carmichael, S., and Hamilton, C.H. (1967). *Black Power: The Politics of Liberation in America*. New York: Random House.

Chestang, L.W. (1974). The Issue of Race in Social Work Practice, in Weinberger, P.E., ed., *Perspectives on Social Welfare: An Introductory Anthology*. New York: MacMillan, p.393.

Cone, J.H. (1992). *Lecture on Malcom X*. New York: Union Theology Seminary.

Cox, F.M., Erlich, J.L., Rothman, J., and Tropman, J.E. (1984). *Tactics and Techniques of Community Practice*. Itaska, IL: F.E. Peacock.

Day, P.J. (1989). *A New History of Social Welfare*. Englewood Cliffs, NJ: Prentice Hall.

Dividio, J.F., and Gaertner, S.L. (1986). *Prejudice, Discrimination, and Racism*. New York: Academic Press.

DuBois, B., and Miley, K.K. (1996). *Social Work: An Empowering Profession*. Boston: Allyn and Bacon.

Evans, E.N. (1992). *Liberation Theology, Empowerment Theory and Social Work Practice with the Oppressed*. New York: Herder and Heider.

Fitzpatrick, J.P., and Parker, L.R. (1981). Hispanic Americans in the Eastern United States. *Annals of the American Academy of Political and Social Sciences, 454*, 106.

Freire. P. (1990). A Critical Understanding of Social Work. *Journal of Progressive Human Services, 1 (1)*, 3–9.

Green, S., Dixon, P., and Gold-Neil, V. (1993). The Effects of a Gay/ Lesbian panel dicussion on College Student Attitudes Toward Gay Men, Lesbians, and Persons with AIDS. *Journal of Sex Education and Therapy, 19 (1)* 47–63.

Gutierrez, L. (1990). Working with Women of Color: An Empowerment Perspective. *Social Work, 35 (2)*, 149–153.

Kerpen, K.S. (1985). Refugees on Welfare. *Public Welfare, 43*, 21–25.

Lipset, S.M., and Schneider, W. (1978). The Bakke Case: How Would It Be Decided at the Bar of Public Opinion? *Public Opinion*, 38–40.

Longres, J.F. (1995). *Human Behavior in The Social Environment*. Itaska, IL: F.E. Peacock.

Macarov, D. (1978). *The Design of Social Welfare*. New York: Holt, Rinehart, and Winston.

Mack, R.W. (1968). *Race, Class, and Power*. New York: Van Nostrand Reinhold.

Marsiglio, W. (1993). Attitudes Toward Homosexual Activity and Gays as Friends: A National Survey of Heterosexual 15–19 year old Males. *The Journal of Sex Research, 30 (1)*, 12–17.

Massey, D.S. (1994). America's Apartheid and the Urban Underclass. *Social Service Review, 68 (4)*, 471–487.

Mirande, A. (1987). *Gringo Justice*. Notre Dame, IN: University of Notre Dame Press.

National Association of Social Workers. (1967). *NASW Code of Ethics-Amendments*. Washington, D.C.: National Association of Social Workers.

National Association of Social Workers. (1980). *NASW Code of Ethics*. Washington, D.C.: National Association of Social Workers.

Newman, W.M. (1973). *American Pluralism: A Study of Minority Groups and Social Theory*. New York: Harper and Row.

Pachon, H., and Moore, J. (1981). Mexican Americans. *Annals of the American Academy of Political and Social Sciences*, 117.

Pinkney, A. (1984). *The Myth of Black Progress*. New York: Cambridge University Press.

Schama, S. (1992). They All Laughed at Christopher Columbus. *The New Republic* (Jan 6 and 13), 30–40.

Schoenberg, R., and Goldberg, R.S. (1989). *Homosexuality and Social Work*. New York: Haworth Press.

Schriver, J.M. (1995). *Human Behavior and the Social Environment: Shifting Paradigms in Essential Knowledge for Social Work Practice*. Boston: Allyn and Bacon.

See, K.O., and Wilson, W.J. (1987). Race and Ethnicity, in Smelser, N.J., ed., *Handbook of Sociology*. Newbury Park, CA: Sage Publications.

Skidmore, R.A., and Thackeray, M.G. (1982). *Introduction to Social Work*. Englewood Cliffs, NJ: Prentice Hall.

Skidmore, R.A., Thackeray, M.G., and Farley, O.W. (1991). *Introduction to Social Work.* Englewood Cliffs, NJ: Prentice-Hall.

Solomon, B. (1976). *Black Empowerment: Social Work in Oppressed Communities.* New York: Longman.

Zastrow, C., and Kirst-Ashman, K.K. (1994). *Understanding Human Behavior and the Social Environment.* Chicago: Nelson-Hall.

Suggested Readings

Aponte, R. (1993). Hispanic Families in Poverty: Diversity, Context, and Interpretation. *Families in Society, 74 (9),* 527–37.

Broken-Nose, M.A. (1992). Working with Oglala Lakota: An Outsider's Perspective. *Families in Society, 73 (6),* 380–384.

Browne, C., and Broderick, A. (1994). Asian and Pacific Islanders: Issues for Social Work Practice and Education. *Social Work, 39 (3),* 298–305.

Castex, G.M. (1994). Providing Services to Hispanic/Latino Populations: Profiles in Diversity. *Social Work, 39 (3),* 288–296.

Daly, A., Jennings, J., Beckett, J.O., and Leadshore, B.R. (1995). Effective Coping Strategies of African Americans. *Social Work, 40 (2),* 40–48.

Dobash, R.E., and Dobash, R.P. (1992). *Women, Violence, and Social Change.* London: Routledge.

Gross, E.R. (1995). Deconstructing Politically Correct Practice Literature: The American Indian Case. *Social Work, 40 (2),* 206–213.

Hall, R.E. (1992). Bias Among African-Americans Regarding Skin Color: Implications for Social Work Practice. *Research on Social Work Practice,* 479–486.

Hidalgo, H., Peterson, T.L., Woodman, N.J., eds. (1985). *Lesbian and Gay Issues: A Resource Manual For Social Workers.* Silver Spring, MD: National Association of Social Workers.

Hines, P.M., Garcia-Preto, N., McGoldrick, M., Almeda, R., and Wiltman, S. (1992). Intergenerational Relationships Across Cultures. *Families in Society, 73 (6),* 323–338.

Kim, Y.O. (1995). Cultural Pluralism and Asian Americans: Culturally Sensitive Social Work Practice. *International Social Work, 38 (1),* 69–78.

Latting, J.K. (1990). Identifying the Ism's: Enabling Social Work Students to Confront Their Biases. *Journal of Social Work Education, 26,* 36–44.

Lukes, C., and Land, H. (1990). Biculturality and Homosexuality. *Social Work, March,* 149–154.

Majors, R., and Billson, J. (1991). *Cool Pose: The Dilemmas of Black Manhood in America.* New York: Lexington Books.

Nagel. J., and Snipp, C.M. (1993). Ethnic Reorganization: American Indian Social, Cultural, Economic, and Political Strategies for Survival. *Ethnic and Racial Studies, 16 (2),* 203–235.

Reiter, L. (1991). Developmental Origins of Antihomosexual Prejudice in Heterosexual Men and Women. *Clinical Social Work, 19 (2),* 163–175.

Romero, M. (1992). *Maid in the U.S.A.* New York: Routledge.

Schoenberg, R., and Goldberg, R.S., eds. *Homosexuality and Social Work.* New York: Haworth.

Stout, K.D., and Kelly, M.J. (1990). Differential Treatment Based on Sex. *Afflia, 5,* 60–71.

Wares, D.M., Wedel, K.R., Rosenthal, J.A., and BoBuec, A. (1994). Indian Child Welfare: A Multicultural Challange. *Social Work, 3 (3),* 1–15.

PART **II**

TWO ATTRIBUTES OF THE SOCIAL WELFARE SYSTEM: SOCIAL WORK AND FIELDS OF PRACTICE

The profession of social work has developed in large part in concert with the social welfare system. In order to fully understand the contemporary system, an understanding of the growth and development of the profession is important. Likewise, contemporary social work practice has been greatly influenced by the development of the social welfare system.

Part Two first considers "The Emergence of the Social Work Profession within Social Welfare," in Chapter 6. The chapter not only discusses the historical roots of the profession but also considers the nature of the profession, the development of professional organizations and professional education, and major attributes of the profession.

Social work practice and service delivery in the U.S. social welfare system are organized around problem areas (child welfare or health care) or around population groups (the aged, families). More recently, fields of practice have developed around a particular environment, such as rural or industrial. This part of the book will examine what is known in social work as *field of practice*, or practice focused on a specific problem or population group. By looking at individual fields of practice in some depth, the complexity of service delivery in the social welfare system is easier to understand. Such study provides a historical perspective on why and how today's services are organized. It also is a good way to learn about the scope of practice and the differences between the fields.

Fields of practice to be considered include: income maintenance, services to children, services to families, health care, mental health care, corrections, and services for the elderly. There is also a chapter on two developing fields of practice, industrial social work and rural social work. Each chapter will first define the field by identifying the population and/or problem it serves. Then, within that field, the history of the social welfare system's response to needs will be discussed. Contemporary practice in the field will be examined using case examples. Issues and current concerns will then be explored. The final chapter of this section looks at some influences in the development of a field of practice. It does this by considering the three traditional methods of social work practice, casework, group work, and community organization.

In addition, this part of the book will identify how the various fields of practice make use of the six arrangements discussed in Part One. It will also note how poverty, racism and discrimination, resource distribution, and social change have affected the population involved.

6

THE EMERGENCE OF THE SOCIAL WORK PROFESSION WITHIN SOCIAL WELFARE

Learning Expectations

- Knowledge about the roots of the social work profession
- Ability to identify the most significant milestones in the development of education for social work
- Knowledge about the characteristics of a profession
- Knowledge about significant social work organizations and their development
- Understanding of the place of the social work profession in the social welfare system
- Capacity to define social work as a profession
- Understanding of the historical development of the social work profession with respect to its concern for the poor
- Identification of major issues or tensions that have faced the social work profession
- Ability to identify the knowledge and value bases that underlie social work practice
- Identification of skills needed in the practice of social work
- Identification of the traditional methods of social work practice
- Understanding of the characteristics of generalist practice
- Understanding of the nature of a field of practice

As the social welfare system in the United States evolved, there arose a need for personnel to staff that system. A major component of that staff, the service providers, carry the title of social worker. As part of the development of the social welfare system, a profession known as social work emerged. However, confusion about who is a social worker continues to this day because not all those who carry the title of social worker are considered part of the profession of social work. This chapter will discuss this ongoing problem as it traces the evolution of the social work profession and the relationship of the profession and the social welfare system.

The chapter will also consider the search for professionalization, the nature of social work organizations, and the development of education for social work. The intermingling of two frameworks for organizing social work practice, methods for practice and fields of practice, will be discussed.

Roots of Social Work

The earliest signs of social work emerged when formal institutions and organizations replaced informal help provided through mutual aid (Dolgoff and Feldstein, 1980). In Europe, the first institution to respond was organized religion. In the beginning, help was given on an individual-to-individual basis. The motivation to assist the needy was inspired by religious teachings that it was a person's duty to help those in need. This religious motivation was evident in many early societies, including those of the ancient Egyptians, Chinese, Babylonians, Hebrews, Greeks, and Romans, and persists throughout the world today. Judaism and Christianity have been the most influential religions in shaping the U.S. social welfare system. Within the Roman Catholic church, Saint Vincent de Paul organized groups of volunteers to serve the needy. These came to be known as the Ladies of Charity (1617) and eventually became the Society of Saint Vincent de Paul (1833). Protestants also made extensive use of their laity in carrying out charitable work (Trattner, 1974).

According to Dolgoff and Feldstein (1980), as responsibility for social welfare shifted from religious institutions to government bodies and private social agencies, the need for paid staff to carry out social welfare functions became apparent. In the public poor relief system established during colonial times, the public officials responsible were called the overseers of the poor. Other early paid staff were employees of the developing institutions. As private philanthropy and charity developed in the late nineteenth century, a British model of poor relief caught the attention of philanthropists in the United States. The New York Society for the Prevention of Pauperism (1819) and the New York Association for Improving the Condition of the Poor (1843) were formed to assist the poor. Both served as models for the development of the Charity Organization Societies (COS). The early forerunners of the COS experimented with a combination of volunteers and a few paid staff in investigating the needs of the poor and providing relief. These organizations employed a paid staff who performed administrative roles, but the volunteers who came to be called the *friendly visitors* provided direct services to people. The paid staff and the friendly visitors were the immediate predecessors of professional social workers in the United States. These pioneer efforts can be viewed as "a major step on the road to professionalization."

Settlement house workers, as mentioned in Chapter 1, used different methods to help people than did their friendly visitor counterparts. Their work style could be described as missionary in nature, working hand in hand with neighbors to improve adverse social conditions. Gradually the settlement workers developed broader goals of social reform through legislation and social policy change. These workers helped bring about changes in child labor laws, in women's labor laws, and in the institutional care of the disabled and the mentally retarded. They were involved in the development of child welfare services and the establishment of juvenile courts. The success of their efforts gave considerable impetus to the movement toward professionalization.

In these two precursors of professional social work, we see two philosophies that are still reflected and still cause conflict in the social work profession. Specification of these philosophies eventually led to what is known as the *cause–function debate*. Porter Lee described this debate in 1929. He defined cause as "a movement directed to the elimination of an entrenched evil—[or] a new way of meeting human need." He discussed function by noting that when a new way of meeting need becomes accepted, it becomes "a function of well-organized community life." The COS represented the function approach and the settlement house the cause approach (Lee, 1930).

Early in the twentieth century, the friendly visitors, through their experiences in working with people, had begun to see the complexities of human needs and problems. Their original philosophy that poverty was caused by moral defects gave way to a new understanding of the interaction between people and their immediate environment and the problems that arise from that interaction. No longer could they place the locus of the problems within the individual, even though many still attempt to do this to this day. Environmental factors such as crowded housing, disease, unemployment, discrimination and prejudice, and problems within the family had to be taken into consideration when assessing an individual's needs and developing plans for assistance. This additional knowledge led to development of additional assessment and intervention techniques for mitigating the complex human problems that helpers were called on to deal with. Society began to understand that assisting people involved far more than simply providing financial aid, and that love in one's heart for people was not the sole qualification for a person engaged in charity work. If helping was to grow beyond the concept of mutual aid, it needed to become scientific through the development of knowledge, problem-solving methods, and professional skills. With these changes in philosophy, the movement toward professional charity work, later called social work, further developed.

A step toward making charity work more scientific was taken when the COS began to identify the needed knowledge base and to establish specified methods and procedures for doing their work. These were formalized into what was later called *casework*. Casework methods called for a careful investigation and diagnosis of problems in the interaction between people and their immediate social environment. Charitable relief was redesigned to meet needs based on these new perceptions and techniques.

Friendly visitors and paid agents alike needed to be trained to use these procedures appropriately. At first the training consisted mainly of apprenticeship. New volunteers and staff simply observed the work of experienced staff and thus learned the methods of charity work. In addition to apprenticeships, agencies gradually began to use more formal training, which consisted of lectures, reading, and discussion. Another opportunity to broaden the understanding of charity work and to learn new methods and techniques was provided by the Conference of Charities. Founded in 1870 and expanded in 1894, this organization later became the National Conference of Charities and Corrections. Its annual conference, attended by state public welfare administrators, institutional administrators, those involved in the COS and the settlement houses, and others concerned about social welfare issues, acted as an exchange, where the ideas and work experiences of charity workers were discussed (Trattner, 1974).

The settlement houses also recognized the need for training their resident workers. They began to organize in-house training, often inviting sociology, economics, and political science professors from nearby colleges and universities to lecture staff on various topics.

Late in the nineteenth century, the COS and the settlement houses realized that formal education, perhaps even higher education, was needed to professionalize what eventually was to be known as social work. Charles Kellogg, the general secretary for the New York Charity Organization Society, frequently commented on the need for more "intelligent agents" (Becker, 1963). He believed that agents' abilities to perform their duties depended on how well educated they were. Leaders in the field began to voice this concern publicly. The first formal plea came in 1893 from Anna L. Dawes, who presented a paper at the National Conference on Charities and Corrections in 1893, "The Need for Training Schools for a New Profession." In this paper, Dawes (1893) presented the case for the establishment of formal training schools for

In the early part of this century, a friendly visitor comes to a home where there are serious unmet needs.

charity workers. Although she did not provide much detail about how this could come about, she did suggest that those who had retired from charity work could become *teachers*, passing on the knowledge they had gained in their work. The use of the words "new professional" in Dawes's paper clearly demonstrates the extent to which the early leaders in charitable work were concerning themselves with moving toward a new profession, social work.

Four years later, at the National Conference in 1897, Mary Richmond of the Baltimore Charity Organization Society presented a paper entitled "The Need for Training Schools in Applied Philanthropy" (Richmond, 1890). Richmond argued that there was a need to attract educated young people to charitable work. She expressed the view that if these young people were willing to commit themselves to a life of charitable work, they needed opportunities for education and professional development. Noting that only limited opportunities could be provided, because charity work was not an established profession, she argued that professionalization could not be established without the development of a professional school. Richmond urged that "we should begin to move without delay in the direction, at least, of some definite system of training." She also set forth the conditions under which she felt a school should be established, including what curriculum should be taught, by whom, and where a school should be located. Most important, Richmond felt that course work should consist of both theoretical and practical field training. The impact of this presentation provided the impetus for the establishment one year later of what was to become the first school of social work in New York.

A Profession: Social Work

Before continuing with this discussion of the development of the social work profession, it is necessary to develop an understanding of the nature and attributes of a profession. Several points of view will be presented. First there is what has been identified as the *trait–attribute approach*. This approach is the one most often referred to in social work literature and is exemplified in the work of Dr. Abraham Flexner (1915) and Ernest Greenwood (1957). Recently two new approaches have been presented, the *process model*, as discussed by Leslie Leighninger (1987), and the *power–control model*, as presented by Gary Lowe, Laura Rose Zimmerman, and P. Nelson Reid (1989).

As early as 1915, social work's professional status came into question. Dr. Abraham Flexner, an authority on graduate education who had intensively studied the medical profession, presented a paper at the National Conference on Charities and Corrections, "Is Social Work a Profession?" In this paper Flexner concluded that social work had not yet achieved professional status. His basis for this view was that social work lacked a specific and unique knowledge base of its own. Although Flexner agreed that social work did meet some of the criteria of a profession, he denied that it was a *profession* in "the same sense in which medicine and law are professions."

As an early and ongoing response to the Flexner paper, efforts were made to identify and develop the knowledge base of social work practice. One of the first efforts to conceptualize practice methods came in 1917 with the publication of Mary Richmond's *Social Diagnosis*. This book established guidelines and norms for professional practice, greatly needed at the time. It also provided impetus for an ongoing development of literature about social work practice. The book was a pioneer in developing the unique methods that Flexner had stated social work lacked.

In the 1920s social workers became interested in psychological theory. The writings of Sigmund Freud and others reshaped the thinking of social workers and provided new understandings of human behavior. This resulted in a change in direction in casework, considered the main method of social work at this time. Social workers began to focus on and develop a knowledge base in the area of psychological functioning and individual adjustment, as contrasted with earlier concerns about poverty, environmental factors, and social reform. This change has been referred to as social work's estrangement from the poor (Ferguson, 1975). It resulted as much from the social and political climate of the times as it did from the new understandings about human behavior. In the early 1900s, social reform was considered a legitimate function of social workers. However, in the aftermath of World War I, social reform became an unpopular activity, largely because of a popular reaction against perceived radical influences, such as fascism and communism, in political and social structures. Social reform was seen as radicalism. Casework, now influenced by psychological theory, seemed a safer and more legitimate approach to assisting people. Social workers also felt that movement in this direction would increase the prestige of the new profession in the eyes of the general public (Borenzweig, 1971).

Periodically, the question of whether or not social work was a profession continued to be asked. Ten years after Flexner stated his position, William Hodson (1925), then president of the American Association of Social Workers, reopened the debate. He delivered a paper at the 1925 National Conference of Social Work in which he reexamined social work's professional status. He argued that Flexner's position was no longer valid because social work had developed a knowledge base, expanded methods of education and training, and increased the number of trained persons in the field. Hodson maintained that in most ways social work was a profession; he said that the final test would come in public acceptance of the profession. He hoped that the American Association of Social Workers, organized in 1919, would provide the leadership needed to bring this about.

In 1932 Esther Lucille Brown compared social work with other professions in a paper read at the National Conference of Social Work. In this comparison, Brown (1932) concluded that social work needed to increase its professional prestige by continuing to fill social work positions with trained people, by increasing the salary levels of social work positions, by maintaining the quality of fieldwork in education, and by obtaining graduate-level status in the educational process. This would, in her estimation, further legitimize social work's claim to being a profession.

In 1957 an article by Ernest Greenwood appeared in the new National Association of Social Workers' journal, *Social Work*, which specified what Greenwood believed to be the major attributes of a profession and his assessment of how well social work adhered to those attributes. These attributes are:

1. *A systematic body of theory:* Professions have general and specific knowledge and understandings that underlie and guide the professional's use of technique in the performance of duties.
2. *Professional authority:* The professional possesses authority based on expertise gained from an extensive education, knowledge, and use of technique. The consumer or client of the professional's services gains a sense of security from the professional's use of authority.
3. *Community sanction:* The professional's authority is sanctioned by the community in informal and formal ways. Informally, the community sanctions the professional's author-

ity and expertise, and the profession's regulation of itself. Formally, sanction is given to some professions through law or the police powers of the community.

4.   *Code of ethics:* All professions possess formal and informal codes of ethics that its members must uphold. Formal codes are written, and professionals affirm their intention to uphold the provisions of the code. Informal codes are unwritten and exist in the context of mutual relationships among professionals. A code of ethics protects clients from unethical conduct in the provision of services by the professional. A code of ethics also performs a self-regulatory function within the profession itself.

5.   *Professional culture:* All professions possess a professional culture that has both formal and informal aspects. Formal aspects of professional culture include the settings in which professional and client come together for their work and the professional–client relationship. The informal aspects of professional culture are the values, norms, and common symbols to which the professional is socialized and must adapt.

In his analysis, Greenwood (1957) examined how well and to what extent social work had acquired these attributes. He concluded that "social work is already a profession; it has too many points of congruence with the model to be classified otherwise." Greenwood's article continues to be the most often referenced one regarding the nature of a profession in social work literature.

Lowe, Zimmerman, and Reid, in a paper presented at the Annual Program Meeting of the Council on Social Work Education in 1989, suggested that a power–control approach might be used when considering the professional status of social work. This view "emphasizes the profession's need to establish a monopoly over the provision of a service." Authority and monopoly are appropriate indicators of professional status. This attribute is related to Greenwood's community sanctions attribute and to the current emphasis in the profession on licensing for social workers.

Leighninger (1987) found that when using the power–control approach in considering the professional status of social work historically, some questions become apparent. Beginning in 1930, the Bureau of Census recognized social work as a profession. According to the 1930 census, 30,500 people were counted as social workers. During the 1930s, because of the increased involvement of government in social welfare, the number of social workers increased dramatically, with the federal government alone employing over eight thousand workers. Because of educational standards, few of these people were eligible for membership in a professional organization. This trend continues today as employees of public social service agencies often carry the civil service title of "social worker" or "caseworker." A majority of them, however, do not possess professional social work education.

There is a two-tiered social welfare employment picture, including a large segment without professional preparation, often employed in public agencies, and a small "professional social work" segment, usually found in the private sector. This situation is the cause of much confusion about who is a social worker. It also indicates that the social work profession does not have a monopoly on the provision of services in the social welfare system.

One means of clarifying the confusion has been for "professional social work" to claim a monopoly only over certain parts of the social welfare system, specifically the social services area. The profession has also worked very hard in recent years for the enactment of state licensing laws that protect the title "social worker." However, the total picture remains confused, as many of the new laws exempt public employees, and many laws "grandfathered in" all those now in social work positions without a professional education.

Leslie Leighninger (1987) uses what she identifies as the "process model" for studying professionalism. This model focuses on the movement toward professional status. Of particular importance is her discussion of the development of professional organizations and professional education. She also identifies four major issues that have been important in the specification of what professional social work is. These issues are:

1. An emphasis on profession building or public service
2. The relationship of social work to social welfare (particularly the national system)
3. An appropriate role in political activity and fostering social change
4. A broad or narrow definition of who is a professional social worker

Consideration of the process model leads to a need to understand the development of social work professional organizations and professional social work education, with particular attention given to the four identified major issues.

Further Professionalization: The Establishment of Professional Organizations

Professional organizations have been important in the development of social work as a profession. Three are of particular interest: the National Conference on Charities and Corrections and its successor organizations; the American Association of Social Workers and other organizations that preceded the formation of the National Association of Social Workers; and the National Association of Social Workers (for further reading, see Chapter 7).

The National Conference on Corrections and Charities came into being in 1874, when representatives from state boards of charities saw a need for a national forum on social welfare issues. Also included were representatives of private charity organizations. This organization had two thrusts. The first was a concern for conditions and circumstances that caused poverty. Included in this thrust was a call for political action aimed toward enactment of preventative legislation. The second was a concern for the development of professionalism in the provision of services. Eventually a private sector focus and the development of professionalism came to dominate. This resulted in a name change in 1917 to the National Conference on Social Work.

Gradually, as other professional organizations developed that began to carry the "call for professionalism" banner, the Conference became the most all-encompassing organization of the social welfare system. The name was changed again in 1948 to the *National Conference on Social Welfare* (*NCSW*), and, after a slow demise, the organization faded from the scene (Leighninger, 1987).

Informal interest among social workers in developing professional organizations began around 1900. This was a frequent discussion topic among social workers at the National Conference of Charities and Corrections. At the same time, because of an increase in the number of paid social work positions, the National Social Workers Exchange was formed in 1917. The exchange provided placement of social workers in paid and volunteer positions, and offered vocational counseling. In 1921 the exchange responded to interest in moving from its informal structure to the creation of a formal professional organization. It became the *American Association of Social Workers (AASW)*. Membership was originally limited to paid social workers, but by 1922 the AASW had begun to develop additional standards based on both experience and education. These standards were continually raised, so that by the 1950s the minimum requirement for membership in the AASW was a two-year graduate degree, the *Master of Social Work (M.S.W.)* (Leighninger, 1987).

Social workers from specific fields of practice also began to organize into professional organizations. In the beginning, these social workers organized what were called discussion clubs, which were located in a few large cities, including Boston, Philadelphia, New York, Milwaukee, and St. Louis. Medical social workers were the first to do this. These discussion clubs soon gave way to structured professional organizations. Lubove (1965) found six such organizations that came into existence, including:

> The American Association of Medical Social Workers (AAMSW), 1918
> The National Association of School Social Workers (NASSW), 1919
> The American Association of Psychiatric Social Workers (AAPSW), 1926
> The American Association of Group Workers (AAGW), 1946
> The Association for the Study of Community Organization (ASCO), 1946
> The Social Work Research Group (SWRG), 1949

By 1949, there were seven separate professional organizations, the largest being the AASW. In the early 1950s strong interest and new leadership unified the profession, leading to the merger of the seven separate organizations in 1955 into what is known today as the *National Association of Social Workers (NASW)*.

Originally, membership in the NASW was open only to those with a master's degree from a school of social work accredited by the *Council on Social Work Education (CSWE)*. This reflected a continuation of the principle of narrow definition of a social worker, which had been the practice of the AASW and several of the other predecessor organizations. According to Leighninger (1987), this requirement was changed in 1969 to open membership to baccalaureate graduates (those with B.S.W.'s) from CSWE-recognized programs. With this change, the NASW moved to a more inclusive stance. In reality, however, few B.S.W.'s have chosen to join the NASW. Recently the NASW has begun to focus on the needs of the B.S.W. and to actively recruit them for membership.

With the formation of the NASW, the profession of social work began to define itself further. In 1960 it adopted a *code of ethics*, which was revised in 1980 (see Figure 6–1) (NASW, 1980). Also, various attempts were made to define the nature and purpose of social work. In 1958 a *Working Definition of Social Work Practice* appeared in Social Work, the NASW journal [see *Social Work* Vol 3 (Apr. 1958) 5–8]. This statement was organized around the following components: value, purpose, sanction, knowledge, and method. In 1981 a *Working Statement on the Purpose of Social Work* appeared, also in *Social Work* (see Figure 6–2). Although these efforts did much to clarify the definition of social work practice, there are still considerable differences within the profession concerning appropriate emphasis on the various activities and concerning the role of the B.S.W.

FIGURE 6–1   National Association of Social Workers Code of Ethics: Summary of Major Principles

---

I. Social Worker's Conduct and Comportment as a Social Worker.
  A. *Propriety.* The social worker should maintain high standards of personal conduct in the capacity or identity as social worker.
  B. *Competence and Professional Development.* The social worker should strive to become and remain proficient in professional practice and the performance of professional functions.
  C. *Service.* The social worker should regard as primary the service obligation of the social work profession.
  D. *Integrity.* The social worker should act in accordance with the highest standards of professional integrity.
  E. *Scholarship and Research.* The social worker engaged in study and research should be guided by the conventions of scholarly inquiry.
II. The Social Worker's Ethical Responsibility to Clients.
  F. *Primacy of Clients' Interests.* The social worker's primary responsibility is to clients.
  G. *Rights and Prerogatives of Clients.* The social worker should make every effort to foster maximum self-determination on the part of the clients.
  H. *Confidentiality and Privacy.* The social worker should respect the privacy of clients and hold in confidence all information obtained in the course of professional service.
  I. *Fees.* When setting fees, the social worker should ensure that they are fair, reasonable, considerate, and commensurate with the service performed and with due regard for the client's ability to pay.
III. The Social Worker's Ethical Responsibility to Colleagues.
  J. *Respect, Fairness, and Courtesy.* The social worker should treat colleagues with respect, courtesy, fairness, and good faith.
  K. *Dealing with Colleagues' Clients.* The social worker has the responsibility to relate to the clients of colleagues with full professional consideration.
IV. The Social Worker's Ethical Responsibility to Employers and Employing Organizations.
  L. *Commitments to Employing Organizations.* The social worker should adhere to commitments made to the employing organizations.
V. The Social Worker's Ethical Responsibility to the Social Work Profession.
  M. *Maintaining the Integrity of the Profession.* The social worker should uphold and advance the values, ethics, knowledge, and mission of the profession.
  N. *Community Service.* The social worker should assist the profession in making social services available to the general public.
  O. *Development of Knowledge.* The social worker should take responsibility for identifying, developing, and fully utilizing knowledge for professional practice.
VI. The Social Worker's Ethical Responsibility to Society.
  P. *Promoting the General Welfare.* The social worker should promote the general welfare of society.

Source: Reprinted with permission from *Code of Ethics,* July 1980, pp. 1–2. Copyright 1980, National Association of Social Workers.

At present, NASW has two major areas of concern: professional recognition and social policy and action. The professional recognition area led to the development of the *Academy of Certified Social Workers (ACSW)* in 1960 as a means for developing quality assurance. Requirements for the ACSW are examination and two years post–master's degree experience. The NASW has also worked for vendorship and reimbursement of social workers in the mental health system. A major activity has been working for *licensing* laws relative to social workers in the various states. At this point, most states have social work licensing laws.

FIGURE 6-2   Working Statement on the Purpose of Social Work

The purpose of social work is to promote or restore a mutually beneficial interaction between individuals and society in order to improve the quality of life for everyone. Social workers hold the following beliefs:

- The environment (social, physical, organizational) should provide the opportunity and resources for the maximum realization of the potential and aspirations of all individuals, and should provide for their common human needs and for the alleviation of distress and suffering.
- Individuals should contribute as effectively as they can to their own well-being and to the social welfare of others in their immediate environment as well as to the collective society.
- Transactions between individuals and others in their environment should enhance the dignity, individuality, and self-determination of everyone. People should be treated humanely and with justice.

Clients of social workers may be an individual, a family, a group, a community, or an organization.

Objectives

Social workers focus on persons and environment in interaction. To carry out their purpose, they work with people to achieve the following objectives:

- Help people enlarge their competence and increase their problem-solving and coping abilities.
- Help people obtain resources.
- Make organizations responsive to people.
- Facilitate interaction between individuals and others in their environment.
- Influence interactions between organizations and institutions.
- Influence social and environmental policy.

To achieve these objectives, social workers work with other people. At different times, the target of change varies—it may be the client, others in the environment, or both.

Source: Reprinted with permission from *Social Work*, Vol. 26, No. 1, January 1981, p. 6. Copyright 1981, National Association of Social Workers.

In the social policy and action area, a *Center for Social Policy and Practice* has been established. In addition, the NASW has become active in the political arena with a strong program to work for desirable legislative action on a wide variety of social welfare issues. Further, through the *Political Action for Candidate Election* (*PACE*) mechanism, it works to elect political candidates who support social welfare legislation in keeping with the NASW's objectives.

Since its inception in 1955, the NASW has continued the push for quality standards of social work practice. It has greatly broadened its concern for social welfare issues, particularly in the political arena. Yet it still cannot be considered an organization that has a monopoly on social welfare employment. Many of those employed in the public sector are still ineligible for membership because they do not possess the necessary educational credentials. In fact, in recent years the public sector has been characterized more and more by *deprofessionalization*. That is, positions in the system are less apt to require certain educational prerequisites.

The Emergence of Education for Social Work

In 1898, the New York Charity Organization Society organized a six-week annual training course in applied philanthropy. Twenty-seven people attended the program, most of whom were college graduates and already working in the field. This first course work consisted of lectures and practical fieldwork. Some years later the curriculum was expanded to an academic year, with emphasis on training college graduates without experience.

In the early 1900s other programs came into existence. In 1901 in Chicago, cooperative efforts between the University of Chicago and Chicago settlement houses created a series of courses that were later organized into an independent *training school*. Training schools were also organized in Boston (1904), Philadelphia (1908), St. Louis (1908), Cleveland (1913), and Houston (1916). At first, these schools functioned independently of institutions of higher learning.

With the emergence of these new training schools came a need to establish standards for common curriculum among the schools. There was a great deal of argument between the schools concerning the appropriate curriculum content. Many schools were committed to teaching casework: This had received considerable impetus from Mary Richmond's book *Social Diagnosis* (1917). The Chicago School of Civics and Philanthropy had established a broader curriculum with emphasis on research, social policy, and administrative issues. Western Reserve University had begun to teach courses in group work. Standards for common curriculum often became a topic of conversation between the directors of these schools when they met each year at the National Conference of Charities and Corrections. It became clear that some sort of curriculum standardization was needed. In 1919, under the leadership of Porter R. Lee, then director of the New York School of Social Work, the American Association of Schools of Social Work (AASSW) was established. The creation of this organization was a giant step forward in the professionalization of social work.

The early training schools remained for many years under the auspices of the social agencies that supplied the instructors and the fieldwork apprenticeship training experiences. Even though the AASSW attempted to set curriculum standards, disagreement continued among the schools over what should be taught. Gradually, beginning in the late 1920s, a movement toward including professional social work education in the higher education systems began. The Chicago School of Civics and Philanthropy was a leader in this effort. This school eventually became part of the University of Chicago.

Edith Abbott, in *Social Welfare and Professional Education* (1931), stressed that social work methods needed to consist of more than casework. She felt that social workers needed a much broader knowledge base that included the biological sciences, sociology, anthropology, economics, psychology, research, and the law. Abbott also advocated that social work education be housed in a university setting.

The AASSW provided further impetus for this in 1935 when it began to require any school desiring membership to be a part of an institution approved by the Association of American Universities. The AASSW also developed minimum curriculum standards for its member schools, and mechanisms for reviewing the schools to ensure compliance.

There developed a growing concern about social work education at the baccalaureate level. AASSW members tended to be schools in large cities and on the East Coast. Developing baccalaureate programs tended to be located in state universities and land grant colleges in the

Midwest and South. For a time, one-year graduate programs were allowed by the AASSW as a compromise with the state universities.

In 1942, another organization, the *National Association of Schools of Social Administration* (*NASSA*), emerged. Its membership included social work programs in state universities and land grant colleges, as well as a few private colleges. This organization was concerned with training for public social welfare agencies. It did not stipulate standards for these programs.

The next ten years were a period of confusion and sometimes even hostility between the AASSW and the NASSA. Eventually, negotiation and compromise resulted in the merger of the two organizations to form the Council on Social Work Education (CSWE). This new organization was dominated by the AASSW philosophy, and two-year graduate education became the accepted mode for social work education. Baccalaureate education continued, usually as an emphasis in a sociology department, as a social welfare program, or as a preprofessional program, particularly in midwestern and southern institutions of higher education. These programs, although not eligible for membership in the CSWE, continued to have a relationship with the CSWE by attending the annual program meetings of CSWE. At these national meetings, specific educational sections were made available to undergraduate educators (Leighninger, 1985).

As early as 1951, when the Hollis-Taylor report, *Social Work Education in the United States*, was published (1951), the elitism of graduate social work education began to be seriously questioned. The Hollis-Taylor report affirmed the legitimacy of undergraduate education in preparing people for professional tasks. It states: "In view of this report social work education will be in a sounder position when the profession officially recognizes that the area of undergraduate concentration (major and minor) offered prospective social workers is an organic part of professional education and should not be characterized by the nondescript term 'preprofessional.' "

During the 1960s, serious questions arose about the capacity of the graduate schools of social work to supply enough professionals for the social welfare system. With increased recognition of social problems and human needs, it became evident that the supply of trained workers was inadequate. This was particularly true in the public sector, where the social service arrangement was expanding in size and importance. It was hoped for a time that the manpower needs of these agencies could be met by graduate-level workers. Even though the number of graduate-level workers doubled from 1950 to 1967, the need for trained workers increased at a faster rate, causing a shortage in the supply. It was also found that most master's degree (M.S.W.) holders were not interested in employment in public social services. This was due in part to low salaries but was also true because graduate education, with its emphasis on individual therapy, did not prepare them for practice in public settings. By 1965 public agencies began to abandon efforts to employ people with master's degrees and started using baccalaureate-level workers in direct service delivery positions (Ferguson, 1975).

During this same period several organizations began to concern themselves with manpower issues. The CSWE, the NASW, the Department of Health, Education and Welfare, and the Southern Regional Education Board all studied how to utilize social services manpower effectively.

For example, in 1960, the CSWE completed a study of the curriculum structure in social work education that considered whether undergraduate social work programs should be recognized as capable of producing professionally trained personnel for the social services (Bisno, 1959). In 1965, the Task Force on Social Work Education and Manpower of the Department of Health, Education and Welfare published a report, *Closing the Gap in Social Work Manpower*. In this report the task force made the following recommendation: "There is a critical need for the advancement of undergraduate education in social welfare both for direct entry of graduates into practice and as preparation for graduate education" (U.S. Department of Health, Education, and Welfare, 1965).

In 1968, another manpower study was published by the NASW: *Differential Use of Social Work Manpower*. The study concluded that there was an inefficient use in the delivery of social services of what is called subprofessional manpower, including workers trained in baccalaureate social welfare programs.

Also strengthening the position of baccalaureate education in social work was the work of the Southern Regional Education Board Task Force. In 1971 it published *A Core of Competence for Baccalaureate Social Welfare and Curricular Implications*. The recognition by these studies of the ability of undergraduate programs to produce graduates capable of performing professional social work tasks and functions brought pressures on the NASW and the CSWE to change their positions on the baccalaureate-level worker. These pressures led to a decision by the NASW, as a result of a referendum in 1969, to allow graduates of baccalaureate programs approved by the CSWE to join the association with full membership entitlements. As a result of the NASW's action, the CSWE made the decision to develop guidelines for the approval of undergraduate programs. In 1973 the CSWE, as a result of further study of the approval process, developed stringent *accreditation* standards for undergraduate programs. The focus of the accreditation standards was on preparing students for professional practice. The accreditation standards and accreditation process were fully implemented in 1974. Baccalaureate programs that had since 1970 been approved constituent members of the CSWE were now eligible for accreditation and full membership in the CSWE, and the Bachelor of Social Work (B.S.W.) degree was now considered the first professional degree (Lowe, 1985).

The broadening of the educational arm of the social work profession has resulted in many more accredited social work programs and thus a greatly expanded pool of individuals with professional social work degrees. In 1995 there were 116 master's-level programs and 391 baccalaureate programs accredited by the CSWE. Many B.S.W.'s are now employed in public social service agencies. There is hope that when issues of deprofessionalization are resolved, social work can move toward a more dominant place in the social welfare system.

The Nature of Contemporary Social Work Practice

Despite the fact that the social work profession has "done its work" for nearly a century, people still have trouble understanding exactly what social work is and what it is supposed to do (Fink, Pfouts, and Dobelstein, 1985). Part of the difficulty lies in the fact that there is no single definition of social work. Social work can be defined in many different ways, reflecting the diversity that exists in the profession. In some ways, this can be viewed as a strength, but it also contributes to the confusion about the nature of the profession. The general public often confuses social work and social welfare. This confusion is easily understood, particularly given the close ties between social welfare, social work, and the system of social services identified in this book.

The National Association of Social Workers defines *social work* as "the professional activity of helping individuals, groups, or communities enhance or restore their capacity for social functioning and creating social conditions favorable to that goal" (NASW, 1973). Social workers help people, singly or collectively, to solve life problems so their lives can be more satisfying and rewarding. In attempting to enhance or restore people's social functioning, social workers also become "concerned with the interactions between people and their social environment, which affects the ability of people to accomplish their life tasks, alleviate distress, and realize their aspirations and values" (Pincus and Minahan, 1973). Social workers intervene to facilitate change, to enhance, restore, or promote a better relationship between people and their environments. This might include, but is not limited to, the following:

1. Counseling individuals, groups, or families
2. Linking people with resources, services, and opportunities to improve their functioning
3. Bringing about changes in environmental systems, institutions, and organizations so they become more responsive to people's needs
4. Bringing about changes in existing policies or creating new social policies that provide for people's needs and well-being (Pincus and Minahan, 1973)

These definitions help develop an understanding of what social workers do. But, there is still a need to discuss further the nature of the profession.

Social work has often been described as a science. Its scientific nature is best illustrated by pointing out that when social workers help people, they employ the problem-solving process, which is an application of scientific principles and methods. In carrying out their tasks, social workers use a knowledge base that includes theories and knowledge extracted from several disciplines, among them sociology, anthropology, political science, and psychology.

Social work has also been described as an art. People's needs, concerns, and problems are complex. Environmental conditions that affect people are also complex. Thus, solutions to problems in people's social functioning can be difficult to find. The social worker's possession of knowledge alone is not sufficient for effective problem solving. Creativity in blending knowledge with action is required. Just as a sculptor or artist uses creativity to produce a work of art, a social worker creatively blends knowledge, experience, values, and skills to help individuals, groups, or communities find solutions to life's problems. This is the *art of social work*.

The 1958 NASW working definition of social work practice has as a basic premise the proposition that professional practice is guided by a body of knowledge that helps the social worker to understand the nature of people's problems with their immediate environment and the causal relationship between the two. Another premise is that the profession possesses a set of values regarding human beings and the human condition that serves as a foundation for practice. The working definition also states that the knowledge base and values of the profession are put into action through a set of skills. Skills are the tools the social worker uses to effect change resulting in beneficial consequences for the people served. It is this constellation of knowledge, values, and skills that organizes the responses made to the concerns, needs, and problems of the people with whom the social worker is confronted (Johnson, 1992).

Social Work's Knowledge Base

One of the basic criteria for any profession is a body of knowledge. The *knowledge base* of social work generally consists of the following:

1. Knowledge borrowed from the natural, social, and behavioral sciences
2. Knowledge developed from social workers' own experiences in assisting and helping people, referred to as "practice wisdom"
3. Knowledge developed by social workers through research efforts

This knowledge base is of little relevance unless it can be integrated into the helping endeavor. Siporin (1975) has suggested that the knowledge base can be divided into two practical component parts, assessment knowledge and intervention knowledge. Assessment knowledge enables the social worker to assess and understand a person's concerns, needs, and problems, as well as the situation in which they exist. It shows the social worker where and how to intervene effectively. Intervention knowledge is that knowledge utilized by the social worker to carry out the interventive process, thus helping individuals, groups, or communities deal effectively with the problems they face. Intervention knowledge is usually specific to the client problem, agency setting, and specific field of practice.

In today's world, a social worker must possess a broad knowledge base that includes but is not limited to the following:

1. Knowledge of human development and behavior, encompassing a holistic view of the person and the reciprocal influences of the environment, including social, psychological, economic, political, and cultural influences. The main source of this part of the knowledge base comes from a strong and broad liberal arts education. It includes (a) knowledge extracted from the social and behavioral sciences (sociology, psychology, anthropology, history, political science, and economics); (b) knowledge from the natural sciences for understanding the physical aspects of human functioning; and (c) knowledge gained through study in the humanities that helps explain the human condition by an examination of cultures, philosophies, and ways of thinking about and expressing the human condition.
2. Knowledge about human relationships and interactions. This includes knowledge of human communication, understanding person-to-person, family, small group, and group-to-group relationships and interactions, as well as the relationships and interactions between individuals, groups, and community organizations and institutions.
3. Knowledge of social work practice theories that embrace helping interactions, processes, and intervention methods and strategies appropriate for a variety of practice situations.
4. Knowledge about social policy and services, including knowledge of professional and institutional structures that deliver services to people in need of help, and knowledge of the history of the movements that have influenced social policy, the impact of social policy on people's functioning, and the role of the social worker in the development of social policy.
5. Self-knowledge, which makes the social worker aware of and take responsibility for his or her own emotions, values, attitudes, and actions, when they would influence professional practice.

6. Specialized knowledge that enables the social worker to work with specific population groups or particular practice situations. This includes knowledge of specific clients, practice settings, and agencies.

Social work's knowledge base has as its source a strong liberal arts background, professional practice, and research base (Johnson, 1992; Morales and Sheafor, 1986; Baer and Federico, 1978).

Social Work, a Value-Based Profession

Social work practice is guided by a set of values about human beings and the human condition. *Values* are strong beliefs that emerge from the way one feels and guide human actions and behaviors. Social work's value base also serves as an ethical guide for the individual social worker in day-to-day work. Individuals hold values learned through socialization at many levels within society. Individual values are diverse, differing from individual to individual. Some human values are held in common by most people and become societal values.

Social work's values are somewhat reflective of individual and societal values, but they are also unique to the profession. They fall into three areas, according to Morales and Sheafor (1986): (1) values that reflect preferred conceptions of people, (2) values that reflect preferred outcomes for people, (3) values that reflect social workers' ethical responsibilities to the people they serve. The following value statements are generally agreed upon as belonging to the profession:

The worth and dignity of people: Social workers believe in the inherent worth and dignity of all people, regardless of their individual or collective characteristics or status.

The self-determination of people: Social workers believe that people have the basic right to self-determination as long as their individual or collective actions do not endanger themselves or infringe upon the rights of others.

The purposefulness of human behavior: Social workers believe that all human behavior has a purpose, however unusual it may appear and however destructive it may be. Social workers strive to discover the meanings and purposes of behavior, rather than to label it, stereotype it, or otherwise react to it in a negative fashion.

People's capacity to grow and change: People should never be viewed by the social worker as incapable of changing and growing in ways that will make their lives more rewarding. No person is beyond the capacity to accept constructive help.

People's need for opportunities for growth and development: Society and the profession must help people by providing the opportunities necessary for them to achieve their full potential in all aspects of their social functioning.

People's right to participate actively in social work practice: Social workers believe that people are capable of making decisions, and that social work is a mutual and cooperative endeavor between worker and client.

Confidentiality: In most instances, unless otherwise prohibited, social workers must respect people's right to privacy (Levy, 1973, 1976; Morales and Sheafor, 1986; Ferguson, 1975).

Social work values are operationalized for use by social workers in their professional practice, through the social work *code of ethics* (see Figure 6–1). All professional social workers are expected to adhere to this code of ethics in their day-to-day work.

The Skills of Social Work

Harriett M. Bartlett (1970) has referred to the *skills* component as an "interventive repertoire"—a "bag of tricks," so to speak, that gives the social worker the means to facilitate change. The skills used by social workers are thought of in terms of the methods and techniques involved, as well as the ability to use knowledge effectively by transforming it into action in the helping process. Social work skills from a more contemporary perspective are defined as "the social worker's capacity to set in motion with a client interventive processes of change based on social work values and knowledge in a situation relevant to the client" (Morales and Sheafor, 1986).

The skills that social workers use can be organized into three general skill-areas: (1) interpersonal helping skills, (2) social work process skills, and (3) evaluation and accountability skills.

Interpersonal helping skills are basic to any professional people-helping endeavor. These skills include the following:

1. Communication and listening skills include the social worker's ability to communicate clearly with a client, to understand and interpret the client's verbal and nonverbal communication; to help clients become clearer in their own communications; to be able to actively listen to the needs, concerns, and problems expressed by clients and so understand them in the reality of their situation; and to be able to transform that which is understood through listening into action with clients, and so assist them in improving their social functioning.
2. Helping relationship skills include the social worker's ability to establish working relationships with clients, who either reach out for help or to whom the profession reaches out to help. Involved here is the social worker's conscious use of self, including values and attitudes. Remaining honest, open, trustworthy, dependable, and nonjudgmental will promote the establishment of helping relationships.
3. Interviewing-counseling skills include the social worker's listening skills and such specific skills as confrontation, limit setting, support, ventilation, empathy, and self-disclosure to assess, question, and respond to the client's expressions of concerns, needs, or problems in their life situations.

Social work process skills are the nuts and bolts of social work practice activity. Here the knowledge base and values of social work come into play. Social work process skills involve creatively integrating interpersonal helping skills with the problem-solving approaches contained in various methods of social work practice for work with individuals, groups, and communities. Use of these skills allows the social worker to be able to do the following:

1. To identify and assess problematic relationships between people and social institutions, where intervention is needed to promote, enhance, restore, protect, or terminate the relationships to improve social functioning

2. To develop and implement appropriate intervention plans based on the assessment of problems involved in the client's situation, that address the client's concern and need

3. To enhance or restore the client's capacity for problem-solving, coping, growth, and development

4. To provide the link between people and community systems that will give them resources, services, and opportunities for improving social functioning

5. To intervene effectively with and on behalf of vulnerable, disenfranchised, and discriminated-against people, to promote and restore their opportunities for social justice

6. To promote the effective and humane functioning of community systems that provide people with resources, services, and opportunities

7. To be involved with others (e.g., clients and professionals) in the development of new service or the modification and improvement of existing community service and resource systems so that they become responsive to the needs of the clients or consumers (Baer and Federico, 1978)

Evaluation and accountability skills are the social worker's conscious use of self in evaluating the effectiveness of practice and being accountable to the people they serve, the delivery system they represent, and society in general. Again, value and ethical considerations in social work practice provide the guidelines against which social workers measure themselves.

Methods and Approaches of Social Work Practice

Discussion of the elements of social work practice—its constellation of knowledge, values, and skills—has provided insight into the foundations on which practice is based. Attention will be given now to discussing how knowledge, values, and skills are organized into methods and approaches for working with people. As social work evolved as a profession, a number of practice methods and approaches have emerged. The development of these methods and approaches has been influenced by several factors: by contributions to the knowledge base of the profession; by advances in technology; by advances in social work education; and by the ever-changing social, economic, and political climate. Three practice methods, casework, group work, and community organization, were developed from the early 1900s to the 1960s. Social workers before the 1970s were primarily educated in only one of these three methods. These methods are referred to as the *traditional methods* of social work practice.

1. *Casework:* Casework was the first method to be developed. It is the method of social work practice that assists individuals or families on a one-to-one or family group basis. A large majority of social workers were educated in this method.

2. *Group work:* Group work is the process of working with individuals within groups and with the group itself. The focus of the group work process is placed on its individual members and on the group as a whole. According to Knopka (1972), the role of the group worker is to enable the group to function so that group interaction and program activity help the individual members to grow, and so that the group as a whole reaches its mutual goals.

3. *Community organizing:* Community organizing is harder to define. One useful definition is as follows: Community organizing is the social work process of bringing about de-

sired change in social welfare services, human relations, or social institutions by a variety of methods. It is the process of organizing a community to bring about desired change, focusing on specific areas and processes, such as changes in the law, improvement in existing service provisions, or improvement in community social conditions that are problematic for people. It differs from casework and group work in that the client of the community organizer becomes the whole community, or designated parts of it (Ross, 1955).

In the late 1960s, social work practice within these three traditional methods began to change as a result of a rethinking using a broad perspective about what constitutes social work practice. The new conceptualization incorporated new theoretical developments in the social sciences, particularly social systems theory (Johnson, 1992). *Social systems theory* brought new understandings about the earlier social work view of people's reciprocal relationship with their environment, and further developed the notion that social work processes should focus on what was called "the person in the situation"—that is, that people are involved in life situations that include interaction with various social systems in the environment that affect their social functioning. Assessing the person in the situation now involved understanding the relationship between individuals and environmental systems, and the problems of social functioning that arise out of that interaction.

New practice approaches surfaced in the early 1970s. In part, these new approaches solved long-standing arguments about the most desirable way for social workers to facilitate change. This argument can be stated as follows: Should intervention be focused on the individual or family, to improve their coping skills and thus improve their interaction with their environment (as the traditional caseworker would believe)? Or should the change occur in the environmental systems that cause difficulties for people and families (as community organizers would think)? It was argued that the traditional methods "encourage the dichotomous thinking of changing the individual or changing the environment, instead of maintaining the primary focus of social work intervention on the person–situation interaction" (Siporin, 1975; Compton and Galaway, 1984; Pincus and Minahan, 1973).

Integrating the knowledge and skill bases of the traditional methods with the broadened person–situation practice perspective was first termed *integrated social work practice.* Also, what were termed the micro and macro approaches became popular. *Microintervention* focuses on intervention by the social worker with small client systems (individuals, families, and groups). Practice principles from the methods of casework and group work are integrated here. *Macrointervention* focuses on intervention with large client systems (communities; societal organizations; and institutions at the local, state, and national levels). Education in macrointervention also prepares social workers to assume administrative, social policy, and program evaluation roles. Macrointervention, then, incorporates the principles of community organizing practice with knowledge about administration and evaluation.

With the recognition of the bachelor's degree in social work in 1974 came concern over how undergraduate social work programs should educate beginning-level practitioners, and how to identify the knowledge and skills needed by the bachelor-level social worker, to prepare them for practice. What eventually emerged began to be called the *generalist approach.* It was based on integrated practice, particularly the focus on the person–situation interaction, but did not lead to a jack-of-all-trades approach. Rather, the generalist social worker assesses the needs, problems, and concerns of people in situations, and then uses knowledge and skill to develop and implement change strategies with a client system of any size. The case study that follows illustrates the generalist approach to practice.

According to Federico (1980), the generalist social worker is sufficiently skilled to assume the following roles in social work practice:

Outreach: The social worker recognizes that some people who need services and are eligible to receive them are often unaware of them or are blocked in some way in their attempts to gain access to them. The worker identifies such individuals and assists them in finding the appropriate social services.

Broker: The social worker has knowledge of and the skills to link individuals with appropriate community resources that will meet their needs and assist them in solving their problems.

Advocate: The social worker has the ability to intervene on behalf of people seeking community resources or experiencing problems in gaining access to such resources. Advocacy may be on an individual-case basis (case advocacy) or in behalf of a number of individuals whose needs are not being met or who are being disadvantaged in some way (cause advocacy).

Teacher: The social worker has the knowledge and skill to teach clients useful specific behaviors and skills in such areas as job seeking, parenting, or homemaking.

Enabler–mobilizer: The social worker has the ability to form productive professional relationships with people and, through encouragement, support, and role modeling, to enable or mobilize the client system to make changes, engage in problem solving, or use social services appropriately.

Behavior-changer: The social worker has the knowledge, experience, and skills to help clients change their problem-causing behaviors through the use of individual or group counseling or other interpersonal methods.

Consultant: The social worker has the skills to work along with community professionals to help the community resource system become more responsive to the needs and problems of community members.

Community planner: Within limits, the social worker assists community groups in planning for the development of needed services or changes in existing services.

Another role that has recently received considerable attention and can be appropriately filled by the B.S.W. generalist worker is that of *case manager.* In this role the worker assesses with the client which services are needed and then obtains those services for the client. The worker may also provide some of the needed services. In addition, the worker assumes responsibility for seeing that the services are delivered, are delivered in a way that is usable by the client, and complement other services being provided (see Rapp and Chamberlain, 1985; DeGennaro, 1987).

Currently, undergraduate social work programs prepare beginning-level social workers to use the generalist approach. Graduate schools prepare social workers for advanced specialized practice. This level of training focuses on a client population or field of practice, such as family therapy or mental health, or on specific training in administration or social planning.

A Case Study

Bobby L., an eight-year-old boy, was referred to the local Family Services agency by his principal upon the request of his parents. A social worker at the agency was assigned to his case, and she proceeded to conduct an initial interview of the family.

Bobby was having academic and behavioral difficulties at school according to the parents. He was inattentive in class, disruptive, and sometimes belligerent towards both peers and teachers. Upon further questioning, the parents admitted Bobby was "a handful at home too." The parents frequently thought of placement in a foster home or residential facility when they had a difficult week with Bobby.

The social worker developed a tentative contract for services based on what she saw as the needs of the family. But first she thought she would contact the school for information about Bobby's behavior. One of her questions was whether Bobby had a long history of behavioral problems in school. Another question she had was whether Bobby had particular teachers and children he didn't get along with. The teachers thought the problems had been going on for the past two years, so the behavior was not a long-standing problem. In the second instance, the answer was no, too: there wasn't any particular situation that set Bobby off.

The social worker suggested to the parents that Bobby have a physical examination by their family doctor to rule out any physical causes such as juvenile diabetes or attention deficit disorder. The social worker also suggested the parents receive parenting training to help them deal more effectively with Bobby's behaviors. Family therapy was suggested for a period of five sessions to see if Bobby's behaviors could improve with increased family communication skills.

Results of the physical examination found higher than normal lead blood levels. Appearantly, the parents had moved two years ago to an older house, and the paint and plaster dust was everywhere. Bobby's behaviors abated with a complete house clean-up. Academic performance improved, and the complaints about his relationships with parents, teachers, and peers decreased.

The social worker continued working on the case, however. She wanted to find out whether the lead problem of Bobby's was an isolated experience, or whether other physicians were finding cases in young children in the area. She contacted the pediatricians in town and conducted a survey. Her findings were remarkable.

Forty-two percent of Doctors surveyed told her that they had noticed increased lead blood levels in area children. The numbers were growing by about 5 to 6 children per year, too. The social worker decided to take action and get the word out to the parents of young children in town. She arranged a community meeting and set up a task force to publicize the problem.

The town started a public awareness campaign and made available handouts on the importance of lead removal in older homes. Not only was Bobby helped by the social worker's interventions, but other children in the community were helped.

Fields of Practice: An Organizing Framework for Practice

Because the social welfare system is involved in many different social concerns, it has been necessary for both the social welfare system and the social work profession to use some mechanism for organizing services or developing *specialist practice*. To do this, a *field of practice* framework has developed. These fields of practice may be organized around a particular social problem area such as child welfare or income maintenance. They may be organized around practice in what are often referred to as host settings, those settings where social work is not the predominant profession. Health care, mental health, and corrections are such fields of practice. They may be organized around a particular population group, such as gerontological social work. Recently, context has developed as a focus of fields of practice—for example, industrial and rural. In addition, there are fields of practice that focus on a particular social system, such as group services, family services, and community organization.

Bartlett (1961) identifies three frames of reference that affect any field of practice. First are the essential elements of any social work practice. Second are the characteristics of the particular field. Third is social work practice as it develops for the particular field. The essential elements of social work practice, regardless of which field of practice workers find themselves in, include values, knowledge, methods, purpose of the practice, and sanctioning of the practice. The characteristics of any field include the problems or conditions of central concern, the system of organized services, societal sociocultural attitudes, the characteristic responses and behaviors of persons being served, and the specialized body of knowledge, values, and methods relative to a field of practice. It is the blending of the essential elements of all social work practice and the characteristics of a field of practice that result in the specific practice within any field of practice.

For a field of practice—a practice with special characteristics for a particular population—to develop, there must be a concern for that population. Both society in general and the professionals in particular must have responded to unmet needs or problems that exist within that population. In addition, both society and the social work profession must understand the system within which the needs and problems exist and the characteristics of the groups affected.

The remaining chapters in this section will deal in some depth with the fields identified here. It is as these fields were defined and developed that the social welfare system developed, as did the social work practice specific to each field. Development of each field includes consideration of social conditions and public attitudes affecting the field, the laws and programs that respond to the human needs related to the field, and the specific social work practice approaches and techniques used in that field. Professional social work is as it is today in part because of the demands of the fields of practice within which it has used its knowledge, values, and skills.

Summary

This chapter has discussed the emergence of social work as a profession within the social welfare system. Attention has been paid to the development of professional organizations and education for social work, as well as to the nature of social work practice. Four points of tension within the profession have been identified: emphasis on the profession or on service to those with needs, the relationship of the profession to the social welfare system, the role of the profession in political or social change activity, and a broad or narrow definition of the profession. Consideration of the development of the profession has shown that from time to time the predominance and content of each issue have changed. Yet they remain today as the unfinished business of the profession. With the possibilities of a new federal social welfare policy in the Clinton administration and the Republican congress, there may come new programs and new ways of delivering old services and entitlements. The evolution of the social work profession will continue with the evolution of the social welfare system.

Key Terms

Academy of Certified Social Workers (ACSW)
accreditation
advocate
American Association of Social Workers (AASW)
art of social work
Bachelor of Social Work (B.S.W.)
behavior-changer
broker
case manager
casework
cause–function debate
Center for Social Policy and Practice
code of ethics
community organizing
community planner
consultant
Council on Social Work Education (CSWE)
deprofessionalization
enabler–mobilizer
field of practice
friendly visitors
generalist approach
grandfathered in
group work
integrated social work practice
knowledge base

licensing
macrointervention
Master of Social Work (M.S.W.)
microinvertention
National Association of Schools of Social Administration (NASSA)
National Association of Social Workers (NASW)
National Conference on Social Welfare (NCSW)
outreach
Political Action for Candidate Election (PACE)
power–control model
process model
profession
Register of Clinical Social Workers
settlement house workers
skills
social systems theory
social work
specialist practice
teacher
traditional methods
training school
trait–attribute approach
values
Working Definition of Social Work Practice
Working Statement on the Purpose of Social Work

References

Abbott, E. (1931). *Social welfare and professional education.* Chicago: University of Chicago Press.

Axline, J., & Levin, H. (1982). *Social welfare: a history of the American response to need* (2nd ed.). New York: Harper & Row.

Baer, B. L., & Federico, R. (1978). *Education of the baccalaureate social worker: report of the undergraduate curriculum project.* Cambridge, MA: Ballinger.

Barker, R. L., & Briggs, T. L. (1968). *Differential use of social work manpower.* New York: National Association of Social Workers.

Bartlett, H. (1961). *Analysing social work practice by fields.* New York: National Association of Social Workers.

Bartlett, H. M. (1970). *The common base of social work practice.* New York: National Association of Social Workers.

Battle, M. G. (1987). Professional associations: national association of social workers. In A. Minahan (Ed.), *Encyclopedia of social work* (18th ed.), Silver Springs, MD: National Association of Social Workers, pp. 333–341.

Becker, D. G. (1963). Adventures in social casework: the charity agent. *Social Casework, 44* (May), 255–262.

Bisno, H. (1959). *The place of the undergraduate curriculum in social work education.* New York: Council on Social Work Education.

Borenzweig, H. (1971). Social work and psychoanalytic theory: a historical analysis. *Social Work, 16* (January), 7–16.

Brown, E. L. (1932). Social work against the background of other professionals. In *Proceedings of the national conference on social work.* Chicago: University of Chicago Press, pp. 520–553.

Compton, B., & Galaway, B. (1984). *Social work processes.* Homewood, IL: Dorsey Press.

Council on Social Work Education (1995). *Directory of colleges and universities with accredited social work degree programs.* Alexandria, VA: Council on Social Work Education.

Dawes, A. (1893). The need for training schools for a new profession. *Lend-A-Hand, 2,* 90–97.

DeGennaro, M. (1987). Developing case management as a practice model. *Social Casework, 68* (October), 1987.

Dolgoff, R., & Feldstein, D. (1980). *Understanding social welfare.* New York: Harper & Row.

Federico, R. (1980). *The social welfare institution.* Lexington, MA: D. C. Heath.

Ferguson, E. A. (1975). *Social work: an introduction.* Philadelphia: Lippincott.

Fink, A., Pfouts, J. H., & Dobelstein, A. W. (1985). *The field of social work.* Beverly Hills, CA: Sage Publications.

Flexner, A. (1915). Is social work a profession? In *Proceedings of the national conference of charities and corrections.* Chicago: Hildman, pp. 576–590.

Greenwood, E. (1957). Attributes of a profession. *Social Work, 2* (July), 45–55.

Hodson, W. (1925). Is social work professional? A reexamination of the question. In *Proceedings of the national conference of social work.* Chicago: University of Chicago Press, pp. 629–636.

Hollis, E. V., & Taylor, A. L. (1951). *Social work education in the United States .* New York: Columbia University Press.

Hoops, J. G., & Pinderhughes, E. B. (1987). Profession of social work: comtemporary characteristics. In A. Minahan (Ed.), *Encyclopedia of social work* (18th ed.) Silver Springs, MD: National Association of Social Workers, pp. 351–356.

Johnson, L. (1992). *Social work practice: a generalist approach* (4th ed.). Boston: Allyn and Bacon.

Knopka, G. (1972). *Social groupwork: a helping process.* Englewood Cliffs, NJ: Prentice-Hall.

Lee, P. (1930). Cause and function. In *Proceedings of the national conference of social work, 1929.* Chicago: Chicago University Press, pp. 3–20.

Leiby, J. (1978). *A history of social welfare and social work in the United States.* New York: Columbia University Press.

Leighninger, L. (1985). Graduate and undergraduate social work education: roots of conflict. *Journal of Education for Social Work, 20* (Fall), 66–77.

Leighninger, L. (1987). *Social work search for identity.* New York: Greenwood Press.

Levy, C. S. (1973). The values base of social work. *Journal of Education for Social Work, 9* (Winter), 37–38.

Levy, C. S. (1976). *Social work ethics.* New York: Human Services Press.

Lowe, G. R. (1985). The graduate-only debate in social work education 1931–1959, and its consequences for the profession. *Journal of Social Work Education, 21* (Fall), 52–62.

Lowe, G. R., Zimmerman, L. R., & Reid, P. N. (1989). How we see ourselves: a critical review of text versions of social work's professional evolution (unpublished paper).

Lubove, R. (1965). *The professional altruist: the emergence of social work as a career.* Cambridge, MA: Harvard University Press.

McPheeters, H. L., & Ryan, R. M. (1971). *A core of competence for baccalaureate social welfare and curricular implications.* Atlanta, GA: Southern Regional Education Board.

Morales, A., & Sheafor, B. W. (1986). *Social work: a profession of many faces.* Boston: Allyn and Bacon.

National Association of Social Workers (1973). *Standards for social service manpower.* Washington, DC: National Association of Social Workers.

Pincus, A., & Minahan, A. (1973). *Social work practice: model and method.* Itasca, IL: F. E. Peacock.

Rapp, C., & Chamberlain, R. (1985). Case management services for the chronically mentally ill. *Social Work, 30* (September–October), 417–422.

Richmond, M. (1890). The need of a training school in applied philanthropy. In *Proceedings of the national conference of charities and corrections.* Boston: George H. Ellis, pp. 181–188.

Richmond, M. (1917). *Social diagnosis.* New York: Russell Sage Foundation.

Ross, M. (1955). *Community organization.* New York: Harper & Row.

Siporin, M. (1975). *Introduction to social work.* New York: Macmillan.

Trattner, D. (1974). *From poor law to welfare state.* New York: Free Press.

U. S. Department of Health, Education, and Welfare, departmental task force on social work education and manpower (1965). *Closing the gap in social work mampower.* Washington, DC: U. S. Government Printing Office.

Suggested Readings

Baer, Betty L., and Federico, Ronald. *Education of the Baccalaureate Social Worker: Report of the Undergraduate Curriculum Project* (Cambridge, MA: Ballinger, 1978).

Bartlett, Harriett M. *Analyzing Social Work Practice by Fields* (New York: National Association of Social Workers, 1961).

Battle, Mark G. "Professional Associations: National Association of Social Workers." In Anne Minahan, ed., *Encyclopedia of Social Work*, 18th ed. (Silver Springs, MD: National Association of Social Workers, 1987), pp. 333–341.

Bernard, L. Diane. "Professional Associations: National Association of Social Workers." In Anne Minahan, ed., *Encyclopedia of Social Work*, 18th ed. (Silver Springs, MD: National Association of Social Workers), 1987, pp. 330–333.

Chambers, Clarke A. "Women in the Creation of the Profession of Social Work." *Social Service Review*, 60 (March 1986), 1–33.

Constable, Robert T. "Social Work Education: Current Issues and Future Promise." *Social Work*, 29 (July–August 1984), 366–371.

Dinerman, Miriam, and Geismar, Ludwig L. *A Quarter Century of Social Work Education* (Silver Springs, MD: National Association of Social Workers, 1984).

Dolgoff, Ralph, and Feldstein, Donald. "Social Work: The Emergence of a Profession." In Dolgoff and Feldstein, eds., *Understanding Social Welfare* (New York: Harper & Row, 1980), pp. 223–250.

Flexner, Abraham. "Is Social Work a Profession?" *Proceedings of the National Conference on Charities and Corrections* (Chicago: Hildman Printing, 1915), p. 576.

Franklin, Donna L. "Mary Richmond and Jane Addams: From Moral Certainty to Rational Inquiry in Social Work Practice." *Social Service Review*, 60 (December 1986), 504–525.

Greenwood, Ernest. "Attributes of a Profession." *Social Work*, 2 (July 1957), 45–55.

Hollis, Ernest V., and Taylor, Alice L. *Social Work Education in the United States* (New York: Columbia University Press, 1951).

Hopps, June Gary, and Pinderhughes, Elaine B. "Profession of Social Work: Contemporary Characteristics." In Anne Minahan, ed., *Encyclopedia of Social Work*, 18th ed. (Silver Springs, MD: National Association of Social Workers, 1987), pp. 351–365.

Jimenez, Mary Ann. "Historical Evolution and Future Challenges of the Human Services Professor." *Families in Society*, 71 (Feb. 1990), pp. 3–12.

Johnson, Louise C. *Social Work Practice: A Generalist Approach*, 4th ed. (Boston, MA: Allyn and Bacon, 1992).

Leighninger, Leslie. "Graduate and Undergraduate Social Work Education: Roots of Conflict." *Journal of Education for Social Work*, 20 (Fall 1984), 66–77.

Leighninger, Leslie. *Social Work: Search for Identity* (New York: Greenwood Press, 1987).

Lloyd, Gary A. "Social Work Education." In Anne Minahan, ed., *Encyclopedia of Social Work*, 18th ed. (Silver Springs, MD: National Association of Social Workers, 1987), pp. 695–704.

Lowe, Gary R. "The Graduate-Only Debate in Social Work Education, 1931–1959." *Journal of Social Work Education*, 21 (Fall 1985), 52–62.

Lubove, Roy. *The Professional Altruist* (Cambridge, MA: Harvard University Press, 1965).

Morales, Armando, and Sheafor, Bradford W. *Social Work: A Profession of Many Faces*, 4th ed. (Boston, MA: Allyn and Bacon, 1986).

Reeser, Linda Cherrey. "Professionalization, Striving, and Social Work Activism." *Journal of Social Service Research*, 14 (No. 3–4), pp. 1–22.

Saxton, Paul M. "Vendorship for Social Work: Observations on the Maturation of the Profession." *Social Work*, 33 (May–June 1988), pp. 197–201.

Trattner, Walter I. "The Quest for Professionalization." In *From Poor Law to Welfare State: A History of Social Welfare in America* (New York: Free Press, 1979), Chap. 11.

U.S. Department of Health, Education, and Welfare. *Closing the Gap in Social Work Manpower* (Washington, DC: U.S. Government Printing Office, 1965)

7

INCOME MAINTENANCE AS A RESPONSE TO HUMAN NEEDS

Learning Expectations

- Understanding of the various forms of income maintenance
- Knowledge of the historical development of income maintenance in Western society
- Understanding of two major value perspectives that undergird the U.S. system of income maintenance
- Ability to explain three ways to conceptualize societal responsibility for income maintenance
- Understanding of major income maintenance programs being used in the current U.S. social welfare system
- Knowledge of some of the proposed reforms for the U.S. social welfare system relative to income maintenance, historically and currently
- Understanding of major contributors and impacts of the low-cost housing shortage in the United States
- Knowledge of the role or possible roles of social work in the income maintenance field of practice

Chapter 1 discussed the arrangements that the U.S. social welfare system uses to provide for human needs, including the major societal values, locality-specific cultural ethos and values, philosophies, and historical changes that have shaped its response. That introduction clearly indicated that one important function of any social welfare system is to provide for those who, temporarily or permanently, lack sufficient income to meet their basic needs.

This chapter examines public-governmental income maintenance services, the core response made by the social welfare system in the United States to persons unable to meet their own needs. Other social welfare responses designed for this purpose, such as private-charitable responses and in-kind income transfer programs, will be discussed throughout this text, as they affect particular populations or fields of practice. Emphasis is placed on developing an understanding of what constitutes the income maintenance system, its structure, including philosophies and values that have impacted its development, a brief overview of governmental income maintenance programs and services, and a look at current issues, trends, and changes in this field of service delivery. The involvement of social work in income maintenance will also be examined from historical and contemporary perspectives.

What Is Income Maintenance?

The concept of *income maintenance* can be more easily understood by separating and studying the terms *income* and *maintenance* separately. In a monetary society like the United States, income, simply defined, means the amount of money necessary for people to purchase life-sustaining resources, material goods, or services. The term maintenance means to continue, hold, preserve, or perpetuate the existence of something at some level. Combining these two terms, a program of income maintenance is designed to keep income at a level that will at least provide people with needed resources to meet human needs, while controlling the extent and means of satisfying those needs.

The concept of helping people who cannot support themselves is a very old one, as we shall see later, but the government's institutionalized program of income maintenance is fairly new to the United States. The Social Security Act of 1935, with its subsequent amendments, most recently P.L. 100–485, The Family Support Act of 1988, is responsible for shaping current income maintenance programs. Prior to 1935, responses to persons lacking sufficient income to meet their needs consisted of a patchwork system of private charity and state and local poor law assistance. Income maintenance programs and services today are entitlement programs, in that they are guaranteed to those persons meeting eligibility requirements. The primary goal of income maintenance programs is to provide a safety net of resources for people with inadequate income, ensuring that they are able to live at a minimum level of subsistence and satisfaction (Brieland, Costin, and Atherton, 1980).

The Structure of Income Maintenance

How a society structures responses to people without adequate income is a direct reflection of its values and philosophies about the human condition (Dolgoff and Feldstein, 1984). A number of values and philosophies have shaped the structure and development of income maintenance programs over the years, some of which will be discussed here and later in this chapter. However, two major value perspectives, which are diametrically opposed to each other, have served as guiding forces in the development of the U.S. income maintenance structure. One value perspective stems from societal concern for human suffering and calls for mechanisms that provide fair and equitable means for the elimination of such suffering. This value perspective is a reflection of the American social value of democratic egalitarianism and of religious ethics, primarily charity values of Judaism and Christianity (Dolgoff and Feldstein, 1984). The charity and philanthropic movements of the late 1800s are examples of this, as are, to some degree, governmental responses, first the state poor laws, and then the Social Security Act of 1935.

The other value perspective influencing income maintenance structure is based on the view that poor, deprived, or disadvantaged people are somehow responsible for their conditions. Rather than viewing such persons as victims of societal social and economic conditions, they are blamed and held responsible for their status in life. This value perspective has several sources, including the notions of individual self-sufficiency, the Protestant work ethic, and a basic rudiment of capitalism, that is, to work for economic gain (Dobelstein, 1990).

These value perspectives undergird the basic goals of U.S. income maintenance programs, providing for those who cannot meet their needs (the humanitarian side), and maintaining the right to control the means and extent to which this occurs (the social control side).

Another way to analyze the structure of income maintenance is to examine the approaches a society uses to provide for unmet human needs. In U.S. society, several approaches have influenced the income maintenance response, although none has been totally adopted or accepted as a guiding principle.

Harold Wilensky and Charles LeBeaux (1958) have offered two approaches in their book *Industrial Society and Social Welfare*. The first is called the *residual approach*, whereby assistance should be offered only when the normal means by which people obtain income—for example, from the family or the workplace—becomes inadequate or nonexistent. In this view, society has only minimal and limited responsibility to provide income maintenance, and should do so only when the customary channels are blocked. When the usual income channels again become available, income maintenance would be withdrawn. One example of the residual approach is the case of factory workers who have been laid off. They might receive unemployment compensation and food stamps while not working. When they return to work, however, these income resources are withdrawn. In this case, the assistance is offered only for a limited time and is categorical in that the recipient must meet defined eligibility requirements.

The second view presented by Wilensky and LeBeaux is the *institutional approach*, whereby the provision of income maintenance is recognized as a legitimate first-line responsibility of a modern industrial nation. This view recognizes that unmet human needs exist as a consequence of living in any industrial society. Therefore, income maintenance is a permanent and necessary part of the social structure. Assistance is then based on universal, rather than categorical, need. Assistance for the elderly, who, because of their age and social status, are in considerable risk of lacking sufficient income, is an example of the institutional approach.

A third way to conceptualize societal responsibility for income maintenance is called the *developmental approach*, which starts from the position that most income maintenance programs and services have been developed to solve the problems of unmet human needs. Thus it is possible, and perhaps desirable, to use income maintenance to provide a better quality of life and to promote and enhance human development. A program based on this philosophy would be universal and would embrace human needs from a preventive and growth-potential perspective.

An example of this is allowances for children, in which families with young children receive assistance to ensure the appropriate and healthy growth and development of their children.

Similar to Wilensky and LeBeaux's approaches, Ashford (1987) suggests that there have been three predominant approaches that have influenced the development of the income maintenance response. The first of these approaches is based on industrialization and the needs of people who live in an industrial society, recognizing that some needs of people will go unmet in such a society. The second approach is based on the social theory, structural functionalism, which asserts that there is a need for balance in society and to maintain social control and order. Meeting people's unmet needs through the provision of welfare assistance programs is seen as a way of doing this. The third approach is more philosophical and contends that the meeting of people's needs is a societal obligation and a social right of people who live in that society.

More recently, Garvin and Tropman (1992) argue that income maintenance programs could be, and in some societies have been, structured around certain groups of people that government should assist. There are three choices: the all-people approach, in which whatever government does to assist people is done for all people (guaranteed annual income programs are an example of this); the some-people approach, in which only some people (those with special needs such as the disabled or elderly) would be assisted; and the poor-people approach, which argues that only poor or economically disadvantaged persons should receive assistance from the government. The structure of the current U.S. income maintenance programs and services is a compromise, containing something from all of these approaches.

Precursors of Income Maintenance Programs and Services

Formal types of income maintenance began to emerge by the eleventh century. (See Table 7–1 for a chronological history of income maintenance programs.) Feudalism, a complex social class and political system that existed from about the tenth to the sixteenth century, could perhaps be considered one of the earliest forms of income maintenance in Europe and England. Feudalism's economic underpinnings depended on serfs who were attached to the land and who supplied the ruling class with a stable labor force. Under the control of the lord of the estate, serfs essentially traded a large measure of their individual freedom for protection against sickness, unemployment, and old age (Trattner, 1989).

People who were not serfs and who lived in cities could look to the social, craft, and merchant guilds for help in time of need. These guilds not only helped their own members but also lent assistance to others. According to historian Walter Trattner, "they distributed corn and barley yearly, fed the needy on feast days, provided free lodgings for destitute travelers, and engaged in other kinds of intermittent and incidental help" (p. 4).

Two of the most vital sources of aid to the poor and needy were the medieval hospital and the church. Early hospitals were attached to monasteries and located along roadsides; they served a much wider function than they do today. Not only did they care for the sick but they "housed and cared for weary travelers, for orphans, the aged, and the destitute." The church's role was, of course, pivotal at this time to society's ability to care for the poor and needy. Trattner explains that, "The bishop in each diocese was charged with the duty of feeding and protecting the poor within his district. He was directed to divide the total revenue of the diocese,

TABLE 7–1   **Important Dates: Income Maintenance**

	British
1350–1530	A series of statutes known as the laborers' laws forced able-bodied people to work and provided relief assistance to the worthy poor, such as children, the aged, and the handicapped.
1536	The Act for the Punishment of Sturdy Beggars and Vagabonds imposed severe penalties for begging.
1601	The Elizabethan (English) Poor Law was enacted.
1621	The Act for Settlement was enacted.
	United States
Late 1600s–1840s	Initially, colonists dealt with human needs by mutual aid. Later, colonial poor laws became the response to human needs. Several religious groups and ethnic societies also provided charity to the poor. State poor laws replaced the colonial poor laws after the American Revolution.
1843	The New York Association for Improving Conditions of the Poor was founded.
1870s–1900	The Charity Organization Societies (COS) emerged.
1935	The Social Security Act was passed.
1956	Amendments to the Social Security Act added an income maintenance program for the physically and totally disabled.
1962	ADC was changed to AFDC; income maintenance and social services were separated.
1964	The Food Stamp Act was passed.
1969	The Family Assistance Plan (FAP) was established.
1972	Supplemental Security Income (SSI) was established.
1973	The Work Incentive Program (WIN) was established.
1977	The Jobs and Income Security Program (JISP) was established.
1988	Family Support Act was passed.

which came from the church tithe, and to distribute a fixed portion—from a third to a fourth—to those in need" (Trattner, 1989).

Throughout the fourteenth and fifteenth centuries, several factors and events began to erode these forms of income maintenance. The economic and political system of feudalism began to be replaced with a monetary economy. While rampant corruption and general decline weakened the role the church played in people's lives, civil forms of government began taking on more responsibility for organizing and protecting society. Natural disasters—most notably the bubonic plague (1334–1354) and several crop failures—further compounded the economic confusion and added greatly to people's insecurity and hardships. This period of social and economic upheaval "resulted in a tremendous increase in unemployment, poverty, vagabondage, begging, and thievery, especially in the growing commercial centers to which many of the needy gravitated" (Trattner, 1989, p. 6).

According to Trattner, "it was in this context that the modern institution of social welfare emerged" (p. 7). One of the first organized or governmental efforts to deal with these problems, and a forerunner of the 1601 English Poor Law, was the Statute of Laborers, actually a series of laws first passed in England in 1350. These laws were essentially aimed at getting able-bodied people to work and beggars off the streets, with restrictions placed on the granting of charitable aid to these people. By the early 1500s more laws had been enacted that made the practice of begging by any able-bodied person a punishable offense. The Act for the Punishment of Sturdy Vagabonds and Beggars was passed by Parliament in 1536. It imposed even greater penalties for begging by able-bodied people, but it also made public officials responsible for obtaining and distributing resources collected by various means to the needy. Public jobs were also made available, and later amendments imposed a system of compulsory taxation to support the relief efforts. This law further expanded the government's role in social welfare and reflects two values that have continually influenced the social welfare response: Society is responsible for helping people who are in distress and for providing social control and social order.

With the passage of time, it became evident that punishment was not an effective deterrent to poverty. While still feeling a need to maintain the social order, Parliament embarked upon a course of action designed to apply public resources to human needs. To keep social order, it imposed strict limitations on granting of assistance. Only certain categories of people were eligible for certain kinds of assistance. This action culminated in the passage of the Elizabethan Poor Law of 1601, commonly referred to as the English Poor Law. The able-bodied were given public jobs, or "outdoor relief," as it was called. ("Indoor relief," or assistance, was provided to the aged, sick, and handicapped in institutions.) Dependent children were either indentured (an arrangement by which a dependent child would be given to a family where he or she could learn a trade and become self-sufficient) or put into institutions (Trattner, 1989).

Vagrancy was controlled under the law by the concept of "settlement," whereby individuals could receive assistance only in the parish in which they were born. Settlement is the direct forerunner of modern-day residency requirements for eligibility for income maintenance assistance. Local control and responsibility were among the outstanding features of this law. With assistance from the churches and a system of local taxation, local government carried out the provisions of the law.

The English Poor Law of 1601 serves as the foundation of the U.S. system of social welfare and income maintenance. Its philosophies and practices, which were brought to the new land by those who colonized America in the 1600s, have heavily influenced the scope and direction of social welfare in the United States.

The American colonial response to human needs was based on mutual aid. It was expected that all colonists would work together for everyone's mutual benefit. Their religious beliefs supported this response, as they were mainly Protestants who believed strongly in the work ethic (Axinn and Levin, 1982).

As the population increased in the colonies, so did the human needs. One factor that contributed to this pressure was England's practice of sending people who were considered undesirable to the colonies. Some of these people were political enemies of the state; others were sick, old, or handicapped; still others had criminal records. The colonial government was faced with meeting the needs of these people as well as developing a mechanism that would maintain social order. As a result, poor laws began to be implemented that were patterned after the English Poor Laws (Trattner, 1989). Such features as indoor relief (institutional care) and outdoor relief (care in the community) began to emerge in the colonies. Compulsory taxation to fund the relief effort, as in England, was also a part of the colonial poor laws. Local communities were responsible for the administration of the laws. As this became increasingly difficult, the colonial treasury began the practice of reimbursing the local community for expenditures for providing relief. This practice is much like the modern-day practice of state aid (Trattner, 1989).

Although political, economic, and social discontent with England culminated in the American Revolution, the country's system of social welfare remained unchanged. Individual states, fearing the investment of too much power in the federal government, assumed responsibility for social welfare. They developed state poor laws based on the models of the colonial and English Poor Laws. This arrangement of "public welfare" relief remained virtually unchanged until 1935, except for the development of the private charity and philanthropy movement in the late 1800s.

From just before the American Revolution until the late 1800s, several religious organizations made relief or assistance available to the needy. These forerunners of the philanthropy movement included the Quakers, who first organized relief efforts in the late 1600s, and the Episcopal Charity Society of Boston. Other nonreligious organizations were involved in extending a helping hand to the poor during this period as well. Many were associated with nationality or ethnic groups. The Scots Charity Society, the German Society of New York, and the French Benevolent Society were all involved in the relief-granting efforts (Trattner, 1989).

During the 1800s economic and social philosophies that included different views about aiding poor people developed. Humanitarian values promoted assistance to the needy as a means of distributing society's benefits. In direct conflict with these values were those of Thomas Malthus, a clergyman and philosopher. In his *Essay on the Principle of Population*, Malthus argued that the poor laws caused overpopulation by allowing dependent people to continue to exist on public assistance. Adam Smith, David Ricardo, John Locke, and Thomas Locke all argued that the poor law system was not economically sound, as it interfered with the functioning of the market economy and was an unjust interference with the lives of those who held wealth. Charles Darwin's law of natural selection held that those who had wealth had proved their right to exist, whereas the poor had demonstrated their unworthiness. Darwin held that granting public assistance was contrary to the process of natural selection (Dolgoff and Feldstein, 1984).

These rather negative views, although they influenced public sentiment against what we now call income maintenance, never were completely accepted in U.S. society. Americans have always been concerned with the moral obligation to assist people in need and to eliminate human suffering. Nevertheless, the philosophy of laissez-faire economics, Social Darwinism, and the work ethic have continued to influence social welfare and income maintenance policy in U.S. society.

As noted in Chapter 1, permanent change in the structure of social welfare and income maintenance services occurred in 1935 with the passage of the Social Security Act. The Social Security Act changed the notion that the states should be solely responsible for providing income maintenance assistance. It moved the federal government into the public welfare arena in a partnership arrangement with the states. The programs created by the Social Security Act of 1935 form the core of the income maintenance response in the contemporary American social welfare system.

Current Income Maintenance Programs

Income maintenance programs are designed to distribute or transfer income to people whose income is insufficient to meet their needs. They are often referred to as *income transfers*; that is, income is transferred through taxes from the more affluent to recipients of income maintenance.

All levels of government—local, state, and federal—are involved in providing these programs. The involvement of each will be discussed separately, although it will soon be apparent that the interrelationship of the three levels of government is necessary and inherent in the U.S. social welfare system.

Local Income Maintenance Programs

The major local program of income maintenance assistance is what is known as *general assistance (GA)*. In some parts of the country it is called "poor relief." General assistance is noncategorical; to be eligible, people do not have to possess certain characteristics (e.g., age, marital status) or be in a certain life situation. The main eligibility requirements for general assistance are income deprivation and residency in a particular county or state.

Various modes of administration exist in these programs. Some are under city, county, or parish administration; others are state-regulated. Most, if not all, are funded by some form of local, county, or state tax revenues. Assistance comes in a variety of forms. In some programs, recipients receive a direct cash grant. In many other programs, assistance is given in kind by providing tangible resources such as food, clothing, shelter, funds to pay energy costs, and medical care. Another feature of general assistance programs is that often they require recipients to work off their assistance in public work projects or, in some cases, to pay back the assistance received. In some programs, liens are placed against the property of those who receive this type of assistance.

There are many criticisms of and problems associated with general assistance programs. One problem is that no guarantee is given to the recipients that the assistance they have received will be ongoing. Most general assistance programs are purposely designed to be temporary or to meet emergency needs. If the need is ongoing, recipients are forced to seek out and make application for more permanent assistance programs. This illustrates the fragmentation that exists in the system among the various levels of government in responding to human needs. A major criticism of general assistance programs is that they often have no formal written and common eligibility requirements, standards, or policies. Therefore local authorities have the discretion to either grant or deny assistance to applicants. Decisions are often made in accordance with locality-specific values and attitudes toward particular cultural, ethnic, racial, or other diverse groups, opening the door for discrimination toward particular applicants. For instance, African Americans in southern states sometimes experience this, or the homeless transient, because he or she is not known by the local authorities, may be denied assistance.

Another criticism is that these programs are often administered by people who do not have adequate qualifications, many lacking training in social work or other helping professions. On the positive side, general assistance programs do make available more immediate access to assistance for people, not characteristic of the more permanent programs that may have more time-consuming application and processing procedures.

Federal and State Income Maintenance Programs

Several income maintenance programs or public assistance programs came into existence with the Social Security Act of 1935. They were originally created as a societal safety net, to ensure a basic subsistence level for families and individuals not covered under two other provisions of the act, unemployment compensation and insurance for the aged. These programs were implemented as *grants-in-aid* programs—that is, a partnership relationship between the states and the federal government. The programs were to be administered by the states, subject to federal regulation and policy, with funding provided on a matching basis from both the states and the federal government.

Three original income maintenance programs were created:

1. *Aid to Dependent Children (ADC):* cash assistance provided to children in families that become dependent and deprived of income resources, due to parental absence through separation, divorce, or death.
2. *Old Age Assistance (OAA):* cash assistance to poor people sixty-five years of age or older who are not covered by Social Security benefits. The creators of the Social Security Act realized that many older Americans would not be covered under the provisions of the social insurance for the aged program. Old Age Assistance was created to bridge that gap.
3. *Aid to the Blind (AB):* cash assistance to blind people, who qualified under income eligibility criteria.

For this family, income maintenance services are a necessary resource if they are to provide for their children's needs.

In 1956, the Social Security Act was amended and expanded to add the program Aid to the Permanently and Totally Disabled (APTD). Of these programs, only Aid to Dependent Children, now known as *Aid to Families with Dependent Children* (*AFDC*), remains solely under the administration of the states. The others were combined in 1972 into a federally administered program called Supplemental Security Income, which will be discussed later in this chapter.

Aid to Families with Dependent Children

Since this program remains under state administration, no uniformity or consistency in its structure exists among the programs. In 1962, the original ADC program was restructured and renamed Aid to Families with Dependent Children. This change reflected a concern for the family and a perceived need to assist AFDC recipients to become more self-supporting through social services and employment services (Skidmore, Thackeray, and Farley, 1988).

Families who apply for AFDC must meet two main eligibility criteria. The first is verification that minor children (those under eighteen years of age and attending school) are deprived of parental support as a result of at least one parent's death, incapacitation, or absence through separation or divorce. The second criterion is income verification. A means test is used to determine financial eligibility. This test consists of determining total family need, depending on family size, including shelter (rent and utilities), using a predetermined formula that varies from state to state. Total family needs are then compared with family income resources, within defined limits, including salary, wages, savings accounts, and other liquid assets (such as stocks and bonds, cash-value life insurance, trust accounts, or any other source that can be readily converted to cash). If determined needs exceed financial resources, the family is then eligible for the program.

No single program of income maintenance assistance has been so widely criticized by the general public and policymakers as the AFDC program. Some of the criticism is valid, but some is based on myth. Among the valid criticisms is the fact that there is no uniformity to recipients' payments among the states. Southern states have traditionally provided exceedingly low payments. The state of Mississippi in 1993 provided an average monthly cash grant of only $120, whereas more populous eastern states provide the highest average monthly cash payments to AFDC families: In 1993 Massachusetts paid an average of $549 per month, and Connecticut averaged $560 per month (U.S. Bureau of the Census, 1995).

The lack of uniformity between states and regions of the country in recipients' monthly cash grants occurs because the individual states are given discretionary authority to determine the percent of actual recipient need that will be provided, based on a predetermined formula. For example, the formula includes a maximum amount for a personal allowance per family member, and for housing (rent and utilities). In some states, recipients receive the maximum amount in the formula (100% of pre-determined need), and in other states recipients receive only a percent of the maximum. Again locality-specific ethos and values may come into play in the decisions made about the percent of need that is provided in a particular state.

Several societal myths have brought this program under attack. Chief among them is the belief that AFDC encourages large family size because recipients, who are mainly women, have additional children so they can receive larger monthly incomes. There is no empirical evidence that suggests that this occurs. In fact recent research has shown the opposite: women welfare recipients have a lower fertility rate than women in the general population, and the longer a women stays on assistance, the less likely she will become pregnant and give birth (Rank, 1989).

According to Abramovitz and Davis (1992), single parent families receiving AFDC average only 1.8 children. Other studies show fertility rates not significantly affected by welfare receipt or benefits level (Wilson and Neckerman, 1986). Welfare recipients continue to be blamed for increased fertility even when research shows contrary evidence.

Another welfare myth is that AFDC recipients are able-bodied people who would rather live on welfare than work. Groskind (1991, 1994), in recent studies, reported that the public tends to hold this view more with respect to two-parent welfare families, where they evaluate the work status and motivation of the father in these families. When evaluating mother-only families, Groskind reported that public attitudes focus more on the characteristics of need when judging whether welfare assistance is deserved. He also notes that peoples' ideological biases and preferences play an important part in their beliefs, not necessarily factual evidence. Approximately 60 percent of all AFDC recipients are children. Only 40 percent are adults, many of whom are female single heads of household, who would rather not be on the program and would prefer to be self-sufficient. They are handicapped in their efforts by the need to care for small children, by long-term disabilities, by their lack of education and training, and by sexual discrimination in the employment marketplace (Skidmore, Thackeray, and Farley, 1988).

Some people believe that AFDC recipients are cheaters who have defrauded the government into providing them with assistance. But repeated studies have shown very little fraud among recipients. More significant are the errors made by program officials working within the massive bureaucratic structure; they are responsible for the fact that some ineligible families are on the program. Another myth is that most AFDC recipients are from minority groups. In fact, most AFDC recipients are white. Discrimination, however, does cause minorities to be over-represented in the AFDC programs.

Supplemental Security Income

Supplemental Security Income (SSI) is a major federally funded and administered income maintenance program. In 1971 the federal government, through an amendment to the Social Security Act, assumed responsibility for cash assistance to the aged and to any blind or disabled person of any age. SSI "federalized" the categorical assistance programs the states had been providing under earlier provisions of the Social Security Act. The program is administered by the Social Security Administration and is funded out of general tax revenues, with additional supplements from states that offer them. Financial eligibility for the program is determined by a means test for income. Eligibility for blind and disabled persons may require additional medical documentation of the extent of disability. About six million persons received SSI in 1993 (U.S. Bureau of the Census, 1995).

Although the SSI program has the advantage of more equitable treatment of recipients nationwide, through a federally guaranteed uniform level of payment, it also has some disadvantages:

1. Too much time is needed to determine eligibility and to process applications.
2. Even though income levels are federally guaranteed, these still may not meet the high costs of living in certain areas, particularly where the state does not provide supplemental assistance.
3. The separation of SSI from state administration has caused duplication of administration and has increased administrative costs because the states must still administer the AFDC program.

Although no income maintenance program has existed without some degree of opposition, the advantages of the SSI program outweigh its disadvantages. There is every indication that some changes will be made by the Clinton administration in these programs. One stated thrust will be to make programs for those who do temporary work with job preparatory and job supportive services built in to those programs.

Other Federal Programs

Pensions and other forms of relief-in-kind assistance to veterans of the armed services are provided by the Veterans Administration. Eligibility for a veteran's pension is based, in part, on the extent to which a person's disability is related to military service. As a result, there is less stigma associated with receiving a veteran's pension than with other forms of income maintenance.

The United States Bureau of Indian Affairs (BIA) administers income maintenance programs and other social and rehabilitative services for Native Americans residing in reservation areas. These programs are federally funded. The main program provided by the BIA is general assistance, which is temporary. Recipients are encouraged to apply for permanent programs such as AFDC or SSI. General assistance is provided only until the person becomes eligible for and begins to receive assistance from other programs.

Current income maintenance programs have both positive and negative aspects. On the positive side, these programs transfer income to people in need, while also providing social and economic stability within society. However, because the various programs were developed at different times, they have different objectives and divergent eligibility criteria and are administered by different government jurisdictions. They are inconsistent in their missions and do not form a well-integrated system. Many overlap in their coverage but at the same time exclude many people who are in need, creating gaps in coverage.

Food Assistance Programs

Food assistance programs are a cooperative effort by the states and the federal government. These programs are relief-in-kind rather than direct cash benefit programs. They also are more universal than categorical, with the primary eligibility criterion being low income.

The major food assistance is *food stamps*. In 1994, 27.5 million persons received food stamp assistance (U.S. Bureau of the Census, 1995). This program is administered by the states with assistance and matching funds from the U.S. Department of Agriculture (USDA). (Since the 1930s, the USDA has distributed surplus food to needy families.) In 1964 Congress passed the Food Stamp Act, which created food stamps, which low-income people can purchase for a portion of their face value and use to buy food items. Generally, the program has been quite successful and has, in many ways, achieved its aims. Like the other programs, however, it has had its share of problems. The primary problem is that policies and administrative procedures have constantly changed, causing confusion among recipients and a significant error rate in the program.

Federally aided school breakfast and lunch programs that help meet children's nutritional needs have been provided in some states. Other food assistance programs, such as Meals on Wheels for the elderly, are also being administered by private social agencies with assistance from state and federal government.

Work Experience Programs

Our society's ideology and the value it places on work have had an impact on every aspect of income maintenance programs in the United States. Because the value of work is so integral to the U.S. way of life, great efforts have been made in the structure of income maintenance to provide incentives for work.

Other work experience programs not specifically tied to income maintenance have come into existence over the years. The New Deal in the 1930s; the Manpower Development and Training program and the Office of Economic Opportunity programs of the 1960s; and the Public Service Employment (PSE), the Emergency Employment Act (EEA), and the Comprehensive Employment and Training Act (CETA), of the 1970s have all provided work experience to the unemployed poor.

A feature of the AFDC program was the *Work Incentive Program (WIN)*. The WIN program was designed to prepare or train AFDC recipients for employment or return to employment, by providing on-the-job training and support services like day care and other social services, so recipients eventually would become self-sufficient and no longer need public assistance. From its inception in 1973 until 1980, the federal government required that states participate and offer the WIN program. It was reduced in the early 1980s to an option for the states. The WIN program is an example of the continued influence of the work ethic in public welfare and income maintenance programs.

Another variation is the *Community Work Experience Program (CWEP)*, commonly known as *workfare*. Under the provisions of the Omnibus Budget Reconciliation Act passed by Congress in 1981, states were given the authority and flexibility to design their own work experience programs requiring AFDC recipients to work a predetermined number of hours per week in public or nonprofit organizations in return for receiving continued welfare assistance (Gueron, 1986).

Proponents of this program were of the opinion that work experience would help recipients become more self-sufficient by restoring personal confidence and self-pride. Critics of CWEP countered that the program lacked basic training experiences, was demeaning and dehumanizing, was rigidly controlled, and was devoid of necessary in-kind supports such as day-care assistance. Workfare programs began in several states as demonstration projects and have gradually become a permanent feature of AFDC programs in many states.

The success of CWEP on a national level is a subject for debate. The Manpower Research Demonstration Corporation (MRDC) completed a study, in 1982, to examine state efforts relative to CWEP. Several programs in large urban states (California, Maryland, and Illinois) and several rural states (Arkansas, Virginia, and West Virginia) were studied. Mixed conclusions were reported as to the success of these programs. MRDC reported that workfare programs should not be viewed as a cure-all to the problems of dependency on welfare programs. Other reforms must also occur, such as training and retraining programs, child support enforcement efforts, and job creation programs, before work experience–welfare programs become more politically acceptable and have success in reducing welfare dependency (Gueron, 1987).

Recent studies evaluating workfare programs have also yielded mixed conclusions. On the negative side, one study concluded that workfare programs, because they do not focus on major job creation, perpetuate conditions of subemployment for welfare recipients. It is argued that this intensifies rather than ameliorates the subsistence level living conditions of the poor. Similarly, another study evaluating workfare in Florida reported that over one-half of recipients who go off welfare after being placed in the workfare program go back on welfare within a short period of time. It is concluded that this is attributed to low pay in the workfare job and the lack of additional support services, such as child care, transportation, and job training (Sheak and Dabelko, 1991; Udesky, 1991).

Although much of the evaluation of workfare programs has been negative, other professionals have argued its merits. It is contended that workfare will ultimately lead to real life choices, freedom, and autonomy for welfare recipients by virtue of the job training they receive and the marketable job opportunities made available through workfare programs (Keleher, 1990). Despite its controversies, workfare seems destined to continue as another experiment that exemplifies the ongoing relationship between work and welfare in the U.S. social welfare system. The most recent work experience program is JOBS, the Job Opportunities and Basic Skills Training Program, created by P.L. 100–485, the Family Support Act of 1988. JOBS went into effect in 1990, with full implementation expected to be in place in 1992. JOBS replaced the former WIN Program in AFDC and CWEP (workfare). All nonexempt AFDC recipients to whom a state provides child care assistance must participate in JOBS. Exempt recipients are the same as in the WIN Program, with minor changes. Other AFDC recipients may volunteer to participate in JOBS with some restrictions. States must also require AFDC custodial parents under the age of 20 who have not completed high school to participate in high school, or equivalent education, regardless of the age of their children. In cases in which this type of education is deemed to be inappropriate, the participant may be required to participate in work or job training activity. All participant's life situations are to be assessed, and needed support services are to be provided or arranged for by the state.

Core services provided in the JOBS Program are educational (including high school or remedial education), job training skills, job readiness, job development and placement, and supportive services. States must also offer at least two of the following: job search, on the job training, work supplementation, and community work experience (CWEP).

Again, the basic thrust of JOBS is to reduce welfare dependency and to promote self-sufficiency for AFDC recipients (Harris, 1989). Because JOBS is relatively new, little evaluation of this program has occurred. However, two recent studies have reported that the states have encountered problems with its implementation. The major problems reported are state budget cutbacks and insufficient budgetary resources that have reduced the potential success of this program. One of these studies also reported that the jobs provided to participants in this program have not significantly reduced poverty and, consequently, dependency on welfare (Sherwood and Long, 1991; Sanger, 1990). As can been seen, work experience programs such as workfare and JOBS have become a permanent part of national assistance programs and many state programs, again calling attention to the strong influence of the work ethic on social welfare policy.

Alternatives to Income Maintenance—Welfare Reform

Alternatives to the current income maintenance programs have been a topic of discussion for both the general public and those who formulate social policy. Although many income maintenance programs are small, particularly local programs, many are not as keenly scrutinized by policymakers as are the larger programs, particularly AFDC (Wyers, 1988). Rapid social change, economic fluctuations, and continued debate concerning who should be helped at what level and at whose expense have pushed the nation toward welfare reform. Although there have been numerous welfare reform proposals, two are noteworthy. The first was the *Family Assistance Plan (FAP)*, introduced to Congress in 1969. This plan would have replaced the existing structure of income assistance with an entirely new plan under the complete control and administration of the federal government. This program's primary feature was that it would have provided a minimum guaranteed annual income to every U.S. household. In addition, the program would have provided incentives for working and penalties for not working. Unemployed persons in families of four or more would have received at least a minimum of $2,400 per year. Employed persons in families would have been guaranteed a minimum of $1,600, which would be allowed to rise to nearly $4,000 through earned wages before penalties would be imposed. Eventually the program was to be turned over to the states, in what was called the *New Federalism* (Doblestein, 1980; DiNitto, 1991). Proponents of this program saw it as a positive step toward improving the conditions of the poor. Critics of the proposal labeled it inadequate, costly, and a step in the direction of socialism. In the early 1970s, after much consideration in congressional committees, the proposal died for lack of support.

A second proposal for welfare reform was introduced in 1977. The Carter administration, on the basis of several months of study, determined that the existing income maintenance system was complicated, unfair, and inequitable. They responded by introducing to Congress the *Jobs and Income Security Program (JISP)*. Again, this program would have totally replaced the existing system. The main features of this plan were a jobs program for people capable of working but currently unemployed and income maintenance for individuals unable to work for specified reasons. Under the plan, unemployed people would have been placed in jobs in the private sector of the economy and earned at least the minimum wage guaranteed by law. They also would have received generous earned-income tax credits that in theory would have increased their gross income. For people unable to work because of parental responsibilities, disability, or age, a generous income maintenance was proposed. Under this plan, each household was guaranteed an adequate level of income. Families of four would have received $4,200 per year, aged couples $3,750 a year, and single persons at least $2,500 per year. Incentives to work were also provided that allowed for a substantial increase of income without penalty. The major drawback to this proposal was that it would have been far more costly than the existing system. Although congressional reaction to the JISP was favorable, Congress adjourned without taking action on it.

At the beginning of the 1980s, discontent with the existing social welfare and income maintenance structure, which had been festering for some time, surfaced again. In 1980 a trend toward political, economic, and social conservatism also emerged. A number of alternative proposals that would drastically change the existing system were generated. These proposals were supported by a number of economic issues. Enormous federal budget deficits have forced Congress to rethink the federal government's spending levels in many areas. Actions were taken to reduce government expenditures, with the belief that this would reduce inflation and consequently stimulate the economy so that incentives would be created for increased production, leading to a rise in personal income resources (Trattner, 1989). One target for reduction of government expenditures was social welfare and income maintenance. A laissez-faire attitude toward the role of the federal government in this area returned. It was based on the belief that expenditures for social welfare undermined the natural functioning of the economy. The residual approach discussed earlier supported this view: Government's role was to create a safety net of income maintenance for the "truly needy." But this view naively asserted that someone can determine who the truly needy are. In fact, "truly needy" has never been adequately defined. What happened was that a plan of action was set in motion, with congressional support, to eliminate or drastically cut federal expenditures in the basic income maintenance programs such as AFDC, SSI, food stamps, and Medicare.

The use of the term New Federalism, coined by the Nixon administration, emerged again within welfare reform proposals. It was strongly felt that responsibility for social welfare ought to be transferred back to the states. In this vein, Congress proposed to "federalize" Medicaid and transfer total responsibility for the AFDC program to the states. The resultant gains and losses of such a plan were reviewed by Congress and the governors of the individual states, and it was determined to be inequitable and unworkable. However, political support within Congress did allow some cuts and changes in the structure of income maintenance and social service programs. In addition, cuts were made in unemployment insurance, employment, and child nutrition programs, although the cuts were not as deep as originally anticipated.

Experiments and demonstration projects in welfare reform also began to occur in several states in the early 1980s. A number of states implemented reforms in welfare programs, which mostly took the form of work experience programs such as community work experience programs (CWEP). Other states, such as Wisconsin, targeted welfare reform measures at certain categories of recipients, for example, older children in AFDC households, tying ongoing eligibility for assistance to school attendance—the so-called "schoolfare," or "learnfare" programs. All of this activity provided the impetus for renewed national interest in welfare reform designed to overhaul the existing system. In 1986 a bipartisan effort, spearheaded by Senator Daniel Patrick Moynihan, resulted in the passage by Congress of Public Law 100–485, the Family Support Act of 1988. The stated purpose of this law is to "revise the AFDC program to emphasize work, child support, and family benefits to amend Title IV of the Social Security Act to encourage and assist needy children and parents under a new program to obtain education, training, and employment needed to avoid long-term welfare dependence, and make other necessary improvements to assure the new program will be more effective in achieving its objectives" (U.S. Congress, 1988).

The major provisions of this act include improved procedures for child support enforcement and establishment of paternity, a job opportunity and basic skills training program, supportive services for families such as child care and medical assistance, benefits for two-parent families, periodic evaluation of need and payment standards, early-childhood development programs, and counseling and services for high-risk teenagers. Work experience, job training and employment finding, and supportive services to families are the strongest features of this act.

Although the entire law did not go into effect until 1994, many of its provisions had already been implemented. The positive or negative effects of the act have been a subject of considerable debate recently. Although we do not wish this section of this chapter to be another forum that continues this debate, we feel obligated to discuss at least two salient issues that appear to be at the heart of the controversy surrounding the nation's newest experiment in welfare reform.

An important issue is reflected in this question: How much change has been or will be brought about in the AFDC program as a result of the Family Support Act? Because of ongoing interest in welfare reform and because the two previous reform proposals during the last two decades were legislatively discarded, the passage of the Family Support Act was initially heralded as landmark legislation that would provide widesweeping and significant changes designed to address the problem of poverty and reduce welfare dependency (Reischchauer, 1989). Some policy analysts are less than enthusiastic about the changes, contending that they are modest at best and represent shifts in policy emphasis and direction rather than being real changes in program benefits and services that will aid in achieving the above-mentioned goals. Similarly, others suggest that the changes did not go far enough, and that other social welfare issues need to be addressed (Karger and Stoesz, 1990a). Some of the programs and policy revisions of the Family Support Act expired in 1994, thus the question became: What then? A second salient issue is, what is the real focus of this reform? Is it truly to address poverty, by providing assistance and services that will lift recipients out of a poverty lifestyle? Or is the real focus to reduce welfare dependency? Some argue that it is the latter and are quick to point out that the problem of poverty cannot be solved with a welfare reform approach. What must occur instead is a nonwelfare solution such as redistribution of income. Further support for the contention that the real focus is reducing welfare dependency is the fact that most of the programs and services provided in the Family Support Act are available only to current recipients of AFDC. The only more universal service available to non-AFDC families is child support enforcement. Consequently, it is argued that, as an anti-poverty program, it falls short because it does not address the needs and problems of the working poor and other nonwelfare, low-income persons and families. It is also contended that if the real focus was to address poverty, guaranteed minimum income would be provided to recipients. This was provided for in the original legislation but, through committee amendment, was taken out of the final version of the Act as passed by Congress. The approach seems to be instead to reduce welfare dependency through work experience programs (Peterson and Rom, 1990; Abramovitz, 1989). The passage of the Family Support Act, despite what is contended by its critics, is significant because it has "broken the deadlock" in welfare reform and laid the groundwork for possible reform in the future.

The details of the welfare reform to be proposed by the Clinton administration are as yet unknown. That there will be reform is certain. Whether it will build on the Family Support Act or introduce a new initiative remains to be seen. However, it can be assumed that efforts will be made to move families to self support within a two-year period of time.

Housing Problems, Programs, and Services

Housing programs and services are not ordinarily considered as income maintenance services. They are discussed in this chapter because we believe there is a relationship between inadequate income, poverty, and housing problems, to which income maintenance services should be designed to respond.

The lack of safe, affordable housing, caused by the absence of a national policy to assist low-income families with their housing needs, and by a rapid rise in housing costs throughout the 1980s, has had a negative impact on these families. As a consequence of this situation, families are doubling and tripling up, creating crowded, unsafe housing conditions. Other families are forced to live in substandard housing, or to rely heavily on social welfare programs to meet housing needs.

The most visible housing problem in the United States today is *homelessness*. Many factors contribute to the problem of homelessness. Among them are mental illness, deinstitutionalization, substance abuse, and family violence (American Public Welfare Association, 1989). However, homelessness should no longer be thought of as a problem confined to skid-row alcoholics or deinstitutionalized mental patients. Poor families, many headed by single parents who cannot afford decent housing; the working poor; and the aged are now among the ranks of the homeless, many for the first time in their lives. Aside from homelessness as experienced by many poor families, a more crucial problem facing these families is the lack of safe and affordable housing, combined with inadequate income resources to rent available decent housing. The American Public Welfare Association (1989) has identified the above as the two most critical factors causing housing problems for low-income families and has called for policy action to reduce the number of families living in poverty and to increase the availability of affordable housing. The affordability of housing for poor families has reached almost crisis proportions in recent years. The poor seem to be losing ground and appear to be getting poorer. Since 1975, the number of families with real incomes of less than $10,000 per year has increased by 26.32% (U.S. Bureau of the Census, 1995). These families must rely heavily on income maintenance assistance to meet their housing needs. The problem is that the cost of decent housing generally exceeds the amount of the housing allowance provided in the monthly assistance grant. This forces recipients, if they choose, to spend a larger proportion of their assistance grant on housing. The standard for affordability of housing, set by the U.S. Department of Housing and Urban Development, is that no more than 25 to 30 percent of income should be spent for housing. More than one-half of all low-income families spend substantially more of their income for housing than this, which causes a reliance on other emergency assistance programs to meet their needs for food and other essentials (Gilbert and Gilbert, 1989).

The availability of affordable housing is also a strong contributor to the housing crisis for low-income families. According to Karger and Stoesz (1990b), four major issues are involved in the problem of availability: increases in the cost of rental units, increased utility costs, lack of moderate and low-priced housing, and lessened governmental support in housing services and programs.

The federal government has been involved in housing programs and services since the late 1930s, and today provides the major forms of housing assistance to poor families. One major form of assistance is public housing and the other is rent subsidies for poor families living in private sector housing units. Since the late 1980s there have been cutbacks in federal housing assistance programs, in rent subsidies, and particularly in the number of public housing units available for low-income families. The need for housing assistance continues to exceed the federal resources available.

According to the American Public Welfare Association (1989), this is not just a big city problem—small towns and rural areas also lack decent and affordable housing for the poor. Notwithstanding, if it were not for federal housing assistance and services, the problem of housing the poor in the United States could be far worse. However, we can and do need to do better. The social welfare system can no longer be the low-income housing agency of last resort for the poor. Deliberate changes must be made in housing policy, and funding for low-income housing programs must increase, or the crisis will become worse. It is hoped that the Clinton administration, as part of its welfare reform package, will seek to increase the amount of affordable housing for low-income families and individuals.

The Role of Social Work in Income Maintenance Services

Provision of financial assistance was motivated by humanitarian concern for human needs. One of the mechanisms developed to meet human needs in the United States at the turn of the century, the private charity movement, was responsible in part for the emergence of social work as a profession. The primary responsibility of the charity workers (later to be called social workers) was to assess the needs of the poor and provide financial assistance to them. As professional education evolved (1900–1950), many social workers were educated in the social casework method, which enabled them to better serve their clients. They were better prepared to assume positions not only in private relief-granting agencies, but also in the public welfare agencies that were created by the Social Security Act of 1935. A variety of roles were performed by professional social workers in these agencies, including child welfare workers and caseworkers in public assistance, now called income maintenance. Some schools of social work throughout the 1930s, 1940s, and 1950s focused on educating social workers for employment in the public welfare field (Weissman and Baker, 1959).

Although social work continued to evolve and move into other areas of need, it has remained involved in public welfare. Today, large numbers of social workers are employed in public social agencies or have been at one time. But direct involvement by professionally educated social workers in income maintenance services has declined over the years, particularly since the 1970s, when income maintenance was separated from social and rehabilitative services in public welfare agencies. Prior to this time, workers involved with income maintenance recipients were also offering social services that assisted in solving problems associated with economic needs. Many people needed income maintenance as a result of social or psychological problems that interfered with their attempts to be self-supporting. Social work placed an emphasis on utilizing the knowledge and skills of professionally educated workers who could interact effectively with recipients, with the goal of reducing or eliminating their need for economic assistance. This model of service to public assistance recipients was created through the 1962 amendments to the Social Security Act, which required that recipients of AFDC be offered a broad array of social services in addition to income maintenance. In the 1970s, people in the system started to realize that this pattern of service delivery had not achieved the desired results. Some believed that services should not be imposed on income maintenance recipients. Consequently, income maintenance and social services are officially separated in public social agencies today. Many professionally educated social workers, as a result of this separation, became involved in social service delivery in the public agencies and are no longer involved in income maintenance services. Some professional social workers, usually M.S.W.'s, remain in income maintenance services, mostly as administrators, supervisors, researchers, and program planners (Ginsberg, 1983).

In recent years, some B.S.W.'s have begun to assume direct-service positions in income maintenance services. Wyers (1981) reported that over one-half of the administrators surveyed would prefer to have direct service positions in income maintenance filled by baccalaureate-level social workers. The administrators feel that many recipients do indeed have additional needs, and that professional knowledge and skills are needed by direct service workers to establish the relationship with clients, discern both their economic and social needs, and link them with appropriate social services. The need for staff with such qualifications is even more important today, due to the newly created support service programs mandated by the Family Support Act, and it will likely create new roles within income maintenance services for the B.S.W. Below is a case example that illustrates direct service roles performed by a B.S.W. employed in income maintenance.

Social work has also done much to improve public social welfare policy affecting the delivery of income maintenance services. Much of this has been done through the work of pro-

A Case Study

Pamela M, a twenty-two-year-old woman with two preschool-age children, recently separated from her husband, came into the agency to apply for Aid to Families with Dependent Children (AFDC). Her case was assigned to Mr. B, a B.S.W. social worker employed as an economic assistance caseworker. During her initial interview with Mr. B, he assisted Pamela in completing the necessary AFDC eligibility applications and determined that she was eligible. In discussing her situation and her need for AFDC, Mr. B learned that Pamela's husband had abandoned the family, leaving them without economic support. Pamela seemed to be distraught and stated that the family had been having difficulties, including some abuse of her and the children by the husband. One of the children had a genetic disorder and special medical needs. She had no friends or extended family on whom she could call for assistance or support. In addition, Mr. B learned that although Pamela had a high school education, she had no particular employment or vocational skills. Because she had been left totally

responsible for the care of the children, she said she felt overwhelmed, was beginning to lose her temper with them, and was afraid she might abuse them. She also stated she had been thinking about having the children placed in foster care or possibly giving them up for adoption.

Using the knowledge and skills he had received in his professional education, Mr. B assessed Pamela's situation and concluded that she was experiencing problems that would certainly require additional social services in addition to AFDC. He referred her to the county general assistance office and explained that they would help her with her immediate financial needs until her AFDC check arrived. He made an appointment for her to apply for food stamps. He asked the community's Easter Seal Society about assistance for the child with special medical problems. He also referred her to the family services unit of the agency so that a family service social worker could help her sort out her feelings about her children and lend support during her upcoming divorce.

fessional organizations such as the National Association of Social Workers (NASW), and the American Public Welfare Association (APWA). These organizations, whose membership consists largely of social workers, have advocated, endorsed, and supported increases in AFDC and SSI assistance grants to ensure an adequate standard of living for recipients; welfare reform proposals such as Family Support Act national health insurance, and other programs that would provide additional income to those in need; and plans that would allow humane, dignified delivery of the economic assistance programs.

Summary

The provision of income maintenance services has been influenced by more than one predominant philosophy. Three often conflicting philosophies are humanitarian concerns, societal responsibility for meeting human needs, and self-responsibility and the work ethic.

Income maintenance programs have always been structured so as to meet the needs of people who cannot meet their own needs. However, another function has been to control the level of assistance provided, thereby limiting the extent to which needs can be met in this way. With the passage of the Social Security Act of 1935, the current income maintenance system was created. Although this system has provided a safety net and ensured that those who cannot support themselves live at a minimal level of subsistence, some human needs have still gone unmet.

Income maintenance, in our view, is a legitimate field of social work practice, and social workers should not only be involved in direct service roles in this crucial area of human services, but should also advocate for the creation of a sound national policy and effective benefits and services in income maintenance that ensure the meeting of human needs.

Key Terms

Aid to Families with Dependent Children (AFDC)
Community Work Experience Program (CWEP)
developmental approach
Family Assistance Plan (FAP)
Family Assistance Support Act
food stamps
general assistance (GA)
grants-in-aid
Guaranteed Income Programs
homelessness
income maintenance

income transfers
institutional approach
Jobs and Income Security Program (JISP)
Job Opportunities and Basic Skills Training Program (JOBS)
New Federalism
residual approach
Supplemental Security Income (SSI)
welfare reform
workfare
Work Incentive Program (WIN)

References

Abramovitz, M. (1989). Why welfare reform is a sham. In R. E. Long (Ed.), *The welfare debate.* New York: The H. W. Wilson Company, pp. 69–75.

Abramovitz, M., & Davis, M. (1992). "Wedfare"—or welfare? *Washington Post Weekly,*.February 10–16.

American Public Welfare Association (1989). Housing the poor: a policy statement. *Public Welfare, 47* (1), 5–12.

Ashford, D. (1987). *The emergence of the welfare states.* New York: Blackwell.

Axinn, J., & Levin, H. (1982). *Social welfare: a history of the American response to need.* New York: Harper & Row.

Brieland, D., Costin, L., & Atherton, C. (1980). *Contemporary social work: an introduction to social work and social welfare.* New York: McGraw-Hill.

Compton, B., & Galaway, B. (1984). *Social work processes.* Homewood, IL: Dorsey Press.

DiNitto, D. M. (1991). *Social welfare: politics and public policy* (3rd ed.). Englewood Cliffs, NJ: Prentice Hall.

Dobelstein, A. (1980). *Politics, economics, and public welfare.* Englewood Cliffs, NJ: Prentice-Hall.

Dobelstein, A. (1990). *Social welfare policy and analysis.* Chicago: Nelson-Hall.

Dolgoff, R., & Feldstein, D. (1984). *Understanding social welfare.* New York: Longman.

Garvin, C. D., & Tropman, J. E. (1992). *Social work in contemporary society.* Englewood Cliffs: Prentice Hall Inc.

Gilbert, N., & Gilbert, B. (1989). *The enabling state: modern welfare capitalism in America.* New York: Oxford University Press.

Ginsberg, L. H. (1983). *The practice of social work in public welfare.* New York: Free Press.

Groskind, F. (1991). Public reactions to poor families: characteristics that influence attitudes towards assistance. *Social Work, 36* (5), 446–453.

Groskind, F. (1994). Ideological influences on public support for assistance to poor families. *Social Work, 39* (1), 81–89.

Gueron, J. M. (1986). Work for people on welfare. *Public Welfare, 44* (1), 7.

Gueron, J. M. (1987). Reforming welfare with work. *Public Welfare, 45* (4), 25.

Harris, S. (1989). *A social workers guide to the family support act of 1988: summary, analysis and opportunities for implementation.* Silver Spring, MD: National Association of Social Workers.

Karger, H. J., & Stoesz, D. (1990a). Welfare reform: from illusion to reality. *Social Work, 35* (2), 141–147.

Karger, H. J., & Stoesz, D. (1990b). *American social welfare policy.* New York: Longman.

Keleher, P. J. (1990). Workfare: servitude or success formula. *Employee-Responsibility-and Rights Journal, 3* (2), 87–124.

Macarov, D. (1978). *The design of social welfare.* New York: Holt, Rinehart and Winston.

Peterson, P. E., & Rom, M. C. (1990). *Welfare magnets: a new case for a national standard.* Washington, D.C.: The Brookings Institution.

Rank, M. R. (1989). Fertility among women on welfare: incidence and determinants. *American Sociological Review, 54* (2), 296–304.

Reishchauer. R. D. (1989). The welfare reform legislation: directions for the future. In P. H. Cottingham & D. T. Ellwood (Eds.), *Welfare policy for the 1990's* (p. 11). Cambridge, MA: Harvard University Press.

Sanger, M. B. (1990). The inherent contradiction of welfare reform. *Policy Studies Journal, 18* (3), 663–680.

Sheak, R., & Dabelko, D. D. (1991). Conservative welfare reform proposals and the reality of subemployment. *Journal of Sociology and Social Welfare, 18* (1), 49–70.

Sherwood, K. E., & Long, D. A. (1991). JOBS: implementation in an uncertain environment. *Public Welfare, 49* (1), 17–27.

Skidmore, R. A., Thackeray, M. G., & Farley, W. (1988). *Introduction to social work.* Englewood Cliffs, NJ: Prentice-Hall.

Trattner, W. I. (1989). *From poor law to welfare state: a history of social welfare in America.* New York: The Free Press.

Udesky, L. (1991). The numbers game: shuttled into dead-end jobs, women forced to participate in the Florida workfare program wind up back on welfare. *Southern Exposure, 19* (2), 14–18.

U.S. Bureau of the Census (1995). *Statistical Abstract of the United States: 1995* (115 th ed.). Washington, DC: U.S. Government Printing Office.

U. S. Congress (1988). *Public Law 100–485: The family support act of 1988.* Congressional Record, October 13,1988.

Weissman, I., & Baker, M. R. (1959). *Education for social workers in the public social services.* New York: Council on Social Work Education.

Wilensky, H., & LeBeaux, C. (1958). *Industrial society and social welfare.* New York: Free Press.

Wilson, W. J., & Neckerman, K. M. (1986). Poverty and family structure: the widening gap between evidence and public policy issues. In S. H. Danziger & D. H. Weinberg (Eds.), *Fighting poverty: what works and what doesn't.* Cambridge, MA: Harvard University Press, pp. 232–259.

Wyers, N. L. (1981). Income maintenance revisited: functions, skills, and boundaries. *Administration in Social Work, 5* (Summer), 20.

Wyers, N. L. (1988). Income maintenance system. In A. Minahan (Ed.), *Encyclopedia of social work* (18th ed.) Silver Springs, MD: National Association of Social Workers, pp. 888–898.

Suggested Readings

Colby, Ira C. *Social Welfare Policy: Perspectives, Patterns, Insights* (Chicago: Dorsey Press, 1989).

Cottingham, Phoebe H. and Ellwood, David T. *Welfare Policy for the 1990's* (Cambridge, MA: Harvard Univ. Press, 1989).

Day, Phyllis J. *A New History of Social Welfare* (Englewood Cliffs, NJ: Prentice-Hall, 1989).

Dobelstein, Andrew W. *Social Welfare: Policy and Analysis* (Chicago, IL: Nelson-Hall Pub, 1990).

Harris, Sunny. *A Social Workers Guide to the Family Support Act of 1988* (Silver Spring, MD: National Association of Social Workers, 1989).

Hefferan, Joseph; Shuttlesworth, Guy; and Ambrosino,

Rosalie. *Social Work and Social Welfare: An Introduction* (New York: West, 1988).

Karger, Howard and Stoesz, David. *American Social Welfare Policy: A Structural Approach* (New York: Longman, 1990).

Long, Robert E., (Ed.) *The Welfare Debate* (New York: H. W. Wilson, Co., 1989).

Peterson, Paul E. and Rom, Mark C. *Welfare Magnets: A New Case for a National Standard* (Washington, DC: The Brookings Institution, 1990).

Trattner, Walter I. *From Poor Law to Welfare State: A History of Social Welfare in America*, 4th ed. (New York: The Free Press, 1989).

8

CHILD WELFARE SERVICES

Learning Expectations

- Ability to define child welfare services and specify which services are usually considered components of the field
- Knowledge of the historical development of the child welfare field of practice
- Awareness of current concerns and problems within the child welfare field
- Understanding of the various manifestations of child abuse and incidence, cause, and response regarding each kind of abuse
- Knowledge of in-home services provided for children
- Knowledge of substitute care services provided to children

Statements such as "the future of America lies in its young," and "children are America's most precious resource," attest to the strong value our society places on children. The well-being of children is a source of social concern; the protection and care of children is one of the oldest forms of charity. In today's world, the social welfare arrangements that respond to children's needs are organized under the broad term *child welfare services*. This encompasses the programs and services provided both by public social service agencies and by private and voluntary service agencies.

Child welfare, like social welfare, is a broad concept and can be defined in broad terms. Two definitions are provided here to demonstrate this breadth. Child welfare is a "series of activities and programs through which society expresses its special concern for children and its willingness to assume responsibility for some children until they are able to care for themselves" (Juvenile Rights Project, 1977). Child welfare is further broadly defined as "whatever is considered essential for the child to develop fully and to function effectively in society" (Child Welfare League of America, 1971). Child welfare can also be defined narrowly. Much of the focus in child welfare services has been on the needs of children and families when family functioning, particularly parental functioning, has broken down, or when children's developmental, emotional, or behavioral functioning has made it impossible for them to remain within the family setting (Cohen, 1992). This definition narrows the perspective on child welfare by considering the relationship between family functioning and the well-being of children. It has been suggested that the key to maintaining the well-being of children is to support and strengthen the family. In recent times the social welfare delivery system and the profession of social work have begun to recognize the importance of the family for the child. Child welfare, then, is our society's way of expressing the high value it places on the well-being of its children.

The Scope of Child Welfare Services

The child welfare service system has traditionally provided two broad areas of service. First, it has provided services to ensure the child's maintenance within the family setting. Second, it has provided services to children who are unable to remain in their own homes. Services in the first area include day-care services, homemaker services, protective services, health services, nutrition services, economic assistance, mental health services, family preservation services, educational services, and services to adolescent parents. Services in the second area include foster family care, institutional care, group homes, and adoption services. These two service areas have become linked together in a service delivery network or system. The system engages in service activities designed to prevent, deal with the consequences of, or otherwise provide solutions to problems potentially jeopardizing the welfare of children. In recent years much effort has gone into developing and providing services to children in their natural homes, as is consistent with the recently renewed interest in and value placed on preserving families and providing permanency for children. When this is not possible, children have been provided with a permanent family arrangement, such as placement with relatives or adoption.

The Historical Development of Services to Children

The emergence of services to children in the United States can be traced to colonial times (see Table 8–1 for a chronological list). The development of formal social welfare arrangements and services to children have taken many forms since then, each influenced by the economic climate of the times, and by ongoing social movements and social change. To attempt to understand today's structure and systems of services to children, it is necessary to understand the events and trends from the past that have shaped its development.

Colonial Times to 1880: Mutual Aid and Poor Law Arrangements

The early colonists, inspired by the sense of freedom gained by being in a new land, emphasized self-sufficiency. Families were the basic social and economic unit in colonial society. Children were afforded no special status or role within the family as they are today. Like all

TABLE 8-1   Important Dates: Child Welfare Services

1727	The Ursuline Convent, the first established orphanage in the United States, was founded.
1853	The New York Children's Aid Society was formed.
1874	The New York Society for the Prevention of Cruelty to Children was founded.
1909	The first White House Conference on Children was held.
1912	The U.S. Children's Bureau was formed.
1920	The Child Welfare League of America (CWLA) was founded.
1921	The Sheppard-Towner Act was passed.
1972	The *Stanley* v. *Illinois Supreme Court* decision was handed down.
1974	The Child Abuse and Neglect Treatment Act
1975	The Title XX amendments to the Social Security Act were passed by Congress. Also, Public Law (P.L.) 94-142, the Education of all Handicapped Children Act, was passed.
1978	The Indian Child Welfare Act (P.L. 95-608) was passed.
1980	The Adoptions Assistance and Child Welfare Reform Act (P.L. 96-272) was passed.
1981	The Omnibus Budget Reconciliation Act reorganized some Title XX services for children.
1986	P.L. 94-142 was amended by P.L. 99-457.
1988	The Family Support Act (P.L. 100-485) and The Child Abuse Prevention, Adoption, and Family Services Act were passed.
1990	P.L. 101-496, The Developmental Disabilities Assistance and Bill of Rights Act, was passed.

members of the family, they were expected to contribute to everyone's maintenance and well-being. Children's individual needs were superseded by family needs. When problems arose that overwhelmed the family's abilities to solve them, mutual aid was the mechanism for assistance. Formal social welfare structures were nonexistent. Colonists were expected to have a sense of duty, to lend a hand, to assist others in the struggle for survival. As the population grew, however, mutual aid became impractical in some situations and was supplemented by formal means influenced by the English Poor Laws.

The harsh and bitter realities of daily living in the colonies resulted in high infant and adult mortality rates. As a result, many children became orphaned and dependent. Colonial officials became concerned about the children from poor, dependent families—the "children of paupers," as they were called. They feared that these children were inevitably destined to a life of pauperism if they were not taught to become self-sufficient (McGowan and Meezan, 1983). Thus, dependent and orphaned children were cared for within the traditions of the poor laws. Several measures of care were employed. Some children were maintained within their own families through provision of outdoor relief—that is, assistance provided directly to the family. Some families and children were actually auctioned off to individuals or families who had agreed to care for them.

One common practice was to apprentice children to families in which they could be taught a trade or skill and thus become self-sufficient. The practice of *apprenticeship* reflected the belief that all individuals should be a part of a family. On a more practical level, it provided a useful way to control and discipline children, reduce unemployment, provide skilled workers to meet the needs of the growing colonies, and to relieve public officials of the responsibility of caring for needy children directly. Other children were placed in the care of relatives. Many other families and children were placed in almshouses by the authorities. Some religious groups cared for children within their group by placing them with members of that faith in either institutions or private homes. During this period, a few special institutions were created for the care of orphaned or dependent children via institutional care arrangements. These *orphanages* were homes that provided care for children whose parents had died or abandoned them. The Ursuline Convent, established in New Orleans in 1727, was the first formally established orphanage in the United States. After the American Revolution, the same patterns of care for children continued virtually unchanged until recent years. Emphasis was placed on low-cost care and on teaching the virtues of industry and self-sufficiency.

Social change in the latter part of the 1800s fostered the development of formal structures in social welfare, including the care of dependent children. Although earlier patterns of response to children's needs continued, some changes occurred that shaped the direction for the future.

One of the most striking changes was the creation of special child-care institutions for dependent and truly orphaned children, under the auspices of the states and private and religious organizations. The impetus for their creation came from a reaction to the evils of almshouses. Children placed in almshouses received no special care and were treated no differently than the adults placed there. Society began to worry about the effects of placing children in institutions with sick, physically disabled, mentally retarded, mentally ill, delinquent, or criminal adults. Conditions were deplorable. Treatment was often harsh and brutal. As a result, dependent and orphaned children began to be placed in orphanages rather than almshouses. Since economic factors were uppermost in the minds of public officials, change was slow to come. It was cheaper and more economically efficient to invest public funds in almshouses rather than to subsidize child care in private institutions. Toward the end of the nineteenth century several states passed laws prohibiting the placement of children in almshouses. Other practices, such as apprenticeship and indenturing, also came under a great deal of attack. *Indenturing* was beginning to be considered a form of slavery. This had become a sensitive issue in the aftermath of the U.S. Civil War.

Private Charity-Philanthropy Arrangements, 1850–1900

Concern over these issues created a climate for additional reforms in formal child welfare structures. The first of these reforms was the emergence of *Children's Aid Societies*. These organizations were concerned with "child saving," rescuing children from the harsh realities of urban life and the insensitive practices of the public poor law system. In 1853 the New York Children's Aid Society was founded, primarily through the efforts of a young minister named Charles Loring Brace. Brace and his followers, though sensitive to the need of dependent children, were far more concerned with the protection of property and the city from what he considered the "dangerous classes, which included homeless and delinquent children." Although he created programs within the city for dependent youth, Brace's main priority was to remove dependent and orphaned children from the city. He rounded up children off the streets and sent them by train to family homes far away in rural areas of the West and Midwest in the belief that such children needed a family upbringing in a clean, moral home, away from the evils of city life. Over the next twenty-five years (1854–1880), the New York

Children's Aid Society placed more than fifty thousand children in such homes. This was heralded as a major innovation in the care of dependent children but also was criticized as nothing more than a form of indenturing. Another problem with Brace's program was that, in some instances, siblings were separated. Some families overworked these children, failed to educate them properly, abused them physically, and fed them poorly. Nevertheless, this program is considered to be the forerunner of the *foster care* service as we know it today (Costin, Bell, and Downs, 1991).

In the years that followed, Children's Aid Societies in other states developed similar practices, but much more care was taken in recruiting and selecting the family homes. Placements were also followed and reviewed periodically. In the beginning, the homes were free homes; families would take in children out of the goodness of their hearts. Gradually, public officials in several states began to place children in foster homes at public expense: Massachusetts in the late 1800s was one of the first states to pay foster parents for child care. This started a new era in child welfare and in some states replaced institutional care as the primary method of dealing with dependent children (McGowan and Meezan, 1983). Institutional care for children with special needs continued to be supplied by both public and private child-care organizations.

In the latter half of the nineteenth century, two additional formal structures for the care of children emerged. These were the Charity Organization Societies (COS) and the settlement houses. The COS indirectly contributed to children's well-being by focusing on their maintenance within the family. The friendly visitors of the COS understood well the effects of poverty on children. Casework services were designed to preserve the integrity of family life. Likewise, but through different approaches and means, some of the settlement workers' social reform efforts focused on child welfare issues (e.g., child labor legislation, the education of immigrant children, and the creation of the first juvenile court). The work of these two private charitable groups furthered the cause of protecting and caring for dependent children.

Toward the middle of the nineteenth century, the United States began to experience the effects of the Industrial Revolution, with its massive social changes. The family's functions as a social institution changed, and society began to assume some of the responsibilities for the socialization of children that families had held exclusively before. The passage of compulsory education laws is one example. With a new understanding of child development came the recognition that children had certain rights that parents were responsible for protecting. If these rights were not protected, states reserved the right to intervene on behalf of the child. States passed legislation providing for legal guardianship and adoption. This principle not only formed the foundation for the juvenile justice system, but was also applied to cases of child mistreatment. Reform in this area came first from the private sector, eventually spreading into the public sector. In 1874 the New York Society for the Prevention of Cruelty to Children was founded. Its purpose was to advocate on behalf of abused children, to ensure their ongoing protection from harm. Although its aims centered on prosecuting individuals suspected of child abuse and not on providing rehabilitative services, its work brought about a public awareness of the child abuse problem.

By the end of the 1800s, formal structures for child care had been created. Although these structures have changed substantially through the years, much remains that can be traced to the developments of this era. The changes of the 1800s were instrumental in preparing the way for innovations that followed.

Public Welfare and Social Services: 1900–1989

In 1909 the first White House Conference on Children was held, marking a shift in child welfare priorities, philosophies, and policies. The delegates to the conference went on record as promoting and supporting the principle that children need stable home environments. At all costs, resources and services should be directed toward maintaining them in their own homes. They recognized that children's basic needs usually could be met through the natural family—if adequate resources, supports, and services were provided. No longer should child welfare systems remove children from their homes solely on the basis of inadequate family income. These new philosophies recognized federal responsibility in this area. In 1912 Congress provided legislation to authorize the development of the *Children's Bureau*. Spearheading the effort to create the bureau were early social workers Jane Addams and Lillian Wald. Julia Lathrop was appointed as the first bureau chief. In the beginning, the Children's Bureau's activities were restricted to broad responsibilities, such as investigating and reporting all matters related to the well-being of all children, including economic, health, child placement, and labor concerns, as well as activities of the juvenile courts and state legislation affecting children (Parker and Carpenter, 1981).

In 1921 the efforts of the Children's Bureau were substantially bolstered by the passage of the *Sheppard-Towner Act*. This legislation gave the bureau the responsibility for administering a grants-in-aid program to the states for maternal and child health services. By 1929, when the program was discontinued, almost three thousand child and maternal health programs had been established in forty-five states, primarily in rural areas. The Children's Bureau, however, continued for many years to be the guiding force in the child welfare system. Its roles and missions have changed over the years, but it remains today as a separate office within the U.S. Department of Health and Human Services.

The Social Security Act of 1935 launched the federal government into a joint partnership with the states in responsibility for broad social welfare programs and services, such as the widows' pension or mothers' aid movement and, later, Aid to Families with Dependent Children (AFDC). In addition, the Social Security Act's social insurance program gradually came to provide benefits to survivors (widows and dependent children). In 1971 the Supplemental Security Income (SSI) program extended income maintenance assistance to families of permanently or totally disabled children. Other forms of federal financial and income maintenance assistance are provided through veterans' pensions. Native American children receive some aid through the U.S. Bureau of Indian Affairs.

The Social Security Act also made funds available on a grants-in-aid basis to the states to develop social and rehabilitative services. Beginning in the late 1930s, the states created child welfare programs within their public welfare agencies. Public welfare departments at first focused on traditional child welfare services, such as child protection, foster care, institutional care, and adoptions. In the 1960s, the Department of Health, Education, and Welfare mandated the separation of social and rehabilitative services that previously had been combined with income maintenance services. Child welfare services, which had always been a separate function, were reorganized under this structure. Additional funding fostered growth in child welfare services. New service programs like day care, family homemaker services, and services to unmarried parents were added. In the late 1960s, public social service agencies were permitted by amendments to the Social Security Act to purchase services from private child welfare agencies, family service agencies, and mental health centers. This solidified the overall delivery system and linked the public social service system with the private system.

Private child welfare agencies, as outgrowths of the private charitable organizations, had for many years provided many of the same types of child welfare services as public agencies. The movement to organize the system of private agencies received its major impetus from the Child Welfare League of America (CWLA) founded in 1920. The mission of the CWLA is to set standards, coordinate, and accredit child welfare agencies. In addition, the CWLA has expanded its roles to include research, information sharing, and the education of social workers working in the field. The CWLA is a powerful force, shaping the direction and future of child welfare services (Cohen, 1992).

In the 1970s and early 1980s, changes in social welfare policy had an impact on social programs for children. In 1975 Congress passed the Title XX Amendments to the Social Security Act, which reorganized public social services by shifting some administrative, planning, and policy decision making back to the individual states. The impact of Title XX on child welfare services was minimal. Most states continued to provide a complete program of child welfare services, despite the fact that Title XX created ceilings on federal funding for social services. Perhaps the most controversial aspect of Title XX was its gradual shifting of responsibility for social welfare from the federal government to the states. This became a source of concern because less populated rural states found that federal funding reductions made it difficult to maintain the services they were providing to children.

In 1981 Congress passed the Omnibus Budget Reconciliation Act, which again reorganized the social services program created by Title XX. Under this act, funding for some programs, including some child welfare programs, were consolidated into *block grants* with annual reductions in funding. These grants consolidated many service programs into a single source of funding, as opposed to funding each program. Advocacy and lobbying efforts were somewhat successful in keeping many child welfare programs out of the block grants, but some programs experienced recent cuts in federal funding. Most of the cuts were in programs such as AFDC, Medicaid, child nutrition programs, school lunch programs, and others. Traditional child welfare programs, such as protective services, foster care, or adoption, fared somewhat better.

The treatment and services provided to minority children remained a source of concern. Even though laws required that minority children receive the same standards of care as are given to white children, this was not happening; widespread discrimination existed within the system (Billingsley and Giovannoni, 1972). However, the picture for Native American children became brighter, thanks to the passage by Congress of the *Indian Child Welfare Act of 1978.* Under this act, Native American tribes were afforded the right to intervene in child welfare matters that affect a tribe's children. They have the right to assume legal jurisdiction over Indian children and provide plans for their ongoing care. This gave Native American people a voice and a measure of self-determination in the care of their children.

Another problem addressed in the 1980s was the extraordinarily high numbers of children remaining in foster care or some form of institutional care for long periods of time. Priorities in child welfare shifted from out-of-home care to serving children in their own homes. Because thousands of children were remaining in care for extended periods of time, Congress, in 1980, passed Public Law (P.L.) 96–272, the Adoptions Assistance and Child Welfare Reform Act. This act provided funding incentives for the states to develop mechanisms for *permanency planning* for children. Plans are to be developed in cooperation with the courts, by reviewing the legal status of children, by providing services that return children to natural families, or by making permanent arrangements for children through placement with relatives or through adoption.

A strong mandate present in this law was that of "reasonable efforts," whereby family dysfunction that affects children was felt to be best treated by intervention with the family unit without removal of the children if possible. If these efforts failed, efforts were made to clear the child's legal status for permanent placement outside the natural home (Costin, Bell, and Downs, 1991).

Economic security for children remained an issue of concern over the past two decades. Although a slight decrease was seen in the children's poverty rate in the early 1960s, during the next two decades it rose. The American Public Welfare Association (1983) reported that the poverty rate among children was at its highest level since 1965. Cuts in AFDC and Medicaid funding that occurred with the implementation of the Ominibus Budget Reconciliation Act of 1981 also impacted on poor children by reducing income supports for poor families.

This, along with many other issues that were discussed in Chapter 7, prompted Congress to pass the Family Support Act of 1988, P.L. 100–485, which restructured the way income supports are provided to low income families and had the goal to improve their economic status and quality of life.

However, economic security for low-income families remains a stubborn and persistent problem that affects the meeting of children's needs. Buttrick (1992), in a recent editorial published in *Social Work Research and Abstracts*, reported that the U.S. National Commission on Children has found that the current poverty rate for children in the U.S. is higher than in any Western industrialized nation. As stated earlier in Chapter 4, the poverty rate for children has increased over 4 percent since 1970. Recent efforts to combat this have come via the Family Support Act of 1988, but the results have not been encouraging thus far.

Further uncertainty about the economic well-being of children has come about as a result of the recent legislation on welfare reform as discussed previously. Although it is not known at this time what form the final reform will take, there is great potential for a negative impact on children. For instance, if children born out of wedlock to mothers under the age of eighteen are denied AFDC benefits, as proposed, clearly their future economic well-being will be compromised in favor of reduction of the "welfare rolls." There is also potential for other impacts, for example, an increase in the number of children being placed in foster care due to parental neglect and or abuse, stemming from the inability of natural parents to adequately meet the needs of these children. Extra burdens will likely be placed on local and state social welfare agencies as well as on private charitable organizations to fill the void in care of these children to the limited extent they may be able to do so.

Although controversial, proposed welfare reform plans may include taking many of the entitlement programs for child welfare services, like Title IV-E of the Social Security Act, and placing them into block grants with reduced federal funding. If this occurs, funding for crucial services for children, such as foster care, intensive family preservation, and adoption, will be jeopardized.

Current Concerns and Problems

Child Welfare practitioners, social work educators, government officials, and social policy makers have all gone on record recently saying that the field of child welfare services is at a crossroads, perhaps even experiencing a crisis. Many problems of long-standing origin as well as newly emerging problems continue to affect children.

Permanency planning for children in foster care and other substitute care situations continue to be problematic for the child welfare services delivery system. Despite reforms mandated by the Adoptions Assistance and Child Welfare Reform Act—mainly "reasonable efforts" that call for the reunification of families to prevent costly child placements—cuts in funding have thwarted the efforts of the system to fulfill the intent of this policy. It has been pointed out that the majority of funding has gone to support foster care placements rather than to provide services to families to prevent placements (Howing, Kohn, Gaudin, Kurtz, and Wodarski, 1992).

The long-existing problems of child abuse and neglect also continue, so much so as to have prompted the U.S. Advisory Board on Child Abuse and Neglect to declare a national emergency. Its prevalence is well documented, perhaps underestimated, but none the less staggering (Buttrick, 1992). Complicating the ability of the child protection system to respond is the significant increase in the rate of reporting child abuse and neglect. This has overwhelmed child protection agencies who have limited resources to investigate reported incidences, and it has led to a national debate on the issue.

On one side of the debate is the argument that reporting laws need to be clearer, with more specific definitions of what constitutes child abuse and neglect. It is also contended that child protection agencies need to develop better procedures for screening reports so that responses can be made without overreaction. This side of the debate is supported by the fact that well over one-half of reported incidents are unfounded.

The opposite argument is that increased reporting of child abuse and neglect reflects a greater awareness of the problem and is indicative of a large number of previously unreported cases (Besharov, 1990).

Other problems of more recent vintage have emerged to tax the already heavily burdened system. Drug abuse is occurring in epidemic proportions in the nation's largest cities, which has led to new, serious problems that consequently affect children. The delivery system has had to gear up to provide for children born addicted to drugs, the so-called "crack babies," and children infected by the HIV virus, caused by parental intravenous drug use during pregnancy. Of no less importance, the problems of fetal alcohol syndrome (FAS) and fetal alcohol effect (FAE) among children have received national attention, manifesting the effects of parental alcohol abuse on the unborn fetus. Health care for children is also a problem of recent concern. Growing numbers of families are unprotected by private health insurance or public health care programs due to high costs, unemployment, or ineligibility.

Another issue of current concern in the field of child welfare is the "deprofessionalization of child welfare services." As the profession of social work and the field of child welfare have progressed in the last two decades, fewer professional social workers, particularly those with the M.S.W. degree, have been employed in the field, particularly in the public child welfare agencies. Thus, these agencies have found it necessary to employ workers without professional credentials.

Concern about the lack of professionally trained staff in public child welfare agencies, increasing reports of child abuse and neglect, inadequate funding, the complex nature of problems affecting children, the inability of child welfare agencies to hire and retain competently trained staff, and several tragic cases brought to national attention by the media, have all caused grave concerns about the ability of the system to respond to vulnerable children.

Response to these concerns has been made on several fronts. Several organizations: the American Public Welfare Association, the Children's Defense Fund, the Child Welfare League of America, the National Association of Social Workers, and the National Association of Public Child Welfare Administrators, have begun collaborative efforts to bring about reform in the system. These organizations are working together to advocate for legislation that will provide needed resources, particularly adequate and competent staff.

Another response has come in the development of child welfare training and certification programs in several states. Florida, Tennessee, Georgia, Ohio, and Washington have implemented the first such programs (Miller and Dore, 1991).

More recently, North Dakota, South Dakota, and Wyoming have developed and implemented training and certification programs. The American Association for Protecting Children, a division of the American Humane Association, has also developed a national model curriculum for the training and certification of child welfare workers. The thrust of these programs is to provide competency-based training to staffs in public child welfare agencies in which staffs achieve certification by completion of training and passing a certification examination. Some states, for example, Tennessee and South Dakota, have made achieving certification a condition of employment for staffs employed in their public child welfare agency.

The U.S. Department of Health and Human Services, Administration of Children and Families, has also responded to concerns about the deprofessionalization in child welfare services. For several years, federal grants have been made available to educational institutions, under Section 426 of the Social Security Act—Child Welfare Training—to provide staff development and in-service training to employees of public child welfare agencies. More recently, priorities under this policy, as well as in Title IV-E of the Social Security Act, have made dollars available for the "professional education" of public child welfare staffs. Accredited undergraduate and graduate social work programs receiving such assistance would develop specific competency-based child welfare curricula and provide educational stipends to offset tuition costs to students who are willing to commit to employment in public child welfare upon graduation. Other collaborative efforts between social work education and other organizations, e.g., Child Welfare League of America and NASW, have recently begun to plan strategy on how to increase the number of professionally trained personnel in the system. All of these responses and efforts may serve to reverse the deprofessionalization in child welfare services and help to create a system that is more responsive and better equipped to deal with the needs of children and families. Other current concerns include: efforts to require parents to pay for at least a part of the costs of foster care for their children and the plight of children left home alone, sometimes for extended periods of time. Underlying the welfare of children in the United States is the need to give attention to how to provide societal support for parents in their parenting roles.

As can be seen, child welfare services historically protected and provided alternative care for dependent and orphaned children. As time passed, new social welfare structures and arrangements have come into play as responses to the overall economic, social, and emotional needs of children. In today's world, a well-established delivery system provides child welfare services.

Current Child Welfare Services

The current emphasis in child welfare services is on blending together into one framework the two traditional areas of service—those designed to maintain the child in the natural family setting, and those that offer substitute care outside the natural family—called a permanency framework. All child welfare services today primarily focus on creating conditions of permanency in the lives of children.

Protective Services

Recent developments have demonstrated that children can be protected from harm through supportive efforts designed to remedy the social conditions and problems in family functioning that would otherwise result in children being removed from their homes. *Child Protective Services (CPS)*, a broad area of service within the child welfare field, is specifically designed for this purpose. The basic aims of child protective services are as follows:

> *To guard children from further detrimental experiences or conditions in their immediate situations, bring under control and reduce the risks to their safety and/or well-being, prevent further neglect or abuse, and restore adequate parental functioning whenever possible or, if necessary, take steps to remove children from their own homes and establish them in foster situations in which they will receive more adequate care (Costin and Rapp, 1984).*

Protective services places primary emphasis on modifying social conditions and problems in parental functioning, to allow children to remain with the family. Removing children from their homes usually is done only if a child is in immediate danger as a result of parental or family circumstances (for example, because of abuse or neglect) or if, after an extensive period of intervention, circumstances and problems within the family have shown no improvement. In either case, efforts are made to ensure that the child's placement in foster care is brief. Intervention is focused on preparing the family and the child for the child's eventual return to her or his natural home.

Child protective services are mainly involuntary; that is, they are imposed on families. (In rare instances, a family will make a request for such services.) In most states, public social service agencies are mandated by law to protect children. In some states these functions are performed by special protective service providers such as home-based or family preservation units, special units within family or juvenile courts; private child welfare agencies; law enforcement agencies; or child protection teams composed of public social service, medical, mental health, and law enforcement personnel. Whatever the arrangement, the agency or team is responsible, by legal sanction, for receiving referrals, investigating, and intervening with families to ensure that children receive their rights to adequate care and protection from harm (Tower, 1993). Physical abuse, parental neglect, and sexual exploitation and abuse are the most common family problems requiring the attention and intervention of child protection authorities. No social problem in recent years has brought forth such an outpouring of public outrage and concern as has that of *child abuse*. Increased attention in the media and rigorous public education campaigns have brought the plight of victimized children into a national focus.

Child Abuse

Concern for protecting children is exemplified by the *child abuse and neglect reporting laws*, present in all fifty states. These laws usually require selected professionals to report suspected child abuse situations to child protection authorities. The general public is also encouraged to report child abuse and neglect.

The physical abuse of children may be defined as physical injury or anything else that threatens or jeopardizes the well-being or life of a child. This includes violent methods of discipline, including beatings that cause lacerations, abrasions, bone or skull fractures, or intentional burning.

Parental neglect appears to be on the increase and is perhaps even more damaging to children than overt abuse because of its subtle nature and the fact that it occurs over extended periods of time before it is called to the attention of the authorities. Child neglect involves deprivation of the physical necessities of life, emotional security and affection, education, or medical care. It may also involve inadequate supervision, abandonment, or provision of an environment injurious to the child's welfare.

Sexual exploitation and abuse have recently received a great deal of media exposure. Consequently, child protection agencies, law enforcement personnel, and the courts have focused attention and effort on this problem. The sexual abuse of children may include parent–child incest initiated by either or both parents; the case of a child forced into sexual activity by stepparents, relatives, or family friends; the rape of a child by a stranger; and sexual exploitation of children, such as prostitution or pornography. Child victims range in age from infants to adolescents.

The reported incidence of physical and sexual abuse and parental neglect is extensive, and has substantially increased over the last fifteen years. The National Center on Child Abuse and Neglect reported 785,000 cases of child maltreatment in 1980. In 1991, 1,767,674 cases were reported nationwide and, of these, 819,922 cases were substantiated. In 1992, 1,898,911 cases were reported, with 918,263 cases being substantiated. Of the substantiated cases reported in 1991, 366,462 were for parental neglect, 206,235 for physical abuse, 129,425 for sexual abuse, and 46,334 for emotional maltreatment. Substantiated cases in 1992 included 474,945 for parental neglect, 212,281 for physical abuse, 129,982 for sexual abuse, and 48,928 for emotional maltreatment (U.S. Bureau of the Census, 1994).

Causes of Child Abuse and Neglect

The causes of physical child abuse and neglect cannot be isolated into separate, specific factors. Physical abuse and neglect result from multiple interacting events, conditions, and circumstances that vary with the family situation (Wiehe, 1992). Much research has focused on identifying contributing factors and causes. In the 1960s Kempe and Helfer engaged in research stemming from their work with physically abused and neglected children. Several years later, their findings were organized into a theory that they termed the "battered child syndrome" (Kempe and Helfer, 1974). Their conclusion was that a multitude of interacting factors appear to predispose certain families to develop abusive relationships.

Other research (Giovannoni, 1985) concluded that three broad areas of interacting situational factors seem to precipitate physical abuse: (1) environmental and situational stresses, (2) characteristics of the parent or parents, and (3) characteristics of the children that make them vulnerable or prone to physical abuse. Recent studies (Burrell, Thompson, & Sexton, 1994; Ney, Fung, & Wickett, 1994; and Tracy, Green, & Bremseth, 1993) have continued to report that there appear to be situational, environmental, and personal factors that are linked to the causes of both physical abuse and neglect. One of the above studies, Ney, Fung, & Wickett (1994), concluded that neglect, in some cases, appears to act as a precursor to abuse.

Again, it must be made clear that none of these factors alone is sufficient to produce abuse. It is the interaction between them that does so. Environmental and situational stresses may include economic stress resulting from loss of income caused by unemployment, social isolation, physical illness, or dysfunction in the marital or parent–child relationships. Predisposing characteristics of parents include abuse by their own parents; ignorance; poor training in parenting skills; poor socialization in parenting roles; impulsive behavior; inability to resolve frustrations and control anger; psychological disturbances such as depression, personality disorders, and mental illness; unrealistic expectations of children's behavior; and abuse of or dependence on alcohol or other chemical substances. Abused children may also possess characteristics—such as demanding and unacceptable behaviors, rejection of the parents' gestures of love and affection, chronic illnesses or disability—that may lead to episodes of physical abuse.

The physical neglect of children also usually involves a number of interacting and situational factors. It has been suggested (Costin, Bell, and Downs, 1991) that there exists in some families a "cycle of neglect" in which parenting and child-rearing practices that were neglectful were carried into the next generation. It is thought that neglectful parents are often raised in similar family situations that were lacking in acceptable standards of care for children.

Other situational factors that cause and perpetuate physical neglect include low or poverty level family income allowing few resources for coping with the dependency needs of children, marital disruption, parental ignorance or indifference about appropriate child care practices, alcohol and drug abuse or addiction, chronic parental illness or disability, and personality or mental disorders.

Causes of Sexual Abuse

The causes of sexual abuse vary with the type of abuse. However, adults who sexually abuse children appear to share at least two characteristics that serve as prerequisites for sexual abuse: a sexual attraction to children and a willingness to act on those sexual feelings. As with other forms of child maltreatment, there also appear to be several contributing factors to the occurrence of sexual abuse. These include individual, family, and environmental factors (Wiehe, 1992). However, David Finkelhor (1993) cautions that, although some characteristics of both parents who sexually abuse children and child victims appear to be risk factors, none of these factors are strongly enough related to the occurance to sexual abuse that they can be used as identifying factors to confirm or not confirm the existance of the problem.

Children are sometimes sexually abused by adults who are outside their immediate family system. In some instances the adult perpetrator is known to the child; in other cases the perpetrator is a stranger to the child. Some of these adults are *pedophiles*, adults whose sexual orientation is toward children. Other adults who sexually abuse children may have poor impulse control, poor self-concept, or a lack of maturity, and may be abusing drugs or alcohol (Tower, 1993).

Child sexual abuse most often occurs within the family and involves sexual activities between a child and a related family member. This type of sexual abuse is known as incest. The most common form is father–daughter incest. Factors associated with this type of incest include poor parental self-concept, unsatisfactory sexual relationship within the marriage, role replacement whereby the child takes on the spousal role in sexual relations, maternal collusion, other inappropriate intimate situations between parent and child, older sexually active children seeking attention through covert and overt seductive behaviors, and child exposure to adult sexual behavior. Another common factor is that the parent abuser may have been a child victim (Faller, 1988).

Environmental factors found to be associated with sexual abuse are parental unemployment and social isolation of the family. The link between unemployment and sexual abuse exists because unemployment sometimes results in one adult becoming the sole caretaker of the children while his or her spouse works. These long periods of contact with children may create conditions in which sexual abuse can occur. Social isolation or infrequent interaction with the outside community sometimes is fostered by the adult perpetrator in incestuous families. Although many factors are related to child sexual abuse, it is the willingness of adult perpetrators to act on their sexual feelings toward children that is the primary cause of such abuse (Faller, 1988).

Emotional Neglect and Abuse

Just as the physical needs of children must be met in order for them to grow and develop appropriately, meeting the emotional needs of children is an important prerequisite to personality development and psychological well-being. Although exact figures are difficult to obtain, many children's emotional needs go unmet due to what is known as emotional neglect or abuse. It has been only recently that emotional deprivation has been considered to be a form of child maltreatment. What is involved is the quality of relationship between the child and his or her parents or caretakers. Relationships that are not emotionally nurturing have the potential to lead into neglectful or abusive relationships (Costin, Bell, and Downs, 1991).

Emotional neglect and abuse may involve parental indifference to the child's emotional needs for love, affection, and security; unusual and excessive emotional demands placed on the child by the parent; and chronic excessive yelling, involving belittlement and discouraging accusations. Often emotional neglect and abuse occur simultaneously with other forms of maltreatment, e.g., physical and sexual abuse. The tell-tale signs of emotional neglect and abuse are more subtle and difficult to assess for professionals. However, some kind of disturbance in the child's behavior is a usual symptom. The characteristics of parents or caretakers who emotionally neglect or abuse children are many of the same as in other forms of abuse discussed earlier. The major obstacle in protecting children from emotional neglect and abuse is a legal one. Generally speaking, these forms of child maltreatment are not included in most states' legal definitions of neglect or abuse. Even when this is the case, proving abuse is difficult, usually requiring expert testimony, which is subject to judicial interpretation and acceptance (Costin, Bell, and Downs, 1991).

In all forms of child abuse and neglect, cautious assessment of causative factors is imperative to avoid stereotyping. Each case needs to be approached with respect for its individual nature. (See the case study provided later in this chapter for an illustration of how child abuse and neglect might be treated by a protective services worker.)

Intervention Approaches and Roles of Social Workers in Protective Services

Intervention may involve direct counseling with the family and extensive use of agency and community resources, such as homemaker services, foster care, medical and health care services, mental health services, economic assistance resources, nutritional services, parent education services, and drug and alcohol treatment services.

The goal of the above interventions is to eliminate the problem conditions that place children at risk. However, intervention may include, depending on circumstances, removal of children and placement in substitute care situations on a temporary basis with the goal of eventual reunification of children with their families.

Sometimes these traditional interventions are unsuccessful. Some families in which children are at high risk for abuse or neglect need more intensive intervention. In recent years, supported by federal legislation (The Child Abuse Prevention, Adoption, and Family Services Act of 1988), state child protection agencies have developed "home-based or intensive family preservation services" that are provided to high-risk families with the goal of preventing out-of-home placements of children. The initial results of this intervention approach appear to be encouraging based on the findings of a number of researchers who have studied this approach (Wells and Biegel, 1992). This service delivery model has also found support among practitioners and policy makers because it is consistent with current priorities of keeping families together and reducing child placement costs.

The roles assumed by social workers in protective services vary from situation to situation, depending on the needs and problems present within the family. However, social workers in protective services generally assume two primary roles. First and foremost, they must be concerned with the ongoing protection of the child. Second, they must prepare an intervention plan that will help the family remove the conditions or resolve the problems that have caused the intervention and placed the child at risk. Serious cases, or cases where parental cooperation is not assured, may require the further intervention of family or juvenile courts to ensure that the child is protected from parental abuse or neglect. In such situations social workers need to be well prepared, to have gathered and organized evidence that is presented as direct testimony that represents the interests of the child. Sometimes a social worker, particularly a "clinical social worker" who possesses expertise in child and family intervention, may be called upon as an "expert witness" and present, in a neutral way, testimony that assists the court in understanding individual case dynamics (Meyers, 1993).

In consideration of the best interests of children, there is often the need for special representation of children in judicial proceedings. Recently a new program, Court Appointed Special Advocates (CASA), which utilizes volunteers, has emerged and has been found to be an effective, reduced-cost way of providing this representation (Poertner and Press, 1990).

Other In-Home Services for Children

Day-Care Services

Day-care services for children constitute an area of service within child welfare. Today it is very common for both parents in a family to be employed and thus dependent on alternative child-care arrangements. Other family circumstances may also necessitate day-care services. Children from families with parent(s) involved in educational or vocational training or children from troubled families are placed in day-care facilities to give the parents needed respite.

One service that has emerged in recent years to assist parents, particularly high-risk parents, is respite care in a crisis nursery. Parents can bring infants or toddlers to the crisis nursery in times of family stress or when conditions produce the potential for neglect or abuse. Staff of the nursery not only attend to the needs of the child, but also provide referral and informational services to the parents about other community services or resources that can assist with the family's ongoing problems (Ceravolo, 1985). Children with special needs (the physically, mentally, emotionally, or behaviorally handicapped) may also make use of specialized day-care services. Many day-care centers, preschools, and other such agencies receive federal funding to support the costs of child care. Family day care (day care of children in a family or home setting) is another form of this service, and again, depending on family eligibility, may be subsidized by federal or state funding sources. Most states require that child-care agencies, organizations, and family day-care homes be licensed to provide such services. Day-care services for children perform a vital function by providing a substitute for family care that focuses on the health, educational, social, and recreational needs of children.

Homemaker/Home Health Services

Homemaker services to children and families are provided by both public social services and private agencies. They are designed to care for children within their own homes, when they cannot receive adequate parental care. Homemakers are assigned to families to help with overall family maintenance. Homemakers, usually women, are trained in child care, home management, and in some instances home health-care tasks. They may be assigned for a few hours a week or on a full-time basis, depending on family need.

Family situations that may require homemaker services include protective service cases, the absence of one parent, the physical or mental incapacitation of one or both parents, or the death of one parent. Homemakers may also teach home management skills, child-care skills, or home health-care skills to parents whose immaturity or ignorance may have placed family welfare in jeopardy. Homemaker services are most often provided to low-income families; at times, however, almost any family may find them useful.

School Social Services

An integral, crucial part of a child's life are his or her educational experiences. Much of a child's future depends on the opportunity to receive a successful education. In the last century, educators and professional social workers have combined efforts to ensure that the educational needs of children are met. Large numbers of trained social workers have been employed in community schools throughout the country. In the early 1970s, the Education of All Handicapped Children Act (Public Law 94–142) intensified and broadened the tasks and roles of social workers in the schools. In 1986 this law was amended through passage by Congress of P.L. 99–457, which mandated the identification of preschool handicapped children in communities and authorized the provision of family-based services to their families. This further expanded the roles of school social workers (Costin, Bell, and Downs, 1991).

School social workers mediate among students, parents, schools, and the community. Problems that arise from the interaction among these groups or have the potential to jeopardize the child's education are focused on by the social worker. *School social services* provide individual and family counseling, as well as group counseling for children with special needs. They act as advocates with the school or community for educational services, act as a liaison between the home and school environments, help teachers understand the needs of children, assist school administrators with policy formation and planning for educational needs, and act as a liaison between the school and community social service agencies.

Nutrition services are also provided by public and private agencies and organizations supported by federal, state, and local funding. For many years, federal funding has supported nutritional services in public and private schools. Nutritional services are also available under the auspices of state and county public health agencies and county extension programs.

Adolescent Sexuality/Services to Adolescent Parents

Sexual activity among adolescents has increased dramatically in the last two decades. This has resulted in an increase in teenage pregnancy and in the number of adolescents who are taking on the role of parent. Child welfare and family services agencies who have regularly provided services to *adolescents* are experiencing new challenges in intervention with this population. Social workers intervening with adolescents around sexuality issues are now faced with providing services to a group at high-risk for infection with sexually transmitted diseases (STD), including HIV infection, which must be dealt with through aggressive educational and counseling programs. In addition, the issues of contraception and prevention of pregnancy have become major focuses. Studies report that prevention programs for teens usually have two goals: to delay the engagement in sexual activity through promotion of abstinence, or to provide educational and counseling services to encourage youngsters who are already sexually active to use contraception to prevent pregnancy. The first goal, although having the most potential as a long-range way of preventing pregnancy, has not shown significant results. Therefore more emphasis is being placed on identifying sexually active youth and providing needed services (Rabkin, Balassone, and Bell, 1995).

Intervention with teen parents usually begins at pregnancy. These young people need assistance in many areas of their own lives, as well as in planning for their child. For some time it has been agreed that unmarried parents are a population at risk. They face many potential problems as parents. Services for them focus on the prevention of such problems. The most difficult task facing the social worker is helping the parents decide what they should do about their unborn child. Options usually discussed with unmarried parents are abortion, giving up the child for adoption, or keeping it. This is a difficult decision for soon-to-be teen parents.

One option, abortion, may no longer be available, or at least will likely be restricted as an option for teens, due to legal and legislative tampering with human reproductive rights. In a June 1992 decision the U.S. Supreme Court upheld the fundamental right of women to have an abortion but also affirmed the right of states to set conditions for and impose restrictions on abortions. Some states have already placed restrictions on a teen's decision to have an abortion, requiring that the girl must have parental involvement and consent in this decision. It is likely that other states will soon adopt this requirement. The social worker needs to take special care in supporting whatever decisions are made by the youngster through counseling. Other services may include economic assistance for prenatal medical care, delivery, and postnatal care; support counseling for unmarried parents and other family members; child management and parenting skills services; foster care services; preadoption release services; and follow-up services. It needs to be noted here that the aforementioned services for adolescent parents may be reduced or eliminated in the near future if the pending welfare reform legislation, as discussed in previous chapters, becomes policy. If this becomes a reality, the social worker's roles with this population may become considerably more difficult.

Additional Services for Children in Their Own Homes

Other services that help maintain children in natural family settings include health care services, nutrition services, mental health services, and family counseling. Children in AFDC and SSI households are automatically eligible for Medicaid health-care services. Social services are also available to developmentally disabled children with various conditions, including physical and mental handicaps, blindness, and deafness.

These services are provided by both public and private agencies, with funding coming from a variety of federal sources, including P.L. 92–142, P.L. 99–457, and most recently P.L. 101–496, The Developmental Disabilities Assistance and Bill of Rights Act of 1990. This latest legislation has as its main focus to ensure that all persons with developmental disabilities receive the services and opportunities necessary to achieve their maximum potential, independence, and integration into the community.

Community mental health centers also provide a full range of services to families and children, including psychological and psychiatric evaluations, child guidance services, and family counseling and therapy. These services are also provided by private family service agencies. The purpose of these services is to strengthen and support families who are experiencing difficulties and to preserve the family unit. Many of the services provided by these agencies are designed to assist with troubled parent–child relationships.

As can be seen, a large number of services are available to assist children in their own homes. For those children unable to remain in their family settings, the child welfare system provides a multitude of services, with an emphasis on family preservation, reunification of the family, or permanency planning for children.

Substitute Care Services for Children

Every child requires care in order to survive. The process of emotional bonding to other human beings enables the child to develop physically, socially, intellectually, and emotionally. In today's world, many families struggle to perform the child-care tasks and functions expected of them. Social changes that have occurred in this century have placed a considerable burden on the family's independence and self-sufficiency. Lacking supports and under stress, some families find it hard to provide a suitable home for their children. When a child, for whatever reason, is unable to remain in the care of his or her natural parents, *substitute care* is provided to ensure that the child's basic needs are met, and that he or she has opportunities for successful growth and development in a nurturing environment.

When and for what reasons do children need substitute care? The major reason is a breakdown in family functioning or parental incapacity brought on by environmental stresses (Costin, Bell, and Downs, 1991). Children who need substitute care may also have special needs that the parents cannot meet because of their own inability to cope, the lack of family resources, or a lack of community resources to meet the child's needs. Children who are afflicted with medical, physical, intellectual, or emotional disabilities also sometimes need substitute care services. Children may need substitute care because of the temporary or permanent loss of one or both parents as a result of death, abandonment, desertion, hospitalization, incarceration, or a parent's decision to surrender the child for adoption. However, children also sometimes need such services in families where both parents are present, because of chronic physical or mental illness, physical disabilities, mental retardation, ignorance, emotional immaturity, chemical dependency, neglect, and child abuse (Costin, Bell, and Downs, 1991).

To avoid the trap of placing the blame entirely on family and parental functioning, it is important to remember that children may require substitute care services because of the conflict between expected family social roles and environmental conditions that make those roles difficult to perform. Social workers should look closely at the deficiencies in a family's social role performance and at the environmental pressures and stresses that contribute to those deficiencies. Decisions to remove children from their homes and place them in substitute care are not made lightly, but require much careful assessment and planning. Placing children temporarily or permanently also involves the judicial system, where the best interests of children, due process of law, and the rights of all involved are protected.

The courts, under P.L. 96–272, the Adoptions Assistance and Child Welfare Reform Act, maintain ongoing involvement in child placement situations through review every six months. This is to ensure that children are not lost or left in "legal limbo" within the foster care system and to promote intervention that has the primary goal of family reunification or the development of a permanent plan involving other options in the permanency planning framework discussed earlier. The duration of placement appears to be a factor that affects the reunification process. In a recent study by Goerge (1990) it was reported that there is less probability of reunification as placement duration increases. Substitute care of children involves several placement types, including family foster care, group, and residential care.

Family Foster Care

Most children who need substitute care need a stable family environment in which to live. *Family foster care* homes often meet that need. Both public social service agencies and private child welfare agencies are authorized to provide family foster home placements for children. Family foster care is the placement of choice whenever possible, and it is the most commonly used form of substitute care. Ideally, family foster homes give children a chance to experience family living with substitute parents and other family members, in a stable environment that meets their physical and emotional needs (Hacsi, 1995). Foster families are seen to be harmonious and cohesive family units, where foster children can learn appropriate behavior, roles, and responsibilities.

Selecting Foster Parents

The procedures used to recruit and select foster parents vary, but they are usually chosen through some form of home study or investigation. In the last several years, a number of states have begun to train foster parents, as a way of professionalizing their services. Training also promotes the concept that foster parents are team members, working hand in hand with agency staff to provide services to children. In most states, foster homes must be licensed to accept children for placement. The biggest problem that remains is that the number of children needing foster home placement exceeds the number of foster homes available.

In today's world, with the number of dual career families that exist, child welfare agencies have difficulties recruiting families who are able or willing to make the commitment to become foster parents. Another disincentive is the generally low rate of payment provided to foster parents. However, a sincere desire to help troubled children and their families—not financial reward or gain—should be the main motivators for couples willing to become foster parents.

Recently, much effort has also gone into recruiting foster parents from various racial and ethnic groups. Child welfare professionals have become increasingly sensitive to the fact that children need homes that maintain their cultural and racial integrity. But despite efforts to increase the number of minority foster homes, a critical shortage remains.

Some foster children may also have particular educational, medical, or emotional needs, such as FAS, AIDS, or emotional or behavioral problems, that must be addressed in the placement. Child welfare agencies have begun to develop specialized foster care programs for these children. In the past, many of these children were institutionalized, but now professionals recognize that some special-needs children benefit from family foster home placements backed up by supportive community services. Agencies have begun to train foster parents to provide the necessary specialized care.

Recent Trends and Issues in Family Foster Care

The cost of providing family foster care services is extremely high. The number of children entering foster care placements has increased significantly over the years, as it has replaced institutionalization as the placement of choice, putting additional burdens on social agencies. Family foster care services are financed both by federal and state funds and by other private funding sources, but the main funding mechanism is Title IV of the Social Security Act, combined with matched state funds. Children placed in foster homes supported by this funding in most states are also eligible for Medicaid services.

Child welfare professionals have long recognized that some children have stayed in foster care for unnecessarily long periods of time. Thus federal policy in foster care services has focused on shortening the duration of foster care placements. The federal government, through the *Adoptions Assistance and Child Welfare Reform Act of 1980*, mandated permanency planning services in the hope that such planning not only will provide cost savings, but more important, will reduce the time that children spend in temporary placement.

However, in some situations, reunification efforts fail, and other permanent placement alternatives, such as relative placement or adoption, are not feasible or available. Therefore the best solution for some children is long-term foster care, usually until the child reaches the age of majority. To this end, some child welfare agencies have developed specialized long-term foster care services. The Casey Family Program is one such agency whose primary service is to provide quality, long-term foster care for children.

It has also been recognized that older adolescents (sixteen and older) living in foster care will need special assistance in making the transition from foster care to independent living. The U.S. Department of Health and Human Services, under the provisions of Title IV-E, section 477 of the Social Security Act, has made funding available to the states to develop and deliver services that will assist the older adolescent in this regard. Specialized assistance and training programs involving the adolescent, child welfare agency staff, and foster parents have emerged in several states, for example, Georgia, Michigan, South Dakota, Texas, and Pennsylvania. The success of these programs appears to be promising, which is encouraging given that previous research had reported that older teens emancipating from foster care struggle have difficulties with the transition to independent living (Barth, 1990).

Social Work Role in Family Foster Care

Social workers in family foster care have a dual role. First, they are responsible for helping foster parents and children adjust to the placement and for providing other support services. Second, they must engage in permanency planning for the child's future. This includes intervening with the natural parents so the child can be returned to them eventually. If this is not realistic, the workers must explore alternative resources for the child, such as placement with relatives or adoption. The following case example illustrates the roles assumed by social workers in intervention with a troubled family, including the protective service, foster care, and intensive family preservation and reunification roles.

Institutional and Residential Care Services

Institutions continue to care for and treat children with special needs who cannot benefit from placements in family foster homes. Children needing institutional care range in age from preschoolers to adolescents. Most of these institutions, residential treatment facilities, and group homes care for older children and adolescents. These facilities are operated by public, private, and religious agencies. Group homes provide a wide variety of services, including ongoing care; educational, psychological, emotional, and social treatment; and recreational services. Most utilize the community's resources and services. Many also provide services to the families of children placed with them. Children with physical, emotional, and intellectual disabilities; blind or deaf children; children with psychological disorders; delinquent children; and chemically dependent children are all served through these institutions, treatment centers, and group homes. The funding for these services comes from federal, state, and local public tax dollars and from private sources. Although most children placed in such facilities are there because of special needs, they may also require permanency planning services. Social workers in these facilities perform direct service roles, such as individual, family, and group counseling. They also provide indirect services, involving staff coordination and supervision, program planning, advocacy, and staff training.

Adoption Services

The *adoption* of children by people not related by blood ties is a legal process. Families are created or expanded when the ties between biological parents and children are severed by the courts and legally reestablished with adoptive parents. Adopted children become the legal children of the adoptive parents and are entitled to all the rights and benefits that a biological child would have. Adoption serves a number of purposes. Most important, it enables children who are legally free for adoption to have a permanent home that they otherwise might lack. Adoption provides a way for couples who are unable to produce children biologically to become parents. Adoption is a way for children whose parents cannot or are unwilling to care for them to be given an adequate home in which to grow up. Adoption, unlike other forms of substitute care, is permanent and gives children much-needed stability.

New trends and issues have appeared in the field of adoption services over the past twenty years. Most noteworthy are new methods of evaluating which children are adoptable and which

A Case Study

Mark and Julie, ages 7 and 5, were removed from the care of their mother, Jennifer, by the juvenile court because of a long history of both physical and emotional neglect. Jennifer lacked adequate income, and had many emotional problems, including abuse of cocaine and crack. She had established a neglectful pattern of child care in which she failed to provide adequate food, clothing, and medical care. She often left her children unsupervised for long periods of time, and verbally abused them. Despite extensive intervention for a period of eight months by the child protective service unit (CPU) of the state's social service agency, that included provision of homemaker services, counseling at the local mental health center, employment assistance and training through JOBS, and involvement in Narcotics Anonymous, little improvement was made by Jennifer. Thus, the CPU petitioned the court for temporary removal of the children from Jennifer's care. The children were placed in family foster care. The court made it clear that Jennifer would be given six months to improve her situation in order to regain custody of her children. Otherwise, the court would remove them permanently. Jennifer's case was subsequently assigned to the Intensive Family Preservation and Reunification Unit of the agency.

The removal of her children did seem to motivate Jennifer to begin making the necessary changes to improve her situation so that she could regain custody of her children. With the intensive intervention of the social worker assigned to work with her, Jennifer entered treatment for her abuse of substances and maintained sobriety, was able to secure employment and keep it, located better housing, and made arrangements for good child care while she was working. Consequently, the children were returned to her care, with follow-up supervision and supportive services provided by the agency. The intensive intervention provided by the social worker from Family Preservation and Reunification Services made it possible for this mother to regain full custody of her children.

potential families should be eligible to adopt them. An adoptable child is defined as any child who needs a permanent home, who can benefit from a family relationship, and who is—or should be made—legally free for adoption. Essentially, any child, regardless of age, sex, or race, and despite physical, intellectual, or emotional disabilities, should be considered an adoptable child.

New thinking about the kinds of families who should receive adoptive placements has also influenced adoption agencies. Emphasis is now being placed on the needs of the child. Large families, single-parent families, foster families, relatives, and families from the child's racial group are now considered potential resources for adoption.

The scarcity of infants available for adoption is another trend that has brought about new developments in adoption services. In the past, most families wanted to adopt infants, but in the last twenty years the numbers of infants available for adoption has declined markedly. This has been caused by the increased availability of birth control and by the fading of the social stigma against unmarried parents keeping their children. Adoption services provided by public and private child welfare agencies have shifted their focus within the last ten to fifteen years to older and special needs children, who now, by new definition, are considered adoptable. Much time and effort has gone into developing adoption services for older children. The CWLA child welfare agencies and other children's interest organizations have contributed greatly to the development of adoption services for these children. Special needs children are those with physical, emotional, mental, and medical disabilities or conditions that pose special challenges to adoptive parents. Recent research focusing on the functioning of adoptive families of special needs children reports that these families face complex issues that are different from those faced by biological families. These families, according to the data obtained, appear to be more adaptable and cohesive in comparison to other families (Groze and Rosenthal, 1991).

This does not mean that all goes well for these families. On the contrary, parents who adopt special needs children experience a good deal of stress. Adoption agencies, recognizing this, provide supportive post-placement follow-up services to these families. Groze and Gruenwald, in a recent journal article, reported on a special service program located in Cedar Rapids, Iowa, called "Partners"—Post Adoption Resources for Training, Networking, and Evaluation Services—that specializes in providing such services (Groze and Gruenwald, 1991). The adoption of minority children by adoptive families from the same groups has been bolstered substantially by the efforts of the CWLA, the National Association of Black Social Workers, and the Indian Child Welfare Act of 1978.

There are a number of ways in which children become available for adoption. First, children being placed must be legally free for adoption. Most commonly, infants become available for adoption when parents choose voluntarily to surrender their parental rights to their child so it may be adopted. The parental rights of both biological parents must be considered: The 1972 Supreme Court case of *Stanley* v. *Illinois* firmly established the parental rights of biological fathers. Younger children who continue to be at risk from abuse or neglect can be permanently removed from their parents' care by the courts and be placed for adoption. Older children who are legally free for adoption, and who have been in the care of the same foster parents for a long time, can be adopted by those foster parents. This type of adoption is on the increase and has contributed much to the success of permanency planning. Another type of adoption is that of foreign children. These children usually come from Korea, India, and some South American countries.

Types of Adoption

The two primary types of adoption are agency and independent adoptions. An *agency adoption* is arranged by a child welfare or social service agency sanctioned and authorized by law or license to do so. These agencies match as best they can the child available for adoption with an approved family that investigation has shown will be able to meet the needs of the particular child. Supportive services, including legal services and counseling, are also provided to the new family to promote the success of the placement. In situations involving special-needs children, some agencies engage in what is termed a subsidized adoptive placement, which involves placing the child with a family that without financial assistance could not provide for the child's ongoing care. In these instances, agencies provide (under P.L. 96–272) the necessary money that makes the adoption possible.

Independent adoptions can also occur. In most states, families can adopt a child through arrangements made by a third party acting independently of a social agency. This person acts as a facilitator between the biological parents and the adoptive parents and makes the necessary legal arrangements for the adoption. Again, children must be legally free, usually because biological parents have voluntarily released them for adoption. This type of adoption has been called gray-market adoption. In recent years, independent or gray-market adoptions have increased greatly in numbers, often as a way of avoiding the lengthy home-study process in agency adoption and the sometimes very long waiting period.

A variation on independent adoption involves the legal adoption of children by their step-parents or by a relative. Again, the parental rights of the absent biological parent must be terminated legally.

Social Work Roles in Adoption Services

The field of adoption services is one of the most rewarding areas of social work practice. Social workers assume many roles in adoption services, including preparing children and families for adoptive placement, finding adoptive homes, and completing adoptive home studies. Beyond this, social workers are responsible for providing support services to families with adopted children to ensure the success of the placement. This is especially crucial when the adopted child is older or handicapped. In these cases, the social worker can direct the new parents to resources who assist in making the transition smoother for both child and parents. Occasionally, when there are problems with placements, social workers must also be prepared to provide ongoing services to the family. Some placements may require extensive work, particularly those involving special-needs children. Social workers in adoption services may also become involved in community development, public education advocacy, program policy and planning, and administrative roles.

Summary

Child welfare services are dedicated to protecting and promoting the well-being of children, and to ensuring that their needs are met during this vulnerable time in their lives. Formal service delivery structures in child welfare, and the policies that have influenced their purposes and missions, have changed over time in response to social changes that have affected U.S. society as a whole. The two broad areas of child welfare services—those dedicated to maintaining children in natural family settings and those for children at risk and unable to remain within their natural homes—have been organized into a permanency framework. Service today is based on the assumption that all children are entitled to a stable, nurturing family home environment. It is believed that for most children, with support and assistance, natural families can provide the best environment in which children can live and grow. Child welfare services, homemaker services, school social services, day-care services, and other forms of assistance to families can bring this about. When these efforts fail, for whatever reasons, and children cannot remain in their natural homes, they must be guaranteed permanent substitute care. Permanency planning mechanisms, such as placement with relatives or adoption, can provide that. Services to children that protect their well-being and socialize them for living within our society should be viewed as an investment in our nation's future.

Key Terms

adolescent parents

adoption

Adoptions Assistance and Child Welfare Reform Act of
   1980

agency adoption

apprenticeship

block grants

child abuse

child abuse and neglect reporting laws
child neglect
Child Protective Services (CPS)
Children's Aid Societies
Children's Bureau
child welfare
child welfare services
day-care services
family foster care
family preservation
foster care
homemaker services/home health aide

indenturing
independent adoption
Indian Child Welfare Act of 1978
orphanage
pedophile
permanency planning
reunification
school social services
sexual abuse
Sheppard-Towner Act
substitute care

References

Barth, R.P. (1990). On Their Own: The Experience of Youth After Foster Care. *Child and Adolescent Social Work Journal, 7 (5)*, 419–440.

Besharov, D.J. (1990). Gaining Control over Child Abuse Reports. *Public Welfare, 48 (2)*, 34–40.

Billingsley, A., and Giovannoni, J.M. (1972). *Children of the Storm: Black Children and American Child Welfare.* New York: Harcourt Brace.

Burrell, B., Thompson, B., and Sexton, D. (1994). Predicting Abuse Potential Across Family Types. *Child Abuse and Neglect, 18 (12)*, 1039–1049.

Buttrick, S.M. (1992). Failed Policies: The Crisis in Child Welfare. *Social Work Research and Abstracts, 28* (1), 3–4.

Ceravolo, F.M. (1985). The Crisis Nursery: A Metropolitan Island of Safety, in Laird, J. and Hartman, A. (eds.), *A Handbook of Child Welfare: Context, Knowledge, Case Management and Practice.* New York: Free Press.

Child Welfare League of American (1971). *A National Program for Child Welfare Services.* New York: Child Welfare League of America.

Cohen, N.A. (1992) *Child Welfare: A Multicultural Focus.* Boston: Allyn and Bacon.

Costin, L.B., and Rapp, C.A. (1984). *Child Welfare: Policies and Practice.* New York: McGraw-Hill.

Costin, L.B., Bell, C.J., and Downs, S.W. (1991). *Child Welfare: Policies and Practice.* New York: Longman.

Faller, K.C. (1988). *Child Sexual Abuse: An Interdisciplinary Manual for Diagnosis, Case Management and Treatment.* New York: Columbia University Press.

Finkelhor, D. (1993). Epidemiological Factors in the Clinical Identification of Child Sexual Abuse. *Child Abuse and Neglect* 17 (1), 67–70.

Giovannoni, J.M. (1985). Child Abuse and Neglect: An Overview, in Laird, J., and Hartman, A. (eds.), *A Handbook of Child Welfare: Context, Knowledge, Case Management and Practice.* New York: Free Press.

Goerge, R.M. (1990). The Reunification Process in Substitute Care. *Social Services Review 64 (3)*, 422–457.

Groze, V., and Gruenwald, A. (1991). Partners: A Model Program for Special-Needs Adoptive Families in Stress. *Child Welfare 70 (5)*, 581–589.

Groze, V., and Rosenthal, J.A. (1991). A Structural Analysis of Families Adopting Special-Needs Children. *Families in Society: The Journal of Contemporary Human Services. 72 (8)*, 469–482.

Hacsi, T. (1995). From Indenture to Family Foster Care: A Brief History of Child Placing. *Child Welfare 74 (1)*, 162–180.

Howing, P.T., Kohn, S., Gaudin, J.M., Kurtz, P.D., and Wodarski, J. (1992). Current Research Issues in Child Welfare. *Social Work Research and Abstracts 28 (1)*, 5–12.

Juvenile Rights Project of the American Civil Liberties Union Foundation. (1977). *Children's Rights Report.* New York: American Civil Liberties Union Foundation.

Kempe, H.C., and Helfer, R.E. (1974). *The Battered Child.* Chicago: University of Chicago Press.

McGowan, B.G., and Meezan, W. (1983). *Child Welfare: Current Dilemmas and Future Directions.* New York: Child Welfare League of America.

Meyers, J.E.B. (1993). Expert Testimony Regarding Child Sexual Abuse. *Child Abuse and Neglect 17 (1)*, 175–185.

Miller, J., and Dore M.M. (1991). Innovations in Child Protection Services Inservice Training: Commitment to Excellence. *Child Welfare 70 (4)*, 437–449.

Ney, P.G, Fung, T., and Wickett, A.R. (1994). The Worst Combinations of Child Abuse and Neglect. *Child Abuse and Neglect 18* (9), 705–714.

Parker, J.K., and Carpenter, E.M. (1981). Julia Lathrop and the Children's Bureau: The Emergence of an Institution. *Social Services Review 55.*

Poertner, J., and Press, A. (1990). Who Best Represents the Interests of the Child in Court. *Child Welfare 69 (6)*, 537–549.

Rabkin, J.C., Balassone, M.I., and Bell, M. (1995). The Role of Social Workers in Providing Comprehensive Health Care to Pregnant Women. *Social Work in Health Care 20 (3)*, 83–97.

Tower, C.C. (1993). *Understanding Child Abuse and Neglect.* Boston: Allyn and Bacon.

Tracy, E.M., Green, R.K., and Bremseth, M.D. (1993). Meeting the Environmental Needs of Abused and Neglected Children: Implications from a Statewide Survey of Supportive Services. *Social Work Research and Abstracts 29 (2)*, 21–26.

U.S. Bureau of the Census (1994). *Statistical Abstacts of the United States 1994: The National Data Book.* Washington DC: U.S. Government Printing Office.

Wells, K., and Biegel, D.E. (1992). Intensive Family Preservation Services Research: Current Status and Future Agenda. *Social Work Research and Abstracts 28 (1)*, 21–27.

Wiehe, V.R. (1992). *Working with Child Abuse and Neglect.* Itaska, IL: F.E. Peacock.

Suggested Readings

Besharov, D.J. (1990). Gaining Control over Child Abuse Reports. *Public Welfare 48 (2)* 34–40.

Cohen, N.A. (1992). *Child Welfare: A Multicultural Focus.* Boston: Allyn and Bacon.

Costin, L.B., Bell, C.J., and Downs, S.W. (1991). *Child Welfare: Policies and Practice.* New York: Longman.

Fraser, M.W., Pecora, P.J., and Haapala, D.A. (1991). *Families in Crisis: Impact of Intensive Family Preservation Services.* New York: de Gryter.

Miller, J., and Dore, M.M. (1991). Innovations in Child Protective Services Inservice Training: Commitment to Excellence. *Child Welfare 70 (4)*, 437–449.

Pecora, P.J. (1989). *Addressing the Program and Personnel Crisis in Child Welfare.* Silver Spring, MD: National Association of Social Workers.

Tower, C.C. (1993). *Understanding Child Abuse and Neglect.* Boston: Allyn and Bacon.

Wiehe, V.R. (1992). *Working with Child Abuse and Neglect.* Itaska, IL: F.E. Peacock.

9

HEALTH CARE AND SOCIAL WELFARE

Learning Expectations

- Ability to identify the common themes of the social welfare and the health care systems
- Understanding of how the arrangements for service delivery that have historically developed in the social welfare system have had a similar development in the health care system
- Understanding of the major approaches for change in health care funding currently being discussed, including knowledge about the strengths and limitations of each
- Identification of overlaps of the social welfare system and the health care system
- Identification of three major components of the health care system and understanding of the special features of each
- Knowledge about the roles social workers fill in each of the components of the health care system
- Understanding of how work in a host setting affects the practice of social work
- Identification of major concerns regarding the delivery of health care today

Social welfare and health care are usually seen as two different systems. The health-care system is generally responsible for the area of sickness and disability, but there are areas where health care and social work overlap, with common concerns and common themes. One of the areas of overlap between the two systems is the practice of social work in health-care settings.

Before proceeding to discuss these common concerns, it is important to define health. Health is usually considered to be freedom from disease. But this definition fails to consider the relative nature of health. Is the person with a well-controlled chronic disease unhealthy? Is a frail elderly person with minimal health problems other than the fraility of old age unhealthy? What about the differing cultural definitions of illness and disease? Are individualized definitions of illness to be considered? Carel Germain (1984), author of one of the major texts on social work in health-care settings, defines health as "a multidimensional process involving the well being of the whole person in the context of his [or her] environment" (p. 34). The *health-care system*, as defined for this book, then, must by necessity be broadly defined. This system consists of institutions and professionals, including those in private practice, who have as a primary focus the care of the physically ill and the physically disabled, and who are engaged in activity that prevents physical illness and disability. This definition excludes the area of mental health, although it is often included in the health-care field. However, the social welfare response to mental health is extensive and has followed a somewhat different course. Social welfare and mental health will be considered separately in the next chapter.

After the discussion of common concerns of the social welfare and health-care fields, a review of the historical development of social legislation relating to health care and of social services in health care is presented. Next, the contemporary role of the social worker in the health-care system is considered. Finally, some current issues in health-care services affecting the social welfare system are discussed.

Health Care and the Social Welfare System

One of the common themes of health care and social welfare is the nature of human functioning. Both systems are *holistic*; that is, they are concerned with the whole person. This includes the biological, psychological, social, and spiritual aspects of living and functioning. Social functioning, the concern of the social welfare system, cannot really be separated from the other functions. Illness and disability are important reasons that people have difficulty providing for their needs and functioning well in society. They strongly influence a person's self-image and social behavior. The reactions of spouses, children, coworkers, and friends to illness or disability affect how a patient responds to the condition and functions socially. Medical treatment also has psychosocial effects on both the individual and the family. For example, when a mother with young children is hospitalized, plans must be made for child care, children may be upset by the absence of their mother, and the husband may have concerns about his wife and children that may in turn affect his functioning in the workplace. The financial cost of hospitalization adds another concern. The mother's response to treatment would very likely be affected by her worry about her children and husband and perhaps by feelings of guilt for causing their distress. And, of course, the social welfare system must be concerned with the health of the individuals it is serving.

On the other hand, the health-care system must be concerned with the psychological, social, economic, and spiritual aspects of patients, since these aspects have considerable effect on their physical status. For people to comply with prescriptions and recommendations from health professionals, they must have enough money to purchase the health care and to buy the prescribed food and medications. Culture, religious beliefs, and family patterns also affect how a patient responds to medical advice. The emotional or psychological state of an individual has a considerable influence on the capacity of the body to respond to medical treatment. It is the individual in a holistic sense with whom both the social welfare system and the health care system are concerned (Brody, 1976).

Another area of overlap is related to environmental factors. Public health and social welfare have had a long partnership in this area (Austin, Baizerman, and Guzzetta, 1974). Public health workers seek to "prevent disease, prolong life, and promote physical and mental health . . . through community efforts." The same could be said of social workers. Both fields have used social reform and social control approaches to social problems.

A third overlapping area is concern for the family. The family can be a resource or it can be an obstacle during an illness. In turn, illness affects the family's capacity to function. The health-care system must be concerned with the effect family members have on the sick person and the effect of the illness on the family. The social welfare system is concerned with how illness and disability influence the social functioning of not only the ill or disabled individual but also the whole family, the various institutions that serve the individual and family, and the community at large. Illness can place a family at risk of not being able to meet its needs, either because of the energy that must go into supporting or caring for an ill member, or because the illness makes it impossible for a vital role (financial support, parenting, or the marital role, for example) in the family to be filled. Epidemic illness can put entire communities at risk. When the individual, the family, or the community risks not being able to meet social functioning needs through the usual mechanisms and resources, the health-care system depends on the social welfare system to develop means for meeting unmet needs.

Arrangements Used to Deliver Health Care

Another way of looking at the relationship of health care and social welfare is to note the arrangements that have been used to deliver health care. As with social welfare, mutual aid has always been a primary resource. Most individuals depend on family, friends, and neighbors in times of illness. Most minor illnesses are handled by self-care methods, which often are used after consulting other people. In places where medical care was not available (on the frontier or in other isolated areas) medical care was provided by family and neighbors with special experience or skill in the care of the sick. Mutual aid was and continues to be an important component of health care.

Hospitals were among the early institutions created under the charity-philanthropy arrangement. Often these institutions were developed by religious groups. Early hospitals were sometimes set up to separate the sick from the general population in the poorhouses. They were meant to be places where these people could get adequate treatment and where, it was hoped, the indigent could be restored to health and thus become able again to provide for their own needs. Gradually, hospitals came to be places where all sick people could receive the care they needed. Two levels of care evolved. Those who could pay were cared for in private hospitals or in the private services of large hospitals. Those who could not pay, the *charity patients*, were cared for in *charity hospitals* or on charity wards. The care of charity patients was often given by physicians in training, whereas care of the private patient was given by personal physicians.

Charity patient care was not only a part of the health-care system but also a part of the social welfare system. When that care was paid for by government funds, the care given in charity hospitals and on charity wards was seen as public welfare. Many city and county hospitals were created to care for charity patients. Bellevue Hospital in New York City and Cook County General Hospital in Chicago are examples of hospitals supported by local government funds. Such hospitals provide not only inpatient care (for patients who stay in the hospital) but outpatient clinics (for patients who do not stay overnight) as well. People who are unable to pay for the services of private physicians use these outpatient clinics as their primary medical care provider. These medical services are clearly within the public welfare arrangement.

A contemporary public welfare mechanism that covers medical services for those who cannot afford to pay is *Medicaid*, which is provided under the Social Security amendments of 1965. By 1971 Medicaid benefits had been extended not only to the aged and families on AFDC but also to the disabled and the blind. Medicaid is available to people in income maintenance programs and, in some cases, to those who are known as medically indigent—that is, who are not eligible for income maintenance but whose incomes are too low to pay for adequate medical care. Medicaid is jointly funded by state and federal governments and administered by the states. The states are given considerable latitude over which services to provide. But all programs must provide outpatient and inpatient care, laboratory and X-ray service, skilled nursing home care, and physicians' care. A major criticism of the Medicaid programs implemented by the states is their almost exclusive focus on treating illness, with little concern for prevention and rehabilitation.

Social insurance, in the form of national health insurance, has been a topic of discussion in the United States since at least 1912, when the Progressive party under Theodore Roosevelt had a proposal for national health insurance in their party platform (Brieland, Costin, and Atherton, 1975). To date, despite numerous attempts to provide universal coverage through a national health insurance plan, the United States remains one of the few industrialized nations without such a plan. Only one segment of our population is covered by a universal health-care social insurance plan—the elderly (those over sixty-five years of age). In 1965 amendments to the Social Security Act provided the *Medicare* program (passed at the same time that the Medicaid program was established). All persons over sixty-five are covered by Part A of Medicare, which is financed through the payroll taxes, commonly known as Social Security, paid by workers and employers. Part A pays primarily for inpatient hospital care. There are deductibles (an amount to be paid before the insurance payments begin) and co-payments (the insurance covers only a percentage of the costs). Part B is optional and is financed by an insurance premium paid for by the recipient and by federal government contributions. It covers physicians' costs, and it too has deductibles and co-payments (Karger and Stoesz, 1994). In 1973 Medicare was expanded to include those with end-stage renal disease.

Social services have been provided in the health-care system since 1909 (see Table 9–1). Such services are mandatory for nursing home patients whose care is provided under Medicaid. The Veterans Administration facilities have been leaders in providing medical social services. Social services are required in hospitals accredited by the Joint Commission on the Accreditation of Hospitals. They are also part of the services offered by some private medical practice groups, such as health maintenance organizations (HMOs) and maternal and child health services.

Although the United States has not, to date, seen fit to develop a universal provision mechanism for the health care of its citizens, many other countries, including Canada and Great Britain, do have universal provision arrangements that cover the vast majority of the health-care services provided to their citizens. In Canada, national health-care insurance is federally mandated but provincially administered. Funding is from federal general tax funds, a provincial general tax base, and insurance mechanisms. All medical care, including doctor's fees, hospitalization costs, and some prescription drugs, are provided at no cost, although there has been

TABLE 9–1   Important Dates: Social Work in Health Care

1893	The Hull House medical dispensary was opened.
1905	The First medical social worker was employed in outpatient department, Massachusetts General Hospital.
1918	The Amerian Association of Hospital Social Workers was formed.
1921	The Sheppard-Towner Act established child and maternal health centers.
1926	Social services were established in the Veterans Administration hospital system.
1935	The Social Security Act authorized maternal and child health programs (Title V).
1965	Amendments to the Social Security Act provided Medicaid (Title XIX) and Medicare (Title XVIII).
1973	The Health Maintenance Organization Act required social services as one component of care.
1976	Publication began of two social work journals, *Health and Social Work* and *Social Work in Health Care.*
1983	Prospective payment–Diagnostic Related Groups (DRGs) were introduced by the U.S. Department of Health and Human Services for Medicare services.
1988	Catastrophic Health Insurance Act was passed by Congress to increase protection of elderly Medicare recipients from catastrophic illness and conditions—later repealed by Congress because of associated high costs.
1990	Health Care Protection reaches crisis state due to high cost of health care and lack of insurance protection.
1995	Comprehensive Welfare Reform passed by Congress that proposes that states assume full responsibility for Medicaid.

some concern about overuse and the need for minimum fees to prevent this. Patients have free choice of doctors, who receive set fees for services rendered. Most hospitals are also provincially administered.

In countries with universal provision for health care, all people have access to such care. Health care is seen as a right. There are two arguments used against such a provision: excessive cost and inferior quality of services. Counterarguments can be put forth against both. In relation to the cost, is there not a greater long-term cost resulting from poor social functioning due to untreated health problems? As for inferior service, there are examples of both inferior and superior service in the current system.

No social problem is receiving more attention in contemporary U.S. society than the cost of health care. This problem is often described as in a state of crisis. It is estimated that between 31 and 37 million people lack health insurance. Others lack coverage for catastrophic situations or are required to provide often unaffordable out-of-pocket costs. Many providers refuse to participate in Medicare and Medicaid because of perceived low reimbursement rates. For those on Medicare, out-of-pocket costs are higher today than in 1965 when Medicare began.

Another grave concern is long-term care; its costs are tremendous. Few people can afford private insurance that includes long-term care. Thus once assets are exhausted, many people must depend on Medicaid. This is troubling to those who have prided themselves on the fact that they could care for themselves without having to depend on "welfare." It is also a tremendous financial burden on state welfare funds. These costs are rising dramatically, particularly due to an aging population.

In 1990, expenditures for health care in the United States were 666 billion dollars. This is well over the 1980 cost. Not only are costs rising because of the aging population but because of what has been identified as "medical inflation" (U.S. Bureau of the Census, 1995).

A number of proposals continue to be introduced as responses to the problem. Rashi Fein (1992), a medical economist at Harvard Medical School, has identified three approaches that are being put forward. First is the *private market approach*. This approach, generally, calls for people to obtain their health care insurance from their employers or through self-purchase. The government would provide vouchers or tax credits for low-income people. Other tax credits may also be available. The present insurance system would remain in place. This system is often seen as one of the causes of excessive health care costs. It also continues a two-tier system and does not cover long-term care.

A second approach is the *employer based approach*. In this approach, often known as "play or pay," health insurance is made available to everyone either through their employer or through the government. Employers must provide health care insurance, "play," or "pay" a tax that goes to coverage by the governmental plan. Medicare remains in place for those who are now covered by that plan. Some proposals include long-term care and preventive care.

The third approach is the *government based approach*. This plan has been known as *single payer* or *national health insurance*. The government is the sole payer; everyone receives guaranteed basic hospital and doctor coverage; usually preventive care is included; sometimes long-term care is also included. Various funding mechanisms are suggested. A major criticism of this approach is that it increases taxes considerably.

In 1990, NASW proposed its own health care plan that would be administered by the federal government with services delivered by the states. Patients would have a choice of providers and have comprehensive coverage. Private insurance would virtually be eliminated. Funding would come from a progressive income tax and an employer paid payroll tax and would be supplemented by the states. This plan is similar to the one that has been in operation in Canada (Fein, 1992). In addition, three other health care reform proposals surfaced in 1990–1991, two in the form of legislative bills introduced in Congress, and the third coming from the work of the Bi-partisan Commission on Comprehensive Health Care. One legislative proposal, known as the Russo bill (H.R. 1300), Universal Health Care Act of 1991, was introduced by Representative Mary Russo (D-Il), and the other (S. 1227) was sponsored by Senate Majority Leader, George Mitchell. The proposal offerd by the Bi-partisan Commission was known as the Pepper Commission Report. These three proposals represent two of the three approaches previously discussed—the single payer approach and the play or pay approach. The Russo bill had as its major component universal health care coverage for all Americans and was not tied to employment. The others, the Senate bill and the Pepper Commission Report, contained elements of the play or pay approach, tying eligibility for health care coverage to employment. Leadership provided by the Clinton Administration in the movement towards health care reform during these years was spearheaded by the President's wife, Hilary Rodham Clinton. Despite these efforts, no final plan for comprehensive reform in the U.S. health care system emerged or was acted upon by Congress. Scuka (1994) evaluated the three proposals discussed above and concluded that only the Russo bill would have provided the kind of comprehensive reform that is seen to be needed. Scuka contends that the ongoing challenge to the Clinton Administration, and to Congress, is to overcome the forces of opposition to health care reform that exist within their own ranks as well in the medical industry so that needed reforms can take place. The consequences for failing in this effort are grave as there is great potential for the number of medically indigent to rise significantly over the next few years (Scuka, 1994).

The Clinton administration stated that one of its major initiatives would be the introduction of a health care plan. Whether this plan would be employer-based or government-based is unclear. The Clinton Administration favors emphasis on preventative care, cost controls, and universal coverage.

All the arrangements used to provide social welfare services in the United States have been used to provide health-care services. Currently there are at least two levels of health care in the United States. One tier is for those who can pay for their care or who carry insurance that will pay for care. This tier's services are organized around a private-practice system of medical care. Mutual aid, social insurance, and social services also provide services to this tier. The other tier, which provides services for those who cannot pay, relies heavily on mutual aid, charity-philanthropy, public welfare, and social services. Many people are not covered by employer-provided health-care insurance, and as premiums for such insurance continue to increase, many Americans find that health care is beyond their means financially. Also, there are increasing reports that the health-care system is refusing to provide service or is providing only a lesser service to those without insurance coverage. These inconsistencies point to the great need for the health care reform called for by President Clinton and a large segment of the U.S. population.

One overlap between the health-care system and the social welfare system falls in the area of the arrangements used to provide health-care services. In the following sections of this chapter, as social services in health-care settings are discussed, further areas of overlap will also become apparent.

Social Services and Social Policy in Health Care

The relationship between the health-care system and the social welfare system extends at least as far back as the late 1800s. Both the Charity Organization Societies and the settlement houses were concerned with the health care of the people they served. Hull House had a medical dispensary that Jane Addams organized in 1893. The COS were concerned with programs to combat infant mortality, tuberculosis, rickets, and scurvy. Maternal and child health clinics and free dispensaries for the poor were also set up by social workers in some communities (Bracht, 1978).

At the same time, the use of hospitals for health care was growing. In 1905 Dr. Richard Cabot introduced social work at Massachusetts General Hospital. Cabot had identified social factors he believed blocked effective medical treatment, and he identified social workers as understanding the environmental circumstances and having the ability to find ways of overcoming these blocks. Ida Cannon, a trained nurse who also had training in sociology and psychology, worked at Massachusetts General and is considered to be the first medical social worker. Other hospitals, particularly the public hospitals, began to follow suit and use nurses with special training to deliver social services. Cannon traveled widely, attended conferences, gave papers, and generally spread the word about the value of social services in hospitals. By 1918 there were enough hospital social workers to form the American Association of Hospital Social Workers. This group saw the need for professional training, and several schools of social work began to offer a specialized curriculum for medical social workers (Kerson, 1982).

After World War I, the federal government enacted two important pieces of health-care legislation. The first was the establishment of the Veterans Administration (VA) in 1921. Health care for veterans has always been an essential ingredient of the services available from the VA. These services can be seen as a different type of public health service. In the past, public health services were provided by local government for those who could not obtain care elsewhere because of poverty. The VA is a federal health care program offered as a benefit for those who served in the armed forces, with fairly broad eligibility requirements. This organization has always been a pacesetter in the area of medical social services; these were established in 1926. There are 171 VA hospitals, all of which provide social services to their patients. In addition, the VA has an extensive outpatient service made up of not only medical services but also mental health services, supportive personal care services, and professional supervision in the veteran's own home or a wide range of substitute residential services. Over three thousand professional social workers are employed in the various VA facilities (Rothman and Becerra, 1987).

The second important act of that period includes another area where health care and social welfare overlap—child welfare services. In 1921, Congress passed the *Sheppard-Towner Act*, which established child and maternal health centers, most of them in rural areas. Under regulations developed by the Children's Bureau, states were helped to provide more adequate services to women and their children and to significantly lower the infant and maternal mortality rate. This program focused on health care with a preventive and developmental focus. Education of mothers was an important ingredient. Although the act was not funded after 1929, its purpose was carried out after 1935 by the Social Security Act (Rothman, 1978).

Although the maternal and child health program was incorporated into the 1935 Social Security Act, it was not until the amendments of 1965 that health care received major consideration with the establishment of the Medicare and Medicaid programs. But earlier, in 1946, Congress passed the *Hill-Burton Act*, which assisted states in planning for health facilities and communities in building health facilities in underserved areas. It was a forerunner of the federal health planning programs to follow in the 1960s and 1970s.

During the 1980s, with the general cutbacks in federal spending for social welfare came other important social policy developments. There was less emphasis on planning and a general concern with the escalating cost of health care, particularly those services supported by government funds. The Medicare program received particular attention. *Prospective payment* mechanisms were developed. With these, a hospital receives a fixed sum for the treatment of a specific medical condition. If the patient can be served for less, the hospital makes money; if the service costs more, they lose money. These *Diagnostic Related Groups (DRGs)* have caused hospitals to need people with discharge planning skills, one of the roles often filled by social workers (Caputi and Heiss, 1984). Discharge planning involves placement in long-term care facilities and provision of needed services if the patient returns home. These changes contributed to the rise of home health-care services. They point to a change in the health-care system as a response to changes in social policy. They point to changes in the roles and functions of health-care social workers and suggest a change in the relationship between the social welfare system and the health-care system.

Social Work in Health Care

In discussing the role of the social worker in the health-care setting, it is necessary to define some of the characteristics of that setting. Although there is no typical health-care setting, the health-care system can be divided into three major parts: the hospital, the long-term care facility, and the community setting. Each of these major components has different subcomponents. The *hospital* may be a large teaching hospital, a hospital specializing in one or more medical conditions, a general hospital in a large or small community, or a VA facility. For the purpose of discussing roles of social workers, the hospital is considered the component that treats acute and short-term conditions requiring inpatient care. The *long-term care facility*, although it also may be called a hospital, in this discussion will include all health-care facilities where the patient is in residence over long periods of time (a month or more), including nursing homes and rehabilitation centers. The *community setting* includes private and group practices of physicians, HMOs, home health-care units, and outpatient clinics.

The Role of Social Work in the Health-Care System

The use of social workers in hospitals has continued to grow. In 1935 the American Association of Hospital Social Workers became the American Association of Medical Social Workers. For a time, this organization published *The Medical Social Worker Journal.* Social workers became recognized as health-care professionals. Their roles expanded to include participation on health-care teams and in comprehensive health-care projects, clinical treatment, teaching, and consultation. Also, following the trend in medicine, they became more specialized. In 1955, with the formation of the NASW, medical social workers became a part of the unified organization.

During the 1960s and 1970s, social work roles in health care continued to expand, in part due to the growing influence of federal legislation on health care. The Social Security amendments of 1965 that also established the Medicare and Medicaid programs led to the establishment of positions for many social workers in hospitals and nursing homes. The 1966 Comprehensive Health Planning Act was aimed at coordinating health-care facilities, services, and funding with the needs, goals, and priorities of health planning bodies.

Slowly, social services have become an accepted part of all units of the health-care system. In 1970 the Joint Commission on the Accreditation of Hospitals adopted a requirement that "social services must be available to patients and families." The 1973 Health Maintenance Organization Act that oversees HMOs (to be discussed later in this chapter) also requires that they make social services available, thus fueling the gradual growth of social services in group medical practices as well as in hospitals, nursing homes, and maternal and child health programs (Bracht, 1978).

During this period the role of social work in health care has also grown and developed. Graduate social work schools have established specialty areas in social work in health care. Two specialty journals have been established, and books on social work in health care have begun to appear. Some discussion has developed about the role of the B.S.W. and the M.S.W. in the health-care field of practice, although there is still no definitive statement of the role of each level of practice in health-care settings.

It should now be evident that social work practice in the health care field takes place in what is known as a host setting. That is, social work is not the prime profession. In health care, the physician is in charge. Often there are tensions between physicians and social workers about a patient's care when it involves social functioning concerns. Issues about client self-determination is only one example. Social workers believe the patient has a right to choose in many situations; the physician may believe patients should follow advice and prescription. When working in this host setting, it is often important to help other health care professionals to understand the client's social needs. However there are times when medical judgment will overrule. Social workers must be prepared to work within the medical system yet maintain their professional integrity.

Another factor affecting the social worker role in health care is the rise of *private practice* in social work. The private practitioner should be an M.S.W. with previous supervised experience. Because private practice has been a usual form of medical practice, physicians seem to feel comfortable with it. Private practice has also been useful when receiving *third party payments* (insurance reimbursement). What the future of social work private practice in the health care system is, remains to be seen.

Throughout the history of the relationship of the health-care system and the social welfare system, there has been an ongoing debate about the control that physicians have had in the planning and delivery of health care. Although there is no doubt that a doctor must be in charge of the physical care, the psychosocial components of health care (those that focus on social and psychological effects of illness and treatment) and health-care planning (including the development of mechanisms for providing the fiscal supports for care) are areas where social workers have considerable knowledge. Health care can be enhanced by the use of this knowledge. Social workers have been particularly affected by this debate because they are often seen as an ancillary profession in health care. They have had to fight an ongoing battle for recognition of their expertise and contribution to the health-care field of practice (Wallace, Goldberg, and Slaby, 1984).

The health-care system is a multidisciplinary one; important professionals in the system include doctors, nurses, physical therapists, occupational therapists, speech clinicians, and nutritionists. In some settings, psychologists, chaplains, and health educators may also be involved. This means the social worker must find a place among often overlapping areas of concern and must work within a team. Second, the physician is the primary professional in patient care, and either specifically or through previously chosen mechanisms determines the social worker's involvement with any patient. Physicians' desires must be dealt with, and doctors must be kept informed of the social worker's plans and interventions. Third, in contemporary health care, a great deal of emphasis is placed on *accountability*—the means for establishing appropriateness and effectiveness of services. Documentation of work performed and contacts made on behalf of the clients, audits and surveys, and care plans are essential parts of work in the health-care setting. It is usually assumed that social workers will deal with psychosocial problems, that they will work with families of patients, and that they will have knowledge of community resources that can benefit the patient or the family. In many settings, particularly if the worker is an M.S.W., teaching, consultation, and administration are also functions of social workers.

As said before, the differentiation of roles between the M.S.W. and B.S.W. in the health-care setting is still uncertain, as it is in the profession generally. However, M.S.W.'s tend to predominate in large teaching hospitals and hospitals in larger communities. They may direct social services in some long-term care facilities and in community agencies. B.S.W.'s tend to work in small hospitals or under the supervision of an M.S.W. in a large hospital. They tend to be the social worker in a nursing home and to carry case management roles in other long-term facilities. Their role in community settings is still unclear. The B.S.W. tends to provide a good deal of the health-care social work in nonmetropolitan settings.

Social workers are found in a variety of health-care settings. The roles and responsibilities of these workers vary from setting to setting. Four settings are of particular interest in discussing the roles of social workers in health-care settings: hospitals, long-term care facilities, community settings, and maternal and child health programs.

Health Care Settings

Hospital Social Work

When working in a hospital, a social worker must always be aware of the dual authority system existing in such settings. Not only is there the medical authority of the physician, but there is also administrative authority coming from the hospital administrator. Hospital administration has become a discipline in its own right, with responsibility for the ongoing functioning of the hospital facility. Also affecting the social worker's functioning is how patients are assigned. Some social workers are assigned to specialty units such as neonatal, obstetrics, pediatrics, medical and surgical, oncology, and renal disease, to name a few. Each of these specialty units has its own way of functioning and of determining how the social worker will be involved. Other social workers receive referrals from physicians and other health care professionals for social services. In still other settings, *protocols* (rules for treating particular medical problems) have been developed and determine which patients are at risk, psychosocially, and should automatically be referred for social services.

Health-care social workers are routinely employed in the emergency room. In the past thirty years the number of emergency room visits has risen 945 percent. Many people use the emergency room as a source of primary care. Emergency rooms also serve rape victims, battered women, child abuse victims, and suicidal and psychiatric patients. All of these situations call for psychosocial as well as medical care. The role and function of the social worker in these settings still is not well defined, but clearly they are the team members who care not only for the patient but for the accompanying family members as well (Clement and Klingbeil, 1981).

Krell and Rosenberg (1990) have identified eleven services usually provided by hospital-based social workers:

- Referrals to community resources
- Preadmission and discharge planning
- Case finding and social risk assessment
- Counseling patients and families
- Psychosocial evaluations
- Health education and community service activities
- Utilization review under the Professional Standards Review Organization (PSRO)
- Case consultation with hospital staff and community agencies
- Program consultation with hospital staff
- Planning activities to enhance hospital programs and resources
- Assessment of patient outcomes and program evaluation

A Case Study

The social worker on a pediatric unit was made aware that five-year-old John R had been diagnosed as having leukemia. Because of new treatments and the early stage of the disease, the prognosis was good; it is likely that John will experience a remission and survive the disease. However, nursing staff have noted that the parents are distraught and unable to cooperate with the care of the child. The social worker came to the unit at a time when both parents were scheduled to visit. She drew them aside, introduced herself, and asked if she could talk with them in her office. When the parents and the social worker got to the office, it was apparent that the mother was very upset. The father, on the other hand, seemed distant and distrustful. The worker explained that she could understand their shock at John's diagnosis and wondered what questions they might have about it. The mother broke down and became almost hysterical; the father seemed unable to respond to her and remained deep in his own thoughts. The worker told the parents that such feelings were natural and encouraged the parents to talk about how they felt. She listened to an outpouring from the mother and, when this lessened somewhat, encouraged the father to talk about how he felt. He tentatively began to talk about how he found it difficult to express feelings but did talk about his concern

for his wife. The worker probed to help him express his frustration at not being able to do anything for John.

When the feelings had been dealt with to some extent, the worker asked if they understood the diagnosis. It soon was apparent they did not. Both parents had heard only the diagnosis and not the prognosis. They assumed John would soon die. The worker talked a little with them about new treatments and about some children she had known who had survived leukemia. She suggested they set up a joint conference with John's doctor to further explore prognosis and treatment issues. With this, the father asked the social worker how they should treat John, what they could do for him. The worker then discussed the meaning of having a sick child, and together the three discussed some immediate ways the parents could relate to their child. As a follow-up, the worker set up the conference with the doctor and checked with the nursing staff about how the parents were relating to their child. The nursing staff reported a marked improvement in their ability to participate in John's care. The social worker also noted that this situation would require ongoing social services to give the family support, help them to express feelings and ask questions, and help them in parenting their child during his illness.

Social services in hospitals are also affected by outside accrediting agencies. Of primary importance in this area are the "Standards for Hospital Social Service" of the Joint Commission on the Accreditation of Hospitals (Standards for Hospital Social Services, 1978).

Long-Term Care

Three groups of people have usually made up the patients in long-term care facilities: those with lifelong disabilities that require ongoing skilled nursing care; those with sudden disabilities like multiple sclerosis, disabling stroke, or trauma (quadriplegia or other extensive injury) resulting from accidents; and the elderly who are too frail to be cared for in a community setting. The two types of institutions usually considered long-term care facilities are nursing homes and rehabilitation hospitals. Although there are differences in the delivery of social services, depending on the reason for the need for long-term care and the particular long-term care facility, there is a commonality about the role of social workers in these settings. Their role is different from that of social workers in the hospital setting. First, social work plays a more central role, and the physician's role is often diminished. Second, the patients' psychosocial needs are related, in part, to the long-term nature of the setting. Because patients live in the facility, their ongoing needs for relationships, privacy, and activity must receive attention. Third, the medical condition is often chronic and may not improve. Thus, the emphasis is on living with illness rather than curing it.

Recently, skilled nursing homes have experienced a new population, those who have been released from hospitals and are not yet able to return home. This population is largely over sixty-five years of age and subject to the Medicare DRG provisions. Many need a considerable amount of skilled nursing care. In small communities, an arrangement referred to as swing beds is often used. Swing beds are beds in small hospitals that can be used either as hospital beds or as skilled nursing home beds. The social service and activities required for the skilled nursing home beds are usually provided from an adjacent nursing home. Individuals who receive skilled nursing care after hospitalization often can eventually return to the community. Thus, discharge planning is an important component of social services for them.

With patients who have had a lifelong disability, the movement to the rehabilitation facility may come in adolescence or early adulthood, when the family can no longer meet the special needs of the patient. These patients will need help in separating from their families, making plans for how to live life in the most productive way possible, connecting with a variety of resources that may enrich life, and sometimes making plans to move back to supported community living or to a more appropriate living facility.

With patients who have an unanticipated disability, the first task is to help them recognize the nature of the disability and how it will affect their lifestyles. Many feelings will need to be dealt with at this stage. Patients will need a great deal of support for the arduous tasks of rehabilitation. Families need help with their feelings. Ongoing tasks of development, such as education or parenting, also need attention. Patients must be given help with developing ongoing living arrangements after the rehabilitation is completed. Resources must be found to support patients either in a long-term care facility or in the community.

With elderly patients, the nursing home social worker will facilitate their entry into the facility with preplacement services and services to help the families and patients with the decision to enter the home. Families need help learning how to relate to family members in a nursing home and dealing with their feelings about the patient. On admission, a social history and in-depth assessment of the patient's needs must be developed. The social worker participates in the development of care plans. Ongoing tasks with nursing home patients include updating and revising goals and care plans; ongoing counseling or group activity; collaborating and consulting with staff, family, and volunteers about the needs of the patient; financial planning; and working to maintain family support and ties. Some patients progress to the point that they can be discharged. Discharge planning then becomes a social work task.

In long-term care facilities, the social worker carries some responsibility to see that the milieu of the facility is one that supports patient functioning at the highest level possible, one in which all the needs (not just the health-care needs) of the patient are taken into account. To do this, the social worker consults with other staff about psychosocial aspects of care and the impact of the milieu on social functioning, participates in staff meetings where decisions are made about the facility's program and way of operating, and provides educational sessions for other staff in areas where the social worker has expertise. The social worker also coordinates the use of community resources to meet the needs of individuals or groups of patients in the area of social functioning. They will maintain the necessary records and serve as advocates for patients. Social workers in long-term care facilities work with individuals, families, groups, and the in-

A Case Study

The social worker went to see Mrs. B, who had just been taken by ambulance to a nursing home from a local hospital. Unfortunately, the social worker had not had an opportunity to visit Mrs. B or talk with her family prior to admission. Mrs. B was recovering from a fractured pelvis. The hospital asked for admission because she had used up her Diagnostic Related Group days and no longer needed acute care. The worker found Mrs. B confused and angry. She was not sure where she was and said that no one had asked her if she wanted to come here. The worker explained to Mrs. B that she was in Shadydale Nursing Home and that together they would explore whether this was the type of care she would need on a long-term basis. The worker repeated that although Mrs. B still needed care, she did not have to remain in the hospital any longer. The worker briefly described the advantages of being in a nursing home over a hospital and assured Mrs. B that this was not necessarily the "end of the line." Mrs. B became quieter, and the worker asked about her living circumstances prior to hospitalization. She found that Mrs. B lived alone in low-cost senior housing. She told Mrs. B that she would check on how long the apartment could be held for her. The social worker asked Mrs. B if there was anything she would like from the apartment for her room here at the nursing home. They discussed this, and Mrs. B asked for some family pictures. The worker told her that she would get them and check on the apartment for her. Then the worker asked about her family and found that Mrs. B had one daughter, who lived some distance away and had a large family of her own that she could not leave just then. The daughter was notified of the move and gave her permission. The worker told Mrs. B she would like to call the daughter and talk with her. Hesitantly, Mrs. B gave permission for this. The worker then told Mrs. B she would be talking to her quite a bit in the next few days and gave a definite time for the next day.

The worker, in thinking about the situation of Mrs. B, noted that this was the third time in a month that Shadydale had received a patient from the hospital who had inadequate preparation for the move. She noted that plans must be developed to prevent this from happening in the future. She called Mrs. B's daughter and found a guilt-ridden woman who simply did not know what to do about her mother. The worker assured her that her mother was being well cared for, but said that long-term plans would need to be made and that the social worker would keep in touch with her. She shared her plans to look into the apartment situation and bring the requested pictures and some of Mrs. B's clothes to the nursing home. The worker called the apartment manager and arranged to see him first thing in the morning. She also recorded her contact in Mrs. B's chart and discussed her findings with the head nurse. She talked to an able long-time resident who had had a similar experience on admission to the home, and suggested that she visit with Mrs. B.

---

stitution itself, as well as with the community of which it is a part. The social work role in these facilities is indeed a generalist role.

Community Settings

The role that social workers play in community settings is still unclear. For the most part, social workers, usually M.S.W. 's, have negotiated their role with the individual physician or clinic. There is also little information about how many social workers are practicing in community health settings.

One type of primary health-care setting is the *health maintenance organization* (HMO), a voluntary, prepaid health system built around a group medical practice. The federal government has set standards and provided financial assistance to these organizations since 1973. Originally, medical social services were required of those organizations receiving federal assistance, but since 1981 this has not been the case. Social workers do continue to be employed in some HMOs.

Some of the services that social workers perform in HMOs are helping patients adjust to illness and understand and follow medical recommendations, helping patients with personal and behavioral problems that adversely affect their health, providing referral and resource development, and coordinating rehabilitation services. In addition, they provide the medical team with information about social and emotional rehabilitation. They treat crisis-based mental health problems and are involved in educational activities. They also handle grievances and discharge planning (Bracht, 1978).

Maternal and child health programs are other community programs that employ social workers. There programs serve children with special needs, those who have some kind of handicap, or those who are at risk because they live in poor families. Because each state administers its programs within federal guidelines, they differ considerably in practice from program to program. The social worker is a member of the team that serves the child in a holistic manner. Most of these positions require an M.S.W. worker, but B.S.W.'s are also used in some programs.

Another component of the community health-care delivery system, currently growing at a very fast rate, is *home health care*. This growth is due in part to the fact that people are spending less time in hospitals and are going home needing continued nursing and other professional care. DRGs are partly responsible for this trend, as is the rising cost of hospital care. Many hospitals are organizing home health-care units. Nurses, physical therapists, and other health professionals go into the home to provide the necessary care. Social workers also participate in this care. Some of the services they provide include developing a patient's comprehensive social history; considering a patient's psychosocial needs in the admission and referral process; making recommendations for the care plan; helping the patient understand and comply with health recommendations; helping the family understand the patient's needs; counseling individuals, families, or groups; and referring people to and developing needed community resources. Hospice care programs, providing care for terminally ill people, have developed and are providing home care. Social workers are important members of the hospice team.

The social worker's role in delivering health-care services, whether in the hospital, the long-term care facility, or the community setting, is important if holistic health care is to be provided. Social services can prevent some of the long-term negative results of illness and disability. They can facilitate the use of community resources to prevent overuse of hospitals and long-term facilities. As the health-care system in particular and the community in general come to appreciate the value of these services, they cannot help but be in demand. This points to a growing importance of social work in the health-care setting.

Issues in the Relationship of Health Care and Social Welfare

Tremendous change is the contemporary theme in the health-care system. A new method of determining payment (prospective payment) seems to be the method of the future, not only for Medicare patients but also for those covered by health insurance and government payment mechanisms. This is only one response to concerns about the rising cost of health care. In the future there may be more reliance on professionals other than physicians for care. (Nurse-practitioners and physician-assistants provide an increasing amount of primary care service.) There is a growing emphasis on delivery of health care in the community rather than in institutions. (The growth of home health-care services is one indication.) Prevention (health care rather than medical care) and a holistic approach are common themes in the popular literature. All of these changes can be interpreted to indicate that the role of the social worker will grow and become more central in the health-care system. Change brings with it many unresolved issues. The health-care system has many such issues today. Many affect the field of social work in health care. In this section, some of these issues will be raised and discussed briefly.

A primary issue that has not been resolved, although it has been discussed for some time, is whether health care is a right or a privilege. Philosophically, many support health care as a right, but social policy does not grant this right to all people. The employed poor, if they have no employer-sponsored health insurance, cannot afford health care. In addition, federal medical programs and most health insurance programs do not pay for preventive care; rather, they pay for treating illness (Hartman, 1992). Unless some form of health care protection is afforded to all through public social policy, as discussed earlier, health care will remain a matter of privilege for those fortunate enough to have acquired an employment situation that affords health care protection as a fringe benefit, or for those of means who can afford private health care insurance.

Quality-of-life issues also must receive attention. In recent years, enormous progress has been made in maintaining life through medical advances. New treatments and life support systems are examples of these advances. However, little attention has been given to whether the preservation of life at all costs is in the best interest of the individual or society. Kidney dialysis patients, artificial heart recipients, severely handicapped newborns all require expensive medical treatment, yet the quality of life that they can live may be greatly limited. Society hesitates to provide funds for the needed medical care or for the life supports that sustain the lives of people receiving *heroic medical measures*, such as the use of life support systems. Questions of the right to live or the right to die must be answered, and whether public funds should be used for heroic medical measures must be decided. Social workers need to be involved in discussions about biomedical ethics (Dhooper, 1990).

Not only is the health-care system responsible for resolving these issues, so is the social welfare system. Many of the people affected by these controversial medical procedures will become recipients of financial support and services from the social welfare system. Ultimately, the general public will be involved in the resolution as they support or fail to support social welfare programs. The general public needs information from the social welfare system as it makes these difficult decisions.

Another related set of issues concerns preventive health care. The system, as it now operates, is focused on treating and curing illness. Many present-day medical conditions are chronic, incurable, and need to be managed. Prevention exists on both a primary and a secondary level. The primary level is preventing chronic illness by educating the public and motivating change. At the secondary level, screening for chronic disease and managing chronic illnesses prevents more serious effects, including psychosocial effects. Emphasis on a holistic approach and on improving lifestyle is the best way to approach prevention.

Related to lifestyle issues are cultural issues. Little attention has been paid to the cultural aspects of illness and health care. Some cultural groups have their own health-care providers (the *curandero* of the Chicano and the medicine man of the American Indian). These resources can provide care, but few health-care agencies understand how to integrate them into a health-care system that depends on highly trained professionals. Also, an understanding of different lifestyles, attitudes about what constitutes health, how illness should be treated, and self-help remedies is needed if these issues are to be addressed.

The social work profession has understanding and expertise that could be very useful in addressing the issues of quality of life, lifestyle, and prevention. The social welfare system has a considerable interest in resolving these issues, for they are closely related to human needs and the mechanisms for meeting those needs. Both the social work profession and the social welfare system should address the questions involved in these health-care issues.

A health-care concern of major importance is the appearance and spread of the *acquired immune deficiency syndrome (AIDS)*. The World Health Organization (WHO) has estimated that 15 million persons worldwide have been infected with AIDS since the disease began to appear in pandemic proportions, and recently reported that there are currently 4.5 million persons with a confirmed diagnosis of AIDS (CDC, 1995). In the United States, the Center for Disease Control (CDC) has estimated that as many as 1.5 million persons may be infected with HIV, Human Immunodeficiency Virus, which causes AIDS, and recently reported that 450,000 persons are known to be infected with HIV (CDC, 1995). The disease has become the second leading cause of death among men, ages 25 to 44, and is spreading the most within the female population, becoming the sixth leading cause of death for women, ages 25 to 44 (Cowley and Hager, 1993).

Responses to this catastrophic situation continue to be somewhat influenced by the fact that gay men and drug users have shown particularly high susceptibility to AIDS. The resulting negative feelings have complicated attempts to deal with the situation both on a societal level (prevention, treatment, and research) and on an individual level (treatment and compassion). However, because the incidence of AIDS has increased more rapidly within the heterosexual population in recent years, it can no longer be viewed as an exclusively gay men's or IV drug users' disease. If the spread of the disease continues at present rates, it will have the potential to affect each one of our lives in some way, either as a victim, family member, or friend of a victim (Cowles and Rodgers, 1994).

Patrick Haney (1988), an AIDS sufferer, has stated, "The bottom line in helping persons with AIDS is to assist us in focusing on learning to live with AIDS." He calls for social workers to empower AIDS patients to maintain control over what happens to them and to advocate or give support when this is needed.

Catlin C. Ryan (1991), in an editorial issue of *Social Work*, made the following observations:

1. Currently there are not enough trained social workers to provide essential services not only to those with AIDS but to all people.
2. Social workers lack sufficient AIDS-specific training.
3. Agency policy has not adapted to the management of high stress and grief associated with service to people with AIDS.
4. Social workers are overburdened with the breakdowns in the health care and public social services systems that interfere with their ability to provide needed services to AIDS patients.

More recently, Buckingham (1994) stated that due to the changing nature of HIV/AIDS, public health and human services professionals need to examine the adequacy and appropriateness of health and pychosocial services being provided victims of this disease so as to be more responsive to the challenges that lie ahead. Mancoske and Hunzeker (1994) have called for an empowerment approach to the planning for and coordination of comprehensive community-based services so that individual communities may take responsibility for meeting their own unique challenges. Lastly, any proposal or initiated measure of health care reform will be impacted by the HIV/AIDS pandemic. Health care reform must consider the health care needs of those afflicted by AIDS and plans must contain provisions for ensuring adequate medical care for victims (Brennan, 1994).

Medical practices and institutions are now managed as businesses. Some feel that this places the major emphasis not on quality of care but on how much money can be made. With the rise of new professions such as physician-assistants, nurse-practitioners, and mental health professionals in the health-care field, and with old professions providing a broader range of skilled services, questions arise about whether these new professionals should be reimbursed by insurance for their services. There are indications that some health care not only can be provided by professionals other than physicians but can be provided more cheaply. But without a system for reimbursing the new professionals, it is impossible to use this factor to reduce costs. The issues of health care as a business and of insurance coverage also must be addressed.

Another development is the proliferation of professions that function in the health-care field. There is no agreement as to which profession should carry out which tasks. For example, should discharge planning be the task of a social worker or of a nurse? Interdisciplinary turf battles must be settled. Some means must be developed to determine which professionals are best qualified to carry out which tasks. Social work, as a profession expanding its role in the health-care field, will be affected by these decisions. If social work is to take its rightful place among health-care professionals, the profession must give attention to the issue. In addition, the profession should consider and clarify the role of the B.S.W. and that of the M.S.W. in the health-care field. This should not be done on the basis of assumptions about what tasks each level of worker can carry out, but from careful study of the roles and tasks that are being carried out by both levels of social workers in the health-care field. The concern over health care costs referred to earlier in the chapter is of course a major issue. It is hoped that the Clinton administration will be able to bring about the necessary reform in health care provision and that social workers and their professional organizations can have meaningful input into the policy development process.

In this section of the chapter, many issues have been raised, but few solutions have been suggested. Both the social welfare system and the profession of social work have contributions to make in the forthcoming discussions. Individual social workers will need to keep abreast of the unavoidable changes that will come and be prepared to answer the challenges change will bring.

Summary

This chapter has discussed the nature of the contemporary health-care system and the intertwining of that system with the social welfare system. It has noted the role that social work has filled in the health-care system and given some indication of the expanded roles for social workers that can be a part of the future health-care system. One last question needs to be raised: Can the social welfare system and the health-care system really be separate if the needs of individuals in a complex society are to be met?

This may be the most crucial of all issues. Until it is resolved, the social welfare system and the health-care system will continue to overlap and to compete for scarce funds. Social workers will find themselves relating to both systems in the health-care field of practice, with conflicting demands from the two systems. Individuals will continue to have their social functioning needs met by both systems, often in a confusing and clumsy manner.

Key Terms

accountability
acquired immune deficiency syndrome (AIDS)
charity hospital
charity patient
community setting
Diagnostic Related Groups (DRGs)
employer-based approach
government approach
health-care system
health maintenance organization (HMO)
heroic medical measures
Hill-Burton Act
holistic
home health care
hospital

host setting
human immunodeficiency virus (HIV)
long-term care facility
maternal and child health programs
Medicaid
Medicare
national health insurance
private market approach
private practice
prospective payment
protocol
Sheppard-Towner Act
single payer
third party payment

References

Austin, M.J., Baizerman, M., and Guzzetta, C. (1974). Public Health and Social Welfare: An Historical View of the Revitalization of an Old Partnership. *Arte 3*, 16–31.

Bracht, N.F. (1978). *Social Work in Health Care: A Guide to Professional Practice.* New York: Haworth.

Brennan, J.P. (1994). HIV/AIDS: Implications for Health Care Reform. *Families in Society 75 (6)*, 385–92.

Brieland, D., Costin, L.B., and Atherton, C.R. (1975). *Contemporary Social Work.* New York: McGraw-Hill.

Brody, S.J. (1976). Common Ground: Social Work and Health Care. *Health and Social Work, 1*, 16–31.

Buckingham, S.L. (1994). AIDS: The Next Wave of the Crisis. *Families in Society, 75 (6)*, 323.

Caputi, A., and Heiss, W.A. (1984). The DRG Revolution. *Health and Social Work, 9*, 5–14.

Clement, J., and Klingbeil, K.S. (1981). The Emergency Room. *Health and Social Work, 6*, 835–905.

Cowles, K.V., and Rodgers, B.L. (1994). Significant Others of Persons with AIDS: A Preliminary Study. *Journal of Gay and Lesbian Psychotherapy, 2 (2)*, 101–119.

Cowley, G., and Hager, M. (1993). Lifestyle: Medicine: What If a Cure Is Far Off? *Newsweek, 121*, 70.

Dhooper, S.S. (1990). Organ Transplantation: Who Decides? *Social Work, 37*, 322–27.

Fein, R. (1992). Prescription for Change. *Modern Maturity, 35*, 22–35.

Germain, C.B. (1984). *Social Work Practice in Health Care.* New York: Free Press, p.34.

Haney, P. (1988). Providing Empowerment to the Person with AIDS. *Social Work 33*, 251–253.

Hartman, A. (1992). Health Care: Privilege or Entitlement. *Social Work 37*, 195–96.

Karger, H.J., and Stoesz, D. (1994). *American Social Welfare Policy: A Pluralist Approach.* New York: Longman.

Kerson, T.S. (1982). *Social Work in Health Settings.* New York: Longman.

Krell, G.I., and Rosenberg, G. (1990). Predicting Patterns of Social Work Staffing in Hospital Settings. In K.W. Davidson and S.S. Clarke (Eds.), *Social Work in Health Care.* New York: Haworth Press.

Mancoske, R.J., and Hunzeker, J.M. (1994). Advocating for Community Services Coordination: An Empowerment Perspective for Planning AIDS Services. *Journal of Community Practice, 1 (3)*, 49–58.

Rothman, G., and Becerra, R.M. (1987). Veterans and Veteran's Services. In A. Minahan (Ed.), *Encyclopedia of Social Work.* Silver Spring, MD: National Association of Social Workers, pp. 808–817.

Rothman, S.M. (1978). *Woman's Proper Place: A History of Changing Ideals and Practices, 1870 to the Present.* New York: Basic Books.

Ryan, C.C. (1991). Where Do We Go From Here? *Social Work, 36*, 3–4.

Scuka, R.F. (1994). Health Care Reform in the 1990's: An Analysis of the Problems and Three Proposals. *Social Work 39 (5)*, 578–587.

Standards for Hospital Social Services. (1978). *Health and Social Work, 3*, 4–12.

U.S. Bureau of the Census. (1995). *Statistical Abstracts of the United States: 1995* (115th edition). Washington, DC: U.S. Government Printing Office.

U.S. Department of Health and Human Services, Center for Disease Control (1995) *AIDS Daily.* Washington DC: U.S. Government Printing Office.

Wallace, R., Goldberg, R.J., and Slaby, A.E. (1984). *Clinical Social Work in Health Care.* New York: Praeger.

Suggested Readings

Alperin, Diane E. and Richie, Nicholas D. "Community-Based AIDS Service Organizations: Challenges and Educational Preparation." *Health and Social Work,* 14 (Aug. 1989), 165–183.

Blumenfield, Susan and Rosenberg, Gary. "Towards a Network of Social Health Services: Redefining Discharge Planning and Expanding the Social Work Domain." *Social Work in Health Care,* 13 (No. 4, 1988), 31–48.

Bracht, Neil F. *Social Work in Health Care: A Guide to Professional Practice.* (New York: Haworth Press, 1978).

Brody, Stanley J. "Common Ground: Social Work and Health Care." *Health and Social Work,* 1 (February 1976), 16–31.

Cabot, Richard C. *Social Service and the Art of Healing* (New York: Moffat, Yard and Company, 1915) (NASW Classic Series).

Caputi, Marie A., and Heiss, William A. "The DRG Revolution." *Health and Social Work,* 9 (Winter 1984), 5–14.

Cohn, Victor. "Rationing Medical Care." *Public Welfare,* 49 (Winter 1991), 38–43.

Dane, Barbara Oberhofer and Simon, Barbara L. "Resident Guests: Social Workers in Host Settings." *Social Work,* 36 (May 1991), 208–214.

Dhooper, Surjit Singh, "Organ Transplantation: Who Decides?" *Social Work,* 35 (July 1990), 322–337.

Fein, Rashi. "Prescription for Change." *Modern Maturity* 35 (August–September 1992), 22–35.

Gorin, Stephen and Moniz, Cynthia. "The National Health Care Crisis: An Analysis of Proposed Solutions." *Health and Social Work,* 17 (Feb. 1992), 39–44.

Iatridis, Demetrius S. "Cuba's Health Care Policy: Prevention and Active Community Participation." *Social Work,* 35 (Jan. 1990), 29–35.

Mayer, Jane B., and Rubin, Gail. "Is There a Future for Social Work in HMOs?" *Health and Social Work,* 8 (Fall 1983), 283–289.

Minahan, Anne, editor-in-chief. *Encyclopedia of Social Work,* 18th ed. (Silver Springs, MD: National Association of Social Workers, 1987). Articles on "Health Care Specialization," "Health Planning," "Health Service System," "Hospice," "Hospital Social Work," "Primary Health Care," and "Public Health Care."

Oriol, William. "Protecting Quality of Health Care During a Cost-Containment Era: HOW?" *Perspective on Aging,* 28 (July–August 1989), 4–13.

Roberts, Clora S. "Conflicting Professional Values in Social Work and Medicine." *Health and Social Work* 14 (Aug. 1989), 211–218.

Schlesinger, Elfriede G. *Health Care Social Work Practice: Concepts and Strategies* (St. Louis: Times Mirror/ C. V. Mosby, 1985).

Schorr, Alvin L. "What Is Reform in Health Care," *Social Work,* 37 (May 1992), p. 263–265.

Silverman, Ed. "Hospital Bioethics: A Beginning Knowledge Base for the Neonatal Social Worker." *Social Work,* 37 (May 1992), 150–154.

Smith, Vernon K., and Eggleston, Ronald. "Long Term Care: The Medical vs. the Social Model." *Public Welfare,* 47 (Summer 1989), 26–29.

Social Work, Special Issue on AIDS, 36 (Jan. 1991).

Social Work and Health Care, Special Issue, "The Changing Context of Social Health Care: Its Implications for Providers and Consumers," 15 (No. 4, 1991).

Surber, Robert W.; Dwyer, Eleanor; Ryan, Katherine J.; Goldfinger, Stephen M.; and Kelly, John T. "Medical and Psychiatric Needs of the Homeless—A Preliminary Response." *Social Work,* 33 (March–April 1988), 116–119.

"The Past as Prologue: Ten Years of *Health and Social Work.*" *Health and Social Work,* 10 (Fall 1985), Special Tenth-Anniversary Issue.

10

SOCIAL WELFARE AND MENTAL HEALTH

Learning Expectations

- Ability to describe the difficulties in defining mental health
- Capacity to define mental health services
- Capacity to discuss the relationship between mental health services and social welfare services
- Ability to trace the development of mental health services in the United States
- Understanding of the place of institutionalization in the mental health system
- Understanding of the strengths and limitations of the delivery of mental health services in the community
- Ability to trace the development of services to the developmentally disabled in the United States
- Understanding of the various roles filled by social workers in the mental health system
- Awareness of some of the current issues and concerns in the mental health field

One of the factors that contributes to inability to meet basic needs is the state of a person's mental health. The social welfare system has developed partly because of needs that go unmet as a result of mental health problems. Different individuals respond in different ways to both their external environment and their internal state of being. This diversity makes it difficult to define *mental health*. One definition of mental health is "a positive state of personal mental well-being in which individuals feel basically satisfied with themselves, their roles in life, and their relationships with others" (Thackeray, Skidmore, and Farley, 1978).

The extent of mental health problems is difficult to document because many people do not seek help for such problems. However, in 1990, there were 9.3 episodes of hospitalization per 1,000 persons in the United States (U.S. Bureau of the Census, 1995). The numbers of people who seek outpatient assistance is greater.

What, then, is the relationship between social welfare and mental health? Does the social welfare system provide for the needs of people in poor states of mental health or those who are in danger of falling into such states because they lack social and economic resources? Or does attention to their mental health prevent the need for social welfare services? These questions are related to whether a preventive or a residual approach to social welfare is most desirable. Some individuals need help from the social welfare system because of poor mental health, whereas others can, through maintenance of their mental health, be prevented from developing a need for help with problems in social functioning.

Another way in which the social welfare system and mental health services are related is in the functioning of the social worker. Social work is the central profession of the social welfare system. The social worker is one of the major providers of mental health services. Whether the service falls within the social welfare system or the mental health system is often unclear. If social work services in mental health care for social functioning needs, they are a part of the social welfare system as well as of mental health services.

Steven P. Segal and Jim Baumohl (1981) have discussed this issue in relationship to community mental health: "The community mental health movement's focus on community-based treatment and its emphasis on the impact of social life on mental status places it squarely within the domain of social welfare. Indeed, despite the greater authority accorded to the medical profession, social workers staff more full-time positions and provide more services than any other professional group in community mental health centers" (pp. 19–20). Definition of what a mental health service is and what it is not is addressed in the first section of this chapter. Next, the development of mental health services, with particular emphasis on the role of social work in their delivery, is considered. Then, this chapter examines the functioning of social workers in the mental health system, along with current concerns and issues for mental health social workers.

Definition of Mental Health Services

Mental health services can be defined as those services provided to individuals who are defined as mentally ill. Officially, the definition of mental illness, or of who is mentally ill, generally makes use of a medical (psychiatric) diagnosis, using the *Diagnostic and Statistical Manual of Mental Disorders*, 4th edition, (DSM-IV). The DSM-IV is the official reference for diagnostic classifications of the American Psychiatric Association (APA). An informal way of defining mental illness is to describe it as the manifestation of some emotional difficulty. This kind of definition is often used by the general public. But these definitions are not as clear-cut as they first seem. Some individuals who, under stressful or difficult circumstances, might manifest symptoms of mental illness never actually do so because their environment is supportive and lacks excessive stresses, whereas other individuals become ill even in a very supportive, safe environment. Cultural factors also influence the definition of mental illness (McNeil and Wright, 1983). In the mainstream of U.S. society, troublesome people tend to be labeled in some way, and often the label is mentally ill. In other cultures the same behavior would not be considered abnormal and might even be valued. For example, in Puerto Rican culture it is believed that spirits of the dead communicate with the living. If a social worker does not understand this and a Puerto Rican client says that he or she is hearing voices, the worker may label the client as psychotic. Mental illness consists of a wide variety of disorders with varying degrees of severity. Some types are short term, due to loss, stress, or anxiety, but *chronic mental illness* can last a lifetime and sometimes may be incurable. The boundary line between mental illness and mental health is often unclear.

If the definition of *mental illness* is based on the absence of mental health, another difficulty occurs. Using the definition of mental health given earlier in this chapter, it should be noted that what gives one person a sense of well-being does not necessarily do the same for another person. Two people who fill the same role in society may not view that role with the same sense of satisfaction. One person may be satisfied with a fairly small circle of friends and prefer solitary activity for a good part of his or her free time. Another person may want ongoing activity within a large group of people. In addition, culture may provide individuals with different sets of expectations about life satisfactions.

Because of these difficulties in defining mental illness and mental health, no attempt will be made to define mental health services using these concepts. Rather, a functional definition will be used. In this discussion, mental health services will refer to those services that are provided by *mental health agencies*. It is further assumed that those agencies generally use a multidisciplinary approach to provide services, and that psychology, psychiatry, and nursing, as well as social work, are core disciplines. Such agencies include *psychiatric hospitals* or psychiatric units in general hospitals, community mental health centers, and child guidance clinics. Services for those who have been diagnosed as chronically mentally ill and treatment for alcohol and drug addiction are included because those services are part of a community mental health service. Services for the mentally retarded or developmentally disabled are also included because, historically, they have been considered a part of the mental health field.

Development of Mental Health Services

The recognition of mental illness has existed throughout history. Before the development of industrial society, however, scant attention was paid to this phenomenon. Deviant behavior was much more tolerable in an agricultural society. Families could allow the deviant to participate in the work of the household or to be hidden away. For those with no family, monasteries often provided a haven. With the onset of industrialization, the mentally ill became a part of the wandering vagrant group viewed as a threat to society. Mentally ill people became known as *lunatics*. They were considered incurable and dangerous and were often placed in workhouses or almshouses.

Mental Health Care from the 1700s to World War I

This pattern of caring for the mentally ill was generally followed in the early years of U.S. history (see Table 10–1). With the rise of special institutions, the charity-philanthropy arrangement was increasingly relied on. In 1773 a mental hospital was established in Williamsburg, Virginia. This and other mental institutions that followed—the *insane asylums* established during the nineteenth century in most states—were developed in part to separate the mentally ill

TABLE 10–1   Important Dates: Social Work in Mental Health

1773	The first mental hospital was established in Williamsburg, Virginia.
1833	Worcester State Hospital (Massachusetts) established and used "moral treatment."
1840s–1850s	Dorothea Dix worked for adequate treatment of the mentally ill.
1854	Congress passed an act to provide support for care of mentally ill. President Pierce vetoed it.
1908	Clifford Beers' *A Mind That Found Itself* was published.
1909	The National Committee on Mental Hygiene was formed. A child guidance clinic was established in Cook County, Illinois.
1946	The National Mental Health Act was passed.
1961	The Commission on Mental Illness and Health report appeared.
1963	The Community Mental Health Centers Act was passed.
1977	President Carter established the President's Commission on Mental Health.
1980	The Mental Health Centers Act passed.
1981	The Reagan administration repealed budgetary authorizations affecting the Mental Health Centers Act and included federal support for mental health services in the health services block grant.

from the general population of the workhouses, poor farms, and jails. Because the mentally ill were considered incurable, little treatment was offered. Often the "lunatic" was confined in chains or in a barred cell. Care was extremely poor, at best.

Across the Atlantic came word of enlightened ways of caring for the mentally ill being used in Europe. Of particular interest was the work of Phillippe Pinel, in Paris, who used kindness and firmness to "cure" some mentally ill people (DiNitto, 1991). Worcester State Hospital, established in 1833 in Massachusetts, used what was known as *moral treatment*, based on the concept of providing a quiet, supportive environment in which the patient could develop new behaviors. For a time this seemed successful. It was probably useful for newly admitted patients, but its downfall was the growth of a long-term chronic population who did not respond as well to moral treatment. State hospitals tended to house individuals from the poorer classes, many of whom were immigrants and were experiencing difficulties in coping in a new culture. This population, because of their different cultures, was little understood by their caretakers and also appeared not to respond to moral treatment (Rothman, 1971).

In the 1840s and 1850s, Dorothea Dix spent a great deal of time speaking to politicians and others about the needs of the mentally ill. She went from state to state, calling for humane care of the insane—instead of isolation, neglect, and cruelty—and for a special state institution for their care. She also worked to obtain medical care and moral treatment for the mentally ill. She was responsible for founding or enlarging thirty-two mental hospitals in the United States and abroad (Leiby, 1978). She also persuaded the Congress, in 1854, to pass a bill providing public lands for the support of therapeutic programs for the mentally ill. However, President Franklin Pierce vetoed the bill on the grounds that care of the mentally ill was the responsibility of the states, not the federal government.

Another important influence on the care of the mentally ill was Clifford Beers. Early in the twentieth century, he spent several years in mental institutions. His book *A Mind That Found*

Itself (1908) was widely read. In 1908 he founded the Connecticut Society for Mental Hygiene, and in 1909 the National Committee for Mental Hygiene (now the *National Association for Mental Health*). Originally, the purpose of this organization was to advocate for more humane treatment of the mentally ill. To this day, this citizens' organization is very influential in working for public awareness and for the development of services in the mental health field. With over one million members, it is the largest voluntary organization in the field of mental health today.

The National Association for Mental Health became interested in the prevention of mental illnesses and saw the treatment of children who were displaying emotional difficulty as a promising measure. The child guidance movement began with a clinic in Cook County, Illinois, in 1909. By 1930 there were five hundred such clinics. *Child guidance clinics* use the interdisciplinary triad (psychiatrist, psychologist, and social worker) in providing services.

Mental Health Care since World War II

Following World War II, the Veterans Administration began to establish what is now the largest psychiatric program in the country. In part, this was an outgrowth of the military experience of the two world wars. World War I saw the first identification of psychiatric casualties. In World War II, the selective service screening process identified mental illness as a major factor in rejecting men for service. The psychiatric casualties of the Vietnam War were also heavy. Of particular concern has been psychiatric disability resulting from the extreme stress placed on participants in this war. To meet the needs of veterans, then, the Veterans Administration facilities place considerable emphasis on psychiatric care.

Mental hospitals—that is, hospitals caring only for patients with mental illness and other emotional or developmental problems—remained the major resource for the treatment of mental illness until very recently. In 1955 there were 550,000 patients in state psychiatric hospitals (Talbott, 1980). By 1990 there were 90,300 patients in state and county hospitals (U.S. Bureau of the Census, 1995). Often, these institutions became the dumping ground for the unwanted and the nonproductive. This was especially tragic when the unwanted were children. Placed with the general population of these hospitals, they received little treatment, nor did the hospitals make any effort to meet their special needs, including their educational needs. Gradually, this has changed. Now special units for children are provided in some mental hospitals. More often, mentally ill children are placed in residential treatment facilities that provide treatment, education, and an appropriate social environment for the children. Specialized group homes have also been developed as a resource for mentally ill children. Private and religious agencies, once dedicated to caring for dependent children in orphanages, have now changed their focus to caring for emotionally disturbed children.

In 1946, as a result of a growing awareness of problems relating to mental health, the National Mental Health Act was passed. A major thrust of this legislation was research on prevention and treatment of mental illnesses and training of mental health professionals. This led to the formation in 1949 of the *National Institute of Mental Health*. This act also encouraged states to designate an agency as its mental health authority. It provided grants-in-aid and technical assistance to the states for programs treating mental disorders.

Beginning in the 1950s, three developments provided new advances in the care of the mentally ill. First, new *psychotropic drugs*, such as tranquilizers, made management of the mentally ill much easier. These drugs reduced bizarre behavior and relieved anxiety in many patients. Second, the concept of a "therapeutic community," as developed by the British psychiatrist Maxwell Jones, became popular. This called for changing the institutional setting, the ward, into a therapeutic setting, using principles of democratic living. Third, many large state hospitals began to be organized geographically. Patients were assigned to wards or units that served a specific geographic area rather than specific types of illness. This allowed closer ties with outpatient facilities in that geographical area. These three developments laid the groundwork for a shift from an emphasis on inpatient treatment to treatment in the community (Bloom, 1984).

The Development of Community Mental Health Centers

The growing concern about mental health in the United States influenced Congress to pass the Mental Health Study Act. This act resulted in the formation of the Joint Commission on Mental Illness and Health and a publication (1961): *Action for Mental Health*. The report called for the following:

1.   Care for acutely disturbed patients in outpatient clinics and inpatient psychiatric units located in general hospitals
2.   Improved care of chronic patients in state hospitals, to be limited to no more than 1,000 beds
3.   Aftercare and partial hospital and rehabilitation services
4.   Expanded mental health education for the public

In December 1962, President John F. Kennedy sent a special message to Congress that proposed a national mental health program (Bloom, 1984). The Community Mental Health Centers Act of 1963 called for the formation of catchment areas with populations of from 75,000 to 200,000 people, so that no more than one hour of travel would be necessary to reach a community mental health center. The original act made federal funds available for the construction of centers. It also emphasized state planning and called for state plans for the delivery of mental health services. In 1965 amendments to the act allowed grants to cover staffing assistance. In 1966 the Comprehensive Health Planning and Public Health Service amendments required that a minimum of 15 percent of the grant go for direct mental health services. From 1967 to 1975 the provisions of the act were extended for additional periods of time.

The advent of community mental health centers marked a significant change in the mental health field. No longer were mentally ill persons to be confined to institutions, often for life. They were now to be institutionalized only when absolutely necessary and, then, for as short a period of time as needed. Community resources were to be expanded and institutional populations reduced. The result was that there were many more mentally disabled people in the community many of whom were overlooked by the system or were not adequately treated by the mental health system. Many older mentally ill persons who had spent a large part of their lives in institutions were placed in nursing homes ill equipped to provide for their needs.

Community mental health centers were expected to offer five services: inpatient care, outpatient care, emergency services, partial hospitalization, and consultation and education. Later, diagnostic services, rehabilitation services, precare and aftercare services, training, and research and evaluation were also required. Continuity of care was stressed. In 1970 legislation also covered the construction and staffing of facilities for the prevention and treatment of alcoholism and drug abuse and for services for children.

In 1977 President Carter established the President's Commission on Mental Health to identify the mental health needs of the nation and to make recommendations to the president. In 1980 the Mental Health Systems Act was passed by Congress. This act made available funds to continue many of the activities provided for under the Community Mental Health Centers Act. Grants were made specifically for the treatment of the chronically mentally ill, severely disturbed children and adolescents, and other underserved populations. The role of the National Institute of Mental Health was expanded to include ongoing planning activities. This act never had a chance to become fully operational, for in 1981, under President Reagan, the budgetary authorizations of the act were repealed and federal support for mental health services was included under the health services block grant. Some requirements for funding mental health services were retained at least until federal funding commitments were fulfilled (Bloom, 1984).

Assessment of the community mental health movement reveals a tendency to focus on verbal, middle-class, nonpsychotic patients who probably do not need hospitalization. Aftercare and services for the chronic patient have been neglected (Barton and Sanborn, 1977). The philosophy of treatment in a community mental health center is that the center meets the needs of the population it serves with a wide variety of approaches. This is done by using several professional disciplines, often with a team approach. Centers emphasize continuity of care, prevention, avoidance of hospitalization, and linkage with the human service network. They focus on health rather than illness. Citizen participation in their governance is essential.

With the development of mental health centers has come the movement for *deinstitutionalization*. Mental health professionals developed a strong belief that institutions were not therapeutic environments and thus were to be avoided at all costs; when they were used, patients should be discharged as soon as they were stabilized. During the late 1960s and 1970s, a considerable push was made to discharge many long-term patients. Populations in state institutions dropped by one-half or two-thirds from earlier numbers. This movement was due in part to changes in the Social Security Act. Supplementary Income Assistance became available to discharged mental patients. Medicare and Medicaid also could be used for some costs of care. Many of the ex-patients became residents of nursing homes. As a result, problems developed because neither the nursing home nor the community mental health center was prepared to provide these individuals with the needed care and services. Today, the nursing home and group home, rather than the state hospital, are often still the institutions that care for the elderly mentally ill patient.

As the economy worsened in the late 1970s and early 1980s, public attention was given to the growing number of homeless people or "street people" (Stern, 1984; Stoner, 1983). Many of these people are chronically mentally ill and are on the streets because of deinstitutionalization and recent court rulings about the rights of mentally ill persons that prevent their being held in institutions against their wishes (Bloom, 1984). Another group of chronically mentally ill individuals has also been identified—young adults (McCreath, 1984). One problem in treating these new noninstitutionalized people who need mental health services has been the lack of interest of mental health professionals in serving them (Atwood, 1982). The chronically mentally ill do not respond to traditional methods of psychotherapy. A cure is seldom a realistic goal. Rather, these people need long-term (perhaps lifelong) services that support them, give them protected community living and work, and coordinate for them the wide range of community services they need. What have come to be known as *community support programs* offer an approach that supplies the services needed by chronically mentally ill people who formerly would have been institutionalized for life and who are still at risk of repeated hospitalizations (Test and Stein, 1977). B.S.W. social workers have displayed both interest and skill in working with this client group, using a case management approach. However, cutbacks in funding for these programs have meant that many who need the service are not getting it. Thus, there seem to be a growing number of mentally ill persons wandering the streets or living in shelters for the homeless (Belcher, 1988).

The Developmentally Disabled

Until the late 1800s, most mentally retarded people who needed care outside the home were cared for in mental hospitals. In fact, there was little recognition of the special characteristics or needs of the *mentally retarded*, those people who have lower-than-average intellectual functioning, which in turn affects their adaptive behavior. During the latter half of the nineteenth century, large state institutions were founded to care for this population, although many mentally retarded individuals continued to be cared for within the family. These institutions were usually in isolated areas. In the past many retarded people did not live to adulthood because they were particularly susceptible to early death from respiratory disease.

As awareness of the need for educational and training programs for the mentally retarded grew, a few programs were established, but this development halted during the Great Depression and World War II. After World War II, the so-called miracle drugs were used successfully to treat respiratory infections and extend the life expectancy of this population. Other scientific studies expanded the understanding of the causes of mental retardation. Early detection became possible, and thus early intervention came to be emphasized. The National Association of Retarded Children (now the National Association of Retarded Citizens) was founded in 1950. This group of concerned parents and others was influential in gaining attention to the needs of the mentally retarded. Educational programs, community workshop and activity programs, residential alternatives, and legislative reforms resulted. Federal funds became available for training professionals for work with the mentally retarded. The Education for All Handicapped Children Act of 1978 (see Chapter 8) had an important impact on services for the mentally retarded child. Handicapped children are now often referred to as the *developmentally disabled*.

Deinstitutionalization became a theme in services to the mentally retarded. As with the mentally ill, communities often did not have the needed services in place to serve them. With a growing group of mentally retarded adults, it became important to establish new services for this group, including sheltered workshops, activity centers, and community living facilities. Because mentally retarded people often have multiple handicaps, a range of other services are also necessary to support them. Mentally retarded people often have mental health problems and therefore often need mental health services (Menolascino and McCann, 1983). Today, services to the mentally retarded probably should not be classified as mental health services but should be considered a distinct field of practice with ties to mental health as well as to child welfare services and school social work services (Dickerson, 1981).

Substance Abuse

Because the treatment of alcohol and drug abuse is a component service of a community mental health center, the history of modes of caring for this major national problem is important for understanding the range of mental health services. Substance abuse problems can be considered from two points of view. The first is the misuse of alcohol and drugs. Many people who use these substances do not find it difficult to moderate their use; it is overuse that is the chief concern. The second is *addiction*. Some individuals become both physically and emotionally dependent on these substances to such a degree that they are unable to control their consumption. Of course, some drugs are powerfully addictive, others only mildly so. One theory holds that some individuals are prone to addiction and cannot use these substances in moderation.

Alcohol and drug use have been a part of civilization for many years, and there have always been some individuals who had problems controlling their use. In the past society has generally seen misuse as punishable behavior. For a time, in the United States, the response to the problem was prohibition of the use of alcohol, and use of certain drugs is still illegal. But prohibition did not solve the problem and caused a great many other problems. The first attempt to deal with alcoholism other than by prohibition was through the formation of a self-help group, Alcoholics Anonymous, in the early 1930s. Of considerable concern at present is the extent of alcohol related problems among teenagers.

Self-help is still the solution of choice for many people with addiction problems. Public Law 91–61, passed in 1970, established a National Institute on Alcohol Abuse and Alcoholism. This law called for state plans using federal funds to develop both education and treatment programs. A variety of programs, in a variety of settings, with a variety of treatment philosophies are now attempting to address the problems of substance abuse. Some are within the mental health field of practice; some are not (Boche, 1981).

History of Social Work in Mental Health

Social work involvement in the field of mental health began in 1906 with the work of Cabot and Cannon at Massachusetts General Hospital (see Chapter 9). Mary Jarret, in 1913, developed a program at Boston Psychiatric Hospital that was known as psychiatric social work. Other such programs soon followed. In these programs, the social worker was primarily responsible for obtaining data from the patient's family. Later, social workers served as a liaison between the patient, the family, and the institution. In 1918 Smith College developed the first formal training in psychiatric social work. In 1926 the Veterans Administration established a Social Services Department. This department has provided considerable leadership in the mental health field of practice. Because of the limited number of psychiatrists, social workers increasingly became involved in prolonged, intensive psychotherapeutic work under the supervision of psychiatrists. Social workers in the mental health field tended to work with more verbal, middle-class clients in outpatient settings, although some social workers continued to work in institutional settings.

The definition of a *psychiatric social worker* has never been firmly established. Some said that it was a social worker who used psychoanalytic concepts. But eventually, the vast majority of social workers used these concepts. Others said it meant that the social worker worked in conjunction with a psychiatrist. Regardless of the definition used, psychiatric social work became a very prestigious kind of social work, and many social workers called themselves psychiatric social workers. Some sought postgraduate training in psychoanalytic-oriented programs, others engaged in personal analysis for training purposes. One of the member organizations that joined together to form the National Association of Social Workers in 1955 was the American Association of Psychiatric Social Workers, founded in 1926. Today, one seldom hears the term psychiatric social worker. Rather, a new group, similar in character, has developed—the *clinical social worker*. Usually, it is accepted that a clinical social worker must have the M.S.W. degree, with training and supervised experience in providing direct services to clients. Clinical social workers are therapists in the mental health field of practice (Nacman, 1977).

The Social Worker in the Mental Health Setting

In 1972, twenty-two thousand social workers practiced in mental health settings. The number is believed to have increased substantially since that time. About one-third of these workers practiced in state and county mental hospitals. Outpatient clinics accounted for another 25 percent of the workers. Clinical social work remains a strong practice area today for many social workers.

To work effectively in the mental health field, regardless of the particular setting, a social worker should have special knowledge. Because most settings emphasize the use of the interdisciplinary team approach, the social worker must understand how teams function and be skillful in working within teams. The social worker also must understand the roles and ways of functioning of the other professional disciplines that are part of the mental health team. Of course, knowing about mental illnesses and their treatment is also essential, including the terminology, etiology (causes), and symptoms of the various syndromes. The ability to use psychiatric classification such as that of the DSM-IV is important. Understanding psychotropic drug treatment and its side effects, along with other kinds of care and treatment, is essential. There are legal issues to be understood as well. Each specific mental health setting will also have knowledge specific to that setting (e.g., rural clinics, inner-city clinics) and the clients it serves that social workers must master to be effective in that setting.

Workers in mental health settings not only perform clinical social work or in-depth therapeutic direct service. They also use short-term approaches for working with patients/clients, with small groups, and with families. They engage in preventive as well as treatment activity. They use indirect methods to obtain needed services for patient/clients or to strengthen the social support network of the individual or family. Social workers are also involved in community organization, supervision and teaching, planning, and evaluation. Educational and consultation services are a part of many mental health agencies' services. Many social workers also are found in the administration of mental health agencies. One role that has recently become important is the case manager role. The case manager, after assessment and planning, develops an array of resources needed by each patient/client and continually coordinates services. As can be seen, social workers in the mental health setting have many opportunities and many important roles to fill.

Social Work in the Mental Hospital

Robert L. Barker and Thomas L. Briggs (1968), in a study of social workers in state mental hospitals, found they fill twenty roles. Some of the more important include the following:

1. Enhancing the patient's psychological functioning
2. Providing concrete social services to the patient
3. Enhancing the psychological functioning of the patient's family members
4. Enhancing social relationships between patients and their families
5. Providing concrete social services for family members
6. Educating the patient's family about the nature of the treatment of the patient
7. Stimulating healthy patient interaction in a therapeutic community
8. Providing information regarding the patient's social background and situation
9. Contributing to the psychiatric team's diagnostic and treatment program
10. Providing aftercare treatment of former patients
11. Developing service resources to help provide for patient needs

There is a wide variation in social work practice in mental hospitals. Much depends on the treatment practiced in a particular hospital. Also important is the particular population being served, because many hospitals place patients with similar diagnoses on the same ward. Admissions wards are very different from continuing care wards. Units for the treatment of alcohol and/or drug addiction use approaches specific to the problems of addiction. In mental hospitals, the psychiatrist is usually the person in charge. The social worker is usually responsible for developing social histories, working with families, and for contacting community agencies. The work is a team effort. Both M.S.W.'s and B.S.W.'s practice in mental hospitals.

Social Work in Community Mental Health Settings

Again, there is a wide range of work in the community mental health setting. Many M.S.W. workers provide counseling for problems of depression and anxiety; provide help with other individual, marital, and family problems; and are involved in crisis intervention. They may do this through a team effort, but often they work as independent therapists. Other M.S.W. workers are involved in service administration. When working in a child guidance clinic, the M.S.W. is usually a member of the team, often works with parents, and may use play therapy with children either individually or in groups. M.S.W. social workers use individual, family, and group approaches when working with clients. They also may be involved in community activity, training, and research.

Both B.S.W.'s and M.S.W.'s may work with the chronically mentally ill and their families in community support programs. B.S.W.'s often are case managers for these clients. Case managers may supervise work programs or socialization activities. They may also work to develop resources in the community to meet the needs of these clients. This can involve working with the local Social Security Administration offices to see that clients receive benefits for which they are eligible. It can mean working with Job Service to find suitable part-time employment for clients. It can mean helping a landlord understand the particular needs of a client (Linn and Stein, 1981).

A Case Study

Mary B is a twenty-five-year-old woman who has had three hospitalizations since she was eighteen years old. She was discharged three months ago from the state hospital with a diagnosis of undifferentiated schizophrenia. Her most recent hospitalization resulted from Mary's failure to take her prescribed medication. She had been living with her parents and said they were "on her case to get out and go to work." She also reported that they said they would kick her out if she didn't straighten up. Mary has a General Education Diploma and has never been able to hold a job for more than two weeks. Her parents seem to have little understanding of her illness. On discharge from the hospital, she was referred to the local community support program.

The community support program operates a transition living residence, and Mary had been living there since her discharge. While living in the transition residence, she developed skills she will need to live independently. She particularly likes to cook and explained that her mother would never let her do this. She also has attended a day treatment program where she works on socialization skills. The case manager tried to involve Mary's parents in a parents' educational group, but they have refused to participate. The case manager determined that returning home is not in Mary's best interests since she needs to see herself as an adult. Also, the parents seem to make excessive demands on her. The case worker found that Mary is eligible for SSI benefits and helped her make an application for these benefits.

Since Mary had been in the community support program for three months, it was time to review her progress and develop a plan for her next steps. The worker met with Mary to discuss her thinking about what she wants to happen. Mary expressed a desire to move to an independent living situation, but she was afraid to try a work situation. A meeting was called including everyone who had contact with Mary in the community support program. Also included were the housing specialist and the vocational specialist. The staff decided that Mary should be allowed an opportunity to move into an apartment that she would share with another client. In this housing situation, she would receive some supervision. It was suggested that she remain in the day treatment program until she adjusted to the new living situation but that she also be introduced to an evening group that meets once a week for socialization. The vocational specialist suggested that Mary be involved in a protected work situation after she adjusted to living independently. He suggested a project in which clients go as a group, twice a week, to the local newspaper office and stuff advertising material into the daily paper. If she could adjust to this, she would be encouraged to move on to more demanding work experiences later.

Mary seemed to be doing well with the medication she was taking. She achieved some independence in medicating herself in the transitional living situation, but the staff felt this should be carefully watched as she moved out of transitional living. The staff suggested that the case manager discuss with Mary her relationship with her family, and help her make some decision about what she would like to happen. The case manager would remain available to the family in the hope they would decide to become involved with the parents' group.

After the staff meeting, the worker discussed the outcome with Mary. Mary was somewhat hesitant about sharing a minimally supervised apartment but finally said that she would try it. The case manager and Mary discussed these feelings and planned to spend time discussing how it was going in the first few weeks of the new situation. Mary wanted to know when she would get her SSI so she would have some money to spend. The worker explained the time needed for this to go through. She also pointed out that Mary would need to budget her money because she would have to pay rent and buy groceries in her new living situation. The worker decided that Mary had worked enough for one session, but made a mental note of other issues that would need discussion the next time: the work experience, her parents, and other changes.

Of considerable concern to the social work profession has been the issue of social workers' obtaining third party payments for services rendered in the mental health field. *Third party payments* are reimbursements for service paid by insurance plans. Usually these are health care plans that have primarily focused on reimbursement for medical services. Slowly, insurance companies are beginning to recognize services provided by clinical social workers as reimbursable.

Addiction Treatment Programs

Some social workers have always been involved in working with problem drinkers or alcoholics. A few have also been involved in drug treatment programs. Some social workers believe that misuse of alcohol is only a symptom of other problems, and that treatment should focus on the other problems. For some clients this seems to be the case. For others, however, the alcohol abuse seems to be the primary problem. When working with this client population, the social worker combines generalist social work knowledge with specific knowledge of alcohol treatment.

Work with the Mentally Retarded

Charles R. Horejsi (1979), in a study of the literature, has identified six kinds of services social workers provide for the mentally retarded person:

1. Providing individual and group counseling to the retarded individuals, their parents, and siblings
2. Conducting social evaluations as a part of the interdisciplinary diagnostic process
3. Developing alternative living plans
4. Offering protective services, social brokerage, and case advocacy services
5. Performing intake, release, discharge planning, and case management activities
6. Community organizing, social planning, and administrative activity

With the movement of the mentally retarded from the institution to the community, many social workers, especially B.S.W's, are finding positions as case managers in community facilities. Also, with the increased emphasis on rights to education, training, and treatment for the mentally retarded, there is an important role for the social worker in advocacy. Because the educational system has become the prime system to serve mentally retarded children and adolescents, social workers place less emphasis on this age group, and more on the growing number of adult mentally retarded people (Horejsi, 1979).

Social workers in every setting in the mental health field carry many responsibilities and provide a wide variety of services to patients/clients and their families. They also play important roles in developing community awareness of, acceptance of, and responsibility for services to the population served by mental health agencies. Social work in these settings calls for skill in case management and in working on treatment teams. The role of the social worker in mental health services continues to broaden as more emphasis is placed on services in the community and on the role of the community and the family in treating the mentally ill. Also, the growing importance of mental health in our society should bring about increased support for mental health programs.

Current Issues and Concerns in the Mental Health Field

As has been shown in this chapter, enormous changes in the care of the mentally ill have taken place in the last two decades. The move from an emphasis on institutional care to care in the community has been responsible for many of these changes. In addition, there has been a shift in emphasis from mental illness to mental health. These changes have brought about a much greater community concern for mental health services. The need for and use of such services has become much more acceptable to the general public. As a natural consequence of this change, tensions and problems have developed within the system. Those that seem most important are discussed in this section. They include issues arising out of a series of court decisions about the rights of the mentally ill, issues related to health insurance coverage, issues related to staffing of mental health services, and issues related to services for the underserved.

Court Decisions

Over the last fifteen years, a number of court decisions have placed new constraints on involuntary care of the mentally ill and have required better care and treatment for these individuals. Essentially, the courts have developed a principle of the right to treatment in the *least restrictive environment* (Gerhart, 1990). In this setting, which can be either in an institution or in the community, people have relatively few limitations on their movements and rights and are given opportunities to make their own choices as long as they do not endanger themselves or others. Prior to these court decisions, mentally ill individuals could be committed to institutions with little recourse and with considerable loss of civil and personal rights. There is no doubt that there was considerable abuse of the commitment proceedings and that some reform was necessary. However, some people wonder if things have not gone too far, whether it is still possible to protect both the mentally ill patient and the community in general. The attempted assassination of President Reagan in 1981 is an example often used to illustrate problems resulting from deinstitutionalization.

Some people question whether community care is always in the best interest of the client, especially when good community care does not exist. Questions are also raised about whether mental health treatment is a right or a privilege. If courts mandate community care for some clients/patients, should it not be available to all who need it? But then who should be responsible for financing such care? Will the historic experience of two systems of care—institutional and community—be replaced by a single system paid for by public funds for those who cannot pay for their own care, and another system for those who can pay for their care? Will these two systems provide similar quality of care, or will higher quality go to those who pay? What will happen to the relationship between the mental health system and the social welfare system? Will institutional care remain the responsibility of the states while community care continues to be funded jointly by state and federal governments? All these questions will need to be addressed as the new mental health system develops.

These court decisions have also given the legal system a much stronger role in the care and treatment of the mentally ill. They have given rise to much litigation around mental health treatment, making it essential that mental health agencies and professionals be aware of the legal ramifications of any treatment used. The decisions have also forced mental health professionals to carry liability insurance, which adds to the costs of care.

These same court decisions have brought attention to the implications of considering mental illness a medical condition. The statement that "deviance is in the eye of the beholder" has cast doubt on current definitions of mental illness. What is the responsibility of the mental health system, what is the responsibility of the criminal justice system, and what should their relationship be?

Health Insurance

Most health insurance provides some, though usually limited, coverage for hospitalization in psychiatric settings. Some health care plans cover certain outpatient services. Coverage has been a major issue. There are questions not only about the amount of coverage (how many sessions or what dollar amount) but also about which services can be provided by which mental health professionals (Bagarozzi, 1995). Services delivered by psychiatrists and, usually, by psychologists are more often covered than are those given by social workers and other professionals. The services covered can usually be categorized as intensive therapy. Newer understandings about treatment of mental illness indicate that this is not always the treatment of choice. Little or no provision has been made to meet the needs of the chronically mentally ill. The emphasis on prevention, which is receiving at least some attention, is not addressed by health insurance, or in the health care field generally (Hudson and Devito, 1994).

Social work, mostly through the National Association of Social Workers, has made a considerable effort to obtain what is known as *third-party payment* (insurance payment for services) for some social workers who provide mental health services, but this is almost exclusively restricted to M.S.W. workers involved in clinical social work. To facilitate this change, the NASW has issued a *Clinical Register* that lists the social workers the organization considers competent to deliver clinical services. Some insurance plans have accepted M.S.W.'s listed in this register as eligible to receive payment for services under their plan. Because many workers listed in the register are not employed in mental health settings, this raises questions about the definition of mental health services used in this chapter. Of particular interest are M.S.W's in private practice. These workers indeed meet many mental health needs, but their place in the social welfare system is unclear. Also, what about mental health services provided by social workers not included in the register? Should they too not be reimbursed? Many questions remain regarding issues of insurance reimbursement for mental health services.

Staffing in Mental Health Services

The sometimes conflicting roles of psychiatrists, psychologists, and social workers have long been troublesome. Different answers have been worked out in different settings. In the hospitals, psychiatrists have tended, at least officially, to be responsible for treatment, using other disciplines as they see fit. This has often placed social workers in an ancillary position. In the outpatient setting, a more egalitarian relationship has evolved, but often with a blurring of roles of the various professions. In this situation, the particular strengths of each profession are often overlooked. Another development has been the addition of professions (e.g., nurses, occupational therapists, and rehabilitation counselors) to the group delivering mental health services. More study is needed on the relative effectiveness and proper roles of the mental health professionals in different mental health settings.

Third-party reimbursement also affects the staffing patterns of some mental health settings. It is in the best interest of the agency to receive as much reimbursement as possible. This, however, hinders staffing decisions based on which professional can best deliver the service in the most economical and effective way. A related issue and a familiar problem is the validity of the B.S.W. as a professional degree. The role and function of the B.S.W. in the mental health field is still unclear. But because clinical services are not the treatment of choice for many clients/patients, and because many M.S.W.'s do not want to provide these services (Rubin and Johnson, 1985), whereas B.S.W.'s do indeed have the skills to provide these services (the case management function is an example), the mental health system does have a place for B.S.W.s, and insurance coverage should be provided for their services. If the mental health system is to meet people's needs, then all these issues of staffing must be addressed.

The Underserved

With the deinstitutionalization of the mentally ill and the mentally retarded has come a demand for vastly increased community services to meet the needs of this population. Although many programs and projects have demonstrated that these needs can be met in the community (Rubin, 1984), a large group of deinstitutionalized people have not received such services. Some are being served by social welfare programs that are not equipped to meet their special needs. Others are in nursing homes. The chronically mentally ill and mentally retarded remain both an underserved clientele and a serious community problem. Some of the needs of the mentally retarded have already been discussed in this chapter, particularly those related to deinstitutionalization and the growth in the number of adult mentally retarded persons. Also, as more is understood about mental retardation, new and more effective ways of responding become available. The mentally retarded person who is also mentally ill is a client-patient who has long puzzled the professional. Much more needs to be understood about this segment of the population.

Other underserved groups include the poor and the aged, groups that have their own special needs. With the drying up of federal funds to support mental health services, such services for those unable to pay either on their own or through third-party payments have been considerably reduced. Also, the best treatment and services for these groups have not been agreed on. Attitudes in U.S. society about aging and the aged have caused indifference toward their many unmet mental health needs, which must be addressed.

Some geographic areas of the country are also underserved. The rural sections of the United States have always lacked sufficient formal social welfare services, including sufficient mental health services. Individuals are forced to use institutions far from their homes or services developed on an urban model. Some attention has been paid to providing mental health services to this population (Wodarski, 1983), but much remains to be done.

There is a growing realization that services to various ethnic groups should be tailored to meet their particular needs. Some of these needs arise from the discrimination they have experienced. Cultural factors must be taken into account when serving people from minority groups. The current interest in their needs must continue and be expanded.

Summary

In this chapter, the mental health field of practice was defined as including those agencies and institutions that provide mental health services. The complex relationship of the social welfare system and the mental health system was described and discussed. The range of services in the mental health field was considered from both a historical and a contemporary perspective. Included in the discussion of the mental health field of practice was consideration of two areas that might be considered emerging fields: the area of developmental disability (formerly known as mental retardation) and drug and alcohol treatment. Social work's development as a mental health profession was examined. Also, a number of contemporary issues relating to the delivery of mental health services were raised.

This field of practice is undergoing considerable growth and change. There is a change in focus from services within institutions to services in communities. There is also a change from emphasis on mental illness to one on mental health, which calls for more attention to preventive services. These changes require new kinds of service delivery and new roles for the social worker. They offer a challenge for creative and innovative work.

Key Terms

addiction
child guidance clinics
chronic mental illness
clinical social worker
community mental health center
community support programs
deinstitutionalization
developmentally disabled
insane asylums
least restrictive environment
lunatics
mental health

mental health agency
mental health services
mental hospital
mental illness
mentally retarded
moral treatment
National Institute of Mental Health
psychiatric hospital
psychiatric social worker
psychotropic drugs
third-party payment

References

American Psychiatric Association (1994). *Diagnostic and statistical manual of mental disorders* (4th ed.). Washington, DC: American Psychiatric Association.

Atwood, N. (1982). Professional prejudice and the psychotic client. *Social Work, 27* (2), 172–177.

Bagarozzi, D. A. (1995). Evaluation, accountability and clinical expertise in managed mental health care: basic considerations for the practice of family social work. *Journal of Family Social Work, 1* (2), 101–116.

Barker, R. L. & Briggs, T. L. (1968). *Differential use of social work manpower.* New York: National Association of Social Workers.

Barton, W.E., & Sandborn, C.J. (1977). *An assessment of the community mental health movement.* Lexington, MA: Lexington Books.

Beers, C. W. (1908). *A mind that found itself.* New York: Longmans, Green.

Belcher, J. R. (1988). Rights versus needs of homeless mentally ill persons. *Social Work, 33* (5), 398–402.

Bloom, B. L. (1984). *Community mental health* (2nd ed.). Monterey, CA: Brooks/Cole.

Boche, H. L. (1981). Alcohol and drug abuse services. In N. Gilbert & H. Specht (Eds.), *Handbook of the social services.* Englewood Cliffs, NJ: Prentice-Hall.

Dickerson, M. U. (1981). *Social work practice with the mentally retarded.* New York: Free Press.

DiNitto, D. M. (1991). *Social welfare: politics and public policy* (3rd ed.). Englewood Cliffs, NJ: Prentice Hall.

Gerhart, U. C. (1990). *Caring for the mentally ill.* Itasca, IL: F. E. Peacock Publishers, Inc.

Horejsi, C. R. (1979). Developmental disabilities: opportunity for social workers. *Social Work, 24* (1), 40–43.

Hudson, C. G., & Devito, J. A. (1994). Mental health under national health care reform. *Health & Social Work, 19* (4), 279–287.

Joint Commission on Mental Illness and Health (1961). *Action for mental health.* New York: Basic Books.

Leiby, J. (1978). *A history of social welfare and social work in the United States.* New York: Columbia University Press.

Linn, M. W., & Stein, S. (1981). Chronic mental illness. *Health and Social Work, 6* (November Supplement), 54s–59s.

McCreath, J. (1984). The new generation of chronic psychiatric patients. *Social Work, 29* (5), 436–441.

McNeil, J. S., & Wright, R. (1983). Special populations: black, hispanic, and native American. In J. W. Callicutt & P. J. Lecca (Eds.), *Social work and mental health.* New York: Free Press.

Menolascino, F. J., & McCann, B. M. (Eds.). (1983). *Mental health and mental retardation: bridging the gap.* Baltimore, MD: University Park Press.

Nacman, M. (1977). Mental health services: social workers in. In J. B. Turner (Ed.), *Encyclopedia of social work* (17th ed.). Washington, DC: National Association of Social Workers.

Rothman, D. J. (1971). *The discovery of the asylum.* Boston, MA: Little, Brown.

Rubin, A., (1984). Community-based care of the mentally ill: a research review. *Health and Social Work, 9* (Summer), 165–177.

Rubin, A., & Johnson, P. J. (1985). Direct practice interest of entering MSW students. *Journal of Education for Social Work, 20* (Spring), 5–16.

Segal, S. P., & Baumohl, J. (1981). Social work practice in community mental health. *Social Work, 26* (1), 19–20.

Stern, M. J. (1984). The emergence of the homeless as a public problem. *Social Service Review, 58* (June), 291–301.

Stoner, M. R. (1983). The plight of the homeless woman. *Social Service Review, 57* (December), 565–581.

Talbott, J. A. (1980). Toward a public policy on the chronic mentally ill patient. *American Journal of Orthopsychiatry, 50* (1), 43–53.

Test, M. J., & Stein, L. J. (1977). A community approach to the chronically mentally ill. *Social Policy, 8* (May–June), 8–16.

Thackeray, M. G., Skidmore, R. A., & Farley, O. W. (1978). *Introduction to mental health: field and practice.* Englewood Cliffs, NJ: Prentice-Hall.

U.S. Bureau of the Census (1995). *Statistical Abstract of the United States: 1995* (115 th ed.). Washington, DC: U.S. Government Printing Office.

Wodarski, J. S. (1983). *Rural community mental health practice.* Baltimore, MD: University Park Press.

Suggested Readings

Alexander, Rudolph, Jr. "The Right to Treatment in Mental and Correctional Institutions." *Social Work,* 34 (March 1989), 109–112.

Aviram, Uri. "Community Care of the Mentally Ill: Continuing Problems and Current Issues." *Community Mental Health Journal,* 26 (Feb. 1990), 69–88.

Bean, Gerald J., Jr.; Stefl, Mary E.; and Howe, Steven R. "Mental Health and Homelessness: Issues and Findings." *Social Work,* 32 (September–October 1987), 411–416.

Belcher, John R. "Rights versus Needs of Homeless Mentally Ill Persons." *Social Work,* 33 (September–October 1988), 398–402.

Bloom, Bernard L. *Community Mental Health: A General Introduction,* 2nd ed. (Monterey, CA: Brooks/Cole, 1984).

Callicutt, James W., and Lecca, Pedro J. *Social Work and Mental Health.* (New York: Free Press, 1981).

Dickerson, Martha Ufford. *Social Work Practice with the Mentally Retarded.* (New York: Free Press, 1983).

Fraser, Mark and Kohlert, Nance. "Substance Abuse and Public Policy." *Social Service Review,* 62 (March 1988), 101–126.

French, Laurence. "Victimization of the Mentally Ill: An Unintended Consequence of Deinstitutionalization." *Social Work,* 32 (November–December 1987), 502–505.

Generations (Winter 1992). Special Issue: "Aging and Disabilities: Seeking Common Ground."

Health and Social Work, 16 (Feb. 1991). Special Issue: "Social Work with Clients Who Are Chronically Mentally Ill."

Hollander, Russell. "Mental Retardation and American Society: The Era of Hope." *Social Service Review*, 60 (September 1986), 395–420.

Horejsi, Charles R. "Developmental Disabilities: Opportunities for Social Workers." *Social Work*, 24 (January 1979), 40–43.

Human Services in the Rural Environment, 12 (Spring 1989). Special Issue: "Rural Chronically Mentally Ill."

Johnson, Peter J., and Rubin, Allen. "Case Management in Mental Health: A Social Work Domain?" *Social Work*, 28 (January–February 1983), 49–55.

Katz-Leavy, Judith and Lourie, Ira S. "New Directions for Mental Health Services for Families and Children." *Families in Society,* 72 (May 1991), 277–285.

Korr, Wynne S. "The APA Model Law and Three Legal Issues in Mental Health." *Health and Social Work*, 12 (Fall 1987), 259–266.

Kutchins, Herb and Kirk, Stuart A. "The Business of Diagnosis: DSM-III and Clinical Social Work." *Social Work,* 33 (May–June 1988), 215–220.

LeCroy, Craig Winston. "Enhancing the Delivery of Effective Mental Health Services to Children." *Social Work,* 37 (May 1992), 225–231.

Levine, Murry. *The History and Politics of Community Mental Health.* (New York: Oxford University Press, 1981).

Libasse, Mary Frances. "The Chronically Mentally Ill: A Practice Approach." *Social Casework,* 69 (Feb. 1988), 88–91.

Minahan, Anne, ed. *Encyclopedia of Social Work*, 18th ed. (Silver Springs, MD: National Association of Social Workers, 1988): Articles on: "Disabilities: Developmental," "Mental Health and Illness," and "Mental Health Services."

Paradis, Bruce A. "An Integrated Team Approach to Community Mental Health." *Social Work,* 32 (April–May 1987), 101–104.

Robertson, Joan F. "A Tool for Assessing Alcohol Misuse in Adolescence." *Social Work,* 34 (Jan. 1988), p. 39–44.

Salem, Deborah A., Seidman, Edward, and Rappaport, Julian. "Community Treatment of the Mentally Ill: The Promise of Mutual-Help Organizations." *Social Work,* 33 (Sept.–Oct. 1988), 403–408.

Schulberg, Herbert C., and Killilea, Marie, eds. *The Modern Practice of Community Mental Health.* (San Francisco: Jossey-Bass, 1982).

Segal, Steven P., and Baumohl, Jim. "Social Work Practice in Community Mental Health." *Social Work*, 26 (January 1981), 16–25.

"Special Issue: Alcohol Problems." *Health and Social Work*, 4 (November 1979).

Sullivan, W. Patrick. "Reclaiming the Community: The Strengths Perspective and Deinstitutionalization." *Social Work,* 37 (May 1992), 204–209.

Surber, Robert W.; Dwyer, Eleanor; Ryan, Katherine J.; Goldfinger, Stephen M.; and Kelly, John T. "Medical and Psychiatric Needs of the Homeless—A Preliminary Response." *Social Work,* 33 (March–April 1988), 116–119.

Thackeray, Milton G.; Skidmore, Rex A.; and Farley, O. William, eds. *Introduction to Mental Health: Field and Practice.* (Englewood Cliffs, NJ: Prentice-Hall, 1978).

Toseland, Ronald; Palmer-Ganeles, Joan; and Chapman, Dennis. "Teamwork in Psychiatric Settings." *Social Work*, 31 (January–February 1986), 46–52.

VanWormer, Katherine. "Social Work and Alcoholism Counseling." *Social Casework*, 68 (September 1987), 426–432.

Videka-Sherman, Lynn. "Metaanalysis or Research on Social Work Practice in Mental Health." *Social Work,* 33 (July–Aug. 1988), 325–338.

Wilk, Ruta J. "Involuntary Outpatient Commitment of the Mentally Ill." *Social Work,* 33 (March–April 1988), 133–137.

Wodarski, John S. *Rural Community Mental Health Practice.* (Baltimore, MD: University Park Press, 1983).

11

SOCIAL WORK AND CORRECTIONS

Learning Expectations

- Ability to identify the three components of the criminal justice system
- Understanding of the difference between a rehabilitative thrust and a punitive thrust in the corrections system
- Understanding of the structure of both the adult and juvenile corrections systems
- Understanding of the complexity of causality of delinquent behavior and the major components of causality
- Ability to discuss the various treatment approaches used in the juvenile justice system
- Ability to define *status offenders*
- Understanding of the role of a social worker in the juvenile justice system
- Knowledge of societal responses to criminal behavior of adults
- Knowledge of correctional services for adult offenders

The profession of social work and the field of adult and juvenile corrections have historically been partners in society's protection of its members from criminal behavior (acts that violate the law) and in providing rehabilitation and treatment. However, social work and the field of corrections have traditionally experienced difficulties working together, in part because professional correctionalists and social workers have different and conflicting sets of values (Johnson, 1995).

Correctionalists, though adhering to a philosophy of rehabilitation, conceptualize this as the offender's responsibility to make retribution for criminal acts. This position is congruent with dominant societal values. Social workers, on the other hand, conceptualize rehabilitation as social adjustment, education, and preparation for living a normal citizen's life (Skidmore,

Thackeray, and Farley, 1991). In a more practical sense, the correctionalists view social workers as idealistic and too soft-hearted. Social workers argue that correctionalists are too hardnosed and insensitive to offenders' needs.

There has always been disagreement among social workers on the place of the profession in the correctional field. In 1945, Kenneth Pray, then dean of the School of Social Work at the University of Pennsylvania, at the annual meeting of the American Association of Social Work, argued that social work should involve itself in the field of corrections. His address was not well received by many social workers (Fox, 1983). Some social workers argue that since offenders are nonvoluntary clients, social workers who work with them violate the social work value of self-determination. That offender clients must involuntarily consent to treatment places social workers in the position of imposing their services on them, which social workers find unethical, impractical, and ineffectual. However, these same social workers fail to recognize that clients in other fields of practice (e.g., child protective services) are also involuntary clients (Johnson, 1995). Other social workers believe that social work should be involved in the field of adult corrections in order to contribute to needed changes in the field. H. Wayne Johnson states, "If social work refuses to have a role in corrections, then it surrenders this important human services field to other, often more repressive groups" (Johnson, 1995, p. 213).

This chapter assumes that social work and the field of corrections are not two clearly separate and distinct responses to criminal acts. Rather, they should be viewed as a blending together of professional services that reflect concern for the treatment and rehabilitation of offenders. Social work has provided a wide range of services focusing on human needs, and its involvement in correctional services is a part of that response. It is as these services are provided that the corrections system overlaps with the social welfare system.

This chapter examines the following: (1) the structure of the criminal justice system (including a brief overview of the fields of juvenile and adult corrections); (2) correctional services for youth (including the historical development of the juvenile court, types of juvenile offenders, legal perspectives, the provisions of services and treatment approaches to juvenile offenders, and the role of social work in the response); and (3) correctional services to adults (including a brief overview of theories of the causes of crime), an examination of the adult cor-

TABLE 11–1   Important Dates: Social Work and Corrections

1787	The Philadelphia Prison Society was founded to bring about reform in U.S. prisons.
1899	An act to regulate the treatment and control of independent, neglected, and delinquent children created the first juvenile court in the United States.
1964	The *Cooper* v. *Pate* Supreme Court decision established prisoners' rights.
1965	The Prison Rehabilitation Act–Correctional Rehabilitation Study Act was passed.
1967	The *Gault* v. *Arizona* Supreme Court decision gave rights of due process of law to juveniles.
1970	The President's Task Force on Prisoner Rehabilitation encouraged development of community-based corrections for adults.
1974	The Juvenile Justice and Delinquency Prevention Act provided incentives for the deinstitutionalization of status offenders.
1984	Comprehensive Crime Control Act
1986	Anti-Drug Abuse Act

rectional system (including prisons, jails, and the probation–parole system), alternative treatment and rehabilitation approaches in adult corrections, and the roles of correctional personnel (including social workers). Throughout the chapter there are discussions of pertinent social issues and social changes that have influenced society's response to the problem of criminal behavior (see Table 11–1).

Structure of the Criminal Justice System

The *criminal justice system,* both currently and historically, has three component parts: law enforcement, the judicial system, and the correctional system (Johnson, 1995). The correctional system is the main focus in this chapter, although all three are discussed at various points.

To understand both the juvenile and adult correctional systems, it is important to define the term *corrections.* In a broad sense, corrections is the part of the criminal justice system that tries to prevent the recurrence of criminal behavior, to deal with its causes, and to implement measures of social control that treat and rehabilitate both adult and juvenile offenders. Corrections is also thought of in a more narrow sense as a professional service that applies a criminology knowledge base to the control and rehabilitation of the criminal offender (Allen and Simonsen, 1989).

There has long been a great deal of argument over what should constitute corrections. Differing values, philosophies, and ideologies have influenced the structure at different times. These arguments are expressed by such questions as: Should punishment be considered the primary method of corrections? If not, should treatment and rehabilitation be? What is rehabilitation? These issues, along with others, continue to be sources of controversy and debate among criminal justice officials, and will be discussed throughout the chapter.

The Structure of the Juvenile Corrections System

As previously mentioned, corrections implies that prevention, treatment, and rehabilitation processes are provided within the criminal justice system. Juvenile corrections, a subsystem, works with young offenders whose age is less than the legal age of majority (eighteen years old in most states). The structure of the juvenile corrections system consists of both institutional and *community-based correctional services.* Institutional services are those in which the juvenile is placed in a closed setting, separated from the community and from his or her family. Community-based correctional services are those in an open community setting, which serve the juvenile offender without separation from his or her family or community. These two areas of services can be further broken down into formal and informal services. There are formal and informal institutional services, as well as formal and informal community-based services. Formal services are those mandated and sanctioned by law; informal services are those that exist and are sanctioned by means other than law.

Formal institutional services consist of reform schools, training schools, detention centers, youth authorities, and other correctional institutions, such as boot camps, provided for by law (U.S. Department of Justice, 1995). They are usually directly operated by local, county, or state government. Informal institutional services consist of group homes, residential treatment centers, and other child-care institutions under the auspices of private, nongovernment social service providers. Examples of formal community-based services are juvenile probation, court services, family court services, juvenile diversion programs, and youth service bureaus, which are mandated by law and administered by local, county, or state government. Most community-based services are informal. Examples include family counseling agencies, child welfare agencies, mental health centers, Boys' Clubs, Girls' Clubs, and YMCA and YWCA (Young Men's and Young Women's Christian Association) programs, scouting programs, and church-sponsored agencies.

Structure of the Adult Corrections System

The adult corrections system is similar to the juvenile system, with both institutional and community-based services. Most of the services are institutional and formal. Examples include jails, prisons, and other adult correctional institutions. Adult community-based services also tend to be formal, and include probation and parole services. The services provided by community mental health centers, drug and alcohol treatment programs, public social service agencies, employment assistance and vocational assistance programs, and family service agencies are part of the informal structure of community-based services for adult offenders.

The Juvenile Justice System

Both serious and minor crimes are committed by children and youth. In 1993, juveniles were arrested for offenses varying from murder to status offenses. Juveniles accounted for 29 percent of all persons arrested for violent crimes (U.S. Bureau of the Census, 1995). Violent offenses committed by juveniles are on the increase, so much so that a "get-tough" policy has been initiated with violent juvenile offenders via the 1994 Crime Bill. This legislation authorizes the adult prosecution of juveniles 13 years old and over who are charged with certain serious crimes. This represents a clear point of demarcation from previous juvenile justice philosophy and policy and reflects the current trend to punish rather than rehabilitate criminal offenders (U.S. Department of Justice, 1995).

To understand the functioning of the current system, it is necessary to understand the history of the juvenile corrections system. In the United States the system began in the late 1800s with the emergence of the separate juvenile court. However, society's special concern for children and the creation of a separate judicial system for them began long ago.

In Roman common law, the system of law in most European countries, descended from the laws of the Roman Empire, the Latin term *parens patriae* means the power of the state to act in behalf of a child as a wise parent would do. This legal precept has prevailed in most European countries since the 1700s (Boisevert and Wells, 1980). Later, English courts began the practice of implementing separate and special procedures for dealing with juvenile offenders. Rather than holding formal trials for children, as they did with adults, they often dealt with children in hearings in a judge's chamber. Prior to this, children were treated no differently than adult criminals. They were incarcerated in common lockups with adults and were subjected to the same harsh, often brutal, punishments. The "eye for an eye" philosophy seemed inhumane and impractical when applied to the child offender (Ferguson, 1975). Furthermore, by the early 1800s many people came to believe that punishment was not an effective deterrent to juvenile crime.

In the United States, these enlightened practices were not implemented immediately. There were few special institutions for young offenders. Children convicted of crimes were sent either to the almshouses or to adult jails or prisons. These correctional institutions were deplorable places with unsanitary conditions, staffed by violent officials who were ignorant and careless about the needs of children (Trattner, 1979). Gradually, after the American Revolution, the states assumed jurisdiction over children and created juvenile correctional institutions, which at first were nothing more than children's jails patterned after the adult correctional institutions. Only in the late 1800s did the response to juvenile delinquency begin to change. The period of change, referred to as the *juvenile reformation,* was signaled by several events.

First, society began to recognize that the system of juvenile institutions was not adequately dealing with the problems of juvenile delinquency. Children released from such institutions had not improved in behavior, and many committed further crimes, only to be institutionalized again. Punishing juveniles by incarcerating them in institutions had failed to rehabilitate them. Studies, particularly those conducted by the Juvenile Psychopathic Institute, which was located in Hull House in Chicago, indicated that the best way to treat the delinquent was not by incarceration but by special home care (Trattner, 1979). As a result, several states began to create special "juvenile homes" or houses of correction. These special facilities marked the beginning of innovative practices in response to juvenile offenders. Such practices as the use of indeterminate sentences, probation, and parole were implemented by these new facilities.

With the growing emphasis on these new ways of treating young offenders came the realization that the laws needed to change to keep pace with these new developments. As a result, state courts began the use of special court procedures with children accused of crimes, which called for them to be dealt with separately and differently from adult offenders. Massachusetts was the first state to adopt such procedures. In Illinois, a battle had been underway for some time, spearheaded by the Chicago Bar Association and the settlement house workers, particularly Jane Addams, to create separate and special courts for juveniles. This led to the passage by the Illinois state legislature of "an act to regulate the treatment and control of independent, neglected, and delinquent children" (Trattner, 1979, p. 105). This legislation created the nation's first separate juvenile court, which was established in 1899 in Chicago. Several other states followed suit by creating their own juvenile courts.

The *juvenile court* was not a criminal court. Instead of criminal procedure, a nonadversarial proceeding was used that took the best interests of the child fully into consideration. The aim of the court was to educate children, act as a parental guide in assisting the child, and develop a plan of individualized treatment.

Although juvenile courts were philosophically dedicated to the aim of individualized treatment and the best interests of the child, this goal was not realized. Many juvenile courts became paternalistic and punitive in their approach to children. A system was created that in many ways was patterned after the adult court system. Children coming under the jurisdiction of the juvenile court were often removed from the custody of their parents without notification and placed in institutions. Parents had no rights to voice objections or to play a part in decisions made by the court concerning their child's treatment or future. Children from minority groups especially suffered from these shortcomings. There were no attorneys to represent children to guarantee their "best interests."

Naturally, serious questions arose about the constitutional rights of parents and children relative to due process of law. But punitive practices continued until 1967, when the United States Supreme Court, in the case of *Gault* v. *Arizona,* ruled that previous juvenile court procedures were in violation of due process of law, and that children and youths under the jurisdiction of the juvenile court must be afforded their due process rights, such as the following:

1. Adequate notice to parents and child
2. The right to legal counsel
3. The right to confront and cross-examine witnesses
4. Guarantees against self-incrimination

This decision was responsible for overhauling the juvenile court system by forcing the courts to establish new legal procedures that respected the child's due process rights. As a result, states began to revise their statutes and laws pertaining to children to include provisions for guaranteeing these rights.

The Current Juvenile Court System

One of the basic goals of a corrections system is to understand the causes of crime and delinquency and then to try to provide treatment and rehabilitative measures that will prevent crime from recurring. Therefore, it is necessary to understand how children come to be under the jurisdiction of the juvenile corrections system. Historically, children brought before the juvenile court were considered *delinquent.* This catchall label was used for many years. As time passed, however, distinctions began to be made among certain types of offenses that children commit. The Gault decision again helped clarify this. Some children commit offenses that, if they were adults, would also result in criminal charges. These include a range of offenses from burglary to murder, from misdemeanors to felonies. Children convicted of these types of offenses are labeled delinquent. However, the juvenile court also has jurisdiction over children who commit offenses such as running away from home, being out of parental control, or failing to attend school, that are offenses because they are minors. These children are labeled *status offenders.* Currently, the juvenile court system is focusing more attention on children adjudicated as delinquent. The tendency has been for status offenders to be diverted from the formal court system. This issue will be discussed later in this chapter. First, it is pertinent to discuss briefly the causes of delinquent behavior, focusing on the research that has explored this problem.

Causes of Delinquent Behavior

The causes of delinquent behavior, like those of all criminal behavior, are complex. Research in the past attempted to explain delinquent behavior from a specific theoretical orientation. Many biological, psychological, and sociological theories were offered (Whitehead and Lab, 1990). On a more practical level, other factors such as peer influence, the failure of the educational system to provide for the educational needs of young people, the lack of employment opportunities for youth, poverty, and alcohol and drug use have been seen to be causative factors associated with delinquency.

More recently, peer influence and older theories, e.g., social control theory, and strain theory (Smith, Visher, and Jarjoura, 1991; Menard and Huizinga, 1994), have attempted to explain delinquency, particularly group delinquency, and the development of juvenile gangs, that has become a significant problem in many of our nation's largest cities. Other research (Minor, 1993) has suggested that juvenile delinquency is the beginning phase of "career criminality." One factor that has received the most attention by researchers is the relationship between delinquency and problems in the child's family system. Research attempting to isolate specific family problems that cause delinquency have yielded contradictory results. Some studies have shown that family conflict, tension, and disruption, family disorganization, lack of parental control, parental rejection, inconsistent and inappropriate discipline, and child abuse appear to cause juvenile delinquency. Recently other studies have reported a weaker link between broken homes and delinquency (Free, 1991). There is, perhaps, no single factor that provides an overall explanation of juvenile delinquency although many factors seem to correlate with it (Roberts, 1989).

Treatment Approaches

Methods and approaches to the treatment of children who are adjudicated as being delinquent vary depending on the child's individual situation. Juvenile court judges have some discretion in deciding the treatment of such children. The following are examples of possible treatment approaches:

1. The child or youth may be placed on probation for a specific period of time.
2. The child or youth may be institutionalized in a correctional, child-care, chemical-dependency treatment, or psychiatric facility.
3. The child or youth may be ordered, along with his or her parents, into community-based treatment such as family counseling or related mental health services.
4. The child or youth may be required to make *restitution* (repairing or paying for damages, returning stolen goods, etc.), particularly in the case of property offenses such as vandalism or burglary.
5. The child or youth may be required to participate in community service work.

Federal grant dollars have also been made available to the states under the Violent Crime Control and Law Enforcement Act of 1994 to build and operate "juvenile bootcamps," which are an alternative to more traditional juvenile correctional facilities and designed to serve less serious juvenile felons and young adults. The bootcamp model is based on the military bootcamp, with rigorous physical training and harsh discipline designed as a sort of "shock treatment" of offenders in which they learn self-control and discipline and respect for authority that will curb their propensity to commit crime (U.S. Department of Justice, 1995). These treatment approaches may be used alone or in combination to meet the individual treatment needs of each child. Emphasis should be placed on the creation of a package of services that meet each child's particular needs, using any and all available resources in the process.

The treatment of juvenile delinquents has become more complicated recently due to the number of violent crimes committed by juveniles as reported earlier. This has prompted some juvenile justice officials to call for a crackdown on juvenile offenders (Frost and Bloomquist,

1991). Another phenomenon that has provided challenges to the treatment of juvenile offenders is their involvement in sex offenses. Excluding forcible rape and prostitution, 19 percent of all persons arrested for sex offenses in 1993 were juveniles (U.S. Bureau of the Census, 1995).

Specialized treatment programs, both within the formal system and community-based programs have been created to deal with these offenders. Some treatment programs purport to have had good success in treating the adolescent sex offender. Success is based on the number of children treated who do not re-offend (Ryan and Lane, 1991; Hunter, Goodwin, and Becker, 1994; Kaplan, Morales, and Becker, 1993).

Status Offenders

Juvenile codes or laws in many states distinguish between delinquents and status offenders. The latter are children who are viewed by the juvenile court as being "in need of supervision" as a result of inappropriate behavior associated with their status as minors. A large proportion of these children come from dysfunctional, conflict-ridden families; many have been victims of physical, sexual, and emotional abuse. There is considerable debate as to whether the juvenile court should have legal jurisdiction over status offenders. Proponents of court jurisdiction offer the argument that the court should intensively supervise status offenders because, without this control, these youths' continued misbehavior will eventually lead to more serious delinquent acts (Roberts 1989). But others believe that status offenders should be removed from the jurisdiction of the juvenile court because the needs of these children can better be met in community-based social service agencies and programs outside the formal legal system (Boisevert and Wells, 1980). In the late 1960s, the juvenile justice system began the practice of diverting status offenders, away from the system. *Diversion* is any process used by components of the juvenile justice system (police, prosecution, probation, or the courts) to avoid the processing and eventual adjudication of an offender within the juvenile court system (Roberts, 1989). Offenders are usually diverted or referred to ancillary juvenile court-based or non-court-based community agencies or programs for treatment or services. The diversion of status offenders who have committed minor offenses has several main objectives: avoidance of labeling children as offenders, reduction of unnecessary detention, reduction of recidivism, provision of treatment and other services, and lowering of juvenile justice system costs (Palmer and Lewis, 1980). There have been arguments both for and against the practice of diversion, as well as debate about the success of diversion programs in achieving the aforementioned objectives.

With regard to diversion and the reduction of recidivism, mixed opinions exist on this issue. Some believe that decreases in recidivism result from diversion programs and others argue that inconclusive evidence exists to support recidivism rates' being lowered by diverting youngsters from the formal system (Whitehead and Lab, 1990). Despite the lack of evidence documenting the success of diversion, its practice continues and will likely do so in the future. Similarly, alternatives to placement of status offenders in juvenile detention and correctional facilities have emerged over the years.

Recently, a study evaluating Florida's alternative programs to secure detention for juveniles reported a lower rate of detention and a substantial costs savings by keeping youngsters out of high security facilities (Schwartz, Barton, and Orlando, 1991). Contrary to these findings, other studies have been more critical of the deinstitutionalization effort. A study assessing the effect of Illinois's new status offender legislation reported that fewer youngsters are being placed in detention under the new law, but the difference from previous practices was not significant. Another national study reported little change in the number of status offenders being held in custody in detention facilities (Logan and Rausch, 1985; Curran, 1988).

Treatment of Status Offenders

Treatment for status offenders is provided by social service, family service, and mental health agencies, or by juvenile court-based programs. A broad range of services is provided, including individual and family counseling, group therapy, addiction treatment, alternative education programs, foster care, residential treatment, vocational education, training and placement services, runaway shelters, and therapeutic services for abusive parents. Intervention should affect the offender's total world. These agencies also coordinate and link children and families to the community resources that serve youth.

The system also emphasizes prevention by developing new prevention-oriented programs or by coordinating existing ones, such as the YWCA or YMCAs, scouting, Boys' Clubs, Girls' Clubs, 4-H Clubs, church youth programs, and the like. Coordination of services with schools has been another thrust.

Even though an elaborate set of treatment machinery has been set in motion within the juvenile corrections system, the system is not perfect. Rates of recidivism continue to be higher than expected. Therefore, all parts of the system must make a concerted effort to develop additions and alternatives to the present system.

The Role of Social Work in Juvenile Corrections

Social work historically has been more involved in the field of juvenile corrections than in the adult system. Social workers have assumed a variety of roles within both the formal and the informal juvenile corrections system. The juvenile corrections system is based on the philosophy of rehabilitation and treatment, as opposed to punishment, which is congruent with social work values.

Social workers within the formal system work as probation officers or with probation officers and other professionals. They perform administrative roles in youth service bureaus. Social workers also work in juvenile correctional institutions, providing individual, family, or group treatment, as well as planning, organization, and administrative services. Many social workers also provide services to juvenile offenders in the auxiliary informal corrections system. Social workers perform a variety of roles in group homes, residential treatment facilities, family agencies, mental health centers, and traditional youth agencies (YMCA, YWCA, etc.), and in coordinating services with schools. These roles are most important to the overall functioning of the system. Social workers have also become members of police crisis intervention teams, and have intervened in family domestic violence situations and in child protection. Juvenile corrections systems vary from one state to another in their organization; thus, the role of the social worker will also vary from state to state. To illustrate the social work role in the juvenile corrections system, the case example on page 242 is provided.

A Case Study

Fred M, a fifteen-year-old youth, was jointly referred by his school counselor and his mother to the intake unit of a county juvenile court located in a large city. Fred's problems, based on information provided by his counselor and mother, were that he was experiencing poor school performance, was skipping several of his classes, was belligerent and disruptive in class, was beyond the reach of his mother's attempts to discipline him, was staying out late, and was verbally and physically abusing his mother. His mother, a single parent, also worried that he could be abusing alcohol or drugs, and feared that he might be involved in delinquent activity with several of his friends. Because no formal charges were being brought against Fred, the intake worker referred Fred and his mother to the family services unit of the juvenile court. The case was assigned to one of the unit's four social workers.

The social worker contacted the school counselor and the mother by phone for additional information and also arranged to meet with Fred and his mother. The social worker met with them on two occasions to assess their situation and to make suggestions about what could be done to assist the family in their situation. The social worker concluded in his assessment that Fred's difficulties stemmed from unresolved trauma and feelings associated with his parents' divorce, which had occurred several years earlier. His mother had also begun a serious relationship with a man and planned to marry this man in the near future.

Fred, although expressing no particular dislike for this man, seemed fearful or perhaps jealous of his mother's relationship with this man. The social worker also concluded that the supervision and discipline the mother used to try to control Fred's behavior were inappropriate and inconsistent. The social worker made the following suggestions to the family:

1. That the family become involved in individual and family counseling sessions, including sessions with the mother's fiance
2. That the mother and her partner attend the parenting training class being offered through the family services unit
3. That Fred attend the peer influence prevention group and the group for teenagers from divorced families provided by his school and conducted by his school counselor

Although it sounded at this point as though the case of Fred M was on the road to a successful outcome, the situation was not easily resolved. The social worker's empathetic persistence, plus the mother's newly learned parenting skills, began to pay off. As Fred was able to understand and deal with his feelings about his parents' divorce, and as he began to see that his mother's firm disciplinary approach meant love, care, and concern on her part, Fred's behavior began to improve. The problems that precipitated the referral to the juvenile court began to subside. After eight months of fairly intensive work, Fred M's case was closed by the family services unit.

Although the role of the social worker in the field of juvenile corrections can be rewarding, it can also be equally frustrating and challenging. Needleman (1983) has suggested several steps for improving the practice of social work in the juvenile corrections system:

1. Social workers need appropriate training in both direct and indirect service methods.
2. Social workers need to be able to communicate, develop relationships with, and move effectively to utilize community social service resources.
3. Social workers need to develop understanding about the community in which they practice. This includes the community's norms and tolerance around juvenile behavior, and crime, as well as its socioeconomic, cultural, ethnic, and racial factors.

4. In order to reduce friction, hostility, and tension between social workers and other juvenile justice professionals, social workers need to demonstrate the value of their contributions to the overall functioning of the system.
5. More social workers need to be a part of the juvenile justice system. Recruitment methods need to be developed to attract social workers (Needleman, 1983: 176–178).

Social workers can also be effective in this field of practice by advocating for change that allows them increased opportunities to use their knowledge and skills in developing innovative intervention for use with juvenile offenders.

The Adult Corrections System

Almost twelve million adults were arrested in 1993. *Crime* and *criminal behavior* are extremely serious social problems in contemporary U.S. society. Societies develop mechanisms to protect themselves from crime and criminal behavior, and to maintain social order and control. The adult criminal justice system that has developed in the United States provides that protection. The goal of the corrections part of the total system, as discussed earlier, is to understand and to treat the problem. The focus here is on the adult corrections system as a specific response to crime and criminal behavior. This concerns not only the policy issues associated with the correctional treatment of the offender but also the broader issues of treatment of the victim and the prevention of crime. In dealing with these issues, it is helpful to gain an understanding of what causes people in society to commit crimes or engage in criminal behavior. This will further understanding of the nature of the responses to crime and criminal behavior that have emerged within the adult correctional system.

Causes of Crime and Criminal Behavior

Historically, explanations of the causes of crime and criminal behavior have varied. The earliest were based on religious thought—the idea that the criminal was possessed by evil spirits. Later, it was thought that the tendency toward criminal behavior was passed on to the individual through genetic inheritance. Still later theories pointed to racial background, mental defect, and the use of alcohol. In the early 1900s it was widely believed that certain biological characteristics predestined certain individuals to a life of criminal behavior. A number of scientists, both biologists and anthropologists, adhered to this concept of *constitutional criminality* (Allen and Simonsen, 1989). These theories attempted to pinpoint a single cause of crime and criminal behavior, and tended to foster the misconception that criminals were all a part of a large, homogeneous group.

Currently, crime and criminal behavior are not attributed to a single source but to a multiplicity of factors. This has been referred to as the multiple causation theory, which combines biological, social, psychological, economic, and environmental factors in explaining why crime and criminal behavior exist. Biological conditions such as poor health and physical handicaps may predispose certain individuals toward a tendency to commit criminal behavior. Social, economic, and environmental factors, including poverty, racism, child abuse and neglect, socialization in criminal attitudes by family or peers, lack of educational achievement, and family breakup, may also be involved. Mental illness, retardation, and family character development are some psychological factors that can influence the individual toward committing crimes. It must be emphasized here that any one factor or combination of these factors will not necessarily cause an individual to become a criminal. These are solely predictive factors and may or may not be associated with the cause of crime and criminal behavior in any given case.

Responses to Criminal Behavior

There has been considerable debate over whether current correctional policy should be oriented toward punishment or rehabilitation; there has been movement toward a crackdown on crime or a punishment orientation in correctional policy. The criminal justice system currently is in conflict between a philosophy focusing on protecting society from crime and one emphasizing the rehabilitation of offenders. On the one hand, correctional policy seems to be dominated by the notions of "just deserts" or the "justice model," whereby the offender receives deserved or just punishment. This is demonstrated by the fact that more dollars are being spent on building prisons than ever before. The Violent Crime Control and Law Enforcement Act of 1994 provides for mandatory life imprisonment without parole for federal offenders with three or more convictions for serious felonies or drug trafficking crimes. Several states also have similar provisions (U.S. Department of Justice, 1995). The practice of *capital punishment* also reflects this view. On the other hand, rehabilitation efforts in correctional services have achieved some positive results. However, the movement toward changing the structure to a more rehabilitative model continues to be difficult, despite the fact that studies indicate that intervention (rehabilitation programs) with offenders have been shown to be effective (Andrews, Zinger, Hope, and Bonta, 1990; Palmer, 1991). The direction that adult corrections policy will take in the future is uncertain and is open for debate. This is because the punishment-deterrence and the treatment-rehabilitation philosophies are based on strongly held, opposing views of human nature. Gould and Sayles (1990) suggest both the punishment and rehabilitation philosophies focus on an offender-oriented view of corrections. They advocate for a shift from individual offenders and what to do with them, to a more interactional view of crime itself. The interactional view assumes that crime is more than a function of individual criminal behavior and is a social event, also involving the behaviors of victims, control agents, and society as a whole. Focus on these interacting behaviors may provide solutions to the crime problem and should shape the future of correctional policy.

Correctional Services for Adult Offenders

As noted earlier, correctional services for adult offenders include both institutional and community-based services. The institutional services are predominant. Jails, operated on a local community or countywide basis, are usually reserved for short-term *incarceration* (confinement); but *prisons* (operated by the states and the federal government) are the backbone of the U.S. corrections system.

The development of the U.S. prison system has a complex history. Prior to the emergence of prisons, those who committed what were considered to be deviant or antisocial acts were dealt with in ways that today would be considered cruel and bizarre punishment. Both severe corporal (physical) and capital punishment (the death penalty) were used. Public hangings, beatings, torture, and other forms of physical punishment were carried out to make a public example of offenders. Beginning in the late 1700s, reform took place in the methods used to deal with adult offenders. A humanitarian protest by a group of Quakers led by Dr. Benjamin Rush has been credited with beginning the impetus toward the development of the modern penitentiary system in the United States. In 1787, Rush and his followers founded the Philadelphia Prison Society, which in the years that followed brought about vast reform in the prison system in Pennsylvania and became a model to other states, which adopted similar reforms. Reforms included open exercise yards, larger cells, and discussion with prisoners about their lives and future. The developing penitentiary prison system provided a relatively humane way of punishing offenders.

Although reform had taken place in the corrections system through the development of penitentiaries, these changes were not long lasting. As the system grew with the establishment of state prisons, some of the earlier enlightened features were forgotten. State prisons became overcrowded and used severe disciplinary measures to control prisoners. This characterized a return to a punishment-oriented philosophy. The State Penitentiary at Auburn, New York, became a model for these new penal institutions. In the 1930s a wave of reform began in the prison system. Impetus for this reform came from a better understanding of crime, criminal behavior, and rehabilitation, stemming from the new social science disciplines. Better designed prisons with more facilities, better trained staff, and individual and group therapy began to appear. The reorganization of the federal system of prisons in 1929 was at the forefront of these efforts. Although it served as a model, few states have adopted many of the innovative features of the federal system.

It was hoped that the Correctional Rehabilitation Study Act of 1965, which addressed personnel problems in the system, would move the system in the direction of prison reform. This has not proven to be the case. Efforts at reform in prisons are thwarted by overcrowding; personnel shortages; poor sanitation and food; and inadequate education, recreation, and treatment programs.

Violence in prisons remains a serious problem. Other problems such as suicide and homosexual rape also point out the inadequacies of the reform effort in the U.S. prison system. Correctional services in institutions fall far short of meeting the human needs of inmates (Bartollas, 1990).

Despite these problems, some positive changes have occurred in recent years. Numerous state, federal, and Supreme Court decisions have emphasized the protection of prisoners' rights. Prior to the 1960s, the courts had maintained a hands-off policy toward prison administration. In 1964 the United States Supreme Court, in the case of *Cooper* v. *Pate,* ruled that prisoners in state prisons are entitled to the protection of the civil rights guaranteed by the Civil Rights Act of 1971. In this case, the court also ruled that prisoners could bring legal action against prison officials, under a law that imposed civil liability on people who deprive others of their constitutional rights. Since 1964 there has been a great deal of prisoner rights litigation. Several court decisions have protected other rights of prisoners, such as freedom of religious practice, freedom of speech, freedom from cruel and unusual punishment, due process in prison discipline situations, and the right to adequate medical care and rehabilitative services (Clear and Cole, 1986). Another positive change has been programs recognizing female prisoners' parental role and either allowing very young children to live with their mother in prison or making special arrangements for children to visit their mothers.

The most pressing problem today is overcrowding. According to the U.S. Bureau of Justice Statistics (1995), almost 1.5 million people were incarcerated in the United States in 1994, a new record. Federal laws, the Comprehensive Crime Control Act of 1984, and the Anti-Drug Abuse Act of 1986, which require mandatory sentencing, have contributed to this problem. This has given rise to lawsuits being heard by Federal Courts, which in many instances have ordered the states to ease the overcrowded conditions in their prisons. The states have responded to this by the construction of new facilities or have added to existing facilities. Although this has eased the problem somewhat, the ratio of the inmate population to the bed capacity in state prisons has remained steady since 1990 (U.S. Bureau of Justice Statistics, 1995).

Another relatively new controversial development in adult corrections has been the movement toward the "privatization of corrections." This has come about partially as a response to the overcrowding problem, where private, not-for-profit or, in some instances, for-profit facilities are utilized to incarcerate criminal offenders. Legislation has been passed in several states requiring correctional systems to contract with private organizations, in some cases, to build and operate jails and prisons. Private corrections have taken a number of forms ranging from contracts, grants, and subsidies to public-private partnerships. There have been arguments both for and against private corrections. Opponents have argued that it is philosophically and legally wrong for any entity other than government to hold in custody criminal offenders. Proponents, on the other hand, argue that the public system has failed, and more efficient facilities, with better quality services and standards of management can be provided by the private sector (DiIulio, 1991). It is not likely that these arguments will be settled in the near future. Nor is there enough evaluative evidence to either support or refute the claims made by those who advocate for private corrections. It will be interesting to see whether the privatization of corrections is merely a trend or if it will eventually become a part of the field of adult corrections.

Community-Based Correctional Services for Adults

In the 1960s, a new form of adult correctional services emerged known as community-based correctional services. It was designed to provide treatment and rehabilitation in the community, as an alternative to institutionalization. The major goal of community-based correctional services is to make available a wide range of resources from which justice system officials may choose in dealing with offenders.

The impetus behind their development came from a variety of sources. The President's Commission on Law Enforcement and the Administration of Justice in 1967 dealt with the issue of incarceration versus community-based treatment, by making the point that the goals of offender rehabilitation were more likely to be achieved by community-based treatment (President's Task Force, 1970). Later, in 1970, the President's Task Force on Prisoner Rehabilitation strongly urged that incarceration should be avoided in favor of community-based treatment (Clear and Cole, 1986). In the 1970s, the National Council on Crime and Delinquency and the Law Enforcement Assistance Administration also expressed a preference for the development of community-based correctional services.

Probation and parole services had been in existence for some years before the more recent community-based programs and remain the most frequently used forms of community-based services. *Probation* is usually offered to first-time offenders as an alternative to incarceration. The offender is allowed to remain in his or her community, to maintain family ties, and to continue to study or work, but remains under the supervision of the corrections system. Probation usually allows the offender to avoid the embitterment of institutional life, and gives the offender a second chance at a crime-free life. *Parole* is designed as a safeguard for both the offender and the community. It allows the offender, after a specified period of time, to be released from the institution into the community, with a plan for ongoing rehabilitation assistance. Parole offers the offender assistance in reintegrating into community life, while also protecting the community, within certain limits, from further criminal acts by the offender. The offender must meet certain conditions to keep the privilege of parole. Parolees must be under the supervision of local parole officers, who may restrict the work or travel of parolees. The offender must avoid further criminal activity, and with just cause parole can be revoked at any time and the offender returned to prison. Other community-based alternatives include *work release* and *educational release* from institutional care back into the community (such prisoners are allowed short-term release to go to school or work but remain under close supervision); restitution; halfway houses; drug treatment programs; mental health services; and other social, health, and recreational services.

The advantages of community-based correctional services are numerous. To begin with, they avoid isolating the offender from the community. Treatment resources are more available in the community than in correctional institutions. The offender is protected from the ills of the institutional system. Finally, and perhaps most important, community-based services are more cost-effective than institutional care. Although it is estimated that the trend toward community-based services will continue, with the current law and order and punishment orientation of the criminal justice system, it seems unlikely that they would ever totally replace the institutional system.

The Criminal Offender

Criminal offenders are diverse, and not the homogeneous group they are often thought to be. Each is an individual with unique needs. Nevertheless, society, through the corrections system, tends to deal with individual offenders according to their group rather than individual characteristics. For example, members of minority groups are more likely to be arrested, convicted, sentenced, and incarcerated for crimes than are whites. In 1993, 3.6 million African Americans, or 31 percent of all persons arrested in the United States, were arrested. African Americans make up only 12.5 percent of the U.S. population, but they represent 47 percent of all persons who are incarcerated in state prisons. It is easy to ascertain that the forces of racial discrimination are operating here (U.S. Bureau of the Census, 1995).

Socioeconomic status is another factor that can influence the kind of treatment an offender receives from the corrections system. White-collar offenders are more likely to receive lenient treatment than are blue-collar and unemployed offenders, who have a much greater chance of being incarcerated.

There are gender differences in the way the system deals with offenders. Women are less often arrested, convicted, and incarcerated than males. However, the number of female arrests increased 24 percent between 1986 and 1991, whereas male arrests increased only 13 percent during this period. In 1991, 19 percent of all persons arrested were women. Although men are more likely to be incarcerated than women, the number of females incarcerated in state prisons increased by 75 percent in the years 1986 to 1991. Women and men also differ with respect to type of crime committed. Men are more likely to be convicted and sentenced for drug-related and violent crimes, whereas women are more likely to be convicted and sentenced for property and other non-violent crimes. Notwithstanding, the number of women sentenced for violent offenses rose 35 percent from 1986 to 1991. There also appears to be a connection between a women's propensity to commit violent crime and a prior history of child abuse, both physical and sexual abuse. Among females incarcerated for violent crime in 1991, almost 42 percent of them reported that they had experienced prior child abuse. Almost 52 percent of women incarcerated for commiting homicide reported that they had experienced prior child abuse (Snell, 1994). The increases noted above in the rate of incarceration of females point to the influence of the currently predominant philosophy of giving offenders their "just deserts," the societal backlash toward treating all criminal offenders more severely.

The diversity of adult criminal offenders is also evident when one considers special categories of offenders, such as mentally ill or developmentally disabled offenders, sex offenders, aged offenders, HIV-infected offenders, and those classified as dangerous offenders. The issue of the relationship between mental illness and criminal behavior has come into focus in recent years. The plea "not guilty by reason of insanity" has come into serious question as a result of public sentiment and several nationally publicized cases. Several states have made changes in laws that provide treatment to such offenders and protect society by confining these offenders in psychiatric institutions. Whether this practice offers any advantages, or whether mental illness necessitates differential correctional treatment for the offender, has not been decided and remains a dilemma.

Developmentally disabled offenders, including the mentally retarded and those with handicapping conditions such as hearing or visual impairments, pose special problems for the corrections system. The dilemma has not so much to do with ensuring that the offender makes retribution for the crime committed as with how to provide rehabilitation to these offenders given the limitations caused by their handicapping conditions. The corrections system is ill prepared to deal with such offenders.

Age is a basis for diversity in the treatment of criminal offenders. In recent years courts have begun the practice of imposing longer sentences, creating a population of offenders who will likely grow old in penal institutions. This category of special offenders has unique problems, and dealing with them in the corrections system will require careful thought and consideration.

Sex offenders are a special group of offenders who have received considerable attention in recent years. Although sex offenses range from rape, child molestation, and incest to exhibitionism and voyeurism, it is rape, child molestation, and incest that have received the greatest amount of attention from society and from the corrections system. When initially faced with dealing with sex offenders, there was considerable debate on whether they should be incarcerated or should receive treatment. Proponents of incarceration were supported by the societal backlash and public sentiment calling for the punishment of offenders, and the fact that the few treatment programs that existed were reporting discouraging results, with respect to recidivism rates of offenders who had received treatment.

Proponents for treatment of sex offenders argued that there were factors that complicated treatment efforts. Among them are lack of support from the corrections system, and the lack of research identifying the social and psychological characteristics of sex offenders. Currently, there is a growing body of research that has assisted in filling the void of knowledge about this population, resulting in the development of more effective treatment methods (Pallone, 1993;

McGrath, 1993; Marshall, 1993; Quinsey, Harris, Rice, and Lalumiere, 1993). Recent studies are reporting treatment innovations as a result of better knowledge of this offender population, and more encouraging treatment results appear to be occurring. This has provided the impetus for the development of a growing number of treatment programs across the country. Once thought to be a crime mostly committed by men, sexual offenses perpetrated by female sex offenders were largely ignored. As the body of research has grown, attention is now being paid to identifying the differences between female and male offenders and the treatment implications for females (Marshall and Eccles, 1991).

Another characteristic of sex offenders, in general, that has been identified in the literature, is the level of violence associated with these crimes. Studies are reporting a greater level of violence than once thought. Therefore, it is now believed that sex offenders should receive a combination of incarceration, therapeutic treatment, and intensive posttreatment supervision by the corrections system (Stermac, Hall, and Henskens, 1989).

HIV-infected offenders pose a special problem for the corrections system. In 1991, 2.2 percent of inmates in U.S. prisons were infected with HIV: 60 percent exhibited HIV symptoms, and 20 percent had confirmed full-blown AIDS (U.S. Bureau of Justice Statistics, 1995). The recent federal legislation requiring mandatory sentencing for convicted drug users, a high risk group for HIV infection, has likely increased the potential for such persons being incarcerated in penal institutions. Movement has begun to develop policy regarding AIDS in the criminal justice system at all levels. Recent literature has focused on the merits of mandatory HIV testing for both offenders and criminal justice personnel (Blumberg and Langston, 1991; U.S. Bureau of Justice Statistics, 1995). As with most special offenders, the system must become better prepared to deal with the needs of HIV infected offenders.

Assessment and management of dangerous offenders by the corrections system poses a difficult problem. The major difficulty lies in identifying potentially dangerous offenders. Dangerous offenders do not come in neatly wrapped packages, nor do they fall within stereotypical perceptions; they are not all mentally ill, criminally insane, or afflicted with a severe personality disorder. Although 10 percent of offenders classified as dangerous do have these conditions, mental illnesses or personality disorders are not in and of themselves reliable predictors of dangerousness (Davis, 1991). A working definition of the dangerous offender is the degree to which the offender is likely to inflict physical injury, harm, or violence, or to cause death to another person or to him- or herself. Although classification schemas have been developed in recent years to predict the risk of dangerousness, they are not 100 percent reliable.

As can be seen, adult criminal offenders are a diverse group including several special categories of offenders. Each has unique needs, and each poses particular problems for the corrections system.

Social Work Roles in Adult Correctional Services

Social workers have performed a variety of roles, both within community-based correctional services and within some correctional institutions. Most social workers in correctional services have filled positions as probation and parole officers. In these positions, the main method of intervention has been what is termed direct intervention or social casework, which involves the use of the social work problem-solving process, including the following:

Data collection regarding the offender's life situation

Assessment (identifying problems, needs, and concerns)

Developing an intervention plan (individual plus family counseling, and use of community resources)

Intervention (carrying out the plan)

Evaluation (examining the plan to ascertain its effectiveness)

Termination (preparing the offender for release from probation or parole)

In addition, some social workers, acting as probation or parole officers, use group intervention methods, working with groups of offenders for a variety of interventive purposes. Social workers in these positions may also be involved in community organization or advocacy roles. Offenders are often shunned by the community, making access to community resources difficult. Advocacy with the community on behalf of offenders is often necessary.

Social workers have also become involved in police work. Some police departments employ social workers in crisis intervention and in domestic violence intervention programs. As early as 1959, social work began to address the needs of corrections through the development of curriculum in schools of social work. More recently, both undergraduate and graduate social work programs have begun to offer specific course work, including field placements, for students interested in correctional social work.

A Case Study

Bonnie B, a twenty-three-year-old woman, was released on parole from the women's correctional facility. When released, Bonnie returned to live with her parents in a nearby city. As required, she made contact with her parole officer, a trained social worker. The parole officer knew from the parole board's report that in the past Bonnie had experienced a great deal of difficulty with alcoholism. Although she had become involved in Alcoholics Anonymous (AA) groups within the correctional facility, she had not received intensive treatment for her drinking problem. Upon meeting with her, the parole officer also learned that Bonnie's two children had been temporarily removed from her custody at the time of her incarceration and had been placed in a foster home in another part of the state. Bonnie expressed her desire to regain custody of her children once she was settled and able to provide for their care. She requested assistance from the parole officer in this effort. The parole officer knew from the parole report that Bonnie had received two years of secretarial training and had

held various secretarial positions before her arrest and conviction. Bonnie also told the parole officer that living with her parents should be only a temporary arrangement. She worried that her parents would have trouble coping with her living independently because "they are overprotective of me."

In the following months, the parole officer helped Bonnie complete alcoholism treatment, along with continuing involvement in AA; find employment as a secretary with a local business; and secure her own living arrangements. The parole officer spent a great deal of time in intervention with Bonnie's family to help them resolve their feelings about Bonnie's living on her own. The parole officer, working through the public social services department, was able to help Bonnie regain custody of her children. Eighteen months after Bonnie's release from the women's correctional facility, the parole officer recommended to the parole board that she be released from parole. The request was granted.

Many state prisons and most federal penal institutions employ social workers in their correctional treatment programs. Most often, social workers provide direct counseling or therapeutic services to the inmates. Social workers can also engage in group work treatment within the prison, working with inmates who have similar concerns, needs, or problems. Social workers can be part of a treatment team that might include other helping professionals; they can also perform advocacy and resource development roles. Social workers play an important role in preparing inmates for release from the institution. This involves forging links between inmates and community resources to assist the inmates in reintegration into the community. The need for these services within correctional institutions is a crucial one. Social workers who demonstrate competence in working within the corrections system will provide legitimacy for the profession's involvement in the adult corrections field.

Summary

This chapter has examined the responses made on behalf of society to crime, criminal behavior, and delinquency. Both the juvenile and adult corrections systems were explored—the responses they have made, the philosophies and values that have influenced the structure of these responses, and the strengths and weakness of the systems. The overall role of social work as a profession was discussed and illustrated, and the contention was supported that involvement in the correctional system is a legitimate field of social work practice.

Key Terms

capital punishment
community-based correctional services
constitutional criminality
corrections
crime
criminal behavior
criminal justice system
delinquent
diversion
educational release
HIV infection
incarceration

juvenile court
juvenile delinquency
juvenile reformation
parens patriae
parole
prisons
probation
restitution
sex offender
status offender
work release
Youth Service Bureaus

References

Allen, H.E., and Simonsen, C.E. (1989). *Corrections in America*. New York: Macmillan.

Andrews, D.A., Zinger, I., Hope, R. D., and Bonta, J. (1990). Does Correctional Treatment Work? A Clin-

ically Relevant and Psychologically Informed Meta-Analysis. *Criminology, 28 (3)*, 369–404.

Bartollas, C. (1990). The Prison: Disorder Personified, in Murphey, J.W., Dison, J.E. (Eds.). *Are Prisons any*

Better? Twenty Years of Correctional Reform. Newbury Park: Sage Publications, pp. 9–11.

Blumberg, M. and Langston, D. (1991). Mandatory HIV Testing in Criminal Justice Settings. *Crime and Delinquency, 37 (1)*, 5–18.

Boisevert, M.J. and Wells, R. (1980). Towards a Rational Policy on Status Offenders. *Social Work, 25*, 230–234.

Clear, T.R. and Cole, G.F. (1986). *American Corrections.* Monterey, CA: Brooks/Cole, pp. 442–467.

Curran, D.J. (1988). Destructuring, Privatization, and the Promise of Juvenile Diversion: Compromising Community Based Corrections. *Crime and Delinquency, 34 (4)*, 363–378.

Davis, S. (1991). An Overview: Are Mentally Ill People Really More Dangerous? *Social Work, 36 (2)*, 174–180.

DiIulio, J.J. (1991). *No Escape: The Future of American Corrections.* New York: Basic Books, pp. 180–210.

Ferguson, E. (1975). *Social Work: An Introduction.* Philadelphia: Lippincott, pp. 359–360.

Fox, V. (1983). Forward, in Roberts, A.R. *Social Work in Juvenile and Criminal Justice Settings.* Springfield IL: Charles C. Thomas.

Free, M.D. (1991). Clarifying the Relationship Between the Broken Home and Juvenile Delinquency: A Critique of Current Literature. *Delinquent Behavior, 12 (2)*, 109–167.

Frost, M.L., and Bloomquist, M. (1991). Cracking Down on Juveniles: The Changing Ideology of Youth Corrections. *Notre Dame Journal of Law, Ethics and Public Policy, 5 (2)*, 323–375.

Gould, L.C., and Sayles, S.L. (1990). The Interactionist Approach to Crime and Corrections, in Muraskin, R. (Ed.), *Issues in Justice: Exploring Policy Issues in the Criminal Justice System.* Bristol, IN: Wyndham Hall Press, pp. 58–72.

Hunter, J.A., Goodwin, D.W., and Becker, J.V. (1994). The Relationship Between Phallometrically Measured Deviant Sexual Arousal and Clinical Characteristics in Juvenile Sexual Offenders. *Behaviour Research and Therapy, 32 (5)*, 533–538.

Johnson, H.W. (1995). *The Social Services: An Introduction.* Itaska, IL: F.E. Peacock, p. 220.

Kaplan, M.S., Morales, M., and Becker, J.V. (1993). The Impact of Verbal Satiation on Adolescent Sex Offenders: A Preliminary Report. *Journal of Child Sexual Abuse, 2 (3)*, 81–88.

Logan, C.H., and Rausch, S.P. (1985). Why Deinstitutionalizing Status Offenders Is Pointless. *Crime and Delinquency, 31 (4)*, 501–517.

Marshall, W.L. (1993). The Treatment of Sex Offenders: What Does The Outcome Data Tell Us? A Reply to Quinsey, Harris, Rice and Lalumiere. *Journal of Interpersonal Violence, 8 (4)*, 524–530.

Marshall, W.L., and Eccles, A. (1991). Issues in Clinical Practice with Sex Offenders. *Journal of Interpersonal Violence, 6 (1)*, 68–93.

McGrath, R.J. (1993). Preparing Psychosexual Evaluations of Sex Offenders. *Journal of Offender Rehabilitation, 20 (1)*, 139–158.

Menard, S., and Huizinga, D. (1994). Changes in Conventional Attitudes and Delinquent Behavior in Adolescence. *Youth and Society, 26 (1)*, 23–53.

Minor, K.I. (1993). Juvenile Delinquency and the Transition to Monopoly Capitalism. *Journal of Sociology and Social Welfare, 20 (4)*, 59–80.

Needleman, C. (1983). Social Work and Probation in Juvenile Court, in Roberts, A.R. *Social Work in Juvenile and Criminal Justice Settings.* Springfield, IL: Charles C. Thomas.

Pallone, N.J. (1993). Legislatively-Mandated Treatment of Sex Offenders: Unsettled Issues. *Journal of Offender Rehabilitation, 20 (1/2)*, 159–205.

Palmer, T. (1991). The Effectiveness of Intervention: Recent Trends and Current Issues. *Crime and Delinquency, 37 (3)*, 330–346.

Palmer, T.B., and Lewis, R.V. (1980). A Differential Approach to Juvenile Diversion. *Journal of Research in Crime and Delinquency*, 209–227.

President's Task Force on Prisoner Rehabilitation (1970). *The Criminal Offender—What Should be Done?* Washington DC: U.S. Government Printing Office.

Quinsey, V.L., Harris, G.T., Rice, M.E., and Lalumiere, M.L. (1993). Assessing Treatment Efficacy in Outcome Studies of Sex Offenders. *Journal of Interpersonal Violence, 8 (4)*, 512–523.

Roberts, A.R. (1989). Family Treatment, in Roberts, A.R. (Ed.). *Juvenile Justice: Policies, Programs and Services.* Chicago: Dorsey Press.

Ryan, G.D., and Lane, S.L. (1991). *Juvenile Sex Offending: Causes, Consequences and Correction.* Lexington MA: D.C. Heath.

Schwartz, I.M., Barton, W.H., and Orlando, F. (1991). Keeping Kids Out of Secure Detention. *Public Welfare, 49 (2)*, 20–26.

Skidmore, R.A., Thackeray, M.G. and Farley, O.W. (1991). *Introduction to Social Work.* Englewood Cliffs: Prentice Hall.

Smith, D.A., Visher, C.A., and Jarjoura, G.R. (1991). Dimensions of Delinquency Exploring the Correlates of Participation, Frequency and Persistence of Delinquent Behavior. *Journal of Research in Crime and Delinquency, 28 (1)*, 6–32.

Snell, T.J. (1994). *Women in Prison/Bureau of Justice Statistics Bulletin.* Annapolis Junction, MD: Bureau of Justice Statistics, U.S. Department of Justice.

Stermac, L., Hall, K., and Henskens, M. (1989). Violence Among Child Molesters. *Journal of Sex Research, 26 (4)*, 450–459.

Trattner, W.I. (1979). *From Poor Law To Welfare State.* New York: The Free Press, p. 105.

U.S. Department of Commerce/Bureau of the Census (1995). *Statistical Abstracts of the United States.* Washington DC: U.S. Government Printing Office.

U.S. Department of Justice (1995). *The Nation's Prison Population Grew Almost 9 Percent Last Year.* Washington, DC: U.S. Government Printing Office.

U.S. Department of Justice/Bureau of Justice Statistics (1995). *Violent Crime Control and Law Enforcement Act of 1994.* Washington, D.C.: U.S Government Printing Office.

Whitehead, J.T., and Lab, S.P. (1990). *Juvenile Justice: An Introduction.* Cincinnati, OH: Anderson Publishing, pp. 65–105.

Suggested Readings

Cromwell, P.F., and Killinger, G.C. (1994). *Community Based Corrections: Probation, Parole, and Intermediate Sanctions.* New York: West Publishing Company.

DiIulio, J.J. (1991). *No Escape: The Future of American Corrections.* New York: Basic Books.

Masters, R.E. (1994). *Counseling Criminal Justice Offenders.* Thousand Oaks, CA: Sage Publications.

Monk, R.C. (1996). *Taking Sides: Clashing Views on Controversial Issues in Crime and Criminology.* Guilford, CT: Dushkin Publishing Group.

Roberts, A.R. (ed.) (1989). *Juvenile Justice: Policies, Programs, and Services.* Chicago: Dorsey Press.

Snarr, R.W. (1996). *Introduction of Corrections.* Chicago: Brown and Benchmark Publishers.

Whitehead, J.T., and Lab, S.P. (1990). *Juvenile Justice: An Introduction.* Cincinnati, OH: Anderson Publishing.

12

GERONTOLOGICAL SOCIAL WORK

Learning Expectations

- Knowledge about the demography of the aging population
- Biological, psychological, and social factors that affect the aging population
- Knowledge of the arrangements used to meet the needs of the aging population
- Awareness of some of the problems and issues that affect the delivery of services to the aging population
- Awareness of the roles that social workers fill when delivering services to the aging population

Working with the elderly is a fairly recent addition to social work. This is not to say that historically this group has been ignored, only that the elderly have been traditionally considered as a part of the family. But with many of the elderly living alone and with a growing elderly population, the needs of older people have been recognized as an area of concern that must be given separate attention.

Many older people have difficulty in meeting all of their needs. They are susceptible to chronic illnesses that may impair their capacity to function. Often they are lonely and isolated. Insufficient income and even poverty are major problems for this population. And although the elderly have always been recipients of income maintenance services, as life spans lengthen, the number of older people who will need special attention will also grow. To meet these and other needs, a special field of practice has developed that focuses specifically on the problems of older people. This field of practice, which has been referred to as social work with the aged or *gerontological social work,* generally includes work with people sixty years of age or older.

Interest in gerontological social work dates from the mid-1940s. Table 12–1 outlines some of the major milestones in the history of the field. In 1945 the Gerontological Society was formed as a forum for professionals working with the elderly. The promotion of research on issues of aging was one of its goals. Group work with the aged was the predominant mode of

TABLE 12–1   Important Dates in Gerontological Social Work

1935	Passage of the Social Security Act provided income maintenance for older people through both insurance and public welfare arrangements.
1945	The Gerontological Society was formed.
1961	The first White House Conference on Aging was held.
1965	The Older Americans Act was passed.
1965	The Medicaid and Medicare amendments to the Social Security Act were passed.
1974	The Supplemental Security Income provisions of the Social Security Act replaced Old Age Assistance.
1974	The National Institute on Aging was formed.
1981	Title XX becomes a Block Grant.
1983	The Social Security Amendments "rescue OASDI."
1983	Prospective payment—Diagnositic Related Groups (DRG's) were introduced for Medicare services.
1986	Elimination of Mandatory Retirement.
1986	Tax reform eliminated the additional personal federal income tax exemption for individuals over sixty-five and taxed Social Security payments (half of the amount over $25,000 for an individual or $32,000 for a couple).
1987	Nursing Home Reform Act passed.
1988	Catastrophic Health Insurance Act that would have expanded Medicare services was signed into law and then later repealed by Congress.
1995	Congress passes "welfare reform bill" that changes Medicaid from an entitlement program to a state block grant program. Also, budget bill is passed that will substantially change the Medicare program.

service. The National Council on Aging was established in 1960 and became a leader in stimulating interest in social work with older people and in developing practice methods and techniques for the particular needs of that population. In 1961 the first White House Conference on Aging was held. This conference identified the needs and concerns of older people that formed the base for several important pieces of legislation passed in the 1960s. Included in this legislation were the Older American Act and the Medicare/Medicaid amendments to the Social Security Act. In the 1960s and 1970s, many conferences and projects took place that dealt with social work's need to recognize the aged as a special group and with enabling social workers to develop the special expertise needed for working in this new field of practice (Lowy, 1991).

Who Are the Aged?

All human beings start aging from the day of their birth, but the word "aged" generally refers to individuals in the last stage of their life span. It is difficult to determine a definite age for this stage. Some say everyone over fifty-five is old; some, everyone over sixty; and others, everyone over sixty-five. Still others say that there are really two groups of aged people, those under seventy-five and those over seventy-five years of age. This latter group is often referred to as the *old-old* or the *frail elderly.* This does not mean that younger people will not be the concern of gerontological social work, which also helps younger people to avoid some of the problems the aged have. The families of aged people are also of concern because of their heavy involvement in the care and support of older family members.

Demographic Factors

In 1994, 33 million people were over the age of 65, 13 percent of the total U.S. population. Since 1900, the number of older people in the population has increased from 3.1 million to over 33 million, or about 10 times. In 1994 there were over 18 million people in the 65- to 74-year age group. The fastest growing segment of this population are those over 75 years. It is estimated that this group will grow by 26.2 percent by the year 2000; with another 10.1 percent by the year 2010. Life expectancy beyond age 65 was 16.8 years in 1984 (18.6 for women and 14.6 for men) (U.S. Bureau of the Census, 1995).

The aged are not a homogeneous group of people but include individuals with a broad variety of characteristics. In 1994, 13.4 million were men and 19.6 million were women. It is estimated that about 5 percent of the group are in nursing homes or other institutions. About 30 percent live alone. Of those over 65 in the population, 27 million are white, 2.5 million are black, and 3.5 million are other races (U.S. Bureau of the Census, 1995).

Geographically, certain parts of the country have a higher percentage of the older population. It is commonly thought that older people tended to live in the South and the West. According to the 1990 census, 17.3 percent of Florida's population is over sixty-five; other states with more than 13 percent of their population over sixty-five include Arkansas (13.7 percent), Rhode Island (13.4 percent), Iowa (13.3 percent), Missouri (13.2 percent), South Dakota (13.2 percent), and Nebraska (13.1 percent). Further examination of census data shows a considerable concentration of older people in the Midwest (U.S. Bureau of the Census, 1995). More older people live outside metropolitan areas than do younger groups. If the elderly do live in cities, they tend to live in the central city, although this is changing as suburbia ages.

Other Factors

When considering this age group, it is important to identify some of the biological, psychological, and social changes that take place at this time of life and are important in understanding the special needs of this population. Gradual physical changes that have been developing for some time now become apparent. The timing and extent of these changes varies widely from person to person. The skin is less pliable, wrinkles develop, the hair grays, the person begins to look old. The skeletomuscular system is more susceptible to stress, bones break more easily, arthritis can develop, and joints are stiffer. Digestive problems become more common. Sensory functions are reduced, eyesight may dim, there may be a hearing loss, and some sensitivity to touch may be lost. The cardiopulmonary system is subject to stress; high blood pressure, heart attacks, strokes, and chronic respiratory difficulty may develop. These physical changes can require a change of lifestyle and diminish an older person's capability to adapt.

Many psychological and sociological theories have been developed about the later years of life (Hooyman and Kiyak, 1996). Scientists have long concerned themselves with studying the causes of aging in humans. It has been their belief that if the biolological determinents of aging could be discovered, the process of aging in humans could be halted and/or reversed. Although there appears to be a body of promising research that has convinced some scientists that the aging process can be reversed, the real value of their research has been to answer the common question: Is aging caused by disease and environmental stresses, or is it due primarily to physiological and biological determinents that naturally occur as chronological age in humans progresses? It is most widely believed that aging occurs naturally and is due to physiological and biological factors. Several theories have been forwarded, ranging from changes in hormonal levels, to a breakdown in the autoimmune system, to changes in body cell replication and reproduction, eventually causing cell death. Genetic cellular theories are currently the most accepted within the scientific community (Hooyman and Kiyak, 1996).

A useful way of considering the psychological factors involved in aging can be from a human developmental point of view. Erik Erikson (1986), a noted psychologist, has identified this as the stage of integrity versus despair. Robert Peck (1968), director of the Research Development Center for Teacher Education in Austin, Texas, has expanded on this to state that the tasks of this stage include developing a sense of worth apart from the work role, developing a capacity to cope with declining physical capabilities, and developing a capacity to deal with the prospect and meaning of death. Maintenance of a positive self-concept is an important task for the older person. Linda George (1982), a professor of psychiatry at Duke University, has identified four dimensions of the adult self-concept that are particularly important:

1. Interpersonal aspects focused on social relationships
2. Altruistic aspects focused on ethical, religious, and philosophical concerns
3. Mastery aspects focused on competence, a sense of effectiveness, creativity, and autonomy
4. Self-protective aspects focused on maintaining a sense of well-being (pp. 22–37).

The sociological considerations important for older people are those characteristics of the society of which they are a part. Contemporary U.S. society displays considerable prejudice against the elderly. Attitudes toward older people and the aging process are generally negative. This has been referred to as ageism. There are few meaningful or important places for older people in our society. Our culture values youth, physical fitness, and productivity. Because of this, stress is inevitable both for the older individual and for society.

Although not all people over sixty-five are in need of attention from the social welfare system, a considerable number find it a constant struggle to meet their own needs either from their own resources or from their immediate personal network. Factors that put older people at risk are insufficient financial resources, living alone with no family nearby, poor health, negative attitudes about aging, and being over seventy-five years of age. Some individuals with these risk factors manage quite well. But when these risk factors begin to affect the individual's capacity to function and when the stress on the individual increases, social welfare resources become important. With a growing number of people in this population group, with multiple risk factors, gerontological social work has become a field of practice, and the social welfare system has developed specialized means for meeting their needs.

Arrangements Used to Meet Needs

Any consideration of the history of working with the aged must take into account that until the twentieth century very few people lived to be as old as many people are today. The number of older people was very small, and they were generally cared for by family mutual aid. Except for the institutional care provided by some private groups, it is only since the enactment of Social Security legislation in the 1930s that any recognition has been given to the special needs of the elderly. Our present modes of care for the elderly contain vestiges of attitudes and arrangements used in the past. It is important to consider how each of the six arrangements identified earlier in this book has been used to provide for the needs of the elderly in our society.

Mutual Aid

This has been the primary arrangement used throughout history to care for older people. Families have been the major resource, and until very recently their responsibility for relatives was enforced morally, culturally, and through law. *Relative responsibility laws* held adult children responsible for the support of their parents. If children could not take an older parent needing care into their homes, then they were responsible for paying at least some of the costs for caring for that parent in an institution or elsewhere. Today, relative responsibility laws no longer exist. And although moral and cultural influences continue to pressure children to care for their parents, social change has made it increasingly difficult. Thus, there is a gap between our expectations and reality.

Another way that mutual aid has provided care for the elderly is through the personal resource networks that exist in communities and cultural groups. On a short-term basis, if older people are ill or unable to perform some of the tasks of daily living, neighbors and friends may bring in meals or otherwise care for the needs that exist. Transportation for shopping, medical appointments, or church activities is often provided. Studies of community helping show that this mechanism is alive and well and is still very important in providing for the needs of the older person (Patterson and Brennan, 1983).

Charity-Philanthropy

The two historical examples of this arrangement (the Charity Organization Societies and the settlement houses) did not emphasize provision for the needs of the elderly, although both did provide some services. Settlement houses were among the early agencies to develop group activities (Senior Citizens' Clubs) for older people. Present-day family agencies (a contemporary example of this arrangement) provide counseling services for older people and their families, which can be particularly helpful when decisions about care must be made or when support in difficult situations is needed. Another agency that is very active in providing for the needs of older people has been the system of Jewish community centers. The Senior Citizens' Centers developed in the last twenty-five years are yet another manifestation of this arrangement (Lowy, 1991).

Another example of charity-philanthropy was the establishment of institutions for the care of the elderly. Most of these institutions charged either an entry fee or a monthly maintenance fee, or both. In 1929 there were 1,268 such institutions. Of these, 43 percent were sponsored by religious groups, 35 percent by private philanthropic organizations, and 10 percent by fraternal orders. The rest were sponsored by ethnic groups and trade unions. In addition, some were federal and state homes for veterans. Catholic orders, especially the Little Sisters of the Poor, operated homes for those without resources. In many cases, individuals served by these institutions had to be members of the church or other organization that sponsored the institutions (Hall, 1930). The use of the charity-philanthropy institutions for the elderly has declined since the development of social welfare and social insurance programs that provide income maintenance for the elderly. Today, most institutions for the aged care for the frail elderly who cannot live alone or whose health problems prevent their care by families. Nursing home care for those with medical problems is the primary use of institutional care today. It is generally accepted that 5 percent of those over sixty-five years of age live in institutional settings.

Retirement villages or apartment complexes where individuals maintain their own private space provide a popular housing arrangement for some older people. Many of these are developed and maintained by private and religious philanthropic organizations. These, like many of the private homes for the aged, require an entrance fee and/or a monthly maintenance fee. Charity-philanthropy is still a mechanism used to provide for some needs of some elderly people in today's social welfare system.

Public Welfare

Elderly people were one of the groups provided for under the poor laws. If a family could not care for an elderly member, and if the elderly person had no resources, then that person became the responsibility of the town or county, and later of the state. In the early days of the United States, these poor elderly individuals were cared for in families reimbursed by the government unit responsible for caring for the elderly. Later, with the development of almshouses, they were cared for in these all-encompassing institutions, along with children, the mentally ill, and others who could not care for themselves. As children and the mentally ill were removed from the almshouses, these institutions became largely populated by old people who had no other place to go. These institutions often came to be referred to as poor farms, county homes, or old folks' homes. Life in an almshouse was dreary at best. There were many abuses in these institutions. Funds were very limited, staff often cared little about the people in their care, and little attention was given to providing proper food and shelter. Unsanitary conditions, neglect, and even brutality abounded (Warner, Queen, and Harper, 1930).

Many older people were also cared for in institutions for the mentally ill. The diagnosis of senile dementia was popular: In 1936, 7.9 percent of all first admissions to mental institutions were for people with this diagnosis (Kurtz, 1939). The back wards also contained many individuals who, having been confined to mental hospitals, particularly the state hospitals, at earlier stages of life, had grown old in these institutions.

Some communities and some states came to believe that older people with no resources of their own could best be cared for by providing assistance payments so they could remain independent within the community. A few states passed old age pension laws, but it took the Depression and the Social Security Act to make financial aid to the elderly a part of the U.S. social welfare system (Kurtz, 1960). One part of the Social Security Act of 1935 was the *Old Age Assistance* program. Under this program, the federal government provided grants-in-aid to the states if the states set up programs to provide income assistance to those over sixty-five whose income fell under specified amounts. The grant-in-aid provided a percentage of the older person's income maintenance; the states provided the rest. States had to meet certain other requirements to receive this grant. Each state had a different program with different payments. In 1973, when this program was discontinued, average monthly payments ranged from $56 to $121 a month.

In 1974 there was a major change in federal financial assistance to older people. The Supplemental Security Income (SSI) program was established. This program removed responsibility for income maintenance of the elderly from the states and placed it under the Social Security Administration. Eligibility depends on income and resources. In 1994, the average monthly payment was $345 for an individual. Automatic cost-of-living increases are incorporated into the payment system (U.S. Bureau of the Census, 1995).

The SSI program remains the primary means of providing for the financial needs of those over sixty-five who have little or no other means of support. It is the present-day use of the public welfare arrangement for meeting the needs of older people. Another program that falls under this arrangement is Medicaid, discussed in Chapter 9, which is an important means of providing for the health care needs of this group. However, the continuence of Medicaid as a resource that provides for the health care needs of America's poorest elderly is currently in question. In 1995, Congress, as discussed in previous chapters, passed a comprehensive "welfare reform" bill, that, at the time of this writing, has not been signed into law. Notwithstanding, one of its provisions is to change the Medicaid Program from an entitlement program to a "block grant" program that will give the states primary control over how the dollars allocated in their block grants that gradually decrease over time will be spent. This means that the states will have the authority to choose what health care services to what recipient groups will be funded under the block grant, and there will be no federally mandated services to specific groups of people, such as the poor elderly. If converted to a block grant program, there will be no guarentee that the Medicaid program will continue as a "health care safety net" for America's aged poor.

Social Insurance

The best example of this arrangement is the *Old Age, Survivors and Disability Health Insurance (OASDHI)* program, commonly referred to as Social Security. The Social Security Act of 1935 established this program. Changes in the program have been mainly to broaden the number of people covered and to increase the amount of the benefits paid. At present, most people in the labor force are covered, and compulsory contributions from employees, employers, and the self-employed are required. Medicare, discussed in Chapter 9, which provides health care for individuals over sixty-five years of age, is also a form of social insurance.

Over 90 percent of those over age sixty-five receive benefits from OASDHI. It is the major source of income for people over sixty-five. The benefits depend in part on an individual's earnings over the period worked in covered employment. Spouses can receive half the benefits of the worker. A surviving spouse receives benefits equal to those of the deceased worker. Benefits are payable at age sixty-five, with the option of payment at age sixty-two at a permanently reduced amount (Karger and Stoesz, 1994).

With the growing numbers of older people in our society, our present OASDHI program is at risk. There are those who would like to see social security benefits further taxed or otherwise restricted for those with incomes which are in the higher brackets. The Clinton administration has proposed raising the tax liability to 85 percent for individuals with incomes over $25,000 and couples over $35,000 annually. Many proposals have been made to give the program a degree of solvency. In future years, the age for receiving full benefits will be raised. Questions about benefits paid to women have been raised. Women are in the labor force for shorter periods of time, and at lower pay. Widows' benefits are lower than those of couples; thus, women tend to receive lower benefits than men. They are at greater risk of being below the poverty level. There is concern about how to provide more equitable benefits for women. In the coming years, Social Security can be expected to change but will continue to be an important arrangement for meeting the economic needs of older people.

Social Services

The needs of older people include not only a place to live or income maintenance, but also intangible services. In recent years, with the emphasis on maintaining older people in the community, it has been found that a variety of supportive services are needed. These include information and referral services, homemaker and home health services, home-delivered meals, socialization services, transportation services, and legal assistance. Some of these have long been provided by the private social agencies. The Social Security Amendments of 1962 provided the first federal support for these social services. In 1975, Title XX of the Social Security Act's major purpose was to provide services to reduce dependency and promote self-support. Eligibility was limited to those receiving income assistance or to those with incomes below the poverty line (Karger and Stoesz, 1994). Social services for older people under provisions of the Older American Act of 1965 further broadened services for the elderly. Because this provision falls under the universal provision arrangement, it will be discussed in that section of this chapter.

When considering the social service arrangement, it is important to note that this is a recent development. Only since about 1960 have such services been developed specifically for the elderly. Many demonstration projects have come and gone. Established private agencies, newly developed community-supported agencies, government agencies, and volunteers have all been active in developing services. Now it seems well established that an array of such services is desirable both to maintain older people in the community for longer periods of time and to enhance their quality of life. There are still questions about how such services should be structured, supported, staffed, and administered. They are, nevertheless, important in the overall service network for aging persons.

Universal Provision

Growing concern about the plight of the increasing number of older people in the United States resulted in the White House Conference on Aging in January 1961. This conference made a number of recommendations, some of which are encompassed in the *Older American Act of 1965 (OAA)*. White House Conferences on Aging held in 1971 and 1981 made further recommendations and to some extent influenced additional legislation. There have been amendments to the original Older American Act. The result of this activity is a plan for meeting the needs of all older people, a plan that uses the arrangement of universal provision. There are no means tests; it is assumed that older Americans, regardless of income or other characteristics, all have needs that should be provided for within the social welfare system.

It must be noted, however, that funding has never been available to put into action fully either the objectives of the OAA or those set forth by the White House conferences. But what has resulted is the identification of needs of the elderly and a framework for working toward meeting those needs. The framework consists of federal, state, and area (territory within a state) administrative units. The *Area Agency on Aging* is mandated to develop a comprehensive and coordinated service system. At present, because of the lack of funding, it makes considerable effort to get others—private agencies, local community groups, and various government agencies—to provide the needed services. Another strategy that has been used is to strongly encourage voluntary donations for services received by those who can afford to pay for the service.

Services identified as universally needed by the elderly are: information and referral, informing older people of available services including developing and maintaining a data bank; outreach, services that break through the isolation of the elderly; transportation; in-home services; homemaker and home chore services and home-delivered meals; legal services; protective services; counseling services; socialization and recreation services; and educational services. Nutrition programs that provide congregate meals in a central location in the community are a major thrust of the services available.

Although the provision of elder services is far from universal at this time, the philosophy behind such services has been developed. Contemporary U.S. society recognizes that the elderly may need not only some kind of income maintenance but also a variety of other services. Because the family structure no longer supports the elderly, society recognizes the provision of these services as a right rather than as charity.

The material presented in this section of this chapter shows how a system for meeting the needs of older people has evolved by discarding earlier mechanisms that are no longer functional, by adapting some arrangements for use in a new time, and by developing new programs and services. Our social welfare system uses all six of the identified arrangements to care for older people's needs. Although strongly rooted in the mutual aid philosophy of preindustrial societies, the current system emphasizes income maintenance through social insurance if possible, but uses public welfare where necessary. It also acknowledges the desirability of maintaining older people in their communities rather than placing them in institutions. In addition, it recognizes that older people must have a wide variety of services if they are to live satisfying lives and be maintained in the community. There also seems to be a growing preference that these services be provided by a universal provision arrangement. This system of care for elders is evolving, not static, and will continue to change as the social welfare system adapts to changing times and changing needs of older people.

Current Problems and Issues

Current problems and issues in social work regarding the aged relate to each of the conditions that give rise to human need (social change, poverty, discrimination, and availability of resources). In the discussion of how each of these conditions affects aging individuals, service delivery issues will also be considered.

Social Change

It should have been apparent from reading Chapter 2 that a tremendous demographic change has taken place in recent years in the United States. With the lengthening life span, the population of older people has grown at an extraordinary rate, not only in numbers but also as a percentage of the general population. This means there are many more aging and dependent people in our society, with fewer younger people to provide for their support. The growth of the very oldest segment of the population (those over seventy-five) has been even faster. Because of their relative physical frailty and poor health, this group's needs are considerable.

Two other significant factors closely related to demographics must be considered. First, there are more older women than older men. This is a fairly new phenomenon, because in the past many women died at an early age from childbirth complications or from the stress of raising large families under primitive conditions. Until very recently, most women depended on men to provide their financial support, so older women are not apt to have financial resources of their own; after their husband's death, they depend on their husband's Social Security or other insurance. Because most older women outlive their husbands, these widows often find themselves with limited resources. This change in the ratio of older men to older women contributes to the low average income of older people generally and of older women in particular.

The other significant factor is the increased quality of health care, which allows many people to live longer and lengthens the life span so that many individuals live into their eighties or even their nineties. But that also means that many more older people are living with chronic illnesses or are very frail, which increases their need for geriatric health care and their dependency on government programs.

Demography is not the only factor affecting social work with the aged. Changes in the family are also important. Smaller families mean that fewer children are available to care for aging parents. And because of society's increased mobility, adult children often do not live as near to their parents as they once did. Another change that reduces the family's capacity to care for its older members is the increase in the number of working women. Women have been the primary caretakers in our society, but as they have joined the labor force, their caretaking role has been reduced. Because mutual aid, specifically family care, has been heavily used to meet the needs of many older individuals, it is easy to see that changes in the family structure have affected the social welfare system.

Retirement is also a very new concept. Before the passage of the Social Security Act in 1935, only a very few older people were fortunate to have pensions and thus be able to leave the labor force through retirement. Most people were expected to work at some task until death. But mandatory retirement was instituted to make jobs available to younger workers during the Depression. Social Security provided income for retiring workers so they could continue to provide for their financial needs. However, work also gives people a sense of self-esteem, a purpose for being, and these too are essential needs. Retirement forces older people to find new sources of a sense of belonging and individual worth, not an easy task in our youth-oriented culture. Thus, retirement is another social change that affects the needs of aging people.

Social change has challenged older people in still another way. The changes that have taken place in their lifetime have been tremendous and have called for constant adaptation. The lifestyle they observed in older people when they themselves were young no longer fits into today's society; adaptation without patterns or role models to follow is always difficult, and it is doubly hard for the elderly. Older people need to understand what is happening to them as they age and how they can best adapt to modern society.

Poverty

Poverty, as discussed earlier, is indeed a condition that threatens the aging population: 12 percent of persons over sixty-five years old lived below the poverty line in 1993. However, to understand the relationship between poverty and older people, it is important to look at which subgroups of elderly are most likely to live in poverty. Women, particularly those who live alone, are far more apt than men to be poor. Minority elders are poorer than white elders. Whereas 10.7 percent of white elders live in poverty, 28 percent of the black elderly and 21.4 percent of the Hispanic elderly live in poverty (U.S. Bureau of the Census, 1995). Thus, if an older person is a woman who lives alone, is black or Hispanic, and lives in a nonmetropolitan area, the chances of her living in poverty are very great. It is not surprising that those groups of poor older people are the same groups with a history of working in low-paid jobs, which in turn affects the amount of Social Security benefits they receive—the economic "double-whammy" of employment discrimination.

Poverty for an older person means that health care may not be affordable, transportation may not be available, suitable housing may be difficult to find, and good nutrition may be overlooked. Although society tries to give special consideration in each of these areas for the low-income elderly, resources and funds are simply inadequate. Older people in poverty risk living unsatisfying and difficult lives; they also risk unwanted institutionalization, and even premature death.

Discrimination

Ageism is one kind of prejudice practiced by contemporary society, which rewards youth, physical fitness, and productivity. Aged individuals do not fit these "valued person" criteria. Older people are seen as "has-beens," unable to offer much to society, who prevent younger people from getting ahead by continuing to occupy jobs when they are no longer productive. They are out of touch with contemporary society. Their wisdom has no value. In summary, they are incompetent. These damaging misconceptions take a toll on the older members of our society.

Ageism shows up in the contemporary scene in several ways. First, there is the workplace. Discrimination against older workers had become such a problem that in 1967 Congress passed the Age Discrimination Employment Act, which prohibits discrimination in hiring and other employment practices because of age. But laws do not change attitudes, and attitudes lead people to find ways to circumvent laws. It is very difficult for older people who want to work to find employment. The jobs they do find are often minimum-wage jobs where they must compete with young people. There are subtle pressures on older people still in the workplace to retire (Hooyman and Kiyak, 1996).

Discrimination is also manifest in the media. Because media images are so influential in our society, the negative depiction of older people reinforces the already negative thinking of the general public and contributes to poor self-esteem among the elderly. It leads to a sense of rolelessness, one of the major factors contributing to the attitudinal problems of the aged (Hooyman and Kiyak, 1996).

It should also be noted that those groups discriminated against because of conditions other than aging are also discriminated against because of their age. These groups include ethnic and racial minorities, women, and the mentally and physically disabled. Some older individuals are discriminated against in two, three, or even four ways. A woman, who is black, chronically physically disabled, and over sixty-five years of age thus can be said to have a fourfold jeopardy!

Several organizations have worked very hard to counteract discrimination in our society. These include the National Council on Aging, the American Association of Retired Persons, the Gray Panthers, and the Gerontological Society. Older people themselves seem to be the best resource for counteracting the many myths and stereotypes that reinforce prejudicial attitudes and practices. But the social welfare system also must develop advocacy strategies to ensure that the rights of aged individuals are respected and that resources are developed to meet their needs.

The Issue of Resource Availability

Because of decreasing personal capacity or decreasing income, older people must increasingly depend on other resources to meet needs. Traditionally the first line of defense has been the family, but in today's changing world, the family is not always able to meet these needs. So how does society cope with the needs of its older members?

Some of these needs are met informally in the community, through friends and natural helpers, who make up *personal networks.* However, these resources can meet only part of the needs related to companionship, reassurance, and short-term emergency situations. Some older people have a limited circle of friends; others find their friends also less able to serve as resources because of their own declining health or strength; and, of course, death takes its toll. Obviously, the informal network cannot be depended on to meet every need.

For those who can no longer live alone on a short-term basis, the nursing home has often been the resource called upon. With changes in the health care system, nursing homes are used more and more to provide recuperative medical care with the expectation that the resident would return to the community. The nursing home is also considered the resource for those elderly who need considerable long-term medical care. However, for those older people who have problems that would ordinarily require institutionalization, new approaches to service delivery and resources have become available to enable them to remain in their own homes. One such approach to service delivery is the Home and Community Based Waiver Services (HCBWS) under Title 19 (Medicaid) of the Social Security Act. Older persons who are eligible for Medicaid and have medical impairments that would render them appropriate for the skilled level of nursing home care are allowed, under the provisions of a waiver program administered by the states, to receive a variety of services, including homemaker, chore, and other home health services to assist them to remain living independently in their homes. The primary purpose of HCBWS services is to delay nursing home admission for older Medicaid recipients, thereby reducing expenditures for skilled nursing facility care. It has been found in program evaluations of state HCBWS programs that there are considerable cost savings by providing HCBWS services as opposed to skilled nursing home care (Schwartz, 1991). A new resource is developing for those who need assistance in activities of daily living, the assisted living facility. These tend to be smaller facilities with a more homelike atmosphere.

Many older people have been very self-sufficient and have never had to depend on resources outside their families and personal networks. They may think of the use of public resources as "welfare," an affront to their pride, and thus not an acceptable means for meeting their needs. They may have no idea of the resources available to them. Thus, information and referral and educational services for elders are very important.

Community groups and public and private social service organizations have developed services that provide older people with meaningful opportunities to participate in community life. The *senior citizens' centers* fall into this area and are important resources for the older person who is still able to be active outside the home. Food is often a part of the activity offered. Older individuals living alone may not maintain a nutritious diet because most people find it hard to cook for just one person. Nutrition programs, which offer a well-balanced meal several times a week, are funded under a section of the Older American Act.

Transportation services are important for those who can no longer drive or use public transportation. Housing adapted to the special needs of elders is another resource that allows people to remain in their community for a longer period of time. Housing that places older people in close proximity to one another seems to encourage a natural helping network in which older people look out for and provide companionship for each other (Hooyman and Kiyak, 1996). Some older people are abused by family members or other caretakers or are unable to manage their financial affairs. These people are in need of protective services.

Many issues arise concerning how the wide range of resources needed by aged people can be provided. Which resources should be provided by community groups? Which can be provided by natural helpers or by the older person's personal network? Which resources must depend on government financial support? How can the resources be provided so that older people will not feel stigmatized? In a society that has a growing elderly population, limited economic resources, and a changing social structure, answers to these questions are elusive. Only as communities and the professionals who work in these communities come to grips with these issues will answers be found. This is the time to develop new mechanisms within the U.S. social welfare system to meet the resource needs of the aging.

Fiscal support is crucial. Yet, in a time of decreasing fiscal resources for the social welfare system, it is questionable how adequate funding resources can be obtained. But how can we fail to meet the needs of the elderly in the community? If these needs are not met, then the aged are in danger of institutionalization, a much more expensive type of care. It is important at this time to identify the kinds of needs that can be met by the natural helping system or community groups with little or no fiscal resources. The formal social welfare system then can work with these groups and help them. But needs not met by natural helping systems and community groups must be provided to maintain the aged in the community. These services should include supportive services to families caring for frail or disabled elderly members. Respite care, stipends for family care, and support groups for caregivers can be useful in this supportive approach.

Aged people with an adequate income are at less risk of having unmet needs. Therefore, attention needs to be paid to developing income maintenance and social insurance programs that support an adequate income for all aged people. The funds that are available should be used to support those proven services and programs that meet critical needs that cannot be met in other ways. All of this requires a creative and critical approach to the use of all existing resources: personal, fiscal, and formal.

Particular attention must be given to the preservation of older persons' resources that they have set aside to care for themselves during their older years. Although aging advocacy groups have been successful in preserving many services for the aging despite federal administration efforts to cut some established programs, there has simultaneously been a continual push for increased taxation of older people. The 1986 tax reforms eliminated the traditional additional personal federal income tax exemptions for those over sixty-five. This "reform" also provided for taxation of half of the Social Security payments of those who might be considered middle income ($25,000 for individuals and $32,000 for couples). This erosion of the planned income of older people can threaten their capacity to provide for their needs, particularly for those who have a fixed income but face increases in the cost of living and in tax levels.

Coordination

Another important issue is *coordination*. Coordination can be considered on two levels. First is the level of coordinating the services of all agencies and programs that provide resources to the elderly. The Area Offices on Aging are set up, in part, to do this. This effort must be strengthened. The coordination effort must identify and address unmet needs. The second coordination level is the personal resource network of the individual aged person. Social workers need to be given means for coordinating natural and formal systems and for including families in the planning process. For the family and other natural helpers to be used effectively, these systems must be balanced when making decisions about their use.

When thinking about this complex system of elderly services, a framework is needed. Such a framework is presented in Table 12–2. This framework shows four levels of care. The first level, preventive care services, can be provided before an individual reaches the elderly stage of life. If people prepare for this stage, they will be more likely to have resources for meeting their needs and a better understanding of those needs and how to meet them. The second level, socialization, includes those services provided as an individual or spouse retires or changes lifestyle to help the individual cope with the adjustments involved and to develop a new, satisfying, and adequate lifestyle. The third level, supportive and protective care, comprises those services provided to frail, ill, or disabled older people to support them and their caretakers in maintaining their capacity to live in the community. They focus on preventing premature institutionalization and supporting as active and satisfying a lifestyle as possible. The fourth level, institutional care, is for those who can no longer be maintained in a *community living* situation. It focuses on elders' maintenance of as much self-determination as possible and on their maintaining contact with the important people in their lives while developing a lifestyle with a positive and active stance.

The framework also divides service into four categories. These categories cover the most common problems of older people. These areas of service are: (1) economic; (2) attitude (helping elders and society in general develop better attitudes toward aging); (3) role making (services that give the aged persons opportunities to play meaningful roles in society); and (4) health care.

This chart can help assess which services are available in a community and which need to be developed. Note that at levels 1 and 2, preventive care and socialization, services can probably be provided through the natural and community systems and do not require a large amount of government funding. They can prevent or postpone the need for the more expensive supportive and protective care and institutional care. The chart does not indicate which services should be provided by private social service agencies; which by public social service

TABLE 12–2   Framework for Considering the Needs of Aging Persons

	Economic Services	Attitudes	Rolemaking	Health Care
Preventive care	Economic opportunity during adulthood that provides for one's older years Education for self-responsibility in planning	Development of positive attitudes toward aging Development of a sense of self-responsibility	Development of useful roles for older people in society Development of a sense of social responsibility	Good lifetime health care for everyone Development of responsible attitudes toward health maintenance
Socialization	Education and information about financial management for the elderly Information and referral services Opportunity for appropriate employment Transportation services	Peer group self-help experiences Education about aging Counseling services, outreach services	Meaningful and useful roles (volunteer, planning, political opportunities, etc.) for the elderly	Geriatric health care for all Self-responsibility for health maintenance Nutrition services Health-care counseling
Supportive and protective care	Adequate income maintenance for people unable to provide for themselves Support to families and people maintaining elderly in their own homes Suitable and subsidized elderly housing	Assessment of emotional and social needs Maintenance of self-determination	Day-care centers Volunteer visiting-support Supports to families maintaining elderly in the home	Geriatric health care Home help and health-care aids Meals-on-wheels Services to maintain others caring for ill and disabled aged persons
Institutional care	Funding for adequate institutional care when needed	Services to provide social activities, entertainment, and counseling Self-determination as possible	Services to help maintain family community contacts; therapetuic activity	Nursing and other needed health care

agencies; which by other professionals or institutions within the social welfare network; and which by families, natural helpers, or community groups. This varies from individual to individual and from community to community, depending on the resources available and on how a particular community functions. Frameworks like this should receive further study to learn how best to organize the social welfare system as it focuses on the aged person.

Another factor in coordination is the network of services developed to meet the needs of the elderly. Some individuals, particularly the frail and disabled, need many different services. Coordination is necessary for optimal use of resources. The case manager function, where one worker is responsible for seeing that the various services fit together in a coherent whole, seems most important. Social workers with a generalist frame of reference are a natural choice for filling this role.

Long-Term Care

Up until very recently, long-term care was thought of as nursing home care. The growing cost of this type of care has caused concern for policymakers and social welfare officials at both the state and national levels. As our country's population continues to age, with the fastest growing segment being people over eighty-five years old, the need for long-term care resources are likely to increase to the extent that the social welfare system will at some point be unable to provide needed resources to meet the demand, unless alternatives to nursing home care are developed. The preponderance of the burden in funding nursing home placements has steadily begun to fall on the entitlement programs of Meidicaid and Medicare. This is because most older persons in need of nursing home care cannot afford the cost of the care over an extended period of time. Although they may initially start out using their own resources to pay for their care, these resources are depleated quickly, usually within two years. At that point, the older person must begin to rely on public dollars to fund their continued care (Spence and Wiener, 1990). In part, the system of community-based care for the elderly that is considerably less costly has developed out of this concern. In addition, some states with high rates of institutionalization in nursing facilities have initiated diversion or community reentry programs designed to assist nursing facility residents to return to community living. Both national and state data on the characteristics of nursing facility residents has shown that there are many older persons residing in nursing homes who need minimal assistance medically and with activities of daily living. The data also shows that unless these individuals are assisted in reentering the community, they are at risk for protracted lengths of stay in nursing facilities (Chapin and Schwartz, 1994; Redford, 1993; Spence and Wiener, 1990).

There have been numerous attempts in Congress to deal with the funding of long-term care. To date, no definitive plan has been adopted, in part because of the high costs involved. As discussed earlier, the uncertainty of Medicaid as an ongoing resource for this population is yet another long-term care issue that will likely cause concern to the social welfare system.

Social Work Practice with Older People

Social workers work with the elderly both in the community and in institutions. In community settings, social workers are found in Area Agencies on Aging, senior citizens' centers, and the divisions of public social service agencies providing services for older people. Social workers in a variety of other agencies serving families, such as the family service agencies, also may have older individuals in their case load.

Social workers use a wide variety of practice approaches with older people. Some of the more important roles a social worker can fill are:

As a broker providing older people and their families with information about available services
As a case manager coordinating a wide variety of services
As a crisis intervener
As a group worker providing a variety of group services
As a community development and planning consultant working on services for older people

As a coordinator with public and private agencies and with community groups

As an administrator with responsibility for programs that benefit the elderly

As a social worker in a nursing home, hospital, or other residential or institutional setting

The case study below is provided to illustrate how a social worker might perform some of these roles.

The growth of the elderly population in recent years provides evidence that there will be an increased need for professional social workers to work with the aged in the future (Monk, 1990). However, the question is: Will there be sufficient resources available to assist social workers in this effort? Cuts in funding for services to this population that occurred in the 1980s, along with pending projected cuts that will likely occur with the new "welfare reform" legislation, forecast the possibility of great challenges in this regard. A call has been issued for social work to establish itself within the field of gerontology. A suggested pathway for social work's involvement in this field is empowerment-oriented practice with the elderly. Recall from Chapter 2 that empowerment is assisting people to gain sufficient personal and political power to take control over events, circumstances, and decision making in their lives. Empowerment-oriented social work practice is a goal and process by which social workers assist the elderly to use their competencies, abilities, and strengths in obtaining resources that will aid in solving their problems, both on a personal and collective level (Cox and Parsons, 1994). Empowering the elderly is predicated on the belief that older persons have experienced loss of power and control on a personal level, due to a number of factors, such as changes in physical and mental

A Case Study

A hospital social worker was asked by Dr. C to find a nursing home placement for Mrs. F. Mrs. F was recovering from pneumonia, and Dr. C felt she could no longer live alone because she had come into the hospital malnourished. The social worker went to talk with Mrs. F and found that Mrs. F did not want to go to a nursing home. Although she admitted it was difficult for her to get meals, she also found grocery shopping very hard. She did have a group of friends who kept track of her and came to see her, but her family lived in a distant city. The social worker contacted the local social service agency that provided both home-delivered meals and homemaker service to see if they could provide service to Mrs. F. The doctor was notified of the social worker's findings and, though reluctant, was willing to explore an in-home plan.

The social worker from the local social service agency visited Mrs. F and went to look at her home situation. This social worker, together with Mrs. F, developed a plan for Mrs. F to receive a home-delivered

meal five days a week at noon until she regained her strength. A homemaker was provided for three days a week to do grocery shopping and some housework, and to assess just what Mrs. F was capable of doing for herself in daily living. A home health nurse was also involved in providing nursing care for a time.

After six weeks, the situation was reassessed. Mrs. F had made a good recovery and no longer needed home health care. Rather than the home-delivered meals, she would be provided transportation on the senior citizens' bus, so she could receive one meal a day at the nutrition site at the local senior citizens' center. Within a month, she was also attending other activities at the center. The homemaker hours were cut to two a week as Mrs. F found she could do her own shopping on the senior citizens' bus. The social worker remains in contact with Mrs. F through the homemaker and through quarterly evaluations of her needs. At this time the situation seems to be stabilized.

health and functioning, economic security, or losses in support systems. Therefore, the empowering social worker assists the older person, through provision of existing community resources and enabling and motivating the person to use their own competencies, or abilities, to gain the power to overcome the personal problems they experience. Likewise, the elderly in U.S. society have experienced sociopolitical losses which have led to their powerlessness and a diminished collective efficacy. Their collective powerlessness has come about largely from age discrimination (*ageism*), through which negative societal stereotypes have led to the stigmatization of elderly, resulting in discriminatory treatment of them as a group. Other social losses that have contributed to their lack of status and collective power are retirement and role loss. For many elderly, one very strong source of their self-identity and perceptions of self-efficacy has been their employment. Therefore, they may experience difficulties in social and psychological adjustment to retirement, with resultant losses in self-esteem and motivation to take action to deal with their situation. In addition, critical losses in income may occur as a result of retirement, as described earlier. Accompanying losses may also be experienced in expected roles, including work roles, community roles, and family roles, again leading to decreased self-esteem and feelings of powerlessness. Empowering social work practice in this vain would be to assist the elderly to overcome their powerlessness by helping them organize and use their collective strengths to gain participation in the decision-making processes that affect their lives. Empowerment-oriented social work practice with the elderly is all about increasing both their personal and collective efficacy, so that they may be able to take action to get both their personal and collective needs met (Cox and Parsons, 1994).

Summary

Given the growth in the aged population, not only will the social welfare system need to respond to the needs of this population, it will also need to evolve new and different ways of responding. This evolution will be related to the characteristics of the aged population, to the current structure of the social welfare system, and to the problems and issues that confront social work with the aged. In this evolving system, the need for social workers will grow. They will support the elderly, their families, and the case managers for the frail and disabled elderly in the community. They will provide protective services and serve to empower those unable to stand up for their own rights and needs. They will provide services to institutionalized aged persons. They will help the mutual aid systems and communities to become more responsive to the needs of the elderly. They will work to blot out the discrimination caused by ageism. This relatively new field of practice will be very important in the social welfare system of the future.

Key Terms

ageism	coordination
Area Agency on Aging	empowerment-oriented social work practice
assisted living facility	frail elderly
community living	gerontological social work
community reentry	Home and Community Based Waiver Services (HCBWS)

long-term care
Old Age Assistance
Old Age, Survivors and Disability Health Insurance
  (OASDHI)
Older American Act of 1965 (OAA)

old-old
personal networks
relative responsibility laws
retirement
senior citizens' centers

References

Chapin, R., and Schwartz, C.L. (1994). *Comprehensive Annual Evaluation Report on the SRS Community Re-Entry Project.* Lawrence, KS: School of Social Welfare, University of Kansas.

Cox, E.O., and Parsons, R.J. (1994). *Empowerment-Oriented Social Work Practice with the Elderly.* Pacific Grove: Brooks/Cole.

Erickson, E.H., Erickson, J.M., and Kivnick, H.Q. (1986). *Vital Involvement in Old Age.* New York: Norton.

George, L.K. (1982). Models of Transition in Middle and Later Life. *Annals of the American Academy of Political and Social Sciences,* 464, 22–37.

Hall, F.S. (Ed.) (1930). *Social Work Year Book* 1929. New York: Sage Publications, pp. 31–55.

Hooyman, N., and Kiyak, H.A. (1996). *Social Gerontology: A Multidisciplinary Perspective.* Needham Heights, MA: Allyn and Bacon.

Karger, H.J., and Stoesz, D. (1994). *American Social Welfare Policy: A Pluralist Approach.* White Plains, NY: Longman.

Kurtz, R.H. (1939). *Social Work Yearbook 1939.* New York: Sage Publications, p. 253.

Kurtz, R.H. (1960). *Social Work Yearbook 1960.* New York: National Association of Social Workers, p. 36.

Lowy, L. (1991). *Social Work with the Aging: The Challenge and Promise of the Later Years.* Prospect Hills, IL: Waveland Press.

Monk, A. (1990). *Handbook of Gerontological Services* (2nd ed.). New York: Columbia University Press.

Patterson, S., and Brennan, E. (1983). Matching Helping Roles with the Characteristics of Aging Natural Helpers. *Journal of Gerontological Social Work,* 5, 55–66.

Peck, R.C. (1968). Psychological Development in the Second Half of Life. in B.L. Neugarten (Ed.), *Middle Age and Aging.* Chicago: University of Chicago Press.

Redford, L.J. (1993). Factors Associated with Functional Level on Admission to Nursing Facilities. Center on Aging, University of Kansas Medical Center, Kansas City, Missouri (unpublished paper).

Schwartz, C.L. (1991). *Assessment of the South Dakota Title XIX Home and Community Based Waiver Services Program for the Elderly.* South Dakota Department of Social Services, Office of Adult Services and Aging, Pierre, South Dakota.

Spence, D.A., and Wiener, J.M. (1990). Nursing Home Length of Stay Patterns: Results from the 1985 National Nursing Home Survey. *The Gerontologist, 30 (1),* 16–20.

U.S. Department of Commerce, Bureau of the Census. (1995). *Statistical Abstracts of the U.S. 1995.* Washington DC: U.S. Government Printing Office.

Warner, A.G., Queen, S.A., and Harper, E.B. (1939). *American Charities and Social Work,* (4th ed.). New York: Sage Publications.

Suggested Readings

Anastas, Jeane W.; Gibeau, Janice L.; and Larson, Pamela J. (1990). "Working Families and Eldercare: A National Perspective in an Aging America." *Social Work,* 35, pp. 405–411.

Beaver, Marion L., and Miller, Don (1992). *Clinical Social Work Practice with the Elderly.* Belmont, CA: Wadsworth Dorsey Press.

Bloksberg, Leonard M. (1989). "Intergovernmental Relations: Change and Continuity." *Journal of Aging and Social Policy* 1, (3–4).

Cox, E.O., and Parsons, R.J. (1994). *Empowerment-Oriented Social Work Practice with the Elderly.* Pacific Grove: Brooks/Cole.

Generations. Special Issues. "Aging in Place" (Spring

1992); "After 25 Years: Aging Policy and the Older Americans Act" (Summer/Fall 1991); and "Diversity: New Approaches to Ethnic Minority Aging" (Fall/Winter 1991).

Hooyman, Nancy R., and Kiyak, H. Asuman (1996). *Social Gerontology.* Boston: Allyn and Bacon.

Journal of Gerontological Social Work (1990). Special Issue: "Health Care of the Aged: Needs, Policies, and Services," 15 (No 3/4).

Kan-fong, Monst Chenny (1988). "Home Care Services for the Elderly: Cost Savings Implications to Medicaid." *Social Service Review,* 62, 125–136.

Kutza, Elizabeth, and Keigher, Sharon M. (1991). "The Elderly 'New Homeless': An Emerging Population at Risk." *Social Work,* 36, 288–293.

Lee, Judith A.B. (1989). "An Ecological View of Aging: Luisa's Plight." *Journal of Gerontological Social Work,* 14 (No. 1/2), 175–190.

Lowy, Louis (1991). *Social Work with the Aging.* Prospect Heights, IL: Waveland Press.

Matlaw, Jane R., and Mayer, Jane B. (1986). "Elder Abuse: Ethical and Practical Dilemmas." *Health and Social Work,* 11, 85–94.

O'Grady-Leshane, Regina (1990). "Older Women and Poverty." *Social Work,* 35, 422–431.

Richardson, Virginia (1991). "Service Use Among Urban African American Elderly People." *Social Work,* 37, 47–54.

Social Casework. Special Issue: (1988). "Life Transitions in the Elderly." 69.

Stoesz, David (1989). "The Gray Market: Social Consequences of For-Profit Elder Care." *Journal of Gerontological Social Work,* 14 (No. 3/4), 19–33.

Wood, Juanita B. and Estes, Carroll (1988). " 'Medicalization' of Community Services for the Elderly." *Health and Social Work,* 13, 35–42.

13

ORGANIZING FIELDS OF PRACTICE BY SYSTEM TYPE: GROUPS, COMMUNITIES, AND FAMILIES

Learning Expectations

- Understanding of the terms *group services, social group work,* and *social work with groups*
- Knowledge of the development of the group services field
- Knowledge of factors that have led to a lessened appreciation for the place of social group work in the social work profession
- Ability to identify functions that are carried out in the field of community practice
- Ability to trace the development of community practice in social work
- Knowledge of the development of services to families in the social work profession
- Understanding of the difficulties in defining *family* in contemporary society
- Knowledge about attempts to develop a federal family policy and the inherent difficulties in doing this
- Ability to identify and discuss some major family-centered problems

Up to this point, this book has discussed fields of practice that relate to specific social problems. Not all fields of practice relate to specific social problem areas. In this chapter the discussion will focus on fields of practice that are closely tied to specific methods of social work. The historical methods, casework, group work, and community organization, were discussed in Chapter 6. These methods are organized around specific social systems. In this chapter the focus will be on emerging fields of practice that relate to context (the environmental site of the practice).

Casework practice, which has been the method of the vast majority of social workers, is usually related to one of the problem area fields of practice. Thus, no identifiable field of practice or specifically organized network of services grew up around this method. The one exception might be what came to be identified as *family services,* or the work in the agencies affiliated with Family Service America (FSA) or agencies offering similar services, where the emphasis is on providing general counseling services. While these agencies, which have their roots in the Charity Organization Societies (COS), have provided services for a wide variety of needs using a broad range of approaches focusing on individuals, groups, family groups, and in some cases communities, their major focus has been on families. The services fit into many of the identified problem fields of practice.

Agencies that have focused on the provision of group services and those that fall within the community practice area have often been considered fields of practice. This chapter will discuss three fields of practice: group services, community organization, and family services. These can be classified as fields of practice with system type as the organizing theme.

Group Services

Not all services using group modalities fall within this field of practice. The field is usually limited to those services provided by an agency that identifies itself as a *group services agency.* As discussion of this field of practice progresses, the meaning of the term "group services agency" should become clearer.

The roots and early history of both the group work method and the group services field of practice are closely related and thus are often confused. The beginning of *group services* is usually fixed in the settlement movement, which was discussed in Chapter 1. Settlement houses, both historically and at present, have used small groups (clubs, classes, and community action groups) as their core means for service. Historically, youth service organizations, such as Scouts, Boys' and Girls' Clubs, and neighborhood centers, were considered a part of the field, as were the YMCAs and YWCAs. Jewish community centers have always been a strong component of the field. Group services has always placed a strong emphasis on recreational activities as a tool, resulting in confusion about the difference between group services and recreation. Using the definition of social welfare used in this book (see Chapter 1), recreation could be considered as part of the social welfare system. We have not chosen to do this, however, as recreation now seems to be a system in its own right. Much of what was once a part of the group services field now finds its home in the field of recreation. Nevertheless, although group services seems markedly diminished in the contemporary scene, the field is notable for its contributions to the development of the social welfare system and therefore merits consideration here.

As noted earlier, the settlement houses, which first developed in the late nineteenth century to serve the immigrant population, primarily in large cities, have always been the core agencies of the field. The settlement houses focused on self-help, informal education, and improving the environment or the neighborhood in which the agency was located. There is a strong emphasis on "normal" behavior as contrasted with maladjustment, which is the focus of problem-oriented fields of practice. This focus has led to goals of growth and of prevention. Settlement houses have been concerned in particular with helping immigrants adjust to the new environment while also helping them to maintain and value their own cultural heritage. Clubs and classes provided opportunities to learn new skills and to learn democratic ways of governance. They motivated individuals to become involved in self-help, in improving and modifying their environment, and in developing their latent potential. The settlement houses emphasized work with children and youth. Another important ingredient of the service was *volunteerism.* Many of the groups were led by volunteers, and participants (members) were encouraged to volunteer to improve both the services of the agency and the environment (neighborhood) in which it operated.

The Ys, youth-serving organizations, and neighborhood centers had much in common with the settlement house approach in their emphasis on character building and recreational activities. They came to serve a broad base of the population. Jewish community centers were developed to meet the specific needs of the Jewish population. Because Jewish culture places a strong emphasis on the communal aspects of human relationships, this type of communal activity has great importance in the life of the Jewish community. These organizations, using the same basic thrust as other group services organizations, have always made a considerable contribution to the field. They continue to be active in efforts to maintain or regain the place of group services as a distinct field of practice in the broader field of social welfare (Middleman and Goldberg, 1987).

Social Work and the Group Services Field

In its early days, group services was not closely tied to the budding social work profession. Early leaders in the field, however, became involved in the National Conference of Charities and Corrections. This involvement was probably strongly related to their concern for social reform to meet the needs of people living in difficult situations. Jane Addams of Hull House in Chicago became president of the National Conference of Charities and Corrections in 1910. She showed her identification with social work when she supported a name change to the National Conference of Social Work in 1917 (Wilson, 1976). Thus began a slow acceptance that social work was more than casework.

As the group services field of practice began to mature, the need for conceptualization and education for the field became apparent. The emergence of the fields of sociology and, to a lesser degree, psychology helped to motivate the formation of small study groups around the country that were concerned with discussion of various aspects of group services and group work more generally. The nature and use of group process was an important point for consideration. In the mid-1920s, *group work* became one of the fields of specialization at the School of Applied Social Science at Western Reserve University in Cleveland. Other schools of social work followed in developing either a specialization or courses in group work.

In 1935 the National Conference of Social Work added a section on group work. Even at this time W. I. Newstetter discussed the necessity "to distinguish between group work as a field, group work as a process, and group work techniques" (Wilson, 1976, p. 20). In 1936 the National Association for the Study of Group Work was formed. This organization is important, for it became the *American Association of Group Workers (AAGW)* in 1946 and was one of the organizations that came together in 1955 to form the National Association of Social Workers (NASW).

During the early days of group services' identification with social work as a profession, several ongoing concerns arose. The first was the relationship between group work and *group therapy.* The group services professionals saw group therapy as something other than group work.

In fact, in the formation of the American Association of Group Workers, one active participant in the movement, a psychiatrist, left the organization over the issue of group therapy's differences from group work (Wilson, 1976). The issue continues to this day, as manifested by ongoing questions about the relationship between group therapy and social group work. Another concern was the relationship between social group work and the developing group dynamics movement. Other issues were focused on ethical considerations in the use of groups in experimental studies and in the use of experimental research design by *group dynamics* adherents who were interested in the study of the group as an entity. Social group workers, by contrast, were interested in the use of the group in the service of individuals, groups, and the environment. They felt that the experimental use of the group, with manipulation of variables and control groups, was a violation of social work's ethical principles. Social group work benefited from the knowledge developed by the group dynamics movement, but it never had a strong relationship to this movement. Another divisive factor concerned the differentiation between group work, with its concern for social issues and community betterment, and the emerging community organization method. The question here seems to be whether practice that uses small groups as a means toward environmental improvement (a valid goal in the group services organization) is a part of the social group work or community organization field of practice.

During the 1940s and 1950s, the group services field of practice remained viable and seemingly healthy. The 1940s and 1950s can indeed be considered the zenith of group services. Workers in that field continued to be identified with the social work profession and were among the contributors to the growing body of knowledge being developed about work with groups. The late 1940s saw the publication of several important group work texts written by authors with experience in the group services field of practice. Group service workers were considered a part of the social work profession if they had the M.S.W. degree. The group services field seemed headed for the same development that the problem-oriented fields of practice were experiencing. It should be noted, however, that no more than 10 percent of all M.S.W.'s ever practiced in this field, and the number was probably less (Middleman, 1968).

Nevertheless, several new trends that were to contribute to the diminishment of the field were emerging. First was the gradual expansion of the use of groups in other fields of practice. In 1948 the Social Group Work Program of the University of Pittsburgh moved into a Veterans Hospital with a unit of field work students. By the mid-1950s the National Institute of Mental Health had awarded a grant to the AAGW for the exploration of group work in psychiatric settings (Wilson, 1976). Again, discussions began about the relationship between social group work and group therapy. The movement of social group work as a method into the mental health field of practice (or psychiatric field, as it was then called) was followed in the 1960s and 1970s by a movement into all fields of practice. In fact, by the 1970s master's level social workers with a group work sequence were seldom found in group services agencies but, rather, were working in the fields of practice identified with social problems. This was in part because the salaries paid to social workers in these new areas were higher than those in the group services field. The only place where this seemed not to be true was in the Jewish community centers.

Other factors that influenced social workers to leave the group services field of practice may have been related to the development of the conceptual base for practice. Schools of social work placed much less emphasis on sociological knowledge in these years than they did on psychological knowledge (particularly the frameworks of Freud and Erikson). Although group work students continued to study some sociological material in group work courses, they also were expected to incorporate psychological knowledge into their practice. This was easier to do in the problem-oriented fields of practice, with an emphasis on pathology, than in the group services agencies, with their emphasis on "normality." There was much devaluing of the use of activity as a tool of practice in contrast to more valued "talk techniques." Also, "volunteerism," an important source of manpower in the group services field fell out of vogue. Many group workers with a strong identification with the social work profession found that group services was not the most desirable field of practice in which to practice.

During the 1960s, other factors contributed to lessening the importance of social group work and the group services field of practice. Growing numbers of M.S.W.'s with a group work background continued to enter other fields of practice. This forced group services agencies to rely on graduates from other fields, including the developing recreation field, for staff. Often, these new workers had degrees at only the baccalaureate level. In addition, in 1963 the NASW abolished its group work section. Thus, group workers no longer had a vehicle through which to continue development of their specific knowledge and practice. During this period the federal government began to pour money into neighborhood improvement and preventive programs, but group services agencies, though long involved in this type of activity, were bypassed. This drained much of the energy and resources provided by volunteer and indigenous leadership from the group services agencies.

In the late 1960s and early 1970s, social work education began to develop what is now known as generalist practice. The group work sequence was abolished in many schools of social work. Group work was to become an integral part of the new generalist method, but this happened only in a sporadic and partial manner. In this new modality, individual and family work usually received primary emphasis.

There is, however, still a remnant of social group workers, who are attempting to preserve the rich heritage of the group services field of practice. In 1978 two events occurred that have given this group a means for continuing to exchange and develop their knowledge about social work with groups and, to some extent, about the group services field of practice. These two events were the formation of the *Committee for the Advancement of Social Work with Groups* (now known as the Association for the Advancement of Social Work with Groups, Inc.) and the beginning of publication of a journal, *Social Work with Groups*. There is now a voice calling for concern in social work practice for preventive work, for emphasis on group problem solving, for the use of indigenous leadership, and even for attention to the use of activity as a tool of practice. It is a voice that calls attention to the lack of emphasis on social work with groups in the generalist modality. Perhaps group service will again rise in some form as an important field of practice. For now, it is also important that the contributions made by those who practiced in this field be incorporated into contemporary practice.

In a sense, this section has dealt with the rise and fall of a field of practice. It may be assumed that as the profession of social work withdrew from the group services field of practice, that field was weakened in its social welfare functions and took on more of the characteristics of the developing field of recreation. Or it could be assumed that a new field was adopted by group services organizations because they found its thrust and values more compatible with their way of functioning. Or it may be that because of the prevailing problem-oriented view of social welfare, public support for the work of group services agencies and organizations became minimal. However, there is another important factor related to the lack of public support for the goals of group services agencies. Prevention, socialization, and volunteerism have given way to professionalism, therapy, and problem-oriented activity. How can the social welfare system and the social work profession avoid losing the rich heritage of the group services field as they seek to meet the needs of people? With the contemporary interest in the use of volunteers, the rise of self-help groups, and the availability of professional B.S.W. social workers, there may still be a place for group services in the social welfare system. But for this to be accomplished, two influences must develop. First, the profession of social work must accept this type of work more fully as a valued function of the profession. Second, there must be public support for this type of work. An important part of this support would be the valuing of preventive activity. In the history of the field of group services, there is much that could be used to address, at least in part, current social problems such as homelessness and drug abuse, particularly among young people. The field also could serve as a focal point for the use of the rich resources of volunteers.

Community Practice as a Field of Practice

Community Practice, as a reorganized field of social work practice, evolved out of the traditions of community organization, considered to be both a traditional method of social work practice, as well as a field of practice within the social welfare system. While retaining a main focus of community organization, that is, concentration on larger systems, primarily communities and organizations, through coordination, planning, funding, and monitoring of the services they provide, community practice also focuses on a broader range of service activity that includes community change and community building (Tropman, Erlich, and Rothman, 1995). Community practice reflects a broad and more contemporary view of community, including geographic (neighborhood, rural, and urban), communities of interest, such as social welfare and social service agencies, and identificational communities, such as African American, Native American, Gay and Lesbian, and so on. Community intervention describes the activities of a broad range of practitioners working in community settings, including administrators, policy-makers, program planners and evaluators, advocates, and clinical social workers (Tropman, Erlich, and Rothman, 1995). In order to fully understand what is involved in community intervention as a field of practice, it is necessary to gain an understanding of community organization, from which this reorganized field has evolved.

In many ways the development of community organization as a field of practice parallels the development of group services. Unlike group services, however, community organization had its roots in both the COS and the settlement house movement. It developed somewhat later than group services as a field of practice. As with group services, some question whether it ever really was a true field of practice or simply a method of social work practice. At various points in the development of the social welfare system, it was probably both.

The early COS found that focusing solely on individual problems was not enough to solve the problems of those they served. According to Garwin and Cox (1987, p. 32), four influences were present that called for a community focus to complement the individual case influence:

1.   The same resources were being approached again and again in charitable solicitations. There was a need to develop ways to be more efficient and less demanding in requests for help.

2. There was a duplication in providing aid, with several sources helping the same individuals.
3. As paid staff began to function in these agencies, they introduced the notion that activities should be directed by rational thinking and were influenced by a developing pragmatic philosophy.
4. Resources were insufficient, which meant that organized fund raising was necessary.

At this time (the late 1800s), Social Darwinism was a strong influence, with its "view that relief was an interference with the operation of the natural law" (Garvin and Cox, 1987, p. 33). One of the early community organization activities of the COS was the development of social service indexes that registered all who received help in an attempt to prevent duplication. Another COS activity at this time was the organization of case conferences, which allowed various agencies to discuss the help given to specific individuals and families. Also, there were studies of social and economic problems in relation to specific remedial measures. Somewhat later (1908), the COS made important contributions in organizing community welfare planning organizations. It was out of these organizations that social survey techniques developed, with one of the earliest examples being the Pittsburgh Survey of the early 1930s. The community organization activity that grew out of the COS can be characterized as strongly rooted in rational approaches with a residual philosophy (see Chapter 7) (Taylor and Roberts, 1985).

In contrast, the activity that grew out of the settlement house movement was pragmatic. In the earlier section on group services, the concern of the settlement houses for the community as they used small groups to bring about change was noted. This activity too can be considered one of the roots of present-day community organization activity. From this root came the development of needed services such as kindergartens. Settlement houses were involved in reform efforts, in provision of services, and in experimental services to determine what would work in various situations.

Eduard Lindemann (1921) made one of the earliest mentions of community organization as a special field. In 1930 a community organization text by Jesse Steiner (1930) was published.

It should be remembered until the onset of the Great Depression and the development of federal funding for relief activities, the formal social welfare system was made up largely of voluntary agencies with private funding. As these agencies increased in number from 1915 to 1929, there was an increase in the demand for coordination and for better fund raising. These became major functions of the welfare councils during this period.

With the emergence of federal government involvement in social welfare, there came new opportunities for the community organization field of practice. One of the most comprehensive planning activities was that of the National Planning Board, which operated from 1933 to 1944 (Austin, 1987). As the government took over former functions of voluntary social welfare agencies, there was additional need for planning and coordination for the social welfare system. Thus, community organizers began to be found in government agencies. Community planning agencies had considerable importance in this transition as they began to coordinate public and private agencies. *Community welfare councils* came to be local associations of citizens and agencies in which citizen interest and professional planning expertise were concerned with various social and health problems and the services related to those problems. The social problem concern of the community welfare councils was probably an important factor in the organization of the social welfare system according to a problem or field-of-practice framework.

An important milestone in the development of the community organization field of practice was the so-called *Lane Report,* a paper entitled "The Field of Community Organization," presented by Robert P. Lane at the National Conference of Social Work in 1939. It was the first significant discussion of the content of community organization practice. In 1946 the *Association for the Study of Community Organization* was formed (Murphy, 1954). In 1955 this organization merged into the NASW. In 1944, community organization became one of the basic eight subjects of the curriculum of schools of social work. As with group work, an ongoing concern arose as to whether community organization was a method or a field of practice. As community organization was practiced in a particular kind of agency involved in planning, it could be described as not only a method but also a developing field of practice.

During the 1950s, community organization agencies moved from a coordinative approach to a planning approach. There was considerable growth in the use of federated funds and a rational planning approach. The agencies tended to be controlled by prominent citizens, with workers playing more of a staff role, carrying out the desires of the board and assisting them in their tasks. Some of the functions of the staff of the community welfare councils were: collecting facts and information, formulating possible plans of action for the elimination of particular social problems, developing plans for raising the quality of community services, developing plans for better coordination of community services, and developing materials that disseminated information about community problems and services.

By the early 1960s boards of community councils were being challenged as having a middle- or upper-class view of the community and its problems. There was a strong call for the inclusion of those who received services from community agencies in the planning process. Also, the increasing availability of government funds brought a change in the funding sources of the voluntary agencies. They became increasingly dependent on grant and purchase-of-service funds. Many new agencies arose as the War on Poverty became a theme of the federal government. These new agencies often were outside the traditional social work area of concern. Many new and less well educated workers were entering what now came to be known as the human services field.

Major legislation that affected this field included the *Model Cities Act* (1967), the *Economic Opportunity Act* (1964), mental health and health legislation that called for planning activity, and the Social Security amendments of 1974. Through this legislation, the federal government developed policies and programs, set guidelines, and provided funding for many programs that were meant to address social problems. State, city, and other local entities were involved in implementation and development of programs and services. This change was one that called for many workers with education and skill in community organization. It called for a broadening of the community organization field of practice. New and different approaches were developed. A much broader population group was involved in the work to be done, in terms of both board membership and workers in the field. There was an increased call for those with a community organization background. In 1968, 6 percent of all graduate social work students were in a community organization sequence. This would drop to only 5.7 percent in 1974 as change again brought new philosophies to government involvement in the social welfare system (Skidmore, 1976).

With the arrival of the Nixon and later the Reagan presidencies, many of the programs developed by presidents Kennedy and Johnson were terminated. Revenue sharing and block grant funding became the federal government's means of involvement in social welfare. Planning returned to local and state government. In addition, deep cuts in funding affected the planning process. Evaluation, efficiency, and management skills grew in importance. Often the demand was not for a community practitioner but for an administrator. Another development was the rise of self-help groups, which pressured for a response to their specific demands regarding the social welfare system.

Social Workers and Community Practice

Through the years, social workers in the community organization field became specialists. Graduate education with an emphasis on community organization was considered a must. As long as agencies with a social work frame of reference were the focus of the work, there was little question about the need for community organizers to be social workers. During the 1960s the field of community organization expanded. Not only did government agencies become a part of the network that planned for and monitored other service agencies, but new types of community agencies developed as well. Of particular interest were the *Community Action Programs,* with their focus on the delivery of services to low-income people. In part this was a reaction to the fact that many traditional social agencies had moved away from their historical concern for poor people and had turned instead to providing services for the growing middle class.

Unlike group services, the field of community organization attempted to accommodate this significant change. New methods of delivering services were conceptualized, and for a time in the 1960s it seemed that the field of community organization would be the practice of the future for many social workers. With the change to a more conservative political climate, in the 1970s and 80s, all this changed. Advocacy and activist strategies once used to obtain services for those with the greatest needs became suspect.

Developments in the 1960s, along with the expansion of the use of community organization methods in new, non-social work settings, called into question whether community organization was indeed exclusively social work's domain. Today community organization is no longer an area that exclusively involves professionally trained social workers. Many other groups are involved—community planners, public administrators, and business trained individuals, to name a few. Social work has reorganized this traditional field of practice into what is now being termed "community practice," as discussed earlier. Social work education for community practice has also changed as well. At the undergraduate level, the generalist approach to practice involves some aspects of community practice, such as coordination and case management activities, as well as development of services with various interest groups within communities. As discussed earlier in this text, social work education at the graduate level is generally organized into the divisions of micro and macro practice. Education for macro practice in some graduate schools may include a focus on community practice. In addition, new methods and strategies for community practice, (i.e., community change and community building), have been developed. This, along with the new conceptualization of community, discussed earlier in this chapter, have brought about the need for social workers working at the community level, to have a broad range of skills, including administrative and program planning and evaluation skills. For instance, community change, that is, assisting a community to develop the capacity and capability to bring about desired change, may involve use of public relations, advocacy, coalition building, and program planning and evaluation skills. Likewise, community building and working with communities of interest, such as oppressed minority groups, with regard to social justice issues that affect them, will require the use of these, as well as other, specialized skills (Tropman, Erlich, and Rothman, 1995). Unlike the case of the group services field, there remains a firm commitment within the profession to social work practice at the community level.

Services to Families

In contrast to the two fields of practice already discussed in this chapter (group services and community practice), family services has never become a widely recognized field of practice. Yet with the current concern about families both in the general society and within the profession of social work, it would seem that services to families should be an important component of the social welfare system. Perhaps the reason the social welfare system has not recognized this field of practice lies in the fact that families are already an important concern in many of the developed fields of practice, such as child welfare, health care, and mental health. Another answer may lie in the way in which social work developed as a major profession within the social welfare system. These themes will be discussed more fully later in this section of the chapter. Also to be discussed are some of the major problems facing families in the United States today. The contemporary social work involvement with services to families will also be considered. First, however, it is important to define the nature of a field of practice that is concerned with services to families.

As has been pointed out, service to families is an important component of many of the problem-oriented fields of social work practice. The major concern of those fields, however, is the alleviation of problem situations. In these fields, services to families are seen as means of reaching goals with respect to an identified problem such as illness or child abuse. Of course, many practitioners in these fields have a genuine interest in the strength of the family. But a family services field, by contrast, sees the family as the major concern of the services. This field could be made up of agencies, both public and private, with a primary goal of preserving healthy family life and of restoring dysfunctional families to healthy functioning. Also included would be agencies with religious affiliations that provide services to the family unit such as Jewish Social Services, Lutheran Social Services, and Catholic Social Services. Agencies in this field could focus on the family system regardless of the particular social problems that might be involved. This focus would include work with individuals, small groups, organizations, communities, as well as policy development, when the work is in the service of families. In light of contemporary understandings about the importance of the family in preventing and alleviating problems in human functioning, it would seem that this field of practice could be recognized as a valid one.

In the discussion of social change in Chapter 3, emphasis was placed on the effect of social change on the contemporary family. As families are experiencing stress because of social change, a field of practice focused on services to families would seem to be a logical component of the contemporary social welfare system. In fact, there are indications that such a field may be emerging. Many graduate social work programs include services to families as one possible specialty. The NASW, at its annual symposium, now includes "Families, Health, and Mental Health" as one of the four specialty conferences.

Social Work and the Family: A Historical Perspective

In the days of the Charity Organization Societies and of Mary Richmond, the family was indeed a primary focus of the developing social work practice and of the social welfare system. In Richmond's conceptualization of casework (see Chapter 6), the family was the case (Hartman and Laird, 1983). Soon, however, this focus was to change to the individual as psychoanalytic thinking, with its individual emphasis, influenced the development of social work practice.

Despite the individual emphasis, the notion of family services was kept alive in an organization founded in 1911 as the National Association of Societies for Organizing Charity. After several name changes, this organization became known in 1946 as the Family Service Association of America and in 1983 as *Family Service America (FSA)*. This national organization, with member agencies in many cities, has been a leader in the development of services to families. The first professional journal, *The Family* (1920), later known as *Social Casework* and more recently *Families in Society*, is published by this organization (Erickson, 1987). It should also be noted that before the development of government income maintenance programs, it was these family service agencies, the successors to the COS agencies, that bore the major responsibility for providing income maintenance services to families. During the early years of this organization, poor families were a major concern of its member agencies. From 1940 on, however, they became concerned with services to all income groups. With the development of the provisions of the Social Security Act, income maintenance (see Chapters 1 and 7) was no longer a function of these agencies, and services to the poor were deemphasized.

In 1953 a report by the Family Service Association of America stated its purpose as: "to contribute to harmonious family interrelationships, to strengthen positive values in family life, and to promote healthy personality development and satisfactory social functioning of various family members" (Family Service Association of America, 1953). As yet there were no broadly accepted means for working with the family as a system, so services were provided largely to individuals who were members of the family unit.

During the 1950s and 1960s, the family as a unit of attention again became a possibility. Both psychiatry and psychology were beginning to recognize the importance of family dysfunction as a contributor to individual dysfunction. As the family therapy movement spread, social workers became involved. Virginia Satir, one of the recognized pioneers of this movement, was a social worker. Another social worker, Frances Scherz of Jewish Family Services of Chicago, also pioneered in developing knowledge about family treatment. The *Family Centered Project of St. Paul* (1954) was a pioneering research study of the nature of what came to be called *multiproblem families* (Geismar and Ayres, 1958).

A 1963 report of the Family Service Association of America states that casework is to be the central means of service but that the service is to be family centered rather than problem centered (Family Service Association of America, 1963). This report also suggests that service be broadened to serve a second function, improving the social environment. This change came about in part because of the advent of the War on Poverty and the availability of new funding for family services under the 1962 amendments to the Social Security Act as they related to social services (see Chapter 1).

Gradually, family service agencies saw significant changes in the ways in which they delivered services. They broadened their programs, developed outreach mechanisms, and gave more consideration to services to minority families. Their boards of directors came to be more broadly representative of the community population. Some new services, such as homemaker services, were provided by persons without professional training. Family life education became a part of the service thrust of some agencies. Today, family service agencies generally have a broad range of diversity; there is little commonality of purpose as local agencies respond individually to changing times. In many states, the public social service agency provides services other than income maintenance to families and thus is clearly a part of this potential field of practice.

This potential field of practice includes several areas of considerable tension. There is tension between focusing on the needs of disadvantaged families versus the more traditional focus on middle-class families. There is tension concerning funding and the question of whether public or private agencies are best suited to provide services for low-income families. There is tension over the use of traditional casework services versus emerging methods of family therapy. There is tension over whether to use scarce resources to respond to the needs of dysfunctional families or to develop a more preventive thrust instead. Finally, there is concern over what are the most appropriate approaches to working with multiproblem families.

To date no definitive statement of what constitutes a *family* has been forthcoming. Many people still consider the traditional nuclear family as providing the definition; to them, a family must be made up of mother, father, and children. But in contemporary society, with its many manifestations of new relationship patterns, such as single-parent families, blended families, and homosexual partners, this definition is no longer adequate. Ann Hartman and Joan Laird, prolific scholars in the field, have developed the following definition: "Two or more people who have made a commitment to share living space, have developed close emotional ties, and share a variety of family roles and functions" (Hartman and Laird, 1983, p. 36).

Another question that remains unanswered is whether services to families is indeed a valid field of practice or is simply an integral part of generalist social work practice and thus used in many fields of practice. In our view, services to families are indeed a part of generalist practice and a part of many fields of practice, but there is nevertheless a place for a field of practice that focuses its services on the needs of families generally—that is, a field that is not related to a specific problem area. Family Service America member agencies, along with parts of public social service agencies, would seem to be core agencies in developing concern and means for service to the family as a unit.

Family Social Policy

Despite the fact that political rhetoric in the United States continues to emphasize the importance of the traditional family as one means of eliminating many social problems, the United States has no social policy regarding the family. It should be recognized, of course, that many public policies have considerable impact on family life. This is particularly true in the areas of child welfare and income maintenance.

One effort of the federal government to articulate concerns, issues, and recommendations about the family was the *White House Conference on Families (WHCF)* in 1980. One proposal that was made during the planning for this conference was for a new definition of the family. This proposal suggested that the family is taking on new forms: the single-parent family, the unmarried couple who live together with or without children, the homosexual couple, and so on. Unfortunately, however, a growing conservative movement prevented even discussion of this approach to considering the needs of people in their relationships to each other.

The conference was held in three cities: Baltimore, Minneapolis, and Los Angeles. Although many issues and recommendations were raised, the conservative voice generally prevailed. This voice opposed the use of federal resources for social programs. It said that families, churches, and to some extent local government should be responsible for the well-being of the family. In other words, it opposed the development of any federal family policy (Dempsey, 1981). It must be added that development of a federal family policy does create the potential for overly intrusive government interference with a family's ways of functioning. The question must be asked: When is government intervention into family functioning justified, and when is it an invasion of individual and family rights to freedom of action?

The WHCF did make recommendations concerning the family in four areas:

1. Families and economic well-being, including economic pressures on family functioning and income support problems
2. Family challenges and responsibilities, including family-centered relationship problems like divorce, family violence, substance abuse, and juvenile delinquency, as well as the special problems of handicapped, disabled, and aged family members
3. Families and human needs, including education, health, housing, and child care
4. Families and major institutions, including the family's relationship with government, the media, community institutions, and the law and judicial system (White House Conference on Families, 1980)

Looking over this long list of recommendations made some fifteen years ago, it is evident that not much headway has been made in forging social policy regarding the family that incorporates the themes forwarded by the Conference. Most of the problems and issues faced by families at that time continue to be faced today. So why this continued lack of attention to the development of a family-oriented social policy? It is speculated (Berger & Berger, 1983) that, in the past, the establishment of a national social policy on families was thwarted by conservative policymakers who feared that such a policy would bring more government intrusion into the lives of families. This is not unlike the case today, where in the 1992 presidential campaign, much discussion of "traditional family values" was engendered. The Republican Party, especially its very conservative wing, appeared to define this issue as a return to what they envision as the "traditional family," a family where mothers remain in the home and out of the work force, with prohibitions against abortion and homosexuality. This surfaced again in the midterm national congressional elections of 1994, where conservative Republicans gained a majority of seats in both houses of Congress and have pushed through an agenda of legislation that promotes getting government out of the lives of people and families, which they have termed their "Contract with America." Proposed in this legislation are drastic cuts in federal funding of services, including basic "safety net" public assistance programs for poor families, such as AFDC, Medicaid, and Food Stamps. Consequently, the prospect for a national policy on the family within the near future seems bleak.

Family-Centered Problems

Family-centered problems may be those that have been discussed in previous chapters relative to the established fields of practice. The child welfare field has a strong family emphasis, as the family is the most desirable major resource for every child. The mental health field is also one that considers family functioning as a prime concern. In this chapter, however, family-centered problems are seen as those that have a major impact on the functioning of the family or that can be identified as social problems with their origin in the dysfunctioning of a family system. Although this definition could include many of the problems discussed in relation to the problem-oriented fields of practice, this chapter will deal with only a few major problems. It will look briefly at how social policies in the area of economic security affect the functioning of some families. It will also consider two relationship problems that are of major concern for the agencies in the suggested family services field of practice: divorce and violence in the family.

Economic Insufficiency

With the tightening of regulations related to economic security and income maintenance, with changing federal policies regarding low-income housing, with the continuing rise of health-care costs and the lack of affordable health insurance for many low-income people, it seems that poor families are having an increasingly difficult time in the 1990s. There are more *homeless families,* more families lack basic health care, more children are living in poverty. The number of single-parent families (always at risk of having insufficient income) has continued to grow. Single-parent families are often female-headed families as well, a factor that also places them at risk of *economic insufficiency.* A family services field of practice could foster additional understanding of how social policy in the areas of income maintenance and employment contributes to placing families at risk of dysfunction. These issues have been discussed in previous chapters, but the specific concern here is that without federal policy that provides for the economic needs of all families, a major social problem—the lack of economic security for many families—will continue to grow.

It has been suggested by one writer, Louv (1990), that a national family policy should pull together an array of services that would strengthen and support families so that they would not even need social welfare services traditionally provided in the federal/state safety net. Included family supports would be sufficient maternity and sick leave, quality and affordable day care services, national health care coverage for all families, and more generous unemployment insurance benefits. This would allow families to obtain or maintain economic self-sufficiency without reliance on government public assistance.

Families and Economic Security

At the heart of adequate economic security for families is income. The three primary sources of family income are employment, social insurance, and public assistance. Employment income is the most socially acceptable. Unemployment and underemployment undermine the economic and social well-being of the family. For some families, racial or gender discrimination has been an obstacle to finding adequate employment.

As discussed in previous chapters, Old Age Survivors, Disability, and Health Insurance (Social Security) provides benefits to individuals upon retirement; to spouses, widows, and dependent children of deceased or permanently disabled insured workers; and to disabled workers. For survivors, the families of deceased workers, it provides a much-needed supplement to other income sources. For families without income supports, public assistance becomes the alternative. Aid to Families with Dependent Children (AFDC) and its supplementary programs are the primary source of public assistance for these families, providing monthly cash assistance grants to eligible families. Nonmonetary, in-kind assistance is also provided through food stamps, subsidized housing, fuel assistance, and Medicaid. For aged, disabled, or blind family members, the federal government also offers cash assistance through Supplemental Security Income (SSI).

On the other hand, families who accept such aid often face the stigma of being "on welfare," which is demeaning and only adds to their problems.

Many families in today's world continue to struggle with issues of economic security. The status quo in economic security for the family has been maintained. Serious questions need to be asked about whether society can reasonably expect troubled families to maintain themselves as independent and self-sufficient units without adequate help from societal support mechanisms. Decisive action must be taken to ensure adequate supports for these families if we want them to be stable and productive members of our society. But what the future holds for the economic security of all families remains to be seen.

Divorce

The *divorce* rate in the United States has increased dramatically since the end of World War II, but it is predicted that it will stabilize in the near future. The causes of the increase in incidence of divorce are many. Some suggest that our technologically advanced society fosters the attitude that almost anything is replaceable, including a marriage. If it doesn't work, throw it out. If the marital relationship does not meet the partners' expectations or satisfaction, a divorce seems to be the option that couples are choosing to end the relationship. The emergence of liberalized divorce laws, particularly the concept of no-fault divorce, reflects these attitudes. Incompatibility in the marital relationship, perceived by one or both partners, can also contribute to the breakup of the relationship. This may include incompatibility in sex roles, excessive life and marriage demands, unmet emotional needs of marital partners, the inability of the marriage to satisfy the individual, individual conflicts about personal fulfillment, and incompatible social roles for both partners. In part, incompatibility may result when marital couples come from very different cultural backgrounds, with different values. When such incompatibility exists in a marriage, tension and conflict often lead to marital difficulties and even divorce, unless the couple makes conscious efforts to resolve their differences (Henslin, 1985). In recent years, the stigma surrounding divorce has faded, making it a much more attractive alternative than it had been in the past.

It is unnecessary to argue whether divorce causes family problems or whether family problems cause divorce. It is more important to consider the consequences of divorce for the emotional well-being of family members, and how divorce affects family functioning. Children are particularly vulnerable to emotional problems as a consequence of divorce. Children often experience divorce as a terrible and confusing loss in their lives, in much the same way that they experience the death of a loved one. This sense of loss can give rise to many emotions within the child: grief, guilt, depression, anxiety, confusion, and bewilderment. The effects of these feelings on the child can be severe and can last well into adulthood. Studies show that emotional problems and behavioral disturbances in adolescents and adults—including depression, alcoholism, anxiety disorders, and suicide—are often linked to unresolved feelings associated with losses experienced in childhood (Lengua, Wolchic, and Braves, 1995).

The effects of divorce can be just as severe for adults. They also experience divorce as a loss, with many of the same accompanying emotional reactions as children experience. What is of central concern here is that divorce can impair adults' capacity and ability to parent. Although this impairment is usually only temporary, it can sometimes be prolonged.

In recent years, social workers and other professional helpers have focused a great deal of attention on helping families cope with the consequences of divorce. Social service agencies have developed specific programs designed to address those needs, including crisis intervention, divorce mediation, family therapy and counseling, support groups for divorced parents, children's support and treatment groups, and parenting skills groups (Simon, 1994). The legal system has also joined this effort. Family and domestic courts, in recognition of the consequences of divorce for the family, have begun the practice of divorce mediation. Crisis intervention services and family counseling have begun to be offered by professionals employed by the courts, with the goals of either preventing divorce or ensuring that the needs and problems of all the family members will be dealt with if divorce occurs.

Family Violence

Violence in the family encompasses many broad areas, including abuse of spouses, children, and aged family members. This discussion is limited to spousal abuse, more specifically wife abuse or wife battering, because other forms of *family violence* have been discussed in previous chapters. Violence toward spouses ranges all the way from verbal abuse and minor physical assaults to homicide. It has been estimated that 11 percent of all homicides are linked to episodes of spousal abuse (Federal Bureau of Investigation, 1992). Most family violence, however, is limited to verbal and physical abuse. A combination of factors is associated with the development of violent behavior patterns within the family: unstable family relationships; parents' childhood experiences with violence; current situational stresses, both internal and external; poor impulse control; inner rage; alcohol or drug abuse; jealousy; sexual conflict; poor communication skills; feelings of personal inadequacy; and fear of intimacy (Martin, 1978). Patterns of family violence have the potential of being passed on from generation to generation. Children who experience, witness, or are somehow exposed to violent relationships within their families appear to be predisposed to developing the same patterns of abusive relationships in adulthood. This appears to hold true both for men who batter and for women who become victims of abuse. Violence perpetrated toward one family member can set up abusive patterns toward other members. In some abusive families, the husband physically abuses his wife, who then abuses the children.

Violence within families has always existed. Only within the past two decades has a greater awareness of this social problem developed within society at large, the helping professions, and the judicial system. Prior to the 1970s, the problem of spousal abuse was seen as an unfortunate but nevertheless private matter within families, requiring only individual responses to its victims, as opposed to a conscious and deliberate large-scale response to family violence as a legitimate social problem.

Societal attitudes about women and spousal abuse were largely to blame for the lack of attention to this problem. Beliefs—such as the idea that a woman was the property of her husband, or that it was the husband's right to abuse the wife, or that some women have a masochistic desire to be punished, or that women provoke the abuse—prevailed and handicapped society's efforts to respond adequately.

Since the 1970s, awareness of spousal abuse as a national problem has come to the forefront. Sociological research, social work, and feminist research and literature have struck a responsive chord and have forced society, the helping professions, and the legislative and judicial systems to reexamine their beliefs and practices toward violence in the family (McNeely and Robinson-Simpson, 1987).

In recent years, specialized programs for abused women have been created. Crisis emergency shelters for *battered women* and their children have been one such development. The services provided by these shelters include individual counseling, support and self-help groups, legal services, and referral services to social service agencies for economic assistance and educational and vocational training (Roberts, 1981). Services are also provided to the entire family by both public and private agencies. Public agencies are called upon when the violence seems to be caused by situational stresses (unemployment, inadequate income, drug or alcohol abuse). Family service agencies and mental health agencies provide intensive treatment and counseling services to violent families, family therapy, marital therapy, and treatment for abusive men. These services can help control or eliminate the violent and abusive patterns and keep the family together.

The judicial system is starting to concern itself with the legal aspects of family violence. Laws have been passed in several states that protect victims of spousal abuse. The laws have helped law enforcement agencies respond to family violence by spelling out, in clear-cut terms, what their roles and responsibilities are. Law enforcement agencies have begun employing professional social workers to work with law officers as a team in investigating and intervening in situations of family violence. It is hoped that this concerted effort by society, the helping professions, and the judicial system will break the destructive cycle of family violence in the near future.

Social Work Practice and the Family

Social workers have used many different theoretical approaches when working with the family unit. Some have been borrowed from other professions such as psychiatry and psychology, but others have been developed by social workers. Of special concern to social workers has been the development of practice approaches that recognize the effects of cultural factors on family life, the ability of the family to use help, work with multiproblem families, and, most recently, with what might be called *new-pattern families* (single parents, homosexual couples, and the like) and homeless families (McGoldrick, Pearce, and Giordano, 1982; Phillips, DeChillo, Kronenfeld, and Middleton-Jeter, 1988). All this development of practice models for work with the family unit would be important in social work practice in the proposed family services field. Workers would also use a generalist model of practice as they focus on environmental concerns that affect family functioning. Work in and with communities and action to influence social policy and programs would certainly be a part of the practice. Work with individuals and groups in the service of families would also be a part of the worker's practice.

A Case Study

The J family made a request for services from a family service agency. Mr. and Mrs. J were worried about the violent and destructive behavior being exhibited by their ten-year-old son, Eric. According to Mr. and Mrs. J, in recent months Eric had appeared generally unhappy. On several occasions, these episodes were followed by violent and destructive behaviors in which he physically assaulted his sister and damaged or destroyed his own personal possessions and other items in the J home. The Js were at a loss to understand what was causing these "temper tantrums," as they called them. The measures they had employed to control Eric's outbursts had failed. They stated that they were at their "wits' end" and were considering placing Eric in a foster home or institution. Eric also had begun to have problems at school with poor academic performance and physical aggression toward his peers.

The social worker assigned to their case spent the initial session and part of the second session gathering information from Mr. and Mrs. J and Eric. During the session with Mr. and Mrs. J, the social worker discovered that the Js were experiencing marital conflict, associated mostly with Mr. J's reluctance to spend time with Mrs. J and the children—caused, according to Mrs. J, by his excessively demanding work schedule and his other interests outside the family. The worker also learned that Mr. and Mrs. J's sexual activity had been reduced to "almost never." They both said that they had tried to keep their conflict hidden from the children, but Eric's recent misbehavior had "pitted them against each other even more," causing them to fight openly in front of the children. They also discussed their relationships with the children with the social worker. From their perspective, their daughter was a "good girl" who had never caused them any trouble. She was a straight A student, involved in school activities, and well liked by her peers. Concerning Eric, they had often thought that they had failed in their parental roles because he was so different from his sister. The Js felt they had a right to expect the same behavior from Eric that they did from his sister.

In the initial session with Eric, the social worker realized that Eric was concerned about his parents' fighting because "They're fighting about me, it's my fault." He also expressed anger about constantly being compared to

his sister, which, he stated, his parents did frequently and openly with him. He said, "They're probably going to get a divorce, and it's my fault." Eric admitted that he would get so mad at his parents and himself that he would "lose control and beat on people or things."

In the third session, with Mr. and Mrs. J and Eric present, the social worker shared his assessment of their situation. He explained that Eric had been feeling disenfranchised by his family because of the marital conflict and the unrealistic expectations placed on him by his parents. His violent and destructive behavior came from his anger toward his parents and himself, and his attack on his sister resulted from Eric's seeing her as part of the problem because he was constantly being compared to her. The social worker made the following recommendations:

1.   The Js should receive marriage counseling.
2.   Mr. J should realign his priorities and spend more time with his wife and children.
3.   They all should continue in family therapy to work on their excessive expectations of Eric and other relationship problems.

After several months of counseling, Eric's violent behavior subsided and his school performance improved. The Js agreed that they "felt much better about their marriage and family than they had for years." The case was closed shortly thereafter.

Before that was done, however, Eric was referred to a group services agency for involvement in a group experience with other boys his own age so that he could improve his interpersonal skills. Also, the worker noted that he was seeing an increasing number of cases in which children were exhibiting violence in their family relationships and in which parents did not have the skills to handle the situation. After discussion of this observation at an agency staff meeting, the decision was made to develop an opportunity for discussion at an interagency meeting. This discussion would have two foci: determination of the incidence of this type of situation as seen by other agencies in the community, and exploration of the possibility of developing an educational program for parents needing help with children's violent behavior.

Summary

This chapter has considered fields of practice as they are tied to specific social systems: the small group, the community, and the family. These fields of practice can also be discussed as those that are tied to traditional social work methods. Each field has been discussed from several perspectives. Each was defined by identifying social agencies and services that are or could be part of the field. Also, each was considered from a historical perspective in terms of both the social welfare system and the social work profession. Functioning and problem identification were discussed, as was the role and function of the social worker in each field.

The developmental stage in the various fields are somewhat different. Work with groups can be described as having diminished in importance, but with the possibility of again becoming important if it can be flexible enough to meet contemporary needs. Community practice is considered a valid field of practice, which has been able to adjust to new situations. Services to families can be considered a potential field of practice. The development of each of these three fields has been greatly affected by the political thrust of the times. Each has been influenced by social policy. For example, in conservative times, the political interest is more in immediate problem alleviation, with little concern for prevention or for quality-of-life issues. As each of these fields has strong preventive possibilities, the three fields seem to be less highly valued in conservative times. Each reflects major tensions within the social welfare system: concern for direct versus indirect ways of functioning, concern for dysfunction versus concern for enhancing normative functioning, and concern for the individual versus concern for the social environment.

It may not be possible for these three fields to become important components of the social welfare system. Nevertheless, understanding the place of the various fields of practice in the social welfare system calls for a consideration of these possible fields and their potential for meeting human needs. It is also important to appreciate their contribution to contemporary generalist practice and to the prevention of social dysfunction so that these contributions may be incorporated in services to people.

Key Terms

American Association of Group Workers (AAGW)
Association for the Study of Community Organization
battered women
Committee for the Advancement of Social Work with Groups
Community Action Programs
community practice
community welfare council
divorce
economic insufficiency
Economic Opportunity Act
family
family-centered problems
Family-Centered Project of St. Paul
Family Service America (FSA)

family services
family violence
group dynamics
group services
group services agency
group therapy
group work
homeless families
Lane Report
Model Cities Act
multiproblem families
new-pattern families
White House Conference on Families (WHCF)
volunteerism

References

Austin, D. (1987). Social Planning in the Public Sector, in Minahan, A. (Ed.), *Encyclopedia of Social Work, 18th edition*. Silver Spring, MD: National Association of Social Workers.

Berger, B., and Berger, P. (1983). *The War Over The Family*. New York: Anchor Press.

Commission on Methods and Scope, Family Service Association of America. (1953). *Scope and Methods of the Family Service Agency*. New York: Family Service Association of America.

Commisssion on Range and Emphasis of a Family Service Program. (1963). *Range and Emphasis of a Family Service Program*. New York: Family Service Association of America.

Dempsey, J.J. (1981). *The Family and Public Policy: The Issue of the 1980's*. Baltimore: Brooks.

Erickson, A.G. (1987). Family Services, in Minahan, A. (Ed.), *Encyclopedia of Social Work, 18th Edition*. Silver Spring, MD: National Association of Social Workers.

Garvin, C.D. and Cox, F.M. (1987). A History of Community Organizing since the Civil War with a Special Reference to Oppressed Communities, in Cox, F.M., Erlich, J.L., Rothman, J., and Tropman, J.E. (Eds.), *Strategies of Community Organization*. Itaska, IL: F.E. Peacock.

Geisman, L.L., and Ayres, B.(1958). *Families in Trouble: An Analysis of Basic Social Characteristics of One Hundred Families Served by the Family Centered Project of St. Paul*. St. Paul: Greater St. Paul Community Chest and Council.

Hartman, A., and Laird, J. (1983). *Family Centered Social Work Practice*. New York: Free Press.

Henslin, J.M. (1985). Why So Much Divorce. In James J. Henslin (Ed.), *Marriage and Family in a Changing Society*. New York: The Free Press.

Lengua, L.J., Wolchik, S.A., and Braver, S.L. (1995). Understanding Children's Divorce Adjustment from an Ecological Perspective. *Journal of Divorce and Remarriage 22 (3/4)*, 25–53.

Lindemann, E. (1921). *The Community*. New York: Association Press.

Listening to America's Families. (1980). *Actions for the 1980's: Final Report of the White House Conference on Families*. Washington, DC: U.S. Government Printing Office.

Louv, R. (1990). *Chidhood's Future*. Boston: Houghton Mifflin.

Martin, J.P. (1978). *Violence and the Family*. New York: Wiley.

McGoldrick, M., Pearce, J.K., and Giordano, J. (1982). *Ethnicity and Family Therapy*. New York: Guilford Press.

McNeely, R.L., and Robinson-Simpson, G. (1987). The Truth About Domestic Violence: A Falsely Framed Issue. *Social Work, 32*, 485–490.

Middleman, R.R. (1968). *The Non-Verbal Method in Working with Groups*. New York: Association Press.

Middleman, R.R., and Goldberg, G. (1987). Social Work Practice with Groups, in Minahan, A. (Ed.), *Encyclopedia of Social Work, 18th Edition*. Silver Spring, MD: National Association of Social Workers.

Murphy, C.G. (1954). *Community Organization Practice*. Boston: Houghton Mifflin.

Phillips, M.H., DeChillo, N., Dronenfeld, D., and Middleton-Jeter, V. (1988). Homeless Families: Services Make A Difference. *Social Casework, 69*, 48–53.

Roberts, A.R. (1981). *Sheltering Battered Women: A National Study and Service Guide*. New York: Springer.

Simon, R. (1994). Mending Marriages: What's Really Best for the Children? *The Family Therapy Networker, 18 (4)*, 2.

Skidmore, R.A. (1976). *Introduction to Social Work*. Englewood Cliffs, NJ: Prentice-Hall.

Steiner, J. (1930). *Community Organization*. New York: Century Company.

Taylor, S.H., and Roberts, R.W. (1985). *Theory and Practice of Community Social Work*. New York: Columbia University Press.

Tropman, J.E., Erlich, J.L., and Rothman, J. (1995). *Tactics and Techniques of Community Intervention*. Itaska, IL: F.E. Peacock.

U.S. Department of Justice, Federal Bureau of Investigation. (1992). *Uniform Crime Reports 1992*. Washington DC: U.S. Government Printing Office.

Wilson, G. (1976). From Theory to Practice: A Personalized History, in Roberts, R.W., and Northen, H. (Eds.), *Theories of Social Work with Groups*. New York: Columbia University Press.

Suggested Readings

Adams, P. (1990). Children as Contributions in Kind: Social Security and Family Policy. *Social Work, 35*, 492–498.

Allessi, A.S. (1980). *Perspectives on Social Group Work Practice: A Book of Readings.* New York: Free Press.

Bandler, J.T.D. (1989). Family Protection and Women's Issues in Social Security. *Social Work, 34*, 307–311.

Berry, M. (1992). An Evaluation of Family Preservation Services: Fitting Agency Services to Family Needs. *Social Work 37*, 314–321.

Blythe, B.J., Salley, M.P., and Jayaratne, S. (1994). A Review of Intensive Family Preservation Services Research. *Social Work Research, 18 (4)*, 213–224.

Breton, M. (1990). Learning From Social Group Work Traditions. *Social Work With Groups, 13 (3)*, 21–45.

Davis, L.V. (1991). Violence and Families. *Social Work, 36*, 371–373.

Familes in Society 72 (1991). Special Issue: The Coming of Age of Family Policy.

Grella, C.E. (1988). Strategies for Surviving Divorce: The Contradictions of Welfare. *Affilia 3*, 24–37.

Hartman, A. (1995). Ideological Themes in Family Policy. *Families in Society, 76 (3)*, 182–192.

Hartman, A., and Laird, J. (1983). *Family Centered Social Work Practice.* New York: Free Press.

Middleman, R., and Goldberg, G. (1990). From Social Group Work to Social Work with Groups. *Social Work with Groups, 13 (3)*, 21–45.

O'Keefe, M. (1994). Racial/Ethnic Differences Among Battered Women and Their Children. *Journal of Child and Family Studies, 3 (3)*, 283–305.

Rice, R. (1990). Change and Continuity in Family Service. *Families in Society, 71*, 24–31.

Seaburg, J.R. Family Policy Revisited: Are We There Yet? *Social Work, 35*, 548–554.

Toseland, R.W., and Rivas, R.F. (1984). *An Introduction to Group Work Practice.* New York: Macmillan.

Tropp, E. (1978). Whatever Happened to Group Work. *Social Work with Groups, 1*, 85–94.

14

OLD–NEW FIELDS OF PRACTICE: INDUSTRIAL AND RURAL

Learning Expectations

- Understanding of the nature of industrial social work—its definition, history, and present forms
- Understanding of the tensions, issues, and challenges facing the industrial social worker
- Understanding of the history of rural social work and some knowledge of the differences between rural social work and social work in a metropolitan setting
- Knowledge of some of the issues that face those who practice social work in a non-metropolitan area
- Understanding of the implications of developing fields of practice in a contextual arena and some knowledge of the strengths and limitations of using such an approach

Each of the chapters so far in this section of the text has discussed fields of practice. The fields focus either on a particular population (e.g., children or the aged) or an institutional setting (health and mental health services or corrections or income maintenance services). Each field of practice has developed its services and ways of practice in response to the needs of people served by the setting and to societal concerns and demands about the problems encountered in the population or setting. The development of each field also reflects political and philosophical influences on that field of practice. Recently the idea of context (the environment of the practice) seems to be a focus around which fields of practice are developing. We consider two such fields to be developing within a context: rural social work and industrial social work. Both fields represent earlier interests of some social workers that once seemed to have waned in importance but are now reemerging. Educational programs are developing that provide specific preparation for work in each field. Articles and books about each field are being written. A specific body of knowledge is developing for each area. In this chapter, each field is discussed separately.

Industrial Social Work: A Historical Perspective

Defining Industrial Social Work

Before discussing the new–old field of practice of *industrial social work*, a definition needs to be developed that will provide an understanding of the context of this field of practice. Paul A. Kurzman (1983) provides the following definition:

> *Programs and services, under the auspices of labor or management, that utilize professional social workers to serve members or employees, and the legitimate social welfare needs of the labor or industrial organization. It also includes the use, by a voluntary or proprietary social agency, of trained social workers to provide social welfare services or consultation to a trade union or employing organization under a specific contractual agreement. The employing organizations are not only labor unions and corporations, but often government agencies and not-for-profit organizations (p. 57).*

Kurzman notes that industrial social welfare is related to a third welfare system. The first two are the social and fiscal systems. The third system is the occupational welfare system. According to Kurzman, this system was conceptualized by Richard M. Titmuss, a British scholar of social welfare. Titmuss sees the occupational system as the benefits and services in which one may participate because of their employment status.

Where other fields of practice have focused on social functioning within the family, on particular social problems such as poverty, and on the social welfare system, this new field of practice focuses on the world of work. Work generates many tensions and problems for individuals—tensions between labor and management, tensions because of a troubled economy, tensions because of the rapid growth in reliance on sophisticated technology, to name a few. These tensions affect the individual's functioning in the work setting as well as in the larger world of society. When social workers focus on the work world, they enter the industrial field of practice. To get a better understanding of that field of practice, it is important first to look at the history of industrial social work.

Social Welfare and the World of Work: From the Middle Ages to the 1930s

Kurzman (1983) traces the relationship of the social welfare system and the world of work back to the Middle Ages, when the medieval craft guilds set aside funds for members' economic security in case of misfortunes such as accidents, old age, or death. The guild was the major social welfare institution, along with the church, until the development of poor laws in the 1600s (see Table 14–1 for a chronological outline of industrial social work). In the late nineteenth and early twentieth centuries in the United States, some employers started to pay more attention to the well-being of their employees. For example, the cotton mills of New England exercised control over the moral life of their female employees. In many cases, these single women were required to live in approved housing, keep prescribed hours, and to participate only in approved social activities. Large industrial employers like mill and mine companies set up entire towns for employees, including houses, roads, stores, schools, and

TABLE 14–1   Important Dates: Industrial Social Work

Late nineteenth century	New England cotton mill owners grew concerned with the moral life of female workers.
1910	Jane Addams became involved in the Hart, Schaffner, and Marx strike.
1920s	Graduates of New York School of Social Work took jobs as welfare secretaries in industry.
1930s	Social workers supported labor efforts.
1940s	Bertha Reynolds worked with the National Maritime Union.
Late 1960s	Industry began to employ social workers.
1970	The Industrial Social Welfare Center was established at the Columbia University School of Social Work.
1978	The first National Conference on Social Work Practice in Labor and Industrial Settings was held.
1982	*Work, Workers and Work Organizations* by Sheila Akabas and Paul Kurzman was published.

hospitals. There was a large element of social control mixed with this philanthropy, and there was some concern over sanitary conditions and worker safety. Some companies hired individuals known as welfare secretaries to administer these programs and services (Popple, 1981). In the 1920s many graduates of the New York School of Social Work took jobs as welfare secretaries. The 1930 edition of a social work textbook, *American Charities and Social Work,* contains a chapter on "Social Work in Industry" (Warner, Queen, and Harper, 1930). But this system was openly paternalistic and was held in suspicion by workers, who saw that it did not have their best interests at heart. In the 1920s the position of welfare secretary began to die out, and by 1935 it had disappeared.

Another strand of early industrial social work was in the labor movement. Jane Addams, a founder of the settlement house movement, was involved in the clothing workers' strike against the Hart, Schaffner, and Marx store in Chicago in 1910. Other social work leaders supported labor's efforts in the 1930s (Jorgensen, 1981). The work of Bertha Reynolds (1951) with the National Maritime Union during World War II is documented in her book *Social Work and Social Living.* The *Social Work Year Book* for 1929 (Hall, 1930) lists "Industry" as one of its groups of classified topical articles. Articles in that group included such labor-related topics as labor legislation for women, night work in industry, hours of work in industry, minimum wage, child labor, organized labor, unemployment, and vocational guidance. The interest of social workers in the labor movement, with a few exceptions such as Jane Addams and Bertha Reynolds, did not lie in working with the labor union's organization but, rather, in a concern for poor working conditions that affected the people with whom they were working.

During the 1920s and 1930s social work moved away from concern for the environmental factors affecting individuals to focus on psychological concerns, looking not so much at cause as at function. It paid scant attention to the environment, the context of an individual's social functioning. With these changes, the interest in social work with either industry or labor seemed to die. Not until the late 1960s did any real interest in industrial social work resurface.

The Reemergence of Industrial Social Work

Although the involvement of social workers in industry was limited at best from 1945 to 1965, two developments in industry are important to note. First, although the position of welfare secretary went out of vogue, concern for personnel issues by industry did not. In many companies personnel management became a department, with responsibility not only for hiring, promotion, and firing but also for programs that provided health, education, and recreational benefits to employees. This development was important for the evolution of the contemporary industrial social work field of practice, for it is within personnel departments that industrial social workers are now often found.

The other important development is the concern of labor unions for employee benefits. Martha Ozawa (1980) has noted that, in addition to concern about wages, labor unions have sought increases in health, security, and welfare benefits, including pensions, life insurance, and health care, including medical, hospital, and mental health care, which have encompassed programs ranging from treatment for alcoholism to marriage counseling. These fringe benefits may be termed an employee assistance program, a wage supplement program, an employee benefits program, or an industrial social welfare program. Ozawa believes the entrance of women and minorities into the labor force has been one factor in the development of these programs. She believes these groups of employees have special needs that can be met by such programs. She also sees a growing alienation from management in workers, which has given rise to an increase in mental health problems related to the *workplace*.

It should also be noted that during this period, the social welfare system saw the creation of several programs related directly to the workplace. These include Workman's Compensation for medical expenses and loss of work time due to accidents on the job, unemployment compensation, retirement benefits related to the Social Security Act, and special compensation for particular occupational diseases such as the black lung disease affecting coal miners. There was a growing realization that social problems in the world of work were caused not only by factors within the individual but also by the effects of a wide range of conditions within the workplace.

In the late 1960s and early 1970s, several large companies began to employ social workers in their personnel departments to deal with the mental health problems of their employees (Bloomquist, Gray, and Smith, 1979). Early programs tended to focus on problems related to alcoholism. But the number and scope of mental health programs have continued to grow. As the employer-based programs developed, so did programs developed by labor organizations. An early example was the Sidney Hillman Health Center of the Amalgamated Clothing Workers of America, a labor-funded mental health and rehabilitation program (Kurzman, 1983).

By the mid-1970s, not only were employers dealing with a new work force (women and minorities) and with the alienation of workers, but they also were being affected by new legislation such as the Occupational Safety and Health Act, the Age Discrimination in Employment Act, and Title VII of the Civil Rights Act. These, together with an increased emphasis on the quality of life, caused employers to realize the need for expert help in work-related social services. Some industries employed social workers to provide this needed expert help; other employers contracted with social service agencies.

The profession responded to this new demand for social workers. In 1970 the Industrial Social Welfare Center was established at the Columbia University School of Social Work. By 1974 Boston College, Hunter College, and the University of Utah also had industrial social work programs. From 1969 on, articles about social work in industrial settings began to appear in both *Social Work* and *Social Casework*. The National Association of Social Workers and the Council on Social Work Education underwrote a joint project on industrial social work that resulted in the First National Conference on Social Work Practice in Labor and Industrial Settings in 1978 (Kurzman, 1983). This conference yielded the first publication within this field, *Labor and Industrial Settings: Sites for Social Work Practice* by Akabas, Kurzman, and Kolben (1979). Industrial social work was well on its way to becoming an established field of practice.

However other steps were necessary if schools of social work were to prepare students for this field. The knowledge base underlying this field had to be defined and developed. According to Mor-Barak, Poverny, Finch, McCroskey, Nedelman, Seck, and Sullivan (1993), the profession is still struggling with conceptualization and implementation of a curriculum for industrial social work.

In 1982, a project to develop such material resulted in the publication of a book that provided at least a first specification of the necessary knowledge base for industrial social work students and practitioners. This book, *Work, Workers, and Work Organizations,* by Akabas and Kurzman (1982) laid much of the foundation for this area of social work practice. The contents include the meaning of work from a historical perspective, work and social policy, the place of work in human development, work related research, the nature of the workplace, and the special practice of the industrial social worker.

Another expansion of the industrial social work knowledge base was done by the faculty at the University of Southern California's School of Social Work since 1982. This M.S.W. program includes emphasis on cultural diversity in the workplace and trains practitioners in working with the modern ethnically diverse work setting. Another purpose of the program is to highlight social work's unique contribution to work organizations and settings. USC's faculty believe the industrial social worker must know the community's network of services and resources that can be enlisted to assist employers and employees in problem solving (Mor-Barak et al., 1993). The industrial field of practice has emerged.

Practice in the Industrial Setting

The new industrial field of practice came into being to serve a previously unmet need. The working-class population has been underserved by the social welfare system. Workers have not been eligible for many public services and have found the traditional private services unusable because of value conflicts, agencies' lack of responsiveness to their special needs, or high fees. But services delivered in the industrial setting have partially overcome these blocks. There, service is seen as an earned entitlement with no stigma attached to its use. There is no cost or little cost to the worker for using the service. Social workers in this field of practice have developed an understanding of the context of the work world. One very important aspect is the meaning of work to the individual. In our society, appropriately or inappropriately, individuals derive much of their identity from the work they do. If that work is not satisfying or does not provide a sense of accomplishment, people may feel a sense of alienation that affects both their work functioning and their social functioning.

What an industrial social worker does, and how, varies from setting to setting. The industrial social worker has assumed an increasingly expanded role as an advocate, labor negotiator, clinician, educator, and community liaison and organizer, according to Wegener (1992). Typically there are three primary modes of service delivery: within the structure of a company, usually within employee assistance services; within the structure of a labor union; and on a contractual basis with a social service agency. In this last mode, the social worker may actually go to the industrial setting, have a contract to provide services in the agency setting, or receive third-party payments (insurance reimbursement) for the service. Some social workers in industry also work with management as it carries out its civic responsibilities. For example, they may consult on corporate giving.

Ozawa (1980) notes that when social welfare service is provided in the industrial setting (company or union), there are four stages in the evolution of services. First, service is provided to deal with one or two specific problems, like alcoholism. At the second stage, the company or union recognizes that the specific problem is only a symptom of other underlying problems, and plans a more comprehensive program. Some of the services included in this comprehensive program may be counseling for personal, marital, or financial problems; crisis intervention; worker education about preretirement planning or health awareness; information and referrals; institution of self-help programs such as Alcoholics Anonymous; creation of recreational programs; or consulting with management on problems affecting workers and their productivity. At the third stage, the worker/recipient actually participates in identifying problems and proposing solutions. At the fourth stage, a blurring of the boundary between management and employees takes place, and worker/recipients share responsibility for implementing and managing programs.

Steiner and Borst (1980) found that the industry's motivation for providing services rests in one of three areas:

1.   They desire to increase employees' financial rewards. Just as higher wages are seen as a reward, so are social services.
2.   The service is a way of controlling employees, keeping them productive by reducing discontent and increasing well-being.
3.   The desire to increase therapeutic services is similar to the first concern but also includes the assumption that disease is the cause of the problems and should be treated.

It is important for the social worker in industry to be aware of the concerns of the employer and to find means for responding to those concerns while adhering to the ethical principles of social work.

In each field of practice, the social worker needs to be familiar with a special body of information about the history, tradition, functions, laws, and environments that affect the target population. When working in the industrial setting, the social worker must first understand the way industry and labor relate and function together and the structure and functioning of the particular setting. Each setting must be understood as its own social system. The social worker must know something about the history of industry and the history of management–labor relations in the United States. Observing the channels of power, decision making, and communications in the setting is also important. The social worker must learn how to work with new professional groups, such as laser engineers or computer programmers, and understand the culture of the blue-collar wage earner, the office support staffer, and the white-collar professional. The worker also has to become familiar with the local resource possibilities for client referral on a wide range of problems (Kurzman and Akabas, 1981).

An Example

This example will depict some of the activities that a social worker in an industrial setting may engage in.

Daily Schedule

8:00 A.M.	Arrive at work and review the calendar for the day. Note two new referrals. Contact to make appointments.
8:30 A.M.	Meet with vice-president to discuss company's participation in the upcoming United Way campaign. Discuss recent meeting for corporate givers. Answer vice-president's questions about the services of several agencies. Suggest content for a letter to be sent from management to employees urging their contributions to United Way campaign.
9:00 A.M.	Session with a worker and his wife who are having marital problems.
10:00 A.M.	First session with a worker who is in financial difficulty because of overuse of credit. Discuss possible solutions. Make an appointment to meet again in two days.
11:00 A.M.	Set aside for case write-up. A foreman drops in to discuss a worker he believes may be having an alcohol problem. Worker is missing work more often than usual and seems irritable. Suggest means for making a referral. Stress confidential nature of the service.
12:00 noon	Lunch.
1:00 P.M.	New client. Problem is lack of resources for a developmentally disabled child. Social worker explores feelings. Discuss possible resources. Make an appointment for client and wife for later in the week.
2:00 P.M.	Make phone calls to check out resources for the child and the family. Return four phone calls that have come in. Finish case write-up interrupted this morning.
3:00 P.M.	Conduct a session for employees who are approaching retirement.
4:30 P.M.	Spend time with participants who have concerns about some aspect of retirement.
5:30 P.M.	Review schedule for tomorrow.

Industrial social work is new and growing very rapidly. It is an exciting challenge for the worker and the profession to provide this new type of service in the workplace.

Issues in Industrial Social Work

Industrial social work is not only practice in a setting not primarily a social work setting, it is practice in a nontraditional setting focused on production, not service. In such a setting, inevitably there will be tensions and uncertainties between business goals and social work goals. Practitioners in industrial settings should be aware of these issues and work toward their resolution.

A primary issue is social work services' goal in the industrial setting. Is its goal to increase profits and productivity, industry's primary function? Or, if the setting is a labor union, is social work's goal to encourage loyalty to the union? Or is its goal to promote the common good of the workers? This latter goal implies a commitment to improve the quality of life for the work force. If the goal of industrial social work is not the last one mentioned, ethical conflicts for social workers will arise. It is very important that social workers recognize this conflict and seek some resolution for themselves.

Related to the issue of conflicting purposes is the issue of placement of the industrial social work service. If it is located with either a company or a union's offices, the social worker may feel pressure to serve the interests of the union or the industry, rather than the interests of the workers. A skilled social worker helps the sponsoring organization see that the best interest of the workers and those of the sponsoring body are indeed related, that they must recognize the unity of those interests. The best way to address placement issues may be to locate the service in a neutral setting, such as a social service agency, or to use a third-party payment mechanism (Jorgensen, 1981).

Another important issue is confidentiality. Social agency records kept on individual workers must not become a part of the personnel file of that worker. Social workers need to explain skillfully the need for this protection. They also must be skillful in explaining the value of the service to individuals and to the sponsoring body without providing specific client-related information. Because this sometimes makes referrals difficult, referral sources sometimes need special help understanding this stance (Kurzman, 1983).

As in other fields of practice in which social work is not the primary profession, there is competition with other professions, especially psychology, over who should provide employee assistance services. As in other fields, social work must demonstrate just what its expertise is and how it can be of service to employer and employees.

Another issue encompasses many concerns that arise from economic security. In a time of growing unemployment rates, plant closings, relocations, significant frustration and stress are present in the work place. What the role of social work is in responding to these conditions remains unclear. This relates to the tension of identifying the client, the employer, or the employee.

Other concerns of employees that social work could well address are such areas as retirement planning, child care concerns, and concern about care for older family members. One employee concern that is related to the benefit package is the erosion of the value of health insurance coverage. Does social work have a role in decisions about health care benefits or other elements of the benefit package? The question can still be asked whether employment assistance programs are a luxury fringe benefit or a right for all workers.

As this new field of practice, industrial social work, develops, it has great potential to become a needed resource in the social welfare system. Workers can be served in the workplace where their special needs can be considered. The workplace can become a more humane place, and thus some problems can be prevented. The provision of universal services, so necessary in a complex society, can be closer to reality in the near future.

Rural Social Work: A Historical Perspective

The second emerging field of practice is rural social work. Like industrial social work, this context received the attention of social workers in the past but seemed to die out before it became an established field of practice, only to reemerge in recent years.

It is hard to define *rural social work*: it is hard to define the word *rural*. The U.S. Census Bureau considers areas rural if they have under 2,500 people in any incorporated area. This would include very small towns and open country. Others define rural in terms of cultural characteristics (Bealer, Willits, and Kuvlesky, 1965). Louise Johnson, one of this text's authors, has suggested that *nonmetropolitan* might be a better classification. That is, rural social work is practiced in any community with fewer than 50,000 people (the minimum U.S. Census designation for metropolitan communities). There are two reasons for this suggestion. First, services to small communities are not delivered from towns with a population of 2,500 or less but, rather, from larger communities whose services reach out to the very small communities. Second, there is a distinct difference in both the service delivery system and some of the practice strategies once a community falls into the nonmetropolitan category (Johnson, 1977). Finally, this classification takes into account the cultural definitions of rurality. The nonmetropolitan community does function within a rural culture. In this chapter, then, rural social work will refer to social work practice in nonmetropolitan communities.

If the context of practice is the identifying characteristic, it is important to identify how rural social work practice differs from practice in metropolitan areas. First, the service delivery system is smaller and depends very heavily on the public social service agency. Second, that system functions more informally in its relationships with its component parts, agencies and service deliverers. Third, the people living in these areas are most comfortable with an informal rather than a formal style of functioning. Fourth, the rural helping system places much more reliance on self-help, natural helpers, and grass-roots groups, with fewer of the traditional services found in metropolitan communities. Fifth, the rural culture is more interested in individuals than in the degrees or positions they hold. And rural roles overlap; that is, people carry several important roles at the same time. For example, local politicians may also be full-time business people. Sixth, there is more attention paid to ecological concerns, such as weather. The definition of rural social work, then, is a contextual definition that takes into account not only a census classification but the characteristics of that population.

Before 1969

Because the modern social welfare system developed in response to the industrialization of society, it is no wonder that the system has not considered the particular needs of the rural society. The earlier heavy reliance on the self-help approach continued to be the major means of providing for human needs in rural areas. As institutions, poorhouses, mental hospitals, orphanages, and the like developed, they were used to meet the needs of some rural people, particularly "outsiders." The COS and settlement house movements had little effect on rural areas, and public welfare has never been an acceptable approach in rural areas. The Social Security Act's social insurance arrangements did not originally cover farmers and other self-employed people, thus offering little protection to rural populations. Overall, the system of social welfare that developed in the United States had limited impact on rural people.

However, the specific social functioning needs of rural people were not completely ignored. Table 14–2 gives a brief chronological history of rural social work. In 1908 Theodore Roosevelt appointed the Country Life Commission, whose functions included developing awareness of the needs of rural communities. Emilia E. Martinez-Brawley (1981), the historian of rural social work, considers this the "genesis of rural social work." As a result of the Country Life Commission, the National Conference on Charities and Corrections and several

TABLE 14–2   Important Dates: Rural Social Work

1908	The Country Life Commission was appointed by President Theodore Roosevelt.
1920s	The 4-H Clubs were established.
1927	Grace Abbott, chief of the Children's Bureau, discussed rural child welfare standards.
1933	*The Rural Community and Social Casework* by Josephine Brown was published.
1969	Leon Ginsberg presented a paper, "Education for Social Work in Rural Settings," at the Annual Program Meeting of the Council on Social Work Education.
1972	The Rural Task Force of the Southern Regional Education Board Manpower and Education and Training Project was created.
1973	The Council on Social Work Education workshops on "Education for Social Work in Rural and Small Communities" were presented.
1974	*Social Work in Rural Communities: A Book of Readings*, edited by Leon Ginsberg, was published.
1976	The first annual National Institute on Social Work in Rural Areas was held in Knoxville, Tennessee.
1976	The journal *Human Service in the Rural Environment* began publication.

schools of social work gave some attention to the need for services to rural people. *Survey* the most important social work journal of the time, also published articles on rural problems and needs. During World War I, the Home Service of the Red Cross developed a regional approach to social service delivery and recognized the special characteristics of rural people and their social service needs. During the 1920s, some attention continued to be paid to the rural culture. 4-H Clubs were established in the U.S. Department of Agriculture Extension programs. These became the group work mechanism for rural youth, much as scouting was the mechanism for urban youth. In fact, Extension Services provided many programs for farm families that can be seen as a part of the social welfare system. It is interesting to note that these services were universal and nonstigmatizing.

Many economic problems plagued the rural United States in the first two decades of the twentieth century, but the farmer and the surrounding community still seemed to have the capacity to provide for their basic needs. Farming still had a subsistence aspect, which helped people provide for at least their own needs. With the onset of the Depression, however, the problems of rural America were especially great. Not only were farm prices down, but drought prevented the raising of subsistence crops. The emergency measures of the early 1930s benefited urban and rural people alike. The Roosevelt administration's Agriculture Adjustment Act (AAA) addressed farm problems. It was aimed mostly at commercial farmers and provided means for controlling the market and providing farm subsidies. Farm subsidies can be considered a form of social welfare; they are a type of universal provision and thus are seldom seen as welfare, but they have helped meet the fiscal needs of the agricultural segment of U.S. society (Martinez-Brawley, 1980).

In 1927 Grace Abbott, then chief of the Children's Bureau, spoke to the National Conference on Social Work about standards for rural child welfare. The child welfare provisions of the Social Security Act of 1935 included services to these children. Because of these provisions, social workers began to provide social services in rural areas, and they quickly identified the differences between rural and metropolitan social work. Training for these workers was largely done under the Federal Emergency Relief Administration, often in the land grant colleges. Two influential books that showed the differences between rural and urban practices appeared by the late 1930s: Josephine Brown's (1933) text, *The Rural Community and Social Casework,* and Grace Browning's (1941) *Rural Public Welfare. Social Work Year Books* and professional journals contained articles on rural social work. Schools of social work started paying attention to this budding field of practice.

But the growth did not continue. By the 1940s, the farm problem seemed to have ended. Social work was then moving toward a psychoanalytical base for practice, and it showed less and less concern for how the environment affected the individual. Probably the biggest detriment to the development of rural social work was the movement in social work education to demand graduate education for professional practice. The demise of the National Association of Schools of Social Administration (discussed in Chapter 6) meant that the undergraduate programs preparing the bulk of the workers for rural areas were no longer recognized. It should be remembered that practice in rural areas was largely in public agencies that had limited numbers of master's-level practitioners. Also, rural people tend to be suspicious of outsiders with "credentials," who often fail to understand their rural lifestyle and try to impose methods of work developed for metropolitan settings. Public social services in rural areas continued to develop and grow as federal funds became more available. Universities in rural states continued to prepare students for work in public welfare agencies; but these programs, usually found in sociology departments, lacked the sanction of the social work profession. Rural social work disappeared from the professional literature.

Since 1969

During the late 1960s, several changes supported the reemergence of rural social work. The NASW voted to recognize baccalaureate graduates of approved programs as professional social workers, and the CSWE developed accreditation standards for such programs. The social welfare programs that had operated since the early 1950s were again acknowledged. This in turn allowed for the professionalization of services in many rural areas.

The unrest of the early 1960s had led social work to develop many new kinds of practice and to move into many new practice settings. The traditional psychoanalytic framework came into question. Social workers began to consider not only individuals but also the environmental aspects of human behavior. This was in part due to the "discovery" of social systems theory. Interest developed in what at that time was known as integrated practice, a practice that combined casework, group work, and community organization. In retrospect, these new practice approaches were much more acceptable to rural people.

The Appalachian Redevelopment Act of 1965 provided considerable funds for the provision of services to the Appalachian Mountain region. Health and social service agencies were important recipients of the available funds. Most important, different approaches to practice and different service delivery patterns, were created for this rural area.

The contemporary rural social work movement dates its reawakening from 1969, when a paper on "Education for Social Work in Rural Settings" was presented by Leon Ginsberg, then director of West Virginia University's Division of Social Work. In the years that followed, a small group of practitioners in various sections of the rural United States began to organize special knowledge bases for work in these settings and to present papers at national meetings.

In June 1970 a workshop sponsored by the Minnesota Resource Center for Undergraduate Social Work Education, "Effecting Rural Service Delivery through Education," was held. In 1972 a Rural Task Force of the Southern Regional Education Board Manpower and Education and Training Project created a statement of educational assumptions for educators preparing social workers for positions in rural areas. In 1973 the CSWE sponsored a series of workshops around the country called "Education for Social Work in the Rural and Small Community." Joanne Mermelstein and Paul Sundet of the University of Missouri were the resource people for these workshops. Papers continued to be presented at national conferences on rural social work. A few of these found their way into the literature. In 1974 the CSWE published *Social Work in Rural Communities: A Book of Readings,* edited by Leon Ginsberg.

The First Annual National Institute on Social Work in Rural Areas was held in Knoxville, Tennessee, in July 1976. Since then, annual meetings have been sponsored each summer by social work schools and programs with an interest in rural social work. The proceedings of these meetings provide an important contribution to the literature about rural social work. A journal, *Human Services in the Rural Environment,* began publication. It is now published by the School of Social Work at Eastern Washington University. At the Knoxville Institute, the Rural Social Work Caucus was founded. This loose-knit group of social workers with a concern for rural social work meets at most national social work conferences and has strongly advocated with both the NASW and the CSWE for recognition of rural social work as a field of practice. The caucus has been particularly successful in having rural content on the programs at most national social work conferences. Several books have been published on rural social work practice (Johnson, 1980; Farley et al., 1982; Watkins and Watkins, 1984). All in all, rural social work has again emerged as a field of practice.

Practice in Rural Settings

Two important considerations must be kept in mind when working in nonmetropolitan settings. First, the rural human services delivery system is different from that of metropolitan communities. Second, there are greater differences among rural population groups than there are among groups in metropolitan areas. Each of these factors heavily influences the nature of practice in rural areas. Another generally agreed upon assumption about practice in rural settings is that practice should be in the *generalist social work* model.

Not only is the rural service delivery system smaller, but its structure varies. Some communities have a variety of agencies, with emphasis on the public agencies located in the community. Other communities, especially very small ones, have no formal agencies located in the community. All communities must rely on some metropolitan-based services for very special needs—for example, those of a child with a rare disease. The formal agencies located in nonmetropolitan communities often provide outreach services to the smaller communities in their region. There is also a tendency for there to be more informal coordination among agencies than in larger communities. The other important difference in the service delivery system is the strength of the natural helping system. This system is akin to the mutual help network, but at times also takes on a more contemporary organization. This may be in the form of coalitions (e.g., against domestic violence or on aging) or organizations that provide resources (e.g., used clothing stores, food pantries). Community institutions such as churches and organizations such as service clubs are often heavily involved in the response to needs. Social workers must be able to work with a wide variety of people and must understand the differences between formal and informal functioning. Much time is spent linking people with needed resources of which they are unaware, and helping community groups accomplish their goals. Rural social workers also help formal agencies with traditional, large-city modes of functioning to respond to the needs of rural people in ways that are acceptable to and usable by them (Johnson, 1977).

When considering the differences among the various rural population groups, it is important to remember that some of the most discriminated-against minority groups are from rural areas (rural southern African Americans, Native Americans, and Hispanics). These groups often fall outside the mainstream, formal, community helping system. They do, however, have their own natural helping systems. The social worker often must play mediating and advocacy roles on behalf of these groups. There are many other nationality-based ethnic groups in rural areas. These groups have their own cultures; to work with them effectively, the social worker must understand the way the particular culture functions. Not all rural people are farmers; some are engaged in mining, logging, or the recreation industry, to name a few. Each group has its own lifestyle, its own particular problems. There are boom towns; there are dying communities: The social worker in rural areas must adapt practice to people's

A Case Study

A social worker stationed in a community that provides services to five surrounding counties has discovered that in Small Town there are a number of older women who are living alone. As these women reach the age of about seventy-five, they find it a struggle simply to maintain themselves in their own homes. Some are no longer cooking adequate meals for themselves. They are all worried about falling and not being discovered for several days. It is also difficult for them to shop or get to the doctor, let alone go to church or community functions, because they do not drive and are no longer able to walk downtown.

The social worker has previously identified the influential people in this community as the pastor of the major church, a county commissioner, and two women who belong to several organizations and have been helpful in the past in identifying natural helping resources in the community. The social worker talks to each of these individuals about her concern for the elderly. Each names several other people they are aware of who are isolated. They admit that they have known a problem existed but have been unaware of its extent and unsure of what to do. The social worker asks these four people to meet with her so that together they can

decide what might be done. After some discussion, this group calls a community meeting to discuss the problem. In preparation for this meeting, they ask that the weekly paper run an article on the problem and publicize the meeting.

Fifty people attend the meeting. A committee is formed to make suggestions on how the problem can be handled by using community resources. As the result of a long process, four different solutions are implemented: the community organizes a nutrition site; the nursing home provides home-delivered meals; a telephone reassurance system in instituted; and a volunteer network offers essential transportation for these isolated older people. After two years, the worker notes that much more informal helping is going on with these elderly women. They are visited regularly by church visitors and friends; they are provided with transportation for church and other community events. The worker now finds it much easier to serve these individuals because she has a well-developed resource system to rely on. Also, she finds she has much more visibility and acceptance in the community, so that many situations are brought to her attention before they reach the crisis stage.

needs within their cultural constraints and environmental conditions, and use the resources available within that culture.

Observing rural practitioners leads to the conclusion that they must be skilled in the use of crisis intervention, mediation, support, problem solving, resource brokering, working with multiproblem families, coordination, program development, and working for change in organizations. They also need at least some ability to work with various problems and age groups, although there is some tendency to specialize in these areas because of the way service agencies split the work to be done. Rural social workers need to be true generalists (Johnson, 1984).

Issues in Rural Social Work

One of the major problems faced by the rural social worker is recognition by those who work in metropolitan areas and those trained to work in such areas that the rural context indeed calls for a different kind of social work practice. The lack of recognition is particularly troublesome when the rural worker must depend on metropolitan services for specialized needs. It also causes difficulty when the worker is a part of the state social welfare agency. These agencies often are dominated by administrators with a bureaucratic orientation incongruent with the rural way of functioning.

A related concern is the education of rural social workers. Most graduate schools of social work are located in large cities. A few, such as the University of Missouri, do offer a specialized curriculum in rural social work. Many baccalaureate programs are located in rural areas and prepare social workers for rural practice; the University of South Dakota program is one. Some believe that the baccalaureate worker has always been the major provider of service to the rural areas and that the acceptance of the baccalaureate degree as professional has upgraded services in rural areas. Questions continue to be asked about the ideal educational program for rural social work practice. Much still remains to be done to develop the information base and practices needed for such work.

Another concern is how to adapt a profession developed in response to problems of industrialization and urbanization to meet the needs of the rural population. Attention should be paid to defining and differentiating between social work practice for all individuals, families, groups, and communities, and social work practice for only rural or only metropolitan service.

A final concern is how to develop means for coordinating the informal and formal systems of helping. Both are essential if individuals in rural communities are to have their needs met, but because of the different ways the formal and informal systems function, the essential coordination of services is difficult. Social workers need to see that rural communities do not always have fewer resources for helping, but instead have *different* resources.

Each of these issues must be addressed if the rural field of practice is to continue to grow and develop. As social workers gain more experience and carry out the essential knowledge building and research, certainly these issues will be addressed and resolved. The new rural field of practice will meet the needs of individuals often overlooked or inappropriately served by the U.S. social welfare system.

Summary

A comparison of the two new fields of practice, industrial and rural, discussed in this chapter yields some commonalities even though the settings are different. As has been stated earlier, they are both contextual fields of practice; that is, they both take a person's environment into consideration. They both call for the social worker to go where the needs are, to reach out to people in their natural settings. In addition, each has a very strong linking function; that is, they connect people with the resources available to them and facilitate their use of the resources. This also involves helping traditional resources (social service agencies) understand the particular needs and ways of functioning of workers and rural populations. Both fields of practice call for adapting traditional ways of meeting human needs. Both also place social workers in a position where tensions exist—tension between labor and management, and tension between the informal way of rural functioning and the formal functioning of government agencies. Both call for workers who are flexible, who can listen to all parties involved in a situation, and who are creative in designing intervention strategies.

These two fields of practice reflect a perspective that calls for social services to be available within people's everyday environment. They are practices that are ecological in nature, practices that involve a wide range of individuals, influential and otherwise, in the development of the service delivery system. They are also practices that place emphasis on short-term service and the development of strong personal support systems. And they are practices that are moving toward universal provision that works with and supports the self-help mechanisms of communities.

Key Terms

generalist social work

industrial social work

nonmetropolitan

rural

rural social work

workplace

References

Akabas, S. H., & Kurzman, P. A. (1982). *Work, workers, and work organizations: a view from social work.* Englewood Cliffs, NJ: Prentice-Hall.

Akabas, S. H., Kurzman, P. A., & Kolben, N. S. (1979). *Labor and industrial settings: sites for social work practice.* New York: Council on Social Work Education.

Bealer, R. C., Willits, F. K., & Kuvlesky, W. P. (1965). The meaning of 'rurality' in American society: some implications of alternative definitions. *Rural Sociology, 30* (September), 255–266.

Bloomquist, D. C., Gray, D. D., & Smith L. L. (1979). Social work in business and industry. *Social Casework, 60* (October), 457–462.

Brown, J. C. (1933). *The rural community and social case work.* New York: Family Welfare Association of America.

Browning, G. (1941). *Rural public welfare: selected records.* Chicago, IL: The University of Chicago Press.

Farley, O. W. et al. (1982). *Rural social work practice.* New York: Free Press.

Hall, F. S. (Ed.). (1930). *Social work year book, 1929.* New York: Russell Sage Foundation.

Johnson, H. W. (1980). *Rural human services: a book of readings.* Itasca, IL: F. E. Peacock.

Johnson, L.C. (1977). Social development in non-metropolitan areas. In R. K. Green & S. A. Webster (Eds.),

Social work in rural areas: preparation and practice. Knoxville, TN: University of Tennessee School of Social Work.

Johnson, L. C. (1980). Human service delivery patterns in nonmetropolitan communities. In H. W. Johnson (Ed.), *Rural human services: a book of readings* (pp. 65–74). Itasca, IL: F. E. Peacock.

Johnson, L. C. (1984). Nonmetropolitan services delivery revisited: insights from a dozen years of participant observation. *Human Services in the Rural Environment, 9* (2), 21–26.

Jorgensen, L. A. B. (1981). Social services in business and industry. In N. Gilbert & H. Specht (Eds.), *Handbook of social services.* Englewood Cliffs, NJ: Prentice-Hall, pp. 337–352.

Kurzman, P. A. (1983). Ethical issues in industrial social work practice. *Social Casework, 64* (February), 105–111.

Kurzman, P. A. & Akabas, S. H. (1981). Industrial social work as an arena for practice. *Social Work, 1981* (January), 52–60.

Kurzman, P. A. (1983). Industrial (occupational social work). In S. Briar, A. Minahan, E. Pinderhughes & T. Tripodi (Eds.), *1983–1984 Supplement to the encyclopedia of social work* (17th ed.), pp. 57–68. Silver Springs, MD: National Association of Social Workers.

Martinez-Brawley, E. E. (Ed.). (1980). *Pioneer efforts on rural social welfare: firsthand view since 1908.* University Park, PA: Pennsylvania State University Press.

Martinez-Brawley, E. E. (1981). *Seven decades of rural social work: from country life commission to rural caucus.* New York: Praeger.

Mor-Barak, M. E., Poverny, L. M., Finch, W. A., McCroskey, J., Nedelman, H. L., Seck, E. T., & Sullivan, R. (1993). A model curriculum for occupational social work. *Journal of Social Work Education, 29* (1), 63–77.

Ozawa, M. N. (1980). Development of social services in industry: why and how? *Social Work, 25* (November), 464–470.

Popple, P. R. (1981). Social work practice in business and industry. *Social Service Review, 55* (June), 257–269.

Reynolds, B. C. (1951). *Social work and social living.* New York: Citadel Press.

Steiner, J. R., & Borst, E. C. (1980). Industrial settings: underdeveloped opportunities for social work services. *Arete, 6* (Fall), 1–11.

Warner, A. G., Queen, S. A., & Harper, E. B. (1930). *American charities and social work* (4th ed.). New York: Thomas Y. Crowell.

Watkins, J. M. & Watkins, D. A. (1984). *Social policy and the rural setting.* New York: Springer.

Wegener, N. (1992). Supportive group services in the workplace: the practice and the potential. *Social Work with Groups, 15* (2/3), 207–22.

Suggested Readings

Industry

Akabas, Sheila, and Kurzman, Paul A. *Work, Workers, and Work Organizations: A View from Social Work* (Englewood Cliffs, NJ: Prentice-Hall, 1982).

Akabas, Sheila; Kurzman, Paul A.; and Kolben, Nancy S., eds. *Labor and Industrial Settings: Sites for Social Work Practice* (New York: Council on Social Work Education, 1979).

Austin, Michael J., and Jackson, Erwin. "Occupational Mental Health and the Human Services: A Review." *Health and Social Work,* 2 (February 1977), 93–118.

Bakalinsky, Rosalie. "People versus Profits: Social Work in Industry." *Social Work,* 25 (November 1980), 471–475.

Balgopal, Pallassana R. "Occupational Social Work: An Expanded Clinical Perspective," *Social Work,* 34 (Sept. 1989), 437–442,

Googins, Bradley, and Godfrey, Joline. "The Evolution of Occupational Social Work." *Social Work,* 30 (September–October 1985) 396–402.

Jorgensen, Lou Ann B. "Social Services in Business and Industry." In Neil Gilbert and Harry Specht, eds., *Handbook of the Social Services* (Englewood Cliffs, NJ: Prentice-Hall, 1981), pp. 337–352.

Kurzman, Paul A. "Ethical Issues in Industrial Social Work Practice." *Social Casework,* 64 (February 1983), 105–111.

Kurzman, Paul A. "Industrial Social Work (Occupational Social Work)," in Anne Minahan, ed. (*Encyclopedia of Social Work,* 18th ed. Silver Springs, MD: National Association of Social Workers), 1987, Vol. 1, pp. 899–910.

Kurzman, Paul A., and Akabas, Sheila H. "Industrial Social Work as an Arena for Practice." *Social Work,* 26 (January 1981), 52–60.

Mudrick, Nancy R. "An Underdeveloped Role for Occupational Social Work: Facilitating the Employment of People with Disabilities." *Social Work,* 36 (Nov. 1991), 490–495.

Ozawa, Martha N. "Development of Social Services in Industry: Why and How?" *Social Work,* 25 (November 1980), 434–470.

Popple, Philip R. "Social Work Practice in Business and Industry, 1875–1930." *Social Service Review,* 55 (June 1981), 257–269.

Social Work, "Special Issue: Social Work in an Industrial Setting." 33 (Jan–Feb. 1988).

Straussner, Shulamith Lala Ashenberg. "Comparison of In-House and Contracted-Out Employee Assistance Programs." *Social Work,* 33 (January–February 1988), 53–55.

Rural

Bealer, Robert C.; Willits, Fern K.; and Kuvlesky, William P. "The Meaning of 'Rurality' in American Society: Some Implications of Alternative Definitions." *Rural Sociology,* 30 (September 1965), 255–266.

Davis, Laura F. "Rural Attitudes Toward Public Welfare Allocation." *Human Services in the Rural Environment* 12 (Fall 1988), 11–19.

Davis, Laura F. "Rural Attitudes Toward Women, Work, and Welfare." *Affilia* 3 (Winter 1988), 69–79.

Denton, Roy T.; York, Reginald O.; and Moran, James R. "The Social Worker's View of the Rural Commu-

nity: An Empirical Examination." *Human Services in the Rural Environment* 11 (Winter 1988), 14–21.

Edwards, Richard L. "Reaganomics and Rural America." *Human Services in the Rural Environment,* 11 (Spring 1988), 14–19.

Farley, O. William; Griffiths, Kenneth A.; Skidmore, Rex A.; and Thackeray, Milton G. *Rural Social Work Practice* (New York: Free Press 1982).

Fieno, Judith Ivy and Taylor, Patricia A. "Serving Rural Families of Developmentally Disabled Children: A Case Management Model." *Social Work,* 36 (July 1991), 323–327.

Ginsberg, Leon H. *Social Work in Rural Communities: A Book of Readings* (New York: Council on Social Work Education, 1976).

Green, Ronald K., and Webster, Stephen A., eds. *Social Work in Rural Areas* (Knoxville: University of Tennessee School of Social Work, 1977).

Johnson, H. Wayne. *Rural Human Services: A Book of Readings* (Itasca, IL: F. E. Peacock, 1980).

Johnson, Louise C. "Nonmetropolitan Service Delivery Revisited: Insights from a Dozen Years of Participant Observations." *Human Services in the Rural Environment,* 9 (No. 2, 1984), 21–26.

Martinez-Brawley, Emilia E. and Blundall, Joan. "Farm Families: Preferences toward the Personal Social Services." *Social Work,* 34 (Nov. 1989), 513–522.

Martinez-Brawley, Emilia E. "Rural Social Work." In Anne Minahan, ed., *Encyclopedia of Social Work,* 18th ed. (Silver Springs, MD: National Association of Social Workers, 1987), Vol. 2, pp. 521–537.

Martinez-Brawley, Emilia E. "Rural Social Work as a Contextual Specialty: Undergraduate Focus or Graduate Concentration?" *Journal of Social Work Education,* 21 (Fall 1985), 36–42.

Watkins, Julia M., and Watkins, Dennis A. *Social Policy and the Rural Setting* (New York: Springer, 1984).

15

THE CONTEMPORARY SOCIAL WELFARE SYSTEM

Learning Expectations

- Understanding of one framework for use in the analysis of a social welfare system
- Integrative view of the concepts presented in this book
- Understanding of the complexity of contemporary social problems and of the possible approaches to alleviate them
- Understanding of some of the structural changes that could be made in the U.S. social welfare system to make it more responsive to the people it is meant to serve
- Understanding of some of the questions facing the social work profession as it functions within the social welfare system

This book has considered the U.S. social welfare system as the chief means our society uses to meet human needs. The text has done this by discussing factors that have contributed to the development of the contemporary system. First general trends were considered; then specific fields of practice were discussed. In this chapter, discussion again returns to the whole system, to help the reader form an integrated picture of our social welfare system and thus pull together the information provided in the earlier chapters of the book. First, the chapter presents a framework for analysis that shows the relationships among the major themes presented in the book. This framework is used to show how any response by the social welfare system to human needs can be analyzed and better understood. This then provides a basis for considering modifications that may be needed if the system is to fulfill its purposes. Next, the chapter discusses several major issues facing the contemporary social welfare system and several contemporary social problems in relation to the capacity of the social welfare system to respond to them. This leads to a discussion of the present structure of the system as it affects its capacity to meet human

needs in the contemporary world. The future of the social work profession as a part of the social welfare system is also considered. Finally, the chapter suggests some steps for the student to
take to gain a greater understanding of the system.

A Framework for Analysis

One way to understand a complex system like the U.S. social welfare system is to identify several major concepts that explain the nature of that system, and then to develop an analytical
framework that shows the relationships of the parts (the major concepts) to the whole (the social welfare system). Such a framework is presented in Figure 15–1, which shows the relationship of the major themes of this book to each other. The center of the framework is occupied
by the *human needs* concept. Human needs were defined, at the beginning of this book, as
those resources that people must have if they are to survive as individuals and function appropriately in the social situation of which they are a part (see Chapter 1). It should be apparent
from subsequent discussion that human needs are both individual and collective. A major impetus for the development of the social welfare system was the society's need to have a means
for helping individuals, families, groups of individuals, and communities meet needs they are
unable to provide for themselves. The book also developed other major themes that explain, at
least in part, the reasons for unmet needs and how the social welfare system responds to needs.

Conditions giving rise to needs or major contributors to human needs were identified as social change, poverty, lack of resources, and prejudice and discrimination. Other contributors
also could be identified, such as chronic illness or disability, status as a dependent person (children or the frail elderly), or lack of opportunity in education or work; but the four contributors listed here are the major sources of difficulty in meeting human needs, and the other
contributors have their roots in them.

FIGURE 15–1   An Analytic Framework: U.S. Social Welfare System

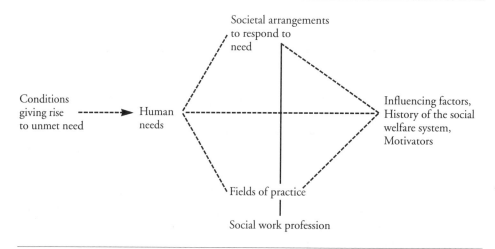

Another theme of the framework is *societal arrangements to respond to need.* This theme was also discussed in Chapter 1. Arrangements identified and discussed were: mutual aid, charity-philanthropy, public welfare, social insurance, social services, and universal provision. These arrangements refer to the different kinds of private and government structures and philosophies that have come into existence to help needy people. When analyzing how any need is met by the social welfare system, it is useful first to determine the arrangement traditionally used to meet the need, the strengths and limitations of that arrangement, and whether the traditional arrangement is the most appropriate one to use.

Contributing to the decision of which arrangement to use are two influencing factors: the *history of the social welfare system* and *motivators.* The historical development of our social welfare system was analyzed in two ways: Chapter 1 discussed the major milestones of its development, and Part Two presented the historical development in each field. The motivators—mutual aid, religion, politics, economics, and ideology—were presented in Chapter 1 and referred to from time to time throughout the book. Usually, more than one motivator has influenced the choice of an arrangement to meet a particular need. To understand the choice, one must first understand the influence of both the historical context of the arrangement and the societal motivations for providing for that need. Looking at the choice in terms of that kind of analysis also provides clues to other choices that might have been made.

Fields of practice was the organizing framework for Part Two. The fields of practice discussed were: income maintenance services, child welfare, health care, mental health services, correctional services, gerontological services, industrial social services, and rural social services. Also discussed as fields of practice were group services, community organization, and family services. In addition, these services could have been divided into other sets of fields of practice. Some would include health and mental health in one field of practice, some would include children and family services into one field, and others would suggest that developmental disabilities constitute a separate field of practice. Still others would not consider rural social work a field of practice. What is important to remember is that the social welfare system developed and is organized around a number of distinct fields of practice and that services do originate in those organized subsystems. Some fields, such as health care and services to children, are seen in a more positive light by the general public than are income maintenance or correctional services. Society's response to needs is influenced not only by the traditional organization of services within a particular field of practice but also by how much that field is valued and supported by the general public. In analyzing how any need is met, it is important to consider which field of practice has traditionally met the need and the structure of its services. Furthermore, it is important to ask if the field being used is the most appropriate one and whether its services are structured to meet the need in the most effective and efficient manner.

It is within the fields of practice that the *social work profession* has evolved. This evolution is discussed in Chapter 6. The fields of practice not only have been a major influence on the development of the profession, but social work practice has influenced the services provided in each field. Thus, the analysis also should ask questions about the social work profession within the field of practice. These questions should include: What social work practice modality(s) are traditionally used to meet the need? Has the response been effective? Why or why not? What changes need to be made in the professional response to the need?

The major themes presented in the book should now fit into a framework for analysis. The following example further clarifies its use. To use the analytical framework, a particular need is identified—whether it is one individual's need or many people's need. Then that need is analyzed from three perspectives: conditions that give rise to the need, arrangements the social welfare system uses to respond to it, and the fields of practice that deal with it. Influencing factors, such as historical development and motivators, are also considered, as are the practice methods used by social workers to respond to the need. With this understanding, current problem(s) in meeting that need can then be examined in order to find solutions.

Identification of Needs

Loneliness and isolation have been identified in a number of needs assessments concerned with services to the elderly in small communities. The population affected comprises primarily single individuals, often widows, over seventy-five years of age, and living alone in small towns or on farms. These people find it increasingly difficult to get out to attend business or social functions, even to shop. Their children tend to live at some distance and thus not be available for day-to-day help and companionship (Johnson, L.C., 1985).

Conditions Giving Rise to Need

Social change is the major contributor to this need. As pointed out in Chapter 2, older people are living longer, and the U.S. population tends to be more mobile than in the past. This creates a longer period of life when people become frail and not able to get around, but at the same time are without the daily support of an extended family, unlike earlier generations. Thus, another contributor to this problem is a lack of appropriate social supports as substitutes. The problems of loneliness and isolation are not simply the lack of vital social interaction with others, there is also a risk that without people to care for them, these older women will face premature institutionalization or a fall, other injury, or illness.

Traditional Arrangement Used to Meet the Need

As noted, the traditional arrangement has been mutual aid, depending on the family for assistance. But the rise in the number of older people with these needs, and mobility and the subsequent removal of traditional family resources, have shifted this responsibility to other parts of the mutual aid arrangement: friends, neighbors, and others. As society ages, some of these resource persons are also reaching a point in life where they not only are unable to meet the needs of someone else but may have loneliness and isolation problems themselves.

More recently, the social service arrangement has been used to provide some monitoring and transportation services. But with cutbacks in funds for social services, it has been impossible to meet these needs fully through the social service arrangement. The social services arrangement may have been a poor choice. The kind of help needed is one where the helper is available fairly often and with a quick response in case of an emergency. The social worker often cannot respond in this way because of large caseloads, and this is probably a poor use of the skilled professional.

The institutional arrangement also has been used, placing these individuals in nursing homes. This is very disruptive to the life-style of older people and is something they often resist. This institutional arrangement is also very expensive, often calling for the use of government funds to support the placement.

The use of traditional mutual aid may indeed be the best response to this kind of need. However, resources other than family and age peers must be developed. Research has shown that this is the most available and usable arrangement (Litwak, 1985). Mutual aid and religious motivators support the use of the arrangement. Current economic and political motivators also support its use because limited funds for services and an uninterested political climate make resources that do not require government funding very acceptable and the resources of choice where possible.

Field of Practice

Two fields of practice traditionally respond to this need, gerontological and rural social work. These two fields are not mutually exclusive, as one responds to an age group and one to a specific context of practice. Both fields have made use of volunteers and natural helpers as part of the service delivery system. Both fields have special understandings that must be drawn on when designing a response to the needs of the rural elderly. Another field of practice that might be concerned is the health-care field. Recently there has been a trend toward "medicalizing the process of aging" and tying the delivery of services to older individuals to medically determined needs. But it is questionable whether loneliness and isolation can or should be related to medical need.

Analysis of the Problem in Meeting Needs

The problem in meeting needs, then, lies not in the arrangement or the field of practice but in the resource being expected to meet the needs. Many social workers who work with elderly people living alone use a community approach within a generalist method and develop motivation for a younger population (largely the younger elderly, those from sixty to seventy-five years of age) to provide the needed friendly visiting, telephone reassurance, and transportation services. This response has been effective in many communities. The strategy used by the social workers places major responsibility for planning and providing those resources in the community. This is congruent with rural culture and with what is acceptable to the frail elderly person. It requires a limited professional input and thus is economically and politically acceptable. The changes that need to be made are as follows:

1. Social workers working with the elderly in rural communities should devote part of their time to motivating and supporting the community in meeting this need.
2. They should continue to make use of the mutual aid arrangement, but with different segments of the informal system than have previously been used. A segment motivated by mutual aid and religion, and also with the time and physical capacity to provide the needed resource, should be used.

Thus we see how the use of an analytical framework enhances the understanding of an identified need. This understanding then gives direction to the choice of responses to the need. Choices made after an in-depth analysis of the need provide some assurance that the response will be one that not only can provide the needed resources but also can do so in a manner that will be supportable by the immediate situation in which the need exists and within the larger societal context. The analytical framework also recognizes the complexity of the U.S. social welfare system.

Contemporary Social Problems

Throughout this book, references have been made to contemporary social problems that the social welfare system should address. These include homelessness (Chapter 7); violence, particularly in the home (Chapters 8 and 13); and AIDS (Chapter 9). Other issues that are also facing contemporary society and that affect the delivery of social welfare services are access to health care, the feminization of poverty, reproductive choice, teenage parenthood, hunger, illicit drug use, and the like.

Solutions to these problems remain elusive and complex, with no consensus on how to solve them. They are problems that cannot be solved only by the efforts of the social welfare system. Homelessness, access to health care, hunger, and the feminization of poverty are economic security problems. They have become more acute in recent years, in part because of changes in U.S. government economic policy. Violence is a criminal justice issue. AIDS, health care delivery, teenage parenthood, and reproductive choice are issues that have strong ties to the health-care system. Illicit drug use is also a health and mental health problem. Many of these problems, at least in part, have their roots in lack of adequate financial resources. Without adequate income, individuals and families do not have access to housing, to adequate food, to health care. The frustration caused by the lack of adequate income often leads persons to turn to illicit drug use or violence. In a society as affluent as ours, it is intolerable that people are homeless or must live below the poverty level. A major task facing our society is the development of feasible and acceptable solutions to the elimination of poverty and also to the provision of basic needs—food, shelter, clothing, and health care—in a manner that preserves the dignity of the individual.

Prejudice and discrimination remain major contributors to the inability of individuals to obtain adequate housing and satisfying, secure jobs that pay an adequate wage. It is becoming increasingly evident that illegal discriminatory practices continue to exist in both housing and employment. Racist behavior seems to be on the increase if one follows current stories in the media. The hard-fought gains of the 1960s and 1970s now seem to be eroded. Prejudice against alternative life-styles seems to be one of the obstacles to provision of adequate services (medical and social) for AIDS victims and their loved ones. These negative attitudes must remain a target for change if human needs are to be met.

Lack of jobs, the cost of health care, and a lack of affordable housing underlies other serious social problems such as the rise of violence, the feminization of poverty, the radical rise in the number of children living in poverty, and the lack of a diversified system for meeting the needs of the growing elderly population. The list could go on and on. The Clinton administration continues to be confronted with a need for major change if human need is to be met in the United States.

It should also be apparent in the discussion of the various fields of practice that a major impediment to meeting human needs is the lack of resources (also see Chapter 4). Questions around this issue are many. Some of the more important are: What resources should federal, state, and local governments be responsible for providing? Which government unit should be responsible for providing which resources? Which resources should be the responsibility of the community's informal helping systems—neighbors, friends, and family? How should government services support these natural helping systems?

When decisions about resource provision are made, attention needs to be paid to social change and its impact on the family, the changing structure and functioning of the family, and thus a changing need for new and different resources. For example, the entry of large numbers of women into the labor force has brought about new needs for child-care resources. Attention also must be paid to the changing population patterns. For example, the growth of the aging population requires an emphasis on resources that provide for community care wherever possible. Changes in other parts of the social welfare system also affect the need for new, expanded, or different resources. For example, the policy of deinstitutionalization calls for a whole range of new community resources to meet the needs of the affected population.

Care must be taken not to pit the needs of children against those of the senior population. Also the growing diversity of the population must be recognized and care taken not to expand institutional racism (discrimination). In fact, as change takes place, it is imperative that institutional racism be eliminated. Also attention needs to be paid to regional differences when deciding upon the preferred means for meeting needs.

As system change is implemented, care needs to be taken that the impending welfare reform plan does not result in blaming the victim for societal problems. Excessive regulation, red tape, and bureaucratization must be avoided. There is an enormous challenge for all parts of the social welfare system, for all levels of government in the remaining years of the 1990s if human need is to be met in the United States.

Given the current political and economic situation, substantial increases in funding for social welfare programs cannot be expected. In fact, it is more likely that we will see cuts. A crucial question is: How can the availability of resources be expanded with little or no expansion in dollars? The use of the informal system must be explored further to determine what resources it can provide. Accountability, effectiveness, and efficiency become important; it is essential that decisions about service provision consider these factors.

The U.S. social welfare system has no unified philosophy for the use of arrangements or for establishing policy that guides the delivery of services. The question of whether the primary purpose of the system is social provision or social control remains unanswered. Depending on the prevailing political and ideological philosophy, the balance changes between care and control; yet the balance is never discussed or identified as such. Far greater understanding needs to be developed about this issue and its influence on both social policy and social work practice (Day, 1981). Decisions about which social arrangement to use have often been related to issues of *social control* and *social provision*. When social provision prevails, there is a tendency to use social insurance and universal provision arrangements. When social control prevails, public welfare arrangements are often the choice.

A closely related issue is whether social welfare should have a *residual* or a *universal approach*. Generally, U.S. policymaking has used a residual approach. As a result, services reach those in need too late to prevent major impacts on their social functioning capacity, thus contributing to the need for more intrusive and expensive interventions. For example, institutional care has often been needed for mentally ill clients because their problems were not identified soon enough or there were not enough resources to support them in the community. Services should be available near potential recipients and tailored to their lifestyles. If hard facts were available comparing the relative costs of the current residual system to a universal system focused on prevention and support, informed decisions could be made about the relative merits of the two systems from both a financial and a humanitarian point of view.

The issues raised in this section are not all-inclusive. Attached to each issue identified are many other issues. Some of these have been raised in earlier sections of this book. Others have yet to be raised. It is hoped that the reader has become aware of the complexity of the issues involved in the ongoing development of the U.S. social welfare system. Only with this understanding can movement be made toward solution of the social problems that currently give rise to many of the situations to which the U.S. social welfare system is called to respond.

Structure of the System

An impediment to meeting human needs that are affected by contemporary social problems is the structure of the contemporary social welfare system. The structure of the social welfare system very much reflects the influences of an earlier time. The use of a particular arrangement to meet a particular need may be more a choice based on tradition than one based on careful analysis. Also, the fields-of-practice structure has allowed the system to develop in piecemeal fashion. An ongoing issue, then, is whether this structure is the most effective and efficient organization for meeting human needs.

Other concerns related to the structure of the social welfare system have to do with whether the present fields of practice should be the organizing mechanism for service delivery. Does this structure segment and compartmentalize problems so that holistic views of individual, family, and community are overlooked? Does it prevent various parts of the system from working effectively together? Are the current fields of practice the most appropriate ones for the contemporary scene, or are they merely a relic of historical development? Should new fields be developed?

Further questions exist about the relationship of the social welfare system to the health, mental health, education, and corrections systems. Are these systems really a part of the overall social welfare system? It might be assumed that they are all part of the social welfare system, but they function as separate but related systems. Social workers are found in all these systems. If they are not a part of the social welfare system, then what should its relationship be to each of these other systems? What should the role and function of the social worker be in these systems?

In a society made up of many special-interest groups, it is difficult to see the overall picture. Yet priorities must be set, decisions must be made. Somehow, society must provide a system that functions equitably across the entire country, yet allows for appropriate local control.

The social welfare system is complex. There is little basic agreement on its role and function in contemporary society. It is costly, it often stigmatizes individuals, it creates multilayered services and responses (those for the person who can pay and those for the person who must rely on government support). The system must change with the changing needs of people in a changing society. The answers to questions about what change is needed, and how that change can be facilitated, are also very complex. The system's change will be heavily affected by ideological, political, and economic motivators.

From time to time, plans arise for changing the social welfare system. Because of political and economic implications for extensive change, that kind of change has proven very difficult to bring about until now. With the unraveling of the liberal paradigm, as discussed in Chapter 2, which began in the 1970s, political ideology and power has gradually shifted to conservatism (Karger and Stoesz, 1994). Over the years, since the 1970s, the foundation for support of what conservatives have called the "liberal welfare state" has been slowly eroding, giving way to a more conservative ideology about the role and function of the federal government in social welfare. The ideology forwarded by conservatives relative to social welfare, favors containment in both the growth and costs of social welfare, elimination of universal type programs replacing them with rigorous means-tested programs, and transfer of responsibility for meeting human need to the private sector or to state government (Karger and Stoesz, 1994). Political support for a conservative agenda for restructuring the current social welfare system was substantially bolstered when the Republican party won a majority of seats in both houses of Congress in the 1994 Congressional elections. In fact, extensive change in the structure, scope, and functions of the U.S. social welfare system are imminent, with both houses of congress having passed extensive welfare reform legislation. Although not signed into law, change in the system will occur as a result of this legislation, the extent to which we have not heretofore seen.

The change that will take place in the structure and function of social welfare will probably not all be for the better of some groups of people, particularly the poor. Drastic cuts in social welfare benefits and social services will likely eliminate the "safety net" which at least guarantees a miminal level of subsistance for impoverished groups. A conservative social welfare ideology also will not foward the philosopy that welfare is an investment in human capital. As President Clinton said in his innaugural address in 1992, "welfare should be seen as a hand up, not a hand out." To counteract the conservative position with regard to the restructuring of the social welfare system, Howard Karger and David Stoesz (1994) have suggested five guiding principles for structuring reform in social welfare policy. They are: (1) increasing economic productivity; (2) strengthening the family; (3) increasing social cohesion; (4) strengthening the community; and (5) greater social choice (p. 429).

The principle of *increasing economic productivity* is predicated on demonstration that social welfare programs can contribute to the country's overall well-being by replacing dependency with productivity. Rather than a single welfare policy that would eliminate welfare dependency by imposing rigorous work requirements, future policy should provide incentives for people to work by providing minimum benefits such as, a minimum wage that is realistic in terms of the cost of living, and universal health care and day-care benefits for all who participate in the work force. *Strengthening the family* calls for the development of a national family policy, as discussed in Chapter 13. Such a policy would include services designed to assist families so that they do not have to become reliant on government public assistance programs. Providing for basic family needs such as housing, medical care, and services that support participation in employment would become part of this policy. The belief that all citizens share in a collective social entity, in which various groups of people accept their mutual interdependentness on one another has declined, and has been replaced by self-interest and individualistic value orientations. This has caused even greater divsions among the population along social class, racial and ethnic lines, and has perpetuated racism and other forms of oppression. Social policy relative to social justice issues then must clearly call for *increasing social cohesion* among the diverse groups in the nation. In part, this calls for social obligation, that is, giving of one's resources to assist those who are less well off, and implies that the obligation extends to more than just paying taxes to support social welfare programs. *Strengthening the community* is based on the fact that many of America's largest cities have experienced extensive deterioration in their infrastructures, schools, buildings, streets, housing, and the like. This seems to have fostered a decay in human capital, involving high crime rates, extensive drug trafficking, use and abuse, high unemployment, and welfare dependency. The communities that have been the most affected are those who have the least resources to deal with these problems. Future social policy should include making available the funding to engage in the restoration of these "poor" communities. Wealth and income afford to many Americans economic security, with a freedom of choice in selecting various kinds of resources by which to meet their needs, for example health care. For many other Americans, however, who are poor or oppressed in some way, freedom of choice is not a reality. These groups must rely on benefits and services provided by government agencies. This is based on the assumption that the poor are incapable of making wise choices. *Greater social choice* is about giving the poor a range of choices in terms of how they might meet their needs in living. Benefit vouchers for housing, day care, and health care that would allow recipients a choice of provider of these services from the private sector. Tomorrow's social policy should make these choices possible (Karger and Stoesz, 1994).

These strategies, though somewhat conservative, are but one method for reorganizing the U.S. social welfare system. A strength of these is that they would demonstrate how social programs can be of benefit to the well-being of the whole nation.

The U.S. social welfare system is not a static entity but an evolving one. Decisions that bring about change originate from and are influenced by many sources: legislative bodies, the executive branches of the various levels of government, judicial decisions, public administrators, professional associations, practitioners, and consumer groups. The student of social welfare or social work must consider not only the past, but also how the past influences the present. Then that student would be well advised to consider what the future may hold and how human needs could more adequately be met as the system evolves. If, as we believe, the U.S. social welfare system is on the brink of another milestone, a time of extensive change in the system, then the present opportunity for influencing the system for change is great.

The Future of Social Work

As the social welfare system changes, the major profession within that system will change as well. That change will come not only from the changing structure of delivery of services to meet needs and respond to contemporary social problems, but also from within the profession of social work as it continues to address the tensions noted in Chapter 6—emphasis on the profession or on service to those with needs, the relationship of the profession to the social welfare system, the role of the profession in political and social change activity, and the broad or narrow definition of the profession.

In order to address these tensions, many questions must be answered. What are the roles and functions best filled by the B.S.W. and by the M.S.W.? Other professionals, such as nurses, psychologists, and the clergy, also work within the system. What should their roles and functions be? What should be the relationship of the social worker to these other professionals? Answers to these questions will come not only from the social work profession but also from the demands of the social welfare system and its various motivators.

The need to expand resources as government-funded resources shrink makes additional use of informal resources essential. The role of professional social workers in developing and working with those informal resources is still in question. There is a growing belief that broker and case management roles are best filled by the B.S.W. A closely related concern is the role of paraprofessionals, volunteers, natural helpers, and self-help groups in the delivery of social ser-vices—which tasks or functions these helping people and groups can carry out—and about the role of the social worker in working with these helping individuals.

Other questions relate to the role of the M.S.W. Social workers at this level generally have been found in two very different types of roles, the clinical or therapist role and the adminis-trative role. Although both of these roles will still be needed in the U.S. social welfare system in the foreseeable future, the numbers of workers needed for each role and which programs and agencies should provide the clinical services are not clear. Also, how interchangeable are these two roles? At present, many M.S.W.'s move from the clinical role into the administrative role without additional administrative education. Are social workers appropriate administrators in the social welfare system? Some insist that to administer a social service program, the adminis-trator must have knowledge derived from practice as a social worker. Others believe this is not the case, that preparation in public administration is required. The supervisory role for the M.S.W. is a related concern, as is the nature of supervision needed by the range of people em-ployed in the social welfare system. The social work profession will wield considerable influence over the resolution of these concerns about professional roles and responsibilities, but political, economic, and social ideology will also be influences.

Predicting the future of social work forces us to gaze into a crystal ball that is not at all clear. Perhaps the best way to accomplish this is to turn to the past as a basis for viewing the future. So-cial work as a profession made significant advances during the 1960s and 1970s, branching out to serve more people than ever before in an expanded human services delivery system. The na-tional political climate nurtured such advancement by placing a high priority on serving the con-cerns and needs of people, which was fostered by a humanitarian spirit. As we moved through the decades of the 1970s through the present time, the political climate has changed, bringing about a shift to more conservative economic, social, and political priorities such as concern for economic stability and national security. These shifts in national priorities have cast doubt on the future of some social welfare and social service programs that traditionally have been staffed by social workers. This has culminated recently in the passage by Congress of welfare reform, as dis-cussed earlier. It is more than likely that cuts will be made in programs that have formed the backbone of the "welfare safety net," casting doubt on the future well-being of people from our country's most vulnerable groups, children, women, the aged, and the disabled. What this should mean for social work, so that it can adequately respond to the needs of such groups of people, as has historically been its mission, is a change in the way social work is practiced. Since the 1970s, the nature of social work practice has changed, but the question is, in what direction? The evidence is that social work practice has largely moved away from work with such groups. This is evidenced by the fact that there has been a significant decline in the number of profes-sional social workers employed in public social service systems, the systems that serve the most disenfranchised population groups (Reid and Popple, 1992). Although a good number of bach-elor's level social workers continue to be employed in such agencies, the same cannot be said for those who hold an M.S.W. Most M.S.W.'s practice today in private voluntary agencies, with the primary practice activity being interpersonal psychotherapy or counseling. A significant number of them are also engaging in private practice. No longer is activism or advocacy on the menu of primary services provided by the majority of M.S.W. social workers today. Harry Specht (1994) posits that social work has become solidly lodged as a major player in the enterprize of psychotherapy, where in 1991, more than one-half of all members of the National Association of Social Workers spent at least part of their week engaged in private practice. Similarly, Walz and Groze (1991) have suggested that factors such as expansion in private agencies and a dominant middle class in which there are many problems, has changed the clientele served by social workers, capturing more of social work's attention and resources. The result has been a weakening in the advocacy and political missions in social work practice. Whether social work will be able to respond to the challenges that it will face over the next few years with regard to its historical mission to assist disadvantaged and oppressed groups remains to be seen. On the more positive side, the profession in recent years has formed a political action coalition known as PACE, which lobbies and makes campaign contributions to candidates who support social policy that benefits the poor or underprivileged. PACE gave support to the Clinton campaign.

Social workers need to react to change by using creative measures to develop and support mechanisms for self-help and empowerment. As Anne Minahan has put it,

> *Social workers have a dual responsibility. In assisting other people to gain control over their lives, they help them establish goals and make plans to adjust to or shape their future. And, if social workers want to do for their profession what they help others to do, they can work to gain some control over the future of their own profession by making a conscious decision to shape the future instead of serving, ignoring, or adjusting to it (Minahan, 1981).*

Social work will survive the changes as it has in the past and will continue to mature as an even stronger profession committed to the ideals of serving humanity.

A Student's Next Step

A major purpose of this book has been to provide a solid knowledge base about the social welfare system for students preparing for work in one of the human service professions, particularly those preparing to become social workers. The survey of the fields of practice should be useful for students who are making a decision about whether social work is the profession for them and, if it is, which of the areas they may be especially interested in. The historical material should help students understand the nature of the contemporary social welfare system in which social work is practiced. The analytical frame of reference should give them one means for looking at human needs and the usual responses to those needs, so they can determine whether the most appropriate response is being used. This, then, can lead to identifying the changes that need to take place in the social welfare system if human needs are to be met. These understandings are needed by all who would work in the social welfare system.

For social work students, the development of these understandings is only a beginning. They will need to develop knowledge and skill in policy analysis, an understanding of legislative processes and of ways to influence those processes, and an understanding of what is involved in the development of social welfare programs and policies. This knowledge is usually taught in a social welfare policy course in a social work curriculum.

Summary

It is hoped that this book has provided the reader with an in-depth understanding of the development and the contemporary nature of the U.S. social welfare system. This understanding should provide a basis for the kinds of decisions that all citizens need to make as they participate in the democratic process. The social welfare system is subject to much criticism. Many issues of values are involved. Much misinformation exists about the system and those who benefit from its provisions and services. Discussions in the political arena, as they affect the development of social policy, need to be influenced by knowledge from the past and understanding of contemporary issues. Citizens need to have this understanding as they vote their political preferences and as they influence the development of public policy. An informed citizenry is essential if the social welfare system is to address the needs of individuals in a changing society.

This book, then, has attempted to present one conceptualization of the U.S. social welfare system in hopes that it will be of value to all who use it to develop their understanding of that system. Human needs are a central concern of social living. The response any society makes to human needs reflects that society's values, political structures and philosophies, economic base, and ecological and demographic makeup. What is functional in one society at any one time may not be functional in another society or at another time. Change in the structure and functioning of the social welfare system is inevitable. For the change truly to benefit the citizens of the United States, it must be influenced by an informed citizenry and knowledgeable professionals who work within that system.

Key Terms

conditions giving rise to needs
fields of practice
greater social choice
history of the social welfare system
human needs
increasing economic productivity
increasing social cohesion
motivators
privatization

residual approach
social control
social provision
social work profession
societal arrangements to respond to need
strengthening the community
strengthening the family
universal approach

References

Day, P.J. (1981). Social Welfare: Context for Social Control. *Journal of Sociology and Social Welfare, 8,* 28–44.

Johnson, L.C. (1985). Services to the Rural Aged: The Application of Community Development. In Summers, A., Schriver, J.M., Sundet, P., and Meinert, R. (Eds.), *Proceedings 10th National Institute, Social Work in Rural Areas*. Columbia, MO: University of Missouri.

Karger, H.J., and Stoesz, D. (1994). *American Social Welfare Policy: A Pluralist Approach.* New York: Longman.

Litwak, E. (1985). *Helping the Elderly: The Complementary Roles of Informal Networks and Formal Systems.* New York: Guilford Press.

Minahan, A. (1981). Social Workers and the Future. *Social Work, 26,* 363.

Reid, P.N., and Popple, P.R. (1992). *The Moral Purposes of Social Work: The Character and Intentions of a Profession.* Chicago: Nelson-Hall.

Specht, H. (1994). *Unfaithful Angels: How Social Work Has Abandoned Its Mission.* New York: Free Press.

Walz, T. and Groze, V. (1991). The Mission of Social Work Revisited: An Agenda for the 1990's. *Social Work, 36 (6),* 500–504.

Suggested Readings

Atherton, C.R. (1992). A Pragmatic Approach to the Problem of Poverty. *Social Work, 37,* 197–201.

Day, P.J. (1989). The New Poor in America: Isolationism in an International Economy. *Social Work, 34,* 227–233.

Kahn, A.J., and Kamerman, S.B. (1990). Do the Public Social Services Have a Future? *Families in Society, 71,* 165–171.

Karger, H.J., and Stoesz, D. (1994). *American Social Welfare Policy: A Pluralist Approach.* New York: Longman.

Meringoff, M.L. (1990). Monitoring the Social Well-Being of the Nation. *Public Welfare, 48,* 35–38.

Reid, P.N., and Popple, P.R. (1992). *The Moral Purposes of Social Work: The Character and Intentions of a Profession.* Chicago: Nelson-Hall.

Specht, H. (1994). *Unfaithful Angels: How Social Work Has Abandoned Its Mission.* New York: Free Press.

NAME INDEX

SUBJECT INDEX